A
Father's Wisdom
for a
Lost Generation

Volume I

DW Carpenter

For permissions contact: **http://afatherswisdom.org**
Any reference to historical events, real people, or real places are used fictitiously.
<u>Copyrighted Acknowledgements and Permissions (Bible scriptures):</u>
KJV: no permission necessary; public domain
NKJV: Scripture taken from the New King James Version®. Copyright © 1982 by Thomas Nelson. Used by permission. All rights reserved.
NIV: Scripture quotations marked (NIV) are taken from the Holy Bible, New International Version®, NIV®. Copyright © 1973, 1978, 1984, 2011 by Biblica, Inc.™ Used by permission of Zondervan. All rights reserved worldwide. The "NIV" and "New International Version" are trademarks registered in the United States Patent and Trademark Office by Biblica, Inc.™
AMP: Scripture quotations marked (AMP) are taken from the Amplified Bible, Copyright © 2015 by The Lockman Foundation. Used by permission.
NLT: Scripture quotations marked NLT are taken from the Holy Bible, New Living Translation, copyright © 1996, 2004, 2015 by Tyndale House Foundation. Used by permission of Tyndale House Publishers, Inc., Carol Stream, Illinois 60188. All rights reserved.
BSB: The Holy Bible, Berean Study Bible, BSB; Copyright ©2016, 2018 by Bible Hub
Used by Permission. All Rights Reserved Worldwide.

ISBN: 978-1-7357589-2-3
First printing edition Oct 2020 in the United States

www.afatherswisdom.org

To my daughters

may you love the Lord as I have learned to,

while on your experiential spiritual life journey

and live a purpose filled and abundant life!

Love

Dad

Thanks and love

goes out to my Lord, my Mother, Aunt BJ, Grandmother MoMo,

Mike, Jeff, Dominic, Tara

A Father's Wisdom for a Lost Generation
Volume I

CONTENTS

i

Introduction

Important note: Before reading Chapter 1, it is very important to read the introduction first, due to how this book is structured.

An Unconventional Approach

The reason I refer to it as unconventional is because I'm going to begin with a cliff-notes style approach then cover in detail the various topics by chapter. The why of this is to pique your interest and bring to your attention the breadth of the topic matter in order to encourage you to read this book in its entirety. This is a book for Believers and non-believers alike, it will significantly transform lives for some, or it will reveal an abundance of golden nuggets for others.

The **intent** of this book is to do whatever I can to help the "lost generations" throughout the world, by conveying important and essential scriptural truths, revealing messages from the Holy Spirit to better understand your spiritual journey, while sharing my diverse journey to give you something to relate to because people generally understand by connecting the dots between the teachings and how it interplays with personal experiences.

The **objective** of this book is to cut your learning curve to a fraction of time that it would've taken without this type of HELP. Its help is with navigating the Guidebook (the Guidebook to life and abundant living; the Bible). I myself was lost until almost reaching 35yrs old (although had a very experiential life during that time; some good and a lot bad). I have for the recent 25years been studying the Bible; the 1st 5yrs dabbling and not asking Jesus into my heart or to be the Lord of my life; then after being saved another 5yrs wondering how this religion thing works; and now the past 15yrs studying with the intent to learn and understand (all the while doing my best to have a life with my family and friends and running businesses fulltime, etc.). Regarding this "religion thing" I just mentioned, I want to communicate up front and make perfectly clear that this book is not about religion and you will see this thread carried through your entire read. This book is about relationships! We are spiritual beings, and this is a guide to connecting in relationship with our creator and with connecting in relationships with other people, and by accomplishing this successfully, it is about having fulfilling and abundant lives while on earth. So this 550+ page, 1st & 2nd Volumes = approx. 80hrs for the "initial" read VS. 15-25yrs; I'd say that is cutting the learning curve into a fraction of doing it trial by error on your own.

1

Important note, this designation * represents a "KEY" foundational precept, topic, point, etc. and is utilized throughout the book; more keys ***indicate a greater importance.

* One of the primary objectives of this book: to relay clear and concise messages of the foundational wisdom of God, the related processes involved and how it impacts our lives daily throughout our entire life on this earth and beyond. And communicate this information so that you can cut through all the years of learning and years of trial by error occurrences which is what I had to go through, and it was not necessary. In other words, * get to living the abundant life sooner in your life than halfway through it, near the end of your life or sadly never. Note also that another couple of objectives of this book is to correct the years and years of misinformation, wrong and false teachings concerning the Bible, then providing you sound and accurate truths of God that will supply you with fulfillment and abundance in your daily life. Also to cut out the unnecessary information that is conveyed by pastors, or should I say in the "church house." Now don't get me wrong or take this out of context, everything in the Bible is relevant but there is a time and place for covering all the stories in the Bible. What I'm communicating in this book are all of the foundational principles and key topics that you need for the basis of your experiential spiritual life journey on earth and nothing more. For those who are babes, you may not realize what I am disclosing here but believe me you will, and for those who are mature Believers you know exactly what I am relaying because it is what you get a large portion of at church from some pastors, or those on podcasts, or TV, or radio, and you're wondering why you've devoted this time to what you feel are irrelevant topics or topics that have catchy phrases and funny anecdotal stories designed to entertain more so than to inform and educate. Let me also add that I've edited this book over and over again, in order to assure that I did NOT relay my bias or my opinions. When I felt a topic needed my input to assist in delivering the message, I mentioned that it was my opinion and on a few occasions I mentioned that the statement was designed not to express my views, but rather to get you to think and meditate on it. I took it to heart not to relay biases and hope that is the way you interpret it as.

I personally have not ever seen a book such as this. One that clearly outlines what you need to know and sets aside all the things you can learn at your own leisure; and that communicates those foundational principles and essential topics in an easy to understand format with dovetailing several passages of scripture to assist in your learning and to justify whatever is being disclosed. There's thousands of Christian books out there but the majority address just a hand full of topics per book and none providing a comprehensive overview of the key topics that you need to understand the Bible, how God's kingdom works in order to receive blessings and act on them so that you have an abundant life.

Pastors for example write "series" which coincide with their sermons; therefore a big encouragement for you to attend church to assist you in the understanding of that series/book/CD and of the Bible. In addition, with your attendance you give your tithe or your offerings and then the books themselves are a significant source of revenues. That statement is not meant to be a knock against pastors, or attending church or the book revenues, rather pastors do provide the sermon in which we are to "hear" the Word spoken, attending church is the avenue to hear the sermon, where you are to give your tithings and to fellowship, etc., and relying on different sources (such as books) to increase revenues is just being creative and smart. The statement was meant to point out that short story books on "series" alone would take you forever (15+yrs) compared to this book and would cost you significantly more than the cost of Volumes I & II, the upcoming Volume III, or any additional.

**This book is unique for an abundance of reasons, just scan the cliff-notes bullet points on the following pages to confirm. Since there are so many various subjects, I felt it important to you the reader to key in on 5 of the most vital topics that will have the most emphasis and focus:

a) This book will explain to you how you can live your life to the fullest and achieve **the abundant life** that <u>Jesus **promised**</u>, as it is written in **(John 10:10)**NKJV "I came that you may have life and have *it* more abundantly." (Additional translations: life till it overflows; better than you have ever dreamed of; on Earth and for an eternity).

b) "**LOST Generation**" relates to not only non-believers but also Believers as well; the emphasis here focuses on how <u>your life and purpose</u> can be "**FOUND**," whether it be the basics of how a non-believer gets saved or how a Believer (whether a recent "babe" or 50yr mature) peels back the onion layer upon layer upon layer (religious doctrine vs. the Bible) so that they can reap the rewards of a Spirit-filled relationship with our triune God!

c) **The message of Glory**: the how's and why's that we must glorify God daily and how this relates to you and impacts everyone and everything on earth.

d) My conversation with God in 2005 and His directive to write this book. Included is the subsequent guidance of the <u>Holy Spirit</u> and **essential prayers** that <u>unlock your access to the fullness of God's Kingdom</u>. **Specifically, ***"My Lord's Prayer"** (Ch3) is one of the primary messages the Lord revealed to me and wants me to deliver to you.

e) **The Bible "a Guidebook to Life and Living"** a comprehensive review of how to understand it and effectively utilize it.

3

This book is truly God inspired and was written for **all** to benefit by it. The last I checked all means all, all genders, all ages, all ethnicities, all economic statuses, all… What it is not, is a replacement for the Bible, it is a supplemental to <u>assist</u> you in navigating it, to <u>help</u> in understanding it and to dramatically <u>cut out years of trial by error approaches</u> by focusing on key topics, so you can ask the Holy Spirit for specific guidance and revelation which significantly speeds up the time for you to achieve living life in abundance. This is also not a sales pitch or gimmick, simply read the book in its entirety along with reading the Bible and you make the determination whether it's transformed your life or at least improved your overall quality of living.

We live in very troubled, uncertain and unstable times and if we do nothing about it to change our course, we're probably looking at self-destruction. I speak the truth and I think that most would agree. Maybe it'll happen in your lifetime or maybe not, regardless that is the direction we're headed. Let me point out here at the beginning that I do not use terror tactics, doom and gloom or other forms of psychological manipulation to deliver messages. As I said, I simply speak the truth and in saying that I take a straightforward approach in the hopes of reaching and positively impacting as many people as I can.

Have you ever heard the saying "if it is to be, it is up to me?" A brief explanation is: accountability starts with you; if you want to see things change whether within yourself or your surroundings it requires action on your part by setting goals and working toward those goals. The saying should not be taken as a selfish statement, meaning that "only you" can do something about it, but rather you must take control or take charge of the <u>circumstances</u> and collaborate and utilize as many other people that are needed to accomplish the set goals. It's not only a way of thinking but a way of doing and a way of accomplishing (i.e. **"Think – Do"** vs. think – exist, or think and do nothing). Along similar lines, another phrase I use often is **"Learn – Do"** which means, **Learn and Just Do It!** To learn and not do, is really <u>not to learn</u>.

Along those same lines, there were a number of instances over the years in which I would get frustrated with trying to balance my life and write this book (a directive God specifically "gave" to me and I could have chosen not to write it). You could imagine what I am referring to since it took me 14+years to date. My point is that my frustrations peaked in the past year and the Holy Spirit said to me in His still small voice, * "If you want it bad enough, you will do it." He was absolutely right. Whether the 30+years as an unbeliever or now as a Believer, anything I wanted bad enough I disciplined myself to go and get it. It's no different with you, whether you want to improve your life, your family's life, live

4

life with purpose and abundance, be a better provider, improve your community, or change the world, it starts with you and God and your relationship with Him, and on and on…and that is where this book picks up to assist you in accomplishing those goals and more.

We can come up with some wild or selfish thoughts to talk ourselves out of work. I could have simply chosen not to write this book, and left it up to someone else to write it (BTW, that is a principle of God, in that if He tells someone to do something and they do not do it, He will find someone else to do it; that is just one reason why it is so important for you to walk in the Spirit and receive His counsel so that you clearly know what is expected of you; this is covered in greater detail in the book). Along those same lines of me choosing to not write the book, you might be thinking why do I need to help save the world, or you may even have the belief that our God will save us from our own self-destruction and if that is the case then why do you need to do anything about it, thus minimizing your responsibility. So let's toss that thought around: Is He capable of doing that? Yes. Will He? No. Why? There are numerous approaches that can be taken to answer this question, such as from an ethical, moral or even a legalistic perspective, or from taking parallel examples from scripture, or taking scripture that has a common relationship with the original question (known as a common thread). The most noted example that should be communicated here is, God gave us a powerful gift when he created us, one of having free will or in other words we make "choices" for ourselves (* note: all **choices** have either positive, neutral or negative **consequences**). In **(Deut. 30:19)** Moses announces a farewell message to the new generation of peoples before they were to enter the Promised Land: "choose life," meaning one with God or "choose death," meaning one without God; he went on to add that this is a simple and straight forward statement and not one that requires analyzing or sending someone to the top of the mountain or the depths of the seas to determine which to choose (God's messages to us are very similar in nature in the respect that they're simple, yet many people over think them and make them overly complicated; i.e. paradoxical; and may use that alone as an excuse to not follow them). Other scripture implies that if God created us solely to give him worship then He could have instead made the trees, or the mountains bow down to him (or create robots to carry out the same function). * He loves us and he wants our praise and he wants our obedience and he wants us to have life and to have it abundantly, but at the same time he's given us the choice to decide how we are going to attempt to achieve it (with or without Him). Thus I responded "no" to the question posed previously: "Will He save us from our own self-destruction?" This was the short answer to the question and the point I'd like to make is that there are no short answers to most ideological questions as it pertains to God and another very important point is that you should read this book in its entirety and by evaluating it comprehensively, most of the questions that you have will be answered (by the many facets, approaches and examples used to illustrate and give explanations throughout this book).

We face challenges and problems in our lives practically every day, whether related to finances, jobs, family, social, political, legal, racial, natural disasters and on and on. They are not only of a new magnitude that we didn't dream of dealing with even just 20 years ago, they're challenges and problems of an entirely different kind. The rate in which technology alone is dramatically changing our world is one of these "different kind" of challenges and problems that I'm referring to (i.e. we must constantly re-educate and re-invent ourselves due to this "kind" of challenge). Additional challenges include the global marketplace and its effect on global economies, terrorism and war, also a shift in values and beliefs in society across the globe. The greater the change, the more difficult the challenges and problems and it is very apparent that the U.S. is having serious enough issues that one has got to question, how long can this go on before people figure out and embrace the idea that a collective group of Americans must initiate the changes needed to redirect our country, not to be great as we once believed we were but to lead the world in every aspect of our being. Not with the intent to gain the respect of other nations (because that will never happen anyway) but to **be the best we can be** regardless of any and all outside influences. I don't believe it will have to come down to an American revolution as some predict but I do believe it will take a revolution in the form of a **spiritual reformation** in massive proportions (not a revival) **along with like-minded leadership** in order to accomplish the significant changes we so desperately need in our society. I hope and pray that this book plays a role in that reformation.

I'm not telling you anything you don't already know by what you've witnessed with your own eyes and experiences. Reality TV is fake yet so many Americans aspire to mimic it. Racial division is tearing the country apart from within its foundation. We used to have the 2%'s but now the share of wealth in this country has narrowed down to the 1%'s the "haves," then we have the rest of us who are the "have-nots" yet striving to "keeping up with the Jones's" by attempting to get the most of the "not" that they can and do so at any cost to others. We live in a "Me" oriented society that takes pride in having established a vindictive "Gotcha" culture that breeds the "Blame" game and keep in mind that the children of blame are "cynicism and hopelessness" (I'm just a puppet that has no control in this system so just tell me what to do); that in turn has contributed to the almost epidemic proportions "Victim" mentality (rather than people humbling themselves and taking responsibility for creatively working his or her way around or through their challenges); which has also birthed an even heightened fleshly emotional response, playing the victim card although this one is the Outrage culture, of people who bend over backward to be offended only to pass judgement on others and scream of the injustice; also an extremely destructive belief: "I think, therefore what I think, I believe, thus is my absolute truth" (denying God's truths); and the signs of the times is our society is devolving; we are now being fed the raw meat of the outrage culture in a neatly wrapped package of complex manipulation that is referred to as the "Cancel Culture." Which is disinformation in its highest form: the devil's tactic of DISTRACTION (fake news = propaganda), which yields destabilization of societies that implode on themselves (referred to as "in crisis") which ultimately leads to its destruction. Why have wars and battles when you can do it this way ("rumors**" of wars; see Matt. 24:6; 7-51). To edify means to build up oneself or one another, which we are all to do "love thy neighbor"; everything described above is just the opposite…it breaks down everybody and everything; to its demise. But if that is not enough then of course next, everyone wants "Instant Gratification" with regards to anything and everything; which in turn gives birth to an offspring called our "credit card" culture. *Strange thing is, **people buy things they cannot afford to impress people who don't care.** We also want to be "Entertained" in every aspect of our lives (whether via Hollywood movies and TV, the shopping mall, the workplace, to even at church): so of course this contributes to people lacking life balance in just about every aspect of their lives, yet again it's all about that FM radio station WIIFM ("What's in it for me") and continuing to chase after all the "nots and Jones's" that they can. All the while this is causing our culture to become more and more secular! Unfortunately you all know that what I've disclosed is true and that I could go on and on, but I thought I'd spare you of the additional pathetic traits and habits we have developed in our society. Is it too unrealistic to believe that we need to pull together as a country or is that even possible? Easier said than done but I for one believe it is possible, for all things are possible with God.

The following is a profound statement that takes into account the prior paragraph and applies to the majority of adults over the age of twenty-five in our society today.

People today are:
- ➤ Trapped due to continuously dwelling on the past
- ➤ Because they are fearful and anxious of the what the future may hold
- ➤ Therefore they are **paralyzed** in the present.
  - o Note: the solution of this is explained in detail in a later chapter.

Have you ever heard an explanation of a **dichotomy**? Take a coin, it has two distinctly different sides (that is if you are playing heads or tails) but if you are spending it, it's simply worth the denomination stamped on it. So although the two sides are very different yet at the same time it is one in the same. Another illustration would be how people who attend a Disney theme park always refer to it as a "magic" place; and Walt Disney often responded by saying "The magic is in the details." On one side of that coin is the magic, while on the other side comprises the enormous amount of resources to create that magic, all the while it is one in the same. Now back to the statement of what "People today are," the "paralyzed" statement above is a dichotomy of our culture which on the one side stands the majority of the population; while on the other side of the coin a small minority of people are:

❖ Thankful and grateful for the past for its fond memories and the lessons learned (so to relay to generations our traditions; then to make it a point not to repeat the negative lessons that we had to so painfully learn ourselves);

❖ And have faith (trust and confidence) in Jesus with regards to what the future holds for us and to set small and BIG goals (this God desires for us to do and will assist us in achieving), so live in hope, but do not get hung up in a "future state";

❖ Rather they choose to live in the present (as we have been instructed by Jesus), and to have life and have it abundantly today in the present moment.

Yet although in stark contrast of each other, the two statements combine to make up our society and functioning for appearances sake, as one in the same. As you can tell, the challenge is to *shift an entire mindset of peoples from the first arrow bullet points to the second diamond bullet points. Easier said than done but I still believe it is possible (all things are possible with God), and if it is to be, it is up to me (to get it started).

Let's get started, so back to what I'd meant by cliff-notes approach is to give you bullet points of summarization, pointing out critical elements and to act as a guide for you to better understand the book and to navigate it. Remember the **objective here is to pique your interest on the vast topics we'll cover and so that you don't just read the first chapter and make a hasty decision not to read any further because it doesn't apply to your immediate need.** Keep in mind that each bullet point will be covered in greater detail in the remainder of this book. Just a reminder, this designation * represents a "KEY" foundational precept, topic, point, etc. and is utilized throughout the book.

- **A journey begins with a first step.**
  - ○ If it is to be, it is up to me (you).
- Just a couple of paragraphs prior, I mentioned "the challenge to shift an entire mindset of peoples." I'd like to rephrase mindset by using another more appropriate word **"Paradigm"** because for one thing it more accurately describes the context in which it is used and that I'll also use it

throughout the book, so would like to make sure you understand its proper meaning. By definition a paradigm is the lens through which we view the world. I once stopped into a costume shop and purchased a pair of clear lenses, black rimmed glasses (Clark Kent style) to illustrate my point in a presentation. I held up the glasses and said this is my paradigm, my lens that I view life. They appear to be constructed with glass and plastic but in reality were created by the culmination of my experiences from since I was born (parents, upbringing, siblings, friends, enemies, teachers, education, bias's, prejudices, peer pressure, sex, money, music, accomplishments, failures, living environments and on and on). I can put them on my nose to illustrate the point but in reality, I don't wear glasses, regardless the lens is there and in place within me as it is within all of us. So to reiterate my earlier point, the challenge is to get an entire group of people to shift their paradigm (their foundational view towards life) and shift it in the direction of Jesus and His teachings beginning with believing in and carrying out the foundational precepts we are to live by, God's Word, the Bible. **Since it starts with you and since I've clarified the definition that the lens in which you view life are from a culmination of all of your life's experiences, ask yourself, from what I am disclosing in this book will you be able to approach this with an open mind to change?**

*As it takes a first step to start a journey, it takes one individual to start the process to change the world.
- o Additional:
- o Most paradigms are simple yet may be difficult to interpret or determine. Others are very deep and in analysis would require the peeling back of many layers of conditioning.
- o Keep in mind: Your perception is your reality!
  - And it may not be the same perception for others or their reality.
- o Don't get too caught up in the complexity of this. Contemplate this example: "You don't know me. What you do know is your life experienced based interpretative perception of me." Again, I threw this in for practice and to expand your thought processes.
- o But remember most paradigms that I will cover within this book has to do with you simply not relying on what or how you've always viewed/thought of something and simply take the time to look at it from a different perspective. Similar to "put yourself in their shoes;" or on the other hand, rather than looking at what is

conveyed in this book with your old dingy rose colored glasses, try putting on a fresh set of clear lenses to evaluate this topic/thing.

- **Paradox**
  - o Contradictory qualities or contradictory statements; contradiction that can go to the extreme (a contradiction between something that is deemed rational but is in reality irrational); other examples: oxymoron, mystery, puzzle.
  - o There are a number of profound paradoxes in the Bible and a few that Jesus specifically points out and teaches on the topic (to be highlighted and reviewed within this book). That is why I've taken the time to define it.
- **Lost Generation**
  - o God is not constrained by time, therefore with regards to "a generation" He is referring to all the peoples currently living. So in terms of the "lost generation" He is referring to all peoples currently living.
  - o Man on the other hand defines "generations" into increments of every 20yrs, then names them and uses various forms of analysis to stereotype that generational group (i.e. Baby Boomers; Boomer echo's; Gen X's, Gen Y's, Millennials, Gen Z's)
  - o I'm going to take the liberty to suggest a name for the next in line as Gen Nex's which sound like nexus (definition: a connected group, a central or focal group). I hope that this name catches on because this generation (a connected group with specific focus) will be responsible for advancing all the efforts for God's kingdom on earth that the current living generations initiated and laid the groundwork for.
  - o How are we lost? Who? Why? What? Solutions?
  - o We are running out of "do over's"
- **Wisdom**
  - o Specifically Jesus's wisdom. Also specifically not man's wisdom.
  - o Jesus is God's word (Bible) made into flesh; the Bible is God's wisdom; therefore Jesus is the wisdom of God. Our creator, God our Father, loves us more than we could ever comprehend, and He always desires the best for us and provides it to those who Believe in His son Jesus.
  - o This book emphasizes the topic of wisdom in every aspect and angle. How to attain wisdom; what path you must take; what options you have; what is wisdom and how does it impact your life, others' lives and the world we live; Jesus's wisdom versus

man's wisdom; the advantages of wisdom and the pitfalls of man's wisdom; and on and on…

- As mentioned, this will cut your learning curve to a fraction of a typical Believer's trial by error approach. * This book covers topics comprehensively with a focused approach on the topics that are specific to you obtaining an abundant living and your experiential spiritual life journey on earth. In brief, we must be born again, and we must walk in the Spirit and renew our minds daily in God's Word (wisdom of Jesus) via reading and hearing via sermons. One of the many points I make throughout the book is that if you are confined to hearing only your pastor at church, then your progress is limited to where he is at in his sermon topics (which he varies from year to year based on current day topics or whatever he and/or the Elders believe should be "taught," etc.), how if anything it relates to you, are you attending 52 weeks a year, or the amount you do attend what messages are you able to receive; and so on… As mentioned previously concerning pastors, the following is an example of how I take the prior question and pair it up to an answer from scripture, then I provide solutions. * If you open yourself up to listening to a wide range of pastors, you will quickly notice that many of them utilize the "Wisdom of words" as Paul points out in **(1Cor. 2:4)**, which means that men and women use their wisdom of words in hopes to persuade others, rather than using the wisdom of God to persuade within the hearts of Believers and nonbelievers alike. Those pastors can often go on and on and on during a sermon with their grandiose eloquence of speech while only conveying one bit or sometimes no useful information. This is exactly what I purposely try to avoid, I tell it like it is and communicate what you need to know for your understanding and applicable aspects for your journey.
- * We are to be **<u>Spirit Dominant</u>**! The entire book is devoted to how to accomplish this. I brought it up here to point out that the Holy Spirit gives us the incredible gift of discernment, which applies too numerous applications than can be mentioned here, but a few are a) discerning what you need to hear during a sermon, b) what words are to jump off the page in scripture as you read it, c) what is contrary to God's Word (Jesus's wisdom), d) how to determine when others are lying and trying to pull the wool over your eyes; e) how to optimize your choices in order to have life abundantly; and on and on…

11

- By now you're probably wondering who I am and what qualifications I have to teach on these topics. I could say I'm a nobody, or just a regular guy that doesn't have any formal seminary training and it was not until my thirties that I had even been to church nor had I been introduced to the Bible, BUT that I've been on a <u>diverse life journey</u> and <u>now a spiritual journey</u> that has much relevance, meaning and worth that God must feel it important that I disclose the aspects of it to you. I think that gives you an adequate initial picture and you'll find out specifics in the book. A parallel that comes to mind is what Simon Peter said to Jesus **(in Luke 5:8)** "I am a mere fisherman and a sinner," you certainly do not want someone as myself following you, or representing you during times you are not present. Now, I am not likening myself to Peter (I am not worthy of tying his sandal laces) but what I am saying is, like Peter I am a mere person and yes I've sinned much in my life too and although our careers are different we both are hard working men, me having spent my life's career in the floor covering industry (and he a fisherman by trade). More importantly, we both over time came to love Jesus; Peter devoting his life to Him and me devoting myself to Him and putting forth incredible hours towards learning, so that I can reveal this information to you (with having received the direction from God and via the help of the Holy Spirit). **So you tell me, after having read this book, why do you think that I've been called to deliver these messages?**
  - o *Point: You are just as important as I, and God gives us all the same opportunity to do small and great things through Christ.
  - o You have the power and authority within you to change the world. You must believe this, embrace it and act on it. As a matter of fact, the Lord wants this of you.

- *** God spoke to me. I've already alluded to it twice and now I'm putting it directly out there. So, don't shut me off just yet, hear me out. I'll give you a chronological account of my life and my journey later on in the book but for the purpose of brevity in 2005 God not only spoke to me we had what I believe was about a 10-minute conversation. Now over the years I've heard pastor upon pastor emphasize that their communications with God are not audible (but internal) and I'd agree with that if they are referring to their relationship and communication with God <u>through</u> the Holy Spirit that dwells in those who are saved, which is the same way my communication is with the Holy Spirit (note: see Ch5 The Holy Spirit for additional information). By 2005 I'd been saved for less than 10yrs., and in that time my relationship and journey started off slow and the progress was slow as well, although in '05 I committed myself to a **"learn and do"** process with regards to my spiritual walk. About 7 months into it, one morning I woke at exactly 5am and due to some back problems I was doing my routine stretching exercises when I felt a presence in front of me and then heard a voice say, "You know the letter that you are considering writing for your daughters, well you will write a book instead but it won't be about what you had planned to write; also it will be written for all people to read and I will guide you in what to communicate." I initially froze sitting on my workout mat, took a deep breath and my mind started racing. It was not uncommon for me on occasions in my life to get lightheaded and/or stutter my words when I'm in an intense or stressful situation, but I didn't do that at all. This was a surreal moment in which I definitely felt His presence and heard His voice whether audible or not it was loud and clear and I believe I spoke audibly to him (or maybe not) because my thoughts and questions seemed to be instantaneously imparted and He responded. For example, the first obvious thought (thus the question I asked) was, "who are you?" and instantaneously He responded, "I AM your God." I've got to give myself credit here for my quick thinking, because I asked Him something that I fully expected to get a non-answer to, "Tell me the title of this book I am to write." Without hesitation He responded, "A Father's Wisdom, for a Lost Generation." I thought, wow that is a good title. Next, I asked him, "Why me, what do I know? I'm no expert." He responded, "Why not you? Don't you realize that throughout your life that I've had a plan for you? I'll bring all this and more to your remembrance through my Spirit who will guide you on these things." A few more specifics were conveyed, then just as quickly as He had first spoke, He was gone.

- o As relayed, I was contemplating writing a lengthy letter to my daughters and had joked that it would probably end up being a book when I finally have everything I wanted communicated in it, but I never meant it literally that I would write a book especially one that would require a title. That is why I asked about the title, because it was never a consideration, therefore I had no clue of what the title would possibly be (moreover this conversation could not have been the "self-talk" that we all do during our waking hours; also note, the voice was not my "self-talk" voice it was distinctly different, and it was loud and clear). Only after hearing the title did it give me a good idea of the topic matter that He was alluding to for the book and not so coincidentally it was of

13

very similar nature to what I wanted to convey to my daughters.

o On a side note, no one should ever have to contemplate writing their children a guidebook on life, unfortunately for all parties concerned their mother's and my relationship did not work out and I was only a part-time participant in their lives from an early age. My advice to anyone in a similar situation and to put it bluntly: live your lives for and with your children and focusing on their overall development. Do not for a minute hold on to the delusional belief that someday when your children get to be a certain age that by writing a lengthy letter or having lengthy talks will compensate for your absence (whether actual absence as mine or like so many today, simply being bodily present but an absentee parent). Then the delusional insanity continues when you hope and pray that the instructions / messages are initially accepted, understood and then acted upon by them. * Thing is, this is what I am up against in writing this book, only it is to you, total strangers! So with having said that, **what motivation do you have to accept this instruction? To work at understanding it? Then actually find the time and the energy it takes to act on it?**

▪ If you are not sure of the answer allow me to relay a few examples:

▪ Maybe you've been going to church for years yet *there* is something missing in your relationship with the Lord or your life is not as fulfilling as you thought it would be; then I believe by reading the book in its entirety you would benefit with the broad range of topic matter that is covered. And remember, you'll at least get out of it the same measure you put into it, or quite possibly a one-hundred-fold increase.

▪ Maybe you are similar to me and was either never introduced to Jesus or you've researched it and decided it wasn't for you. Similar to the prior example, the way I present this topic is easily understandable, relatable and I try to minimize the use of "Biblese" as well as not using any religious doctrine (traditions of men). Again, reading this book in its entirety could benefit you by giving you a greater comprehensive understanding of God, the Bible, Jesus, the Holy Spirit and what role they play and the role you would play in order to have life and have it abundantly. Also how

14

to live a fulfilling life with God for an eternity rather than in hell or purgatory (the outer darkness).

- Maybe you think that you are not worthy of a relationship with Jesus. Please never make the fatal decision that you are too despicable or not worthy or whatever devil inspired thoughts you can come up with (the devil/mind battle will be explained in detail in Ch9 &10 titled "Spiritual Warfare" and "The Mind"). * God loves you and yearns for a relationship with you and all you have to do is open your heart and allow him to be the Lord of your life. That's where you start but then the book will allow you to leap over years of searching for answers and get you on your path to abundant living and a rewarding relationship with the entire triune Godhead.
- These are only a few of the endless examples I could have used. Point being: read this book, keep an open mind and open your heart to Him.
  - o Note: God spoke to me on two other occasions. They were one-line answers to a specific question unrelated to this topic matter. One thing this did for me was justify the first conversation. So on the one hand hearing from Him again comforted me that He did actually respond to my plea, but on the other hand for years I've yearned for more but has resulted in what I interpreted as an unfulfilled desire, but what I've concluded is that our conversation was a miracle and that * **His Holy Spirit is sufficient enough for me to communicate with** in the spiritual realm / human realm.
  - o I want to reiterate and make it crystal clear that I am in no way disclosing that I'm unfulfilled other than the area in which I just mentioned because to the contrary, His Holy Spirit has been an awesome communicator with me which is extremely fulfilling. My relationship with Jesus is extremely fulfilling, as is my relationship with my Heavenly Father sharing my thoughts and expressing my praise and love.

- Why has approximately 14+ years passed before I even started composing the book? I've written well over 1000 pages (legal pad size) of journal entries during that time (although did not know what information would be included in this book). This is an interesting topic I'll expound on later in the book, but for some insight note the following:
  - o Did you know that the Apostle Paul spent 10years in the church before he went out on his first evangelistic mission,

and then began his writings (which comprises over 60% of the New Testament)?

o Did you know that it took David, a man after God's own heart, 20years until God believed him ready to be prospered and made King?

o Did you know that Joseph for 13years (was heavily burdened as a slave and incarcerated; although this time "in the wilderness" was a tremendous growth period for him) between receiving visions from God of his destiny of ruling a nation, to it finally happening 13years later when he was awarded second in command to Pharaoh?

o Do not for one minute believe that I am comparing myself to these men, one point that I am making is that God has a purpose for all of us and in that purpose we have a calling that takes time to seed, nurture and harvest. The harvest part comes when God has "sent" us to accomplish that which He has ordained (defined as prescribed, i.e. doctor prescribes medication) in this case God's prescribed action to complete. I believe that after 14years what God has sent me to do and ordained for me is exactly where I am at now and where I am supposed to be; God only knows, and time will tell.

- *** The Bible is a guidebook to life and abundant living.** Very important and please note: This is not my interpretation but God's revelation to me.

- **Navigating and understanding the Bible**
  o How to get started
  o Purchase an easy to read Bible such as: BSB, NKJV, NIV.
    - I prefer the more difficult read KJV (King James Version, red letter, meaning the words spoken by Jesus are in red) but I often refer to the NKJV, BSB, NIV and occasionally the NLT.
    - These other Bibles listed are for additional reference, also I access additional reference material online via these websites: www.biblegateway.com and www.biblehub.com I utilize Bible Hub frequently; note, by pulling up the scripture of interest then there are tab options such as "interlinear" and "lexicon" in which there is a range of information regarding the Hebrew or Greek texts and translations.

- You will be seeking to understand God's Word so to do just that it often takes researching the passage(s) of scripture; also due to the fact that the original text of the Bible was Hebrew and Greek and our Bibles have been translated to English the meanings at times may be confusing and/or often it is just not expressive enough to convey what the original writer was attempting to communicate in the Greek or Hebrew context. Translating accurately via the actual Hebrew and Greek meanings of words and doing so via a lexicon or interlinear reference book/website (i.e. Bible Hub) will assist you in your understanding; additionally understanding and interpreting the "proper" grammar will assist in translating and can also be found in the lexicon.
- Other reference sources of information are referred to as a "commentary" and a "concordance." Bible commentaries aid in the study of Scripture by providing explanation and interpretation of Biblical text. Please note, be sure to use a legitimate source such as Mathew Henry's Commentary; or Strong's Concordance. Note, a concordance is utilized by providing an alphabetical list of words in the Bible and shows you what page(s) and specific line of scripture in which the word is located by page #; Book title; line of scripture.

o The Bible is a "guidebook" and **NOT a manual**. A manual is a step by step guide and we are not God's robots, we have free will; therefore can choose how we want to approach this thing called life. This is elaborated on in Ch8 and throughout the book.

o **Always read the full context** of what is being communicated, do not just take one line of scripture and try to interpret its meaning. Read either 4 or 5 lines before the line of interest and 4 to 5 lines after; better yet read the full chapter that line is in or a good portion of it. By scanning the other lines you'll easily determine where the context begins and ends for that line of interest.

- Be careful to avoid over analyzing and over interpreting scripture. * There is a term/phrase referred to as "to be legalistic, (or legalism)" what that means is when someone over analyzes every sentence to sometimes every word and they get lost in the analysis. Then they are paralyzed in proving their points rather than trusting in their "beliefs;" they often "argue" their points, point after point after point with others to the extent it becomes absurd and foolish. It is easy to fall into this trap with everyone having an opinion and with the infinitesimal amounts of information on the internet. But rely on your relationship with God including the support you receive from the Holy Spirit that dwells in you.

- As with most words "legalism" has another meaning, legalism is a belief or doctrine of belief for some people in which they believe that their salvation is due to their "good works" and their strict adherence to the laws of God. I don't want to go into detail on this other than to say that this belief is absolutely contrary to the New Testament and that only by God's grace through faith are we saved and will be covered in great detail later on in the book. Although legalism has these two different meanings, one a doctrine of belief and the other an almost obsession of analyzing and over analyzing. The thing is, it's a perfect example of how over analyzation can lead to wrong beliefs, misguided beliefs, conveying false teachings and how people become paralyzed in their tracks, thus not moving forward in their walk and blind to what is actually taking place.

o ***Understanding** the Bible is a key phrase here that needs to be expounded on. You need to seek to understand the KEY things of the Bible and that is what I'm attempting to accomplish with this book. Seek to understand and do so as deeply as possible concerning each topic rather than having blind faith and taking things at face value or believing in things you do not understand. The Holy Spirit dwells in you and assists you in "seeking" the truth of all matters and topics.

o One of my primary objectives is to communicate Jesus's teachings in an understandable and simplistic manner. Actually anyone can make His teachings complex and confusing to the extreme and to the point of being utterly ridiculous, because the devil <u>will</u> eagerly assist them in doing so and assist you in confusing yourself while placing doubts in your mind.

o   * It is imperative that you research everything and **confirm the "truth" and validity** of anything read or heard outside of the Bible. Do not take this book as being 100% accurate (perfect); also with respect to the Pastor (or anyone) of your church, do not take what they say as being 100% accurate (perfect). The Bible is 100% accurate and perfect and is the guideline and reference for you to base all "truths" from.

o   Read all books from "cover to cover," don't skip the preface, foreword, introduction, etc. because often the scope of the book is explained there. Only speed read books to determine whether it is worth your time to read it in its entirety (i.e. reading first paragraph, first and last sentence of every paragraph and last paragraph of each chapter); I do not suggest you try speed reading this book and especially do not speed read the Bible.

     ▪   Option A: for those who are <u>professing Christians (Believers)</u>, read this book from cover to cover then read the Bible from cover to cover. I'm assuming that you know the Gospels and have over the years been exposed to a broad range of scripture but like most have not read the Bible from cover to cover. Option B: since many people do not like hearing that they need to read the Bible from cover to cover, then read this book first and as you read it explore the Bible as it pertains to the topic at hand.

     ▪   You may have purchased this book because when attempting to read the Bible and go to church you are not understanding it either partially or in full; or you may be considering becoming a Christian/Believer and trying to understand the overall concept is overwhelming or underwhelming to you. Regardless, this book should assist anyone in better understanding the comprehensive messages of the Bible.

-   **The Lord's Prayer and My Lord's Prayer**

-   **Holy Trinity** / Triune God / Godhead

(Triune God, Holy Trinity, Godhead all refer to our God, triune or trinity = 3 Godheads; so **"the 1 is 3 and the 3 are 1"** and that means that God (1) is made up of (3) Godheads: the Father, the Son and the Holy Spirit and those (3) "persons" are our God (1). The concept is slightly outside of man's thinking and rationale when there is no reference but when you take a comprehensive read of the Bible [or this comprehensive book] the concept is easily understandable.)

- **God**; the Heavenly Father and part of the triune Godhead.
    - o Old Testament
        - "Shadows" and "Types" of Jesus
            - Concealed and then revealed
        - In the beginning
        - Adam and Eve
        - Moses; Abraham; Isaac; Jacob
        - Joseph; King David
        - Prophets
    - o New Testament
        - The Gospels; Jesus
        - The cross; the crucifixion, death and resurrection
        - Disciples; Apostles
- **Jesus**; Son of God and part of the triune Godhead;
    - o God's Word made into flesh and dwelt among us
    - o He is the wisdom of God
        - We must <u>hunger</u> for His wisdom daily, and we must <u>thirst</u> for His abundant life daily
    - o His life as per the four Gospels; the Passion of Christ
    - o He is the **way** (the only way to having a relationship with the Father)
    - o He is the **truth** (God's word made into flesh)
    - o He is the **life** (He gives life; He came here that we may have life and have it abundantly; etc....)
    - o He made all this possible
    - o By his stripes I am healed
    - o I am the righteousness of Christ in God's eyes (due to Jesus's works on the cross)
    - o **Come and Hear, Go and Tell**
    - o He is to you, your: Savior and King of Kings, Lord of Lords, Teacher, Brother and <u>Friend</u>

- **The Holy Spirit** (HS); the Spirit of God and part of the triune Godhead. The Holy Spirit has been a pivotal part of my journey, not only is there an entire chapter devoted to Him, but the Holy Spirit is mentioned throughout.
    - o Baptism of the Holy Spirit (how and why)
    - o The Holy Spirit dwells in us.
    - o Comforts us (referred to as The Comforter).

- o Counsels / Counselor (speaks to us), (listens to us)
- o The Holy Spirit did exactly what God said he would do for me: bring all things to my remembrance. (For God knew us before the beginning of time; in Spirit)
- o Fills us with God's wisdom so that we would have knowledge and understanding of the Kingdom of God in Heaven and of the things of this world.
- o Teaches us via scripture to understand and gain knowledge.
- o Gives us discernment not only of scripture but of this world.
- o Red light; green light; GPS; (this is the way in which he leads, guides, directs us)
- o Gives us "God Confidence" vs. self-confidence
- o **There were years that rather than enjoying my Saturdays like most people do (especially since I lived in the Cayman Islands), I'd get up at 6am pray, praise and worship, read scripture and begin a writing marathon of journal entries in which many times I had to force myself to stop at noon, while many a time I needed to try to find a stopping point and would write until 2 or 3pm. Often my Sundays would include an average of 3 to 4 hours of writing. I'm not implying that I am some kind of brainiac now with my mind loaded with biblical information because I am not. I have retained much information but only a fraction of what I've been exposed to. That is why I believe I was inspired to write so much of it down for reference. To add to that, the Holy Spirit speaks to us progressively, meaning when you are in the Word either just reading or researching, plus you are writing that teaching and your thoughts down on paper (or laptop/computer) is when the Holy Spirit increases the communication and the revelation more and more as you go. Many a times after 4-6hrs of this when I decided to break for the day I was not exhausted although I was spent and fortunately I could go out and take a casual walk along the beach, walk to get groceries, have a relaxing dinner and a pleasurable evening and feel awesome on Sunday morning to do it all over again; then that would start me off perfectly for a very demanding work week. As mentioned, what an amazing relationship I have with God the Father, the Son and the Holy Spirit. But this is not about me and my relationships, * it is about you and your potential relationships with God and people you come in contact with and about how extremely important all relationships are to

our experiential spiritual life journey on earth and how it impacts living a purposed filled and abundant life.

- Learning how to have an intimate and close relationship with the Holy Spirit. This is NOT an option. We can NOT pray without the Holy Spirit, and He will NOT pray to God for us!
- See chapter 5, The Holy Spirit
  - o The Holy Spirit is the POWER that resurrected Jesus; and we have him dwelling inside us (as Believer's)!
  - o Speaking in tongues
  - o God's Grace; the Holy Spirit replaced the Law.
  - o He convicts and condemns unbelievers in order to get their attention; and some Believers.
  - o He corrects and convinces Believers. In today's world, we all require quite a bit of both correction and convincing. What a special Father we have that does this for us.

- **Prayer**: It's Explosive Power and Significance; plus, How to Pray
  - o Keep it simple
  - o Not a cell call that you hang up and go about your own business; or brief texts; but is ongoing from morning thru to the night
  - o Majority should be prayers of praise because He's already blessed us, only we have to receive the blessings and act on them; the minority would then be petition prayers (meaning asking for something)
  - o <u>Believe</u> it to be and praise as though it is (this is a must)
  - o <u>Declare</u> your prayers in the power and authority of Jesus.
  - o Have patience.
  - o God answers all prayers and your questions (although most are not the answers we wanted)
  - o Miracles (specific petition, urgent circumstances)
  - o "Sinners Prayer," the prayer to say in order to be saved by God
  - o Importance of "relationships" in God's kingdom
    - I can't emphasize enough, with regards to a relationship: our Heavenly Father, Jesus and the Holy Spirit yearn to be in a relationship with you!
    - This is the prayer you pray to begin your relationship with them; also known as the "Sinners Prayer."
    - **"Jesus please come into my heart; I know that I'm a sinner and I repent of my sins (meaning I will change**

my ways); I want to have a relationship with you and have you be the Lord of my life.''

- ▪ If you said that prayer with a sincere yearning to have Jesus enter your heart and be the Lord of your life, <u>then you are saved</u>. But it is only the first baby step that you will take to having life and having it abundantly. Your next step should be to get access to a Bible, in conjunction with reading this book, and research a church that teaches the Bible (<u>and **not** their own doctrine</u>) and that you feel comfortable with. Believe me, this is the optimum way to start and get you on the right path to an abundant, blessed, fulfilling and purpose filled life!
- ▪ Being saved is a one-time thing for an eternity, and you cannot be unsaved. You can although fall out of favor and out of fellowship with God and lose out on His blessing, power, authority, glory, etc., and I discuss how this can happen. But He will never forsake you, which means if you have a change of heart, He will be waiting to welcome you back.

- **Power of Praise and Worship**

- **Reformation** (not revival)
  - o Defined comprehensively; why and what we need to do to make this happen and change the world.

- **Spiritual Warfare**
  - o It's real, do not dismiss it! If you dismiss it, it could be a fatal mistake in your journey for abundant living.
    - ▪ You do although need to dismiss every single Hollywood depiction or book written on this topic and along with that all of your preconceived stereotypes.
    - ▪ This is a true "paradigm shift" for you to commit to and then develop your beliefs based on what your research in the Bible unfolds and reveals, along with what you personally experience.
  - o Defining: satan, his demons, fallen angels, his domain on earth, hell, etc.
  - o Liar, cheater, thief, deceiver, etc., he robs you of an abundant life, uses scripture to create doubt and manipulate Believers;

23

- As for non-believers satan is your god that you worship whether you are conscious of it or not; he has control over you and your decisions which play a role in his objectives and furthering his agendas and domain on earth. What's that, you question that statement? I validate that statement in over a hundred pages in example after example, because I was no different than you in disbelieving in evil and satan/devil, close to 40yrs of my life.
  - Jesus already won the battle and defeated him, but you **must** believe and have faith in this and act on it.
    - Having said that, I worded it that way in order to make it easier to understand as in terms of winning a battle and defeating a foe; but to clarify, in reality Jesus did win BUT an actual physical battle did not take place, He did so by disarming satan, his demons and the devil for all Believers. (See Ch9 for additional information.)
  - Armor of God; why do we need armor if he's been defeated? We live in his domain; our fallen nature (will always have an influence over us) along with disobedience will form portals that allow the devil entry to wreak havoc in a Believer's life.
  - The devil, a daily battle (more aptly described as a tug of war) that takes place in our mind; as examples: do you focus more on your burdens than your blessings? Do you believe that the glass which represents your life is half full or half empty? When you think about either deep past or immediate past are the images and representations primarily negative or positive? (topics such as your family, grade school, high school, your past workplace, your current workplace, your current home life, etc.; point is: most are wired to think negatively due to our fallen fleshly nature; the good news is that Jesus has disarmed that way of "stinkin-thinkin" from happening and wants you to have a life of joy and gives you all the tools you need to accomplish it).
  - Finally, how to rid yourself of satan/devil for good and live the abundant life that Jesus said is a primary reason for Him to come to save us.
- **(Phil. 4:8)**KJV "Brethren, whatsoever things are true, whatsoever things are honest, whatsoever things are just, whatsoever things are pure, whatsoever things are lovely, whatsoever things are of good report, if there be any virtue and if there be any praise, **THINK** on these things."

24

- These are optimal thoughts for us to "think" about. But realistically how we "think" about God, about ourselves, about others, about everything, IMPACTS our daily lives as well as our entire lives. I take a deep dive into a comprehensive analysis in relation to what we think, what we should **filter** out and not think about; what we should think and what we should **focus** our thoughts on.

- Do you feel as if you've been searching and searching for the buried treasure to life? Well for one thing, most of what is buried are past regrets, poor choices, bad consequences, dead bodies, etc. and should remain buried. **Look Up!** I'm telling the world of the treasure that I've found, and it is found in the Lord! And conveyed in this book.
- **Focus = Will, Skill and Filter**
- **A Key concept that I'd like to communicate with clarity pertains to the following words: Focus; Filter; Will; Skill.**
- **Skills** are learned abilities (whereas gifts and talents are God given, therefore a "natural gift or talent" that can far exceed the learned abilities of most others).
  - In regard to this book, much of what I have relayed should as mentioned help you cut the learning curve to a fraction of the time it would normally take. Having said that, the teachings in this book are broad, which allows you to learn "how to do" and learn the 5 W's (who, what, when, where, why, to do's) to the extent of being "skilled" in what is required to successfully navigate your experiential spiritual life journey on earth via your relationship with God. Therefore, it is up to you to learn and acquire these skill sets and that means that you have to first have the will or desire to do so.
- **Will** has to do with a person's willingness, want or desire to do something; or their intent or intention with regards to accomplishing something.
  - In regard to this book, do you have the will to read, then receive the information, then to act on what you have learned? Next, do you have the desire to act on the principles and teachings conveyed that have the potential to change your life, positively impacting it for the better so to live an abundant life? Also, can you develop an intention within yourself to act on the things that have the potential to change the world?
- **Focus** is a thinking skill. Therefore it is commonly a learned behavior, although it can be a natural talent, given of God that a person possesses.

To have the abilities to focus means to begin a task without procrastination and then maintain the attention, effort and energies required to complete that task. Those that aspire and those that attain living life abundantly have this talent in common, in being able to discern those things that require their focused attention from the start in order to optimize the time and energy spent on tasks or projects, thus maximizing the results.

- o In regard to this book, I have focused on what you need to know on each foundational topic matter. But I'm mentioning this because you need to be aware of the structure of the lessons and messages and **the importance of being focused, is to your success.** Not only on the teachings but as you are on your journey the Holy Spirit will give you discernment and in order to optimize it, you need to develop your focus skills. This is where your "filter" comes in and it too needs to be developed by you.

- **Filter** is also a thinking skill and either a learned behavior or natural talent. Successful people know that they have a talent for filtering out information, news, noise, etc. which is irrelevant, insignificant, non-essential, trivial, or anything similarly applicable. By filtering out those things, it allows them to focus on what is important or urgent.

- My desire is for everyone who reads this book to be successful in their journey, and that will happen if you have the will to do so, in developing your skills with filtering out all the unnecessary that there is in the world and focusing on the necessary as outlined in this book, including everything the Holy Spirit guides you through, in respect to God's kingdom, His wisdom (Guidebook) and what His plan is for you.

Thank you for taking the time to read through this intro which gives you a comprehensive outline of what to expect, as well as some specific foundational topics that will assist you in your further reading. I hope that your spiritual journey is positively impacted by the overall messages of this book and that it accomplishes the objectives as disclosed.

Briefing by Chapter

This chapter briefing is for those of you who are impatient, read books leisurely and surf around to only read specific topics, or speed read in order to make a decision on whether to read a chapter in full or in part, or even for those who begin on the first page and are a committed reader through to the last page. That just about covers everybody. This briefing is an overview for you to refer back to if needed, that provides you with a glimpse of what each chapter involves. I have to say though, that if you are truly wanting to develop your spiritual relationship and live an abundant life, you really need to read this book from cover to cover, because doing so in any other manner will keep you from getting the most out of it and keep you from getting the most out of your life journey and spiritual walk.

To begin, this book is uniquely structured in that the Introduction must be read before any of the other chapters due to the broad range of information and primarily for some essential foundational topics. The Introduction gives you a sampling of the extensive topics covered throughout the book and for someone who is just beginning this read, it provides a concise idea of what you are heading into. I wanted to take a quick moment to relay that this book is NOT about religion, it is all about relationships and optimizing your spiritual journey so that you can achieve a truly abundant life on earth. To continue, Ch1 begins as an extension of the intro's foundational topics and background information that some will enjoy, while others may promptly scan and move on (but I expect those who do scan it will return to read it more thoroughly once they get to Ch3). Ch2 is where the rubber hits the road on your reading journey and never really eases up from providing the ripe applicable information you came searching for, continuing through to the end of the book. Whether you are taking the first step of your spiritual journey, or you are taking a quantum leap as a mature Believer this chapter will help you significantly and ultimately rate as one of your favorites. Ch3 as I just conveyed is a hard charging continuation and since everyone is unique, I'm looking forward to hearing which of the chapters you felt provided you with the most important, or informative and/or transformational-critical to your spiritual development. At first glance, it is a comprehensive review of a very special prayer, but after you've read it, you'll probably revisit it more than a couple of times because of the volumes of information that is packed into it. Ch4 is a guide for prayer and gives many examples of prayers. The thing is, I felt it important to isolate as much as I could on this topic for the purpose that you have a point to reference, but the best tips on how to pray are sprinkled throughout the entire book and I did not want Ch4 to be redundant and repeat points stated elsewhere in the book. Ch5 is about the Holy Spirit, but again, so is the entire book. He is God's support team and your personal trainer. Just as Jesus described Him to the disciples before Jesus's ascension, "But do not venture forth until you have received the POWER from heaven." Point being, this is a very important chapter for your journey, but similar to Ch4, I was able to funnel a good amount of information into this chapter to provide a reference point, but the Holy Spirit is discussed from cover to cover. Ch6 do not be misled by the title, Bits and Pieces. What it's referring to is the length of the various topics and allows a break from what I previously coined as hard charging point after point impartation of important information. Thing is, that was my intent and I accomplished it for a couple of pages, but you'll quickly notice that the topic matter becomes a rapid fire of useful and helpful topics and increasing in importance as you read through the chapter. Having said that, there are very important diagrams (associated with

Ch2) at the end of this chapter. Volume II Ch7 is about Jesus, and as you may know the Bible from cover to cover was not only about Jesus, it is Jesus (concealed and revealed from beginning to end; the Alpha and the Omega). So too is this book about Jesus from cover to cover and the significance and direct correlation between you and your spiritual journey and achieving a truly abundant life. Just as with many of the other main topics and chapters, I was able to compile a significant portion of information regarding Jesus and thus a very important chapter. Ch8 is a reiteration and an attempt at surmising this book's topic matter via a broad range of examples and topics, in how it relates to your spiritual journey, abundant life on earth and aspects of your eternal life in heaven. Let me put it this way, I've already begun writing Volume III for the advanced Believer, because the information is endless. Upon completing Ch8, you can summarize the two volumes at this point with regards to God the Father, Jesus, the Holy Spirit, the Bible and how your journey connects to it. Then at the end of Ch10, I'm going to strongly suggest that you revisit your highlighted notes from the Intro thru Ch8, because those notes will support what you encountered in Ch9/Ch10 and bring the entire comprehensive BIG picture together for you. So what about Ch9 & Ch10? You can consider them bonus chapters, because the book takes a big left hand turn, to speak about and relay important-crucial information concerning evil, evil doers, evil ways, satan, his demons and the devil, the reality of this topic, how to identify it in your life and what to do about it to combat and come out a victor. It's an intense read and it will blow some of you away, while others will for the first time relate and understand the why's and how's you have taken the wrong paths in the past and be able to correct it now. You'll see that I could have written an entire book on the subject (and probably will in the future) but the Holy Spirit nudged me to include in this book due to the critical topic matter and how it can impact your abundant life. It can be a sour pill to have to take, but nonetheless is written so that you have a sweet remedy that applies to a plethora of personal, social and spiritual ills.

Enjoy, Bon Appetit! And may you be fulfilled in every step of your abundant experiential spiritual life journey on earth!

Chapter 1 God's Fingerprints

Important note: Before you start reading Chapter 1, it is extremely important that you've read the introduction, due to how this book is structured.

College Influence

I think back to during my college days when my mind was somewhat of a clean slate and I believed the world had infinite opportunities, which were mine for the taking. In other words I was young and naive but full of energy. It was at college that a number of my professors pushed the question of whether there was such a thing as a divine or supreme creator, a god? Keep in mind that up to that point in my life I had not been to church and my knowledge of Jesus was that he was born on Christmas day, so we celebrate his birthday and of course I was told that he was God. Other than that I was ignorant to the true meaning of the: who, what, why, where, when and how of God (note: the sum of the parts of this book will explain all that but for this chapter I'm communicating my view on the existence of God).

I was barely an average grade student throughout my school years all the way until college. The first two years I earned A's and my accounting and economics professors, although unknowing what the other was doing, both respectively had me stand in front of an auditorium style class of approximately 100 students and they touted my note taking abilities (which requires excellent listening skills and by the way is key to doing well in school, in sales, in relationships, etc.) and the earnest attitude I had towards the class and succeeding (I had a very competitive nature growing up but now it wasn't about sports but all about learning, acquiring knowledge, taking charge of my life and taking it to the next level: "success and the materialistic American dream") and my econ professor told everyone that they should buy my notes and study them and in doing so would probably earn an A (good lesson on free enterprise and the entrepreneurial system). Then my junior year my business major required a Philosophy course and I quickly found myself struggling in this class and even heading towards a failing grade. Similarly, I remember talking to a number of the other students who they themselves were struggling but for a different reason, they considered themselves Christians and the professor was aggressively challenging their beliefs. Now, I believed that I was pretty good at arguing to defending multiple areas of thought and because I was not biased in one way or another in regards to God, it would work to my advantage, but according to the professor I didn't get it. As mentioned, I am very competitive and was not going to take a hit, so I went to a tutor for assistance. I didn't get this from my tutor but I figured this out, philosophy to this professor is similar to a game of intellectual and verbal chess that is played on an argumentative platform and the person with the best/solid argument/defense wins. Also, with it being an intangible and subjective course, the non-philosophical questions on the exam needed to be answered verbatim from his lecture (to satisfy his ego) and not the textbook. He was teaching the wrong class; he was teaching apologetics with a heavy dose of narcissism and atheism (from a psychological viewpoint narcissism and atheism are typically close bedfellows). I did make it for a period of time, but the class drop cutoff date was nearing and I didn't want to risk the professor failing me since the course was subjective and he held the cards. I will only give credit to that professor for one thing and that was that the class (not him) opened my mind to thinking about the possibility of the existence of God (thus God left his fingerprint). In regard to the class and the disappointment, it was just another "welcome to the realities of life" point in time with my life journey.

Unfortunately there isn't a continuation of the philosophical or college story, it was the '80's and I got hooked up with the wrong crowd who were also as naïve as I but deep into the music, nightclub and popular drug culture of the time. For 1 year my life took an amazingly quick spiraling nosedive and it literally went to pot. Although I didn't credit Him for it then, in hindsight, God pulled me out of the pit of hell with minimal damage, set me on my feet and allowed me to continue this journey (the continuation of that story is in Ch2).

Miracles, Fingerprints and Footprints

A few years passed from the debacle that ended my college pursuits and I still had no interest or desire to pursue God. Again in hindsight, He was always waiting there for me. Now at 32yrs old He's going to attempt to get my attention again and maybe ignite the kindling that He's been accumulating in my heart over the years (as mentioned, the most significant to date was in college). He certainly got my attention when I witnessed the birth of my first daughter. Even today I have total recall of the birth, from the doctor asking me twice if I was okay and me responding twice, "I'm doing great!" The doctor had not anticipated having to do a cesarean section and within minutes switched to that procedure and even with his focus on the scalpel and the incision, he was concerned that I didn't pass out or create a problem for the process. When my daughter was delivered and began to cry, I too had tears but of joy and was grinning from ear to ear (that was the second time the doctor asked me if I was okay because my surgical mask was hiding my smile). "This is truly a miracle and a gift from God" was my first thought during the birth and that thought has endured ever since. So God left His fingerprint on that event, but it still did not sway me to pursue him (a brief continuation of that story is in Ch2). Point is: for me this was when I knew, that I knew for sure that God exists; and the fingerprints He's left each time points to His existence.

Do you question the existence of God? I did up until I was 32yrs old. Some people use common arguments to convince others on the existence of God, such as look at our complex universe and its order, it had to be created by a God; look at nature and its majestic splendor and its complexities; look at humanity from a couple of perspectives 1) human beings (man is incredibly made, his intelligence, his innate knowledge of right and wrong) 2) the human race (how its managed to grow and prosper throughout history somewhat as a collective unit); and now there are scientists that believe they have proof that God exists, as well as quantum physicists; others yet have a profound need or experience that proves to them that God exists (this is often the case and relayed in peoples testimony's of getting saved, their direct God experience); and there are numerous more examples but this gives you an idea of how you might choose to investigate this topic. I strongly encourage you to do so. As I've disclosed, I didn't pursue Him even after he saved me from the pit of Hell, then I still didn't after coming to the realization that He exists. *My point and suggestion, don't wait like so many do (as per their testimonies) until a tragic life event occurs. If you have an adequate history to evaluate your past, look for the indicators (the fingerprints) then ask Him into your heart and your life. If on the other hand you are young and do not have the history/past to evaluate, no worries because you are actually in a better position with not having layers upon layers of negative conditioning built up and thus able to be easily receptive to His presence, blessings and the communication of His messages to you. You would essentially be knocking at His door and He will surely open the door unto you, with an answer.

> (Matt. 7:7-8)BSB Jesus himself said, "Ask and it will be given to you, seek and you will find, knock and the door will be opened to you. For everyone who asks receives; he who seeks finds; and to him who knocks, the door will be opened."

As mentioned, for me all it requires is to focus on the numerous instances and occurrences in the past which clearly give me an indication that God's fingerprints were ever present throughout my life even as an unbeliever. I also wanted to relay that when I was saved, I initially had so very much going on in my life but as it began to balance out, I was able to focus more on my walk with the Lord. Once I got to that point, I can't emphasize this enough to you to follow my lead on this one because the relationship becomes so real that I was often walking along the beach in meditation in my walk with the Lord and there were times that I'd look behind me to see if I could see Jesus's footprints in the sand. I know that it may sound foolish to some, maybe even delusional to others, but until you surrender your "self" to Him in obedience and walk in relationship with Him and He's giving you precise discernment which answers your questions with His vast wisdom from scripture, that is when it's easy to truly believe in Him and that's also when you catch yourself looking around because you're experiencing His presence or in this case looking for an additional set of footprints in the sand. That is why I'm suggesting that you seek, and knock, and He will surely open the door unto you with experiences you never imagined you could have.

Body of Christ / Unified Collective of Believers

Believers have a lot in common and it's important that we do because we are the body of Christ, which means that we are all individual members that make up the church (one unit/including Jesus) and each plays his/her own role to edify (build-up) the church. Please do not confuse the word church in this context as being a brick and mortar building because it is not; we are what makes up the church which is the body of Christ. Note, that throughout the book I will either refer to the "church house" or "body of Christ" to differentiate the two. In (1 **Cor. 12:27**)BSB "Now you are the body of Christ, and each of you is a member of it" (member meaning having its own unique role as in the members of your body, such as your fingers, toes, forearm, etc.). Additionally, Paul refers to the body 18 times and his conclusion is that *we must be connected to each other in order to be what God wants us to be. Elsewhere in the book I referred to that connection as a "collective" because I wanted to use a term that many would understand. Hopefully by referencing the body of Christ it doesn't throw anyone, simply put, it is the collective of Believers who make up the body of Christ of which Jesus is the head and we are the members.

Regardless of which term is used, * we are a collective whole that are interconnected not just because we are professed Christians, we are more importantly Believers in Christ and thus interconnected supernaturally with each other and with God. That is why Jesus said that we as a collective have the power to tell trees to uproot and move to another place (**Luke 17:6**)BLB "And the Lord said, if you have faith even the size of a mustard seed, you would say to this mulberry tree, be uprooted and be planted in the sea and it would have obeyed you." It is very important to note that He said, if you have faith even the size of a mustard seed you would...many misread it as saying if you "had," implying that our faith is weak, therefore we will always be striving but falling short of even having faith as small the size as a mustard seed, therefore unable to accomplish incredible acts. That is not the case at all, He is telling us how much faith we need as a collective to tell a tree to uproot itself, plus He has given us as a collective the power to do so! In a parallel verse (**Matt. 17:20**) He refers to a mountain rather than a tree; and mountains are commonly used in the Bible as a metaphor for problems, trials and tribulations, therefore He is saying that with the proper amount of faith that we could move mountains rather than having to face it head-on and climb and claw your way up the mountain. Jesus finished that passage by saying, "Nothing will be impossible for you," which conveys that with Him all things are possible and that we can move the mountains that we face. Do not interpret the two verses the same way, one is referring to what we can accomplish as a collective (which empowers individuals), and the other as to what we can accomplish individually (which then can edify/build up the collective powers), there is a difference. Finally what I just covered, points out a few of the very important aspects of the collective / the body of Christ. In addition to that, I communicated in the introduction that if we could ever come together as a unified collective to approach the problems of the world then we could truly change the world and put it on a path of possibilities and not on the path to destruction that it is currently on.

The Uncommon Carpenter

The prior subchapter began by relaying that, Believers have a lot in common and it's important that we do because...and it went on to discuss the topic of the body of Christ, which is referring to the entire collective body of Believers. That body of Believers have a lot in common because God designed it to be that way. All Believers are called by Jesus to be like-minded and in saying that, it is highly recommended that we associate with like-minded individuals in our daily lives, although when we are evangelizing then we should pursue all that we can in the hopes that they allow Jesus into their hearts and transform them into Believers with the following inherent characteristics that are associated with being like-minded:

> **(1 Peter 3:8)**KJV "Finally, be ye all like-minded, compassionate, loving as brothers, tenderhearted, courteous...
> **(Phil: 2:20)**NKJV "Make my joy full, by being like-minded, having the same love, being of one accord, of one mind."
> **(Rom. 15:5)**KJV "Now may the God who gives endurance and encouragement grant you to be like-minded one toward another, according to Christ Jesus."
> **(2 Cor. 13:11)**BSB "Finally, brothers and sisters, rejoice. Aim for perfect harmony, encourage one another, be of the same mind, live in peace, <u>and the God of love and peace will be with you.</u>"

If you are a Believer and you have not experienced fellowshipping with other Believers in working together on a charitable project or simply kicking back as friends and enjoying each other's company then you are really missing out on some of the best times and relationships life has to offer. I'm not at all referring to going to church and socializing, which there is nothing wrong with that, I'm simply saying that being around like-minded individuals who have shared beliefs, ideas and goals, it is quite special and unique (uncommon) when compared to the common place of a wide range of worldly social settings in which most are trying to fit in, to be accepted, to follow the crowd, to be successful, etc.

To further this discussion on being like-minded and uncommon, it is by God's design that these are two of the many characteristics He expects out of a Believer. Therefore Believers are not common folk, Believers are uncommon folk. Now hear me out, I'm not purposely trying to come up with some catchy phrase, rather the Lord does specifically desire for us to be uncommon and for us to have the mindset to be uncommon. You could go as far as to refer to uncommon as part of a Christian creed, because the definition of a creed is: a set of beliefs; therefore to be uncommon would be one aspect of the set of beliefs.

Uncommon means to not be common. To begin, let me make this perfectly clear: uncommon means to stand out from the rest. It does NOT mean low esteem or being inferior to others. It also means to not fit into the crowd, to not chase after the things of this world, to not love the world, etc. Jesus said and made it very clear that * this world is NOT our home. And further into the book I'll relay time and time again that we are on an experiential spiritual life journey on earth which means to experience this journey to its fullest so that God can live through us and that it is only temporary because He will eventually call us home; this is the life we've been gifted with while on earth and one aspect of the journey is to seek life in abundance; and we've been blessed with the opportunity during this journey to grow and mature spiritually which is a major portion of our sanctification process (becoming holy and sinless; to be covered in a future chapter). Holy by the way has many definitions, one of which is to be "set apart" from what, from the rest; in other words to be uncommon. In addition to what I've said here, (1Peter 2:11)NLT "Beloved, I warn you as temporary residents and foreigners, to keep away from worldly desires that wage war against your very souls."

Two of Jesus's disciples were originally fishermen by trade, Simon called Peter and his brother Andrew. When Jesus saw them while He was walking the shore of Galilee He said (Matt. 4:19)KJV "Come, follow me and I will make you fishers of men (and women)." What Peter did not realize at the time was that Jesus was also going to have him become an **uncommon fisherman**. And there is no question that is what he became.

In some similarity I am the **uncommon carpenter**; I build people up (to edify, is to instruct or to improve someone intellectually) and I build up people (in the knowledge of God via His wisdom/Bible; not to mention what I do for my career as a trainer and in management). Originally by trade I was a floor covering installer, stone mason and tile setter, and in the same industry a manager, company trainer, Vice President, CEO and business owner. The Lord has truly blessed all the works of my hands. In the introduction, I referred to myself as nobody special and just an average guy, although who had a miraculous conversation with God and the point that I am conveying to you is that there is nothing different between you and me, so do not think for a minute you cannot achieve the things I have and much more! Now based on the context of this subchapter, I do want to set the story straight in the introduction, I am an average "uncommon" guy, the uncommon carpenter.

On a side note, Jesus's craft/skill before his ministry began, was referred to as a "nagara" in Hebrew or "tekton" in Greek, which has been commonly translated as a carpenter and is accurate in the Greek translation. But, more accurately translated from the Hebrew first designated definition is a "stone mason and a builder / architect." A stone mason is a true artist and finds use for most all stones and rejects very few, as well as an architect that is responsible for carefully and methodically designing complex and simple structures, and a builder that oversees the work. I can relate to all of this because as mentioned, I too was a stone mason / tile setter and was actually certified by the State of Florida as one, when I owned my retail store. Additionally, this is all just a matter of semantics and translations, Jesus fit into every category of the numerous definitions (of that culture), from builder to carpenter to stone mason, to architect, to handyman, to very appropriately a lowly laborer who would do whatever work that would provide a meal, and the word even translates as an author (i.e. "The author of our lives and the finisher of our faith" **Heb. 12:2 NKJV**).

I'm always intrigued by the flow of things, such as when the Holy Spirit is revealing something to me and 8 out of 10 pastors are teaching on the same topic although communicated in varying contexts, but are clearly on "the same wavelength" and believe me that is not a coincidence, it is by design and it is an aspect of how God is in control of things and is also an occurrence that happens on a continual basis. As I mentioned in the prior subchapter, Believers are part of a supernatural interconnected collective so events such as mentioned and numerous more take place worldwide that have a common thread as part of its make-up.

Having disclosed and explained what uncommon means and that the Lord wants all Believers to have that mindset as well as execute it in their lives, there is a current common thread to uncommon, that I at least perceive is one. What I am referring to is that there is a book and a song in the Christian music arena that share the same name: **"I'm Okay, that I'm Not Okay."** I also just heard over the weekend a popular pastor give a sermon that used this saying as an aspect of the sermon. Now, I'm not at all familiar with the context of the book and although I've heard the song, I have not looked up the lyrics and determined its context and message. So in case you are familiar with either one or both, then do me a favor and do not apply its context to what I'm about to relay. Meaning focus only on the context in which I am referring. "Uncommon" is another form of saying "I'm okay, that I'm not okay." A couple of paragraphs prior I pointed out the following which is important to remember: Uncommon means to not be common. To begin, let me make this perfectly clear: uncommon means to stand out from the rest. It does NOT mean low esteem or being inferior to others. So, I'm okay, that I'm not okay is disclosing that I as a Believer know and am okay with the fact that based on a world view which believes that I'm not okay (in other words the world sees us as uncommon but in a negative sense and let them think that); as it is written:

> **(Romans 1:22)**KJV "Although they claimed to be intelligent and wise, instead they became fools," this is referring to * unbelievers and pseudo believers who boast about their worldly knowledge and even their supposed knowledge of Christian teachings that in reality is false teachings and traditions of man.
>
> **(John 15:17-19)**BSB "This is my command to you: love one another. If the world hates you, understand that it hated Me first. If you were of the world, it would love you as its own. Instead, the world hates you, because you are not of the world, but I have chosen you out of the world."
>
> **(John 16:33)**BSB "I have told you these things so that in Me you may have peace. In the world you will have tribulation. But take courage, I have overcome the world!" (overcome means victory over)

Additionally, even if the person is physically impaired in any capacity or if they feel they don't fit in even in Christian circles let alone the world, the word "Uncommon" and the phrase "I'm okay, that I'm not okay" still applies to anyone and everyone that is a Believer and God wants all Believers to have these two similar mind sets which in doing so instills that they stand out from the rest. Not due to ego, or conceit, or vanity, or boasting, etc., but due to taking the narrow path that Jesus directs and only the Uncommon do, also to always do the right thing, to loving God and loving their neighbors as themselves, to forgiving others, to giving of themselves for others, etc….that is what it means to stand out from the rest; so I'm okay, that I'm not okay and that I am Uncommon in Christ!

DO NOT LOWER THE BAR! It's commonplace to see pastors lowering the bar to gain a wider church following and gain in popularity. There are numerous ways to lower the bar, for example to relay a "softer" message or better yet a watered down version of what God truly wants from us, in the hopes of getting more people shaking their head yes in response to a sermon or message that is less strict and restricting, to a more open-minded, accommodating and easygoing one. * I did my uttermost NOT to lower the bar throughout this book and to communicate the truth as God wants it conveyed and how it was revealed to me via the Holy Spirit of God. I see it as an injustice to all if the Word of God is watered down / diluted for any reason whatsoever because if this is done it misguides, misleads, confuses, can create doubt and becomes borderline false teaching, all of which allows the opportunity for the devil to step in; which by the way everything I just mentioned happens to be * the first strategies of the devil in manipulating man in the first place.

I had mentioned that a popular pastor used the phrase "I'm okay, that I'm not okay" in his sermon and in interpreting the context of it, his message was exactly opposite of what I just relayed. I'm not saying that in and of itself is wrong, but what I am saying is that it is not right to plug in a popular buzz phrase into a sermon in which it does not or should not apply. Rather than us being okay that we are Uncommon and apart from the rest, he disclosed that the world is domineering and forceful and we are to be "okay" because we ourselves are rooted in hope and patience and to humble ourselves (which are all extremely accurate in terms of the Bible) but then he went on to say to the point of passivity (and thus saying that we are "not okay," in the respect that we are passive and opposite of a worldly view of domination). Well even out of respect it is hard to sit idly by when someone is conveying a confusing message. In restating my position on "I'm okay, that I'm not okay," the phrase (okay = not okay) is paradoxical just like numerous other topics in the Bible and the way I see it, it is also counter-intuitive also like so many topics in the Bible; meaning that you would immediately assume being not okay is referring to being different, inferior, passive, etc. but counter-intuitively it means * we are different as in Uncommon, principle driven, strong and focused, powerful and with authority, extraordinary, and a step above the rest in our actions towards others and do all these things consistently because of the God we believe in. It's frustrating for me to hear pastor's relaying confusing messages of suffering, passivity, submission, etc., that is in negative context which is out of context of how it is truly communicated in the Bible. This is the manner of past history and of teachers with their outdated approaches to controlling the masses, or present day in controlling their congregation by beating them down. * Yes, we will suffer on more occasions than

37

we would like but because Jesus suffered, we too will suffer and is an important aspect of our journey but we can significantly limit that suffering by allowing Jesus to be the Lord in our lives. Yes, there are times that we are to be submissive and other times passive, but those specific times are pointed out in the Guidebook/Bible, thus another aspect of our "righteousness" journey. But please do not ever forget that we are uncommon and we have the power and authority of the almighty God within us and at all times at our disposal; we can do ALL things through Christ who strengthens me; and on and on and on! This is what needs to be preached and emphasized consistently as supporting those aspects of our journey that many of us struggle with.

DO NOT RAISE THE BAR either! The counter-opposite is to relay messages that make things more difficult to attain. This occurs more often than you would think because it's just another avenue to control the masses, typically by particular groups that want to oppress and keep people stagnant for as long as they can and have those people reliant on them. I'm not going to go off onto a rabbit trail on this topic, but briefly many religious doctrines alive and well today were established over the past thousands of years and are filled with "traditions of man." My point in mentioning this is to simply send a warning out to everyone to be cognizant of it, walk in the Spirit and ask for discernment as to if this is the truth of God or just something someone is telling me and following "tradition" over the millennium. If that is so, then it is your choice to make the bold decision to change and to ask for guidance on what that change should consist of and search earnestly for the answers.

Thank goodness, God is in control. Of not just the bar, but of everything (note: see Ch2 GPS for additional on God is in control). In brief, He doesn't control us like robots because He gave us free will to be independent to choose to follow Him, or not. But that is not the topic of discussion here, rather what I just alluded to in the last paragraph that we live in a fluid world which is ever changing but some things (i.e. traditions of man) never seem to change. We live in a world in which things are just accepted without any thought as to whether they should be questioned and whether there may be a better way. Too often we just accept the way things are and this is often via a distorted worldly perspective by believing that we are able to rationally and logically deduce and evaluate, or not and just taking the path of least resistance and follow the flow of the world; or preferably from a spiritual perspective to ask in prayer, receive guidance and act on what God is telling us to do. That is why I've emphasized the importance of being in an intimate relationship with the Lord in order to live and to live abundantly with the guidance and direction we receive from Him.

God Only Knows: Why He's having Me Pen This Book

"I'm okay, that I'm not okay" and "God Only Knows" are both titles of Christian music singles. Both are great songs and as you've read, I've elaborated on the former quite a bit and now for the latter, "God Only Knows" is popular for many reasons due to the singer, instruments, lyrics but also because a good percentage of the population probably have parents or grandparents who had used that phrase with regularity. I know that is the case for me and it brings back some fond memories. This subchapter title though adds another aspect to the phrase, "God Only Knows: Why He's having Me Pen This Book." Thing is, it is something I've really got to now question and contemplate because I've been such a poor parent. I just mentioned my fond memories and in contrast to that, my now adult children have little to no special memories of me. Let me make it clear that this is not a by my design pity party, also I am not looking for anybody's sympathy, I assume full responsibility for the consequences of the choices I've made in my life; and I am not playing the victim card either. The bottom-line: "God Only Knows: Why He's having Me Pen This Book: A Fathers Wisdom, for a Lost Generation," has just recently got me perplexed.

Maybe He's having me write it simply due to Him predestinating my purpose either before the world began or when I was formed in my mother's womb? Regardless, this may well have been a predestined purpose for me.

And in association with that, He purposed the events and He purposed my drive for understanding everything to date via His Godly counsel?

Maybe it has to do with the trauma I experienced over having lost my children from being with them daily, to then being a Sunday father and then becoming a long-distance father?

Maybe it is that I'm the best person to relay a book such as this due to that riveting experience I endured and have a better understanding than most concerning people who are lost and lonely from a father's perspective for his children. I know and everyone who has children knows this as well and that is: you may think you know love and know what love is, until you have children and as the years pass by, you understand exceedingly more (specifically in my case) that the extent a father's love is all-encompassing for his children and from what I've witnessed with my mother and her mother and others, that it was the same for them. Also as the years have passed I have frequently contemplated God with respect to the love that He has for all of his children, and although my love and experience is a fraction on a scale compared to His, it has still got to somewhat parallel each other in intensity, value and importance. He yet again, being the model for our lives holds true in this example as well.

39

Important note: I stopped writing at this point and went to bed. Twenty hours later after a hectic day of business I return to my laptop, opened the file to this chapter and had a stirring of my spirit. So I took a short break, listened to some music on the radio and a program came on that I don't normally listen to and the pastor said,

"That people like me, or those in similar positions as me, there are a large number of Christians who have the belief and think that we are special and favored in God's eyes, therefore what we preach and teach on various topics we are then able to then go home to our perfect and abundant lives and not have to deal with the problems, trials and tribulations that others endure. I'm here to tell you that is not true, I struggle with many things myself that I preach about and life isn't perfect at home with my husband or my teenage children. Today's topic on 'Why God wants us to enjoy sex in marriage' is one close to my heart because I've counseled on this for years as a psychologist and I myself should have had this topic personally mastered with what I know but for whatever reason God had me experience and endure decades of frustration and even pain with regards to sex up until about seven years ago. So it is sometimes for reasons of trials, tribulations, pain and especially it seems like for many, for reasons of brokenness that they are used by God to communicate important messages to others in need."

Wow, I can't tell you how many times the Holy Spirit for years and years and years has provided me with discernment and has revealed things to me often within 24hours of questioning and contemplating various topics. And this one is no different. I disclosed in the introduction that when I had the conversation with God, in which He instructed me to write this book, I questioned Him, "Why me" and I questioned myself as to "Why me" for only about a few weeks but then set forth on a journey that I had no idea would bring me here. Now in all these years and years of developing and writing this book I never really stopped to question it any further until I just got to the point of starting to wrap up the book. So after reading an overview of the 90% that I've accomplished to date, I penned in this chapter what I thought was a very critical question: "God Only Knows: Why He's having Me Pen This Book." Believe me when I heard that pastor's explanation, I knew immediately that it applied to me, and it was meant for me to hear, as well as it had answered the question I had posed; finally that it was the Holy Spirit who led me to it!

I immediately came to realize that it wasn't only what the pastor said, although it was the most significant answer for "Why me," but that it was also due to all of the points I had entered the night before (listed 2 paragraphs prior). So now I have no doubt it was primarily due to a brokenness that I've carried for years and years. Even knowing all that I do now concerning the love and forgiveness Jesus is all about, also specifically that Jesus chose to have His body broken so that I would be made whole again and no longer broken, I still chose to carry that burden (albeit suppressed) all of these years. Much of it had to do with the trauma of going from loving my daughters more than life itself (this was before my conversion and did not realize that God deserves that kind of love first out of me before anyone else even my daughters) and wanting to spend all my time with them and grow them spiritually, intellectually, physically and emotionally, yet still be able to provide and give them everything I could from a material standpoint, only to have my ex decide practically overnight to end the relationship, which in turn devastated me. I've already, in another chapter, spoke on those immediate devastating results that I endured and how I chose to deal with them, so no need to cover here. Only that if I would have had the Lord in my life when this happened or especially years before, life as I and my daughters now know it, would have been dramatically different. But I now know that I cannot take the route of I shoulda, then I woulda, and then I coulda...but rather I now believe that I am at exactly where God intended for me to be and I pray that it is a place that benefits you and everyone else within the sphere of influence and teaching that I am able to reach! And that is where I'm going to leave this, "God Only Knows: Why He's having Me Pen This Book."

Chapter 2 A Father's Wisdom for a Lost Generation

A Father's Wisdom for a Lost Generation

A Father's Wisdom for a "Lost Generation" is what I heard God say to me, as clear as could be. But at the time it was not made clear to me ,what He wanted me to relay. Now fourteen years have passed since God spoke to me and during that time I have been exposed to an incredible amount of information and experiences. So much information, that I could write a book exclusively on this topic and just about every chapter in this book could have easily been its own book. I'll go ahead and relay this even though some of you may not understand what I am referring to, that the Holy Spirit is guiding me in what is written in this book. For example, the chapter titles (topic matters) were made clear to me, thus the comprehensive flow of what needs to be communicated. In the introduction, I've already disclosed a number of things you can expect in this book, including what was designated not to bother you with, but rather divulged it in brief bullet points in the introduction. * My intent is to stay within the framework of the comprehensive message as outlined by the title of the book and its chapters, by relaying foundational principles, scriptural teachings, giving guidance, inserting a few narrative stories whether from personal experience or other people's stories as they coincide with the messages disclosed, focusing on and making sure specific messages get communicated that are for your immediate practical use, and offering solutions and/or making strong recommendations. Having said that, you will hopefully find this book interesting and highly enlightening, but it's not likely that you'll find it entertaining. We live in a culture that wants to be entertained throughout their waking hours, therefore all I'm saying is I didn't have that in mind while writing it. People today even want to be entertained in church and they've pretty much gotten their way, to the point that most sermons are a maximum of 20 minutes long and often they are comprised of 1-2 messages primarily drowned out by the anecdotal (entertaining) stories the pastors connect to them. Now I did want to say that "worship in song and praise" is an important part of our relationship with God and therefore needs to be achieved, just not 30+ minutes and typically lasts longer than the sermon. Point is, people need to **read** scripture from the Word of God (Bible) and they need to **hear** the Word of God preached, this is how we primarily learn and grow in the Lord (there are numerous versus in scripture that confirm this). This book will assist you in navigating the majority of the processes you will encounter in your journey with God. But I don't want to get ahead of myself.

Lost Generations

I just mentioned that "we live in a culture that..." and a statement such as that generally defines an age group of people living during a specific time and being described by their collective beliefs, viewpoints, lifestyles, etc. That by the way is the definition of "generations." Now due to the analytical nature of man, we have classified generations by segments of years, typically 20yrs. The different generations of our time is: Baby Boomers (1946-1964); Gen X's (1965-1984); Millennial's (1984-2004); and (2005 - 2025) this generation are the Gen Z's (as in catching some Z's; asleep; I hope that's not the case) and I personally would like to see the next generation called Gen Nex's (i.e. next generation, or Nex's sounds like nexus which is defined as: a connected group; the "link" that connects a series of groups or bonds the groups together). One thing for sure is this is not a very scientific process and is not static, it's fluid. When I was in college my age group was never close to being associated with Baby Boomers and at the time we were called the "Echo Boom." Many of you may recall a Gen Y that got assimilated into both X's and Millennial's. The thing is, yes there are definite generational differences due to upbringing and all the variables of the time period involved, but this is not a research paper on the differences and characteristics of the generations of today. Point is: very specifically and succinctly put, we are all a "Lost Generation" that if something drastic is not addressed soon, then life as we know it will cease to exist. I'm not saying that it is the end of the world, by no means is that the case but life as we know it, what was at one time referred to as "the good life" will drastically change and for America it could easily be a game changer. This is NOT gloom and doom designed to scare people towards God. It is although time for a wake-up call and we need to start working towards changing the wide variety of things that are so negatively impacting the world in which we live. And the first most important and urgent step is to do it with a firm relationship with God and by His grace will He save us from the ever-accelerating death spiral we are currently in.

By the way, God does not acknowledge the different classifications of generations. To Him, by what He revealed to me, was that all living peoples are what makes up this "Lost Generation." Typically people that are lost, want to be found (rescued) and in most circumstances once found they are said to be saved. This is a generic reference and should not be confused with how Jesus saves. So let's look at some observations that support these striking concerns for a lost generation.

I realize I may lose some of the readers at this point because they have an entirely different outlook, maybe that being a husband and wife with 2 young children that are living well with their professional careers and who have worked very hard to get where they are at and they don't want to for a minute consider that something devastating would ever happen to their then grown children. So if I'm preaching doom and gloom (as I said, I am not) then that family and those similar to them will just remain in their bubble and wish for the best. One point that I would like to convey to someone in those circumstances is, don't ever be scared or manipulated into seeking out a relationship with God but consider it for the endless opportunities, including improving yours and your family's current life while impacting others and to have the promise of eternal life also for yourself and so that you could try to bring your entire family to the Lord as well. What needs to be communicated now and over and over again moving forward is that I believe that with the proper action on our generations' part that we can change the world and make it a better place to live! That is why I am not preaching doom and gloom. I personally have lived the good life that shifted into a chaotic life and now I'm living the abundant life that is purposeful and fulfilling. I would like for everyone to have that same opportunity and so does our Father in Heaven who inspired this "Father's Wisdom" to save the lost.

Now for the balance of the readers, do I really need to go into example after example after example of the current state of our world in which we live, not to mention where it is headed? I believe the primary difference between the majorities of the population that agrees with me is the extent (or degree) to which this country as well as the entire world is spiraling downward. As in whether you are concerned, worried, afraid, or know beyond a shadow of a doubt that this is the case. The other difference would be whether you believe it's too late, versus we can still change the world. Then finally, for those who believe we can change the world, will you make the difficult choices to change and are up to the task and hard work and sacrifices to do so, therefore taking the position "if it is to be, you can count on me," versus those that will leave it up to "somebody/anybody" else to do it because they cannot be bothered. I think it goes without saying that we all need to take a serious look into this and start putting together viable solutions immediately.

I do not want to stereotype the different generational groups, but that is exactly the purpose for dividing us into these categories in the first place. So that economists, sociologists and psychologists, etc. can analyze (stereotype) these groups by their unique characteristics whether beliefs, buying habits, social skills, etc., then that information can be used in all sorts of ways from marketing to advertising to counseling, etc. If I could just read the minds of the readers of this book, I'd bet that based on whether you are a Boomer, an Gen X or an Millennial, that you are probably sizing up the other's as to who's responsibility this is, or who's going to "have" to clean this mess up, or point fingers on who made the mess, etc. Isn't that what we do? And isn't that exactly what we need to change? * See, if you want things to change then you must be willing to make the changes that are required and then do so, regardless of who did what or who is not doing whatever.

There is much being said about Millennials, whether it's TV commercials, stand-up comedians, articles, books on the generational differences (i.e. the workplace), etc. and again it is unwarranted and primarily due to our current culture of throwing "fiery darts" at every opportunity. So, who should take the most heat for the current state of our country? The Boomers parents and grandparents made it through the depression and the World Wars and brought stability, security and growth to the Boomers who catapulted this country into the modern age and affluence. Then do I continue by discussing things like over-consumption, greed, pollution, nuclear proliferation, wars, abuses of power, etc. and the Gen X's were right in the midst of this so what role do they play and where do the Millennials fit into this? The Boomers are retired or retiring so are they going to take responsibility and help to finance and repair this and are the recipients of progress the Gen X's going to help finance and repair this; or how about the Millennials are they going to carry the full brunt of responsibility on their backs? I know you all are already thinking these sorts of things, so I wanted to air everything out and also to make a point. As I have already said, it doesn't matter! We are ALL responsible for not only our current circumstance but are ALL responsible for now changing the world!

I often strike up conversations that have to do with various topics concerning our country or the world and since I travel often, I'm able to get a broad range of viewpoints. One that stands out in my mind and that correlates with this topic matter had to do with talking to a border line Millennial/Gen X (35yr old) male, divorced, 2 children, affluent, business owner, Christian and active in the church; I asked Him about the 2016 candidates for president and then we got into a discussion regarding the overall state of the country. Allow me to remind you, I will not use this opportunity to entertain and relay our entire conversation as would be the case in a reality TV show, this is for the purpose of brevity and so I can focus on communicating important messages. His summation point was, "the Bible reveals that everything in this world will continue to get worse and worse and I believe that that is exactly the case." Now I know this man well and I know that he's living a very comfortable life and he is not the type to whine or have a pity party, so I was very surprised that he so nonchalantly wrote everything off to that personal evaluation or belief. In the remaining conversation along with subsequent ones regarding various other topics this remained his foundational outlook. Something to also take note of is that he never alluded to what needs to be done or what could be done to avert what he sees as the inevitable. Yes, there is Bible prophecy that divulges that message, but for what age in time? Ours, or 100 years from now? As I said, there is absolutely no reason for him to see his glass as being half empty although that is exactly what he is conveying. If I were to stereotype him I would say he is a Gen X because he took over his father's (Boomer) company, although he comes across more like a Millennial, thus me stating earlier he is "borderline" and I'll soon elaborate on what I mean by borderline in that there are common threads that run through all of the generations that make it practically impossible to differentiate from one to another.

On a side note this brings me to a related topic, I wear various hats in the company I work for and one of the hats is advertising and marketing. I'm always staying up to date on business trends, business analysis, etc., and was reading an industry association article on a study that a large major chain retailer had done for the purposes of marketing and advertising to target markets. The survey, analysis and study were done nationwide with Millennials as the demographic. Keep in mind that this is a business-related article, therefore I was not privy to the complete study, only the graphs and condensed summaries to relay the specific and pertinent points determined by the study. Also, since it was an industry periodical, I trust the validity and that it is not biased or fake news. Again, I'm going to pare this information down to focus on the topic at hand. There are 2 primary categories that dominated their profile assessments that would be utilized in business advertising and marketing strategies. The two categories that are characteristic of the majority of Millennials: a) Lonely and b) Lost. WOW, you could imagine how this screamed my attention. As previously divulged, the Lord has brought so many things to my attention over the past fifteen years and this is no coincidence. Remember, I was simply doing research for my own business advertising strategies and this is a perfect example of when you "walk in the Spirit daily" (I'll elaborate on what this is in detail in other chapters of the book) these are the things that get <u>presented</u> to you so that you are able to <u>discern</u> the <u>message(s)</u>.

I wasn't at all expecting those two categories to top the list. Since I'm a business executive the additional hats I wear is HR interviewer and I'm the company trainer, meaning I am very familiar with all the various age groups characteristics (e.g. we utilize a Jungian theory-based assessment test prior to hiring). What I expected was characteristics like: tech-savvy; connected to social media; work-life balance needs; entitled; instant gratification; self-centered; overtly passionate; open-minded, environmentally conscious; liberal; etc., of which were all listed either as categories (or within them) but that the top two that stood above the rest, lonely and lost. The list I just relayed was not only included in the study, I chose to disclose the ones in which I've personally witnessed and agree with as well. I would like to interject some of my personal observations. To begin with, a unique characteristic that I've witnessed with Millennials is their actions often involve a dichotomy (as defined in the introduction chapter; "two sides of the same coin") and I would like to make clear that I am not referring to being dualistic (this is a derogatory term and it is a term often representing people with dual personalities) because that is not the case at all. Some examples of the two sides of the same coin are: the majority are labeled liberal but in my encounters (w/some college or degree; nationwide pool although concentrated in the southeast and midwest) majority are centrist, second are liberal, while the balance are leaning the conservative direction; they are definitely effective in a collaborative environment of peers but outside their peer group or in first meet (i.e. cold call) situations they are often socially awkward, they come across as being quiet to the point of being aloof (i.e. cool, distant); they are definitely multitaskers and can get a job done in half the time of a Gen X or Boomer but often it lacks attention to detail and their overall production by end of day is no different than the others because they have so many distractions that balance out their day (in other words, they could speedily accomplish the comparative of others work in 4hrs vs 8hrs but by the end of the day everyone's production is the same); their upwardly mobile inclined, many by their own initiative but I've witnessed many unsettling cut throat tactics in the workplace in order to advance (all Gen X and Boomers are considered immediate fair game, also even among their own peers), to add to this I did want to point out that I believe they are a product of our culture, referring to the age of reality TV. All too often in my international travels the conversation leads to American TV and how laughable and pathetic we are perceived; in fact their reality is that we all actually act like what TV portrays. In saying that, why wouldn't that strongly influence the generation of that time; and finally one more observation, they are overtly passionate but not always with the things they themselves or society would benefit from; *Point is, if they focused their passions on more of the things that would positively impact our society as a whole, they could change the world! And I mean that. I hope that none of you are taking what I've said to this point too personally, I'm serious, so please don't. As mentioned, all generations are "stereotyped" and how can anyone accurately place a label on 75 million people?? I only bring up my examples so to encourage some introspection for any attention that you may see needed and/or areas of personal improvement.

I've been very fortunate to have had been mentored by and work alongside a number of true Boomers (meaning the ones from 1942-54), including my oldest brother and sister and numerous cousins; just a different breed; incredible intellect and amazing to watch their thought processes and how they would operate; many of them truly gifted by God. This now leads me to make some other important points that Millennials can take to heart, I'm very impressed with this group as a whole. Primarily with their intelligence (similar to Boomers although more advanced) and their focus and concern with the overall quality of life; next to their interest on a broad range of social matters and issues (from social justice; equality; the quality of life; education; health; to international affairs; etc.); their concerns for the world's environment; their giving nature in terms of volunteering their efforts, that's ongoing and without hesitation; and this is what I believe is their strongest attribute: <u>passion</u>. I believe that God has truly gifted them with passion and a genuine care for others (despite negative cultural influences) and I see a light in them as I had witnessed in the Boomers that is unique. God has His "perfect timing" that I've experienced and witnessed over and over again and He undoubtedly has his hand in your intelligence and especially His perfect timing instilling in you a passion for others, because mankind needs that now more than ever!

My two awesome daughters are a part of the millennial generation and even though I am biased they too are a very close fit to what has been conveyed in this chapter. They both have very giving natures; my oldest has a therapy dog that she spends her weekends at Big Sister events, children's hospital events and nursing homes not to mention that she is on 24hr call with her job as a computer engineer specializing in robotics. My youngest has received her Master's degree and currently teaching a class as a professor's assistant (note: it is sad to divulge, but I know many more millennials better than I know my own daughters; I will elaborate on our strained relationship in this and future chapters). So in case you're wondering I did not use them as the model or factor them into my prior stated observations but as mentioned they pretty much fit the mold. Even possibly being lonely and lost to a certain degree, although you would never be able to tell if you met them. They are both very driven similar to myself throughout my entire life. Maybe they are still in the process of finding out who and what they are in this world. Much of what I've just relayed can probably be attributed to a broken home when they were 4 and 7yrs old. After my relationship failed with their mother I went into a deep depression and lost my job, but somehow that drive I spoke of appeared although very vaguely after about six months just enough for me to somewhat get my act together and I accepted a position half way across the country (only in retrospect did I realize that God was with me during this time, but didn't know it at the time because I had not yet been introduced to Him). The only reason I am bringing up this very personal information is to relay <u>a message to everyone, which is, you are pretty much no good for being a responsible party for others if you are not healthy (spiritually, mentally and physically) yourself, so that's a **wake-up** call for those who need it.</u> Therefore, I left knowing that I had to get my act together if I was going to fulfill my responsibilities as a father. I believe that I did accomplish it but only to the extent that one could do from being a world away. I spoke to them weekly and saw them once (sometimes twice) a year; they knew that I loved them and that they were constantly in my prayers and my thoughts daily and I supported their every needs financially, but not much beyond that. This is why I said they subconsciously or even consciously feel a degree of loneliness and/or being lost (although I have yet to ask them this question and a deep conversation seems to me to be something that is out of my reach, at least at the present moment).

Maybe time for another wake-up call, as mentioned they knew I loved them, I gave my advice and encouragement as I had the opportunities, etc., so they know of me but being absent they didn't know me intimately. I was a child of six, my parents stayed married, so I lived under my father's roof, but he worked all the time to provide a large family with a better than average lifestyle. When he wasn't working, he did attempt to participate in some of the children's lives, but I never knew him intimately. At best I observed him; his actions and words; but his beliefs were not clearly conveyed; etc. As I got into my teens the lack of intimacy (love) strained our relationship beyond repair. Also this is not just a father issue, I know plenty of people who would turn the table of this discussion on the mother or both parents. So point is, does this sound like you, or remotely resemble you? **Wake-up** and change things, start being an active participant in their lives versus an absentee parent whether long distance or a world away under the same roof.

Broken families are probably the primary contributing factor for the "lost and lonely" results of the study although I believe I know of a few other possible ones: possibly due to the growing secularism in this country (secularism as pertaining primarily to a nonreligious culture); the "body of Christ" (the Church) has let them down or was never a factor in their life to begin with; possibly even to a degree video games and social media contributed by isolating individuals and causing them to be less social (we were created to be in relationship with God and with others; if one or both of these falter on a collective scale it will make a resounding negative impact on society).

Nobody wants to admit that deep down inside their inner being that they are lonely and/or lost. So many put on masks (fake facades) to hide their reality, it's referred to as self-deception (this does not mean delusional). Self-deception is a form of self-preservation and although it may accomplish that purpose, it is at the same time negatively impacting how they view themselves and therefore negatively impacts their mental health. This also significantly impacts all of their relationships because in order to perpetuate the lie that has put them into that box, they have to lie (manipulate) all others to fit comfortably into the same deception box they have created and now inhabit. It's too deep a discussion to cover here but I think you can understand that by sustaining negative issues as these, is an unhealthy way to live your life.

Let's take yet a different approach in discussing these topics. Imagine you are a college senior pursuing a career in advertising and your professor assigns you a project to create a TV commercial for a major company (assuming all developmental criteria has been learned by you prior to your senior year; and that all strategies have been predetermined i.e. budget, TV channel, time segment ad would run, projected revenues that factor into determining whether a success or not, etc.), the only 2 remaining specific criteria to relay here would be: 1) product: beer; 2) target demographic: Millennials. As pointed out, you would know to research your target market extensively, one way being the study I mentioned prior at the beginning of this chapter, it has their personality characteristics / attributes; as well as numerous other studies as in buying habits, etc. We already know the study concluded that they are primarily lonely and lost along with a list of other characteristics. Question: What would your TV commercial be comprised of and how would it play out? Answer: Simply watch a Monday Night Football telecast and watch the commercials (whether beer or otherwise). They are all very consistent with each other and are comprised of the dichotomy (the flipside of the coin) to the study. Backyard or apartment common area with a "group" of people laughing and talking and enjoying good eats and beer; or young families having a BBQ outdoors with neighbors; or a group leaving another group at a restaurant or bar and getting into their "new car" (a car commercial) and laughing, having a good time and driving off into the twilight (or sunset). In other words, "the good life" or "the American dream."

You get the picture and I don't need to drill it any further. I also wanted to reiterate that there is a common thread among all living generations and lonely and lost is one of them, in other words it applies to us all. I'm sure by now you want to move on from the topic of "lonely and lost." But remember, a "Lost Generation" in part is what this book is about, although not just continuously reminding you of it <u>but finding solutions to correct it</u>! This chapter is titled "Lost Generation," so a few goals I'm trying to accomplish is defining what is meant by lost and who it involves; why and how this may have gotten to this point (<u>to learn from our mistakes; if you don't learn from your mistakes, you are bound to repeat them over and over and over again; except we are</u> now **running out of "do over's"**); next, to try to achieve a consensus that there is a problem and one in which merits immediate and significant action. The remainder of the book is about: where do we go from here; what steps do we take to change and what all is involved in taking those steps and accomplishing them; how do those steps factor into the goals that need to be set in order to achieve a predetermined end game result. So please bear with me a little longer regarding the continued discussion on "lost."

As mentioned, I haven't left Gen X out of this equation or the Boomers for that matter. There is much more to come on these two generations but for now I wanted to disclose that they too are "Lost." Actually, would you agree or disagree that you cannot label a specific generation as being lonely and lost? My point is, I believe it applies to all living generations and this is for a number of reasons. The most critical reason is because that is what God had originally revealed to me! That is good enough for me. So you could say that I didn't have to even write all the support information for this chapter and the book, just make the statement and relay the answer in a ten page article, post it in a blog and hope for the best. Thing is, who is God's "target market" here that I'm writing to? If someone is lost then they need some form of help: maybe all they need is accurate directions (wisdom; steps to achieving life goals); or they may have tunnel vision and can only see the massive and overwhelming tree in front of them and cannot see the width breadth and depth of the forest they are standing in, yet not even realize they are lost and missing out on a better _____ (abundant, purposeful and fulfilling = life); or they are unsure of their own status but can see that the rest of the world is on a crash course and you are wanting directions to do whatever you can contribute to avoid the crash; or you admit you are lost and that you need help but do not know where to even get started; possibly you are like some that need to be found first (maybe even rescued); this book covers every aspect I just disclosed and I can assure you of that.

Regarding Gen X, they are 65 million in population and are "THE" predominant generation to factor into this discussion. Why? Predominant because you are the "middle child" meaning your generation is smack dab in the middle of the "up and coming" Millennials and the "aging and departing" Boomers. Yes, you are not predominant in or due to sheer population numbers, but you play a KEY role in all matter of things. You are front and center; you are established with regards to your families, careers, business, finances, etc.; you are not exiting the workplace soon or reducing your involvement in the marketplace; you are significantly impacting the economy; you are significantly impacting the government and legislation on policies, etc.; and on and on. You still have influence with your children the "Millennials" and are the grandparents of the "Gen Z's." I realize that many of you are beneficiaries of the Boomers upward mobility, the advancements in almost every subject category, significant increases in earnings, on and on but I also realize that many have paid the price of greed, overconsumption, overspending, abuses of power, and so on. That you were also the beneficiaries of unstable economies with cycles of recessions which quite frankly forced a significant number of Gen X's to pack up all their belongings and move their families or themselves away from their extended families (while moving away from their hometown of generations) chasing after employment. Just one of the many sacrifices that has had to be made over the years. Note: these happenings and occurrences are what also "conditioned" the characteristic ways of the Millennials. Note also: that what I've mentioned is only a small portion of what is wrong with our country and our way of living. So now I'm asking the Gen X's (along with everyone) to make a few more sacrifices (i.e. contributing monies to finance the reformation; to vote for change; to change the status quo in their life and in their communities; and play an active role in this reformation). Great thing with Americans, we are resilient and committed to improving our lives and others lives, and sacrifice runs to the core of our being.

In saying that, the Boomers don't carry any more or any less of the burden of contributing to this initiative and reformation objective as does the Gen X's and Millennials. The same will be asked of you too: as in contributing monies to finance the reformation; to vote for change; to change the status quo in your life and in your communities; and play an active role in this reformation. Additionally, many Boomers are in the workplace because they either don't golf, or they simply want to stay busy. Unfortunately there are many more Boomers that do not have the retirement savings to sustain a living, therefore must hold menial, base or mid-management level jobs to survive. A thought to ponder, a nationwide initiative to reform the country will take a massive effort and would desperately need skilled workers in key role positions yet at base level wages; my recommendation is the Boomers pull out of the current workplace and take on roles fulfilling those positions referred to by utilizing their broad talents and capabilities to succeed, while maintaining close to their current income and could include some other incentives (a win-win for all). Note: these are just recommendations to stimulate thought at this time but will require future consideration on the organizers of this initiative. Also note: there needs to be a concerted effort in the current workplace to work on a transfer of knowledge from the Boomer generation to the others. Finally with respect to all generations contributing monies, a program needs to be put together to design, build and implement a system for the financing of this initiative and would be a priority first step. Note also that I do not want to tackle politics in this book but did want to briefly mention that I am not in any way shape or form suggesting socialism or anything similar. God prospered the United States in so many ways, one of which was with a free enterprise system and a democracy form of government and it should remain that way.

BTW, you've noticed that I use the word "reformation" (definition: making changes to something with the intention of setting it back on the right path; an action or process to change an institution or practice) because it best represents the monumental task at hand. The word "revolution" has been creeping its way into the mainstream and that not only implies violence, it implies an entirely new way of life forced upon the many by the few taking a violent shortcut while not addressing the actual diseases that caused the problems in the first place. Then also another term often used in religious circles, "revival" (definition: a recovery; comeback; restoration, resurrection). I believe it is a limiting term and doesn't convey the magnitude or the breadth of what needs to take place. Also I wanted to briefly point out that this is not at all about religion (especially organized religion). Succinctly, it is about a relationship with God and everything that a relationship entails, which in turn results in abundant, purposeful and fulfilling lives, which in turn yields an opportunity (that God makes certain) to change our thoughts, beliefs, words, actions across the board that it would require to initiate the much needed changes in the world we live.

I really don't like having to break all this down by categorized generations because again you are all included as the "lost generations" and we are all in this together; the workplace, the marketplace, the government, etc. are not broken down by age classification or otherwise. Additionally, when it comes to population numbers and generational categories (figures excerpted from Pew Research) Millennials have surpassed Baby Boomers as the nation's largest living generation, according to population estimates released (4/2016) by the U.S. Census Bureau. Millennials, whom we define as those ages 18-34 in 2015, now number 75.4 million, surpassing the 74.9 million Baby Boomers (ages 51-69); and the Gen X's (ages 35-50) now number 65 million. I alluded to this previously, the Gen X's for example, what's the difference of 10 million in the grand scheme of things and especially if you are currently in the driver's seat for this country. Add it all up as a collective force (or collective problem) and you have 215 million adults that have the capability to contribute to potentially changing the world!

I think initially I had the Millennials concerned that I was suggesting that they were going to carry the burden of this world on their shoulders, but I had a surprise in mind. Point is, this is a matter for all. If we are going to make this world a better place to live and in order to do so it must start with each individual (changing the way they are currently doing things), and then at least a significant amount of the population combining their collective efforts, this cannot be done by categorizing generations but as a total collective group. When communicated in that manner it sounds like a monumental task. Well, it will be. How do you eat an elephant? Or take on a monumental task? One bite at a time.

I haven't left anyone out, the Boomers have their accountability and responsibilities, as do the Gen X's have their accountabilities and responsibilities in changing the world. You should now realize why I made such an emphasis on the Millennials, obviously due to the study that made the connection between them being lost and lonely which related directly to this book (although I believe to a degree the majority of people today, not just Millennials are lost and lonely). But the primary reason why I am highly emphasizing them, is because they've been given special gifts and talents from God. *So (Luke 12:48)BSB "when much is given, then much is expected (or required)," therefore their accountabilities and responsibilities are automatic. Thus they will be the driving force of a reformation in this country and they are the transformational link of initiating change and then successfully passing the baton (via intently and righteous upbringing) to Gen Z's, so they can continue the progress.

There must be a...No, it must be clearly stated in terms of "we must..." WE must have a plan with set goals (targets) if we ever plan on changing the world. In the introduction chapter, I communicated: you can't continue to do the same thing and expect different results (the definition of insanity); also, if you are wanting to change what you are doing then you must change the way you THINK. If you have the opportunity to ask a forensic psychologist what the number one thing a convicted criminal can do to turn their lives around, they will respond, "To change the way they think." BTW, ask the same question to a faith filled forensic psychologist who is walking in the Spirit daily and living an abundant life and they would respond, "Pursue a relationship with the Lord and change the way you think." Elsewhere in the book we thoroughly cover the "renewing of your mind."

I can confidently say that God loves each and every one of you and He yearns to be in relationship with you and that He is the answer to all of your ills. As a collective we need to try to convey to others what they are missing out on and what the true benefits are from the brothers and sisters in Christ who are active in their faith, living and experiencing the abundant life that Jesus has promised. Now you may be thinking I'm not lost and/or I'm not lonely. Then great, but you should still seek out a relationship with God. Because He can improve your overall life, His gift of grace will bless you far beyond what you could ever imagine. For the others that are dealing with some problems or issues, the same goes for you...seek out a relationship with Him through His son Jesus Christ and it may or may not happen overnight but He will lead you on a path of abundant living while you are here on earth and continue for an eternity.

Remember the example of the TV commercial that was the flipside of reality, man's brilliant attempt and strategy to manipulate the masses. On the flipside of that we need to open our hearts to the Lord first, then to others that are in this same boat or worse and relay that this life has its mountain "highs," but also has its valley "lows." That it ebbs and flows and that we have a God that loves us and will guide and direct our paths to a more balanced lifestyle in which abundant living prevails. So we have our work cut out for us in communicating this "good news" of Jesus Christ to the majority of a 200+ million population that the majority (up to 80%) claim they are Christians but most are not practicing and those that practice (estimated less than 20% of total; or less than 40M) are active in the church body. Note: the church body is not necessarily referring to a brick and mortar building, but the body of Christ, the active Believers that have their faith and trust in Him.

Regarding churches, even they are not exempt from problems and pains of this world. For now though exposing all their issues is not relevant to this topic, but to give you an example of a big issue in terms of what is considered right versus wrong or confused priorities, there was a day in which the church helped the needy of this country but now it is primarily the responsibility of the government. For a dramatic example of a wider spread problem, a natural disaster flood had occurred and people looking for shelter were turned away from a large church. The church claimed that they were not equipped to provide the needs of a shelter, but in reality many a church are a business first and this one needed to focus on having the church available for services which provide the revenue stream and could not afford/allow the sanctuary to be tied up for weeks or months as a shelter. Remember earlier in the chapter when I made the point that sometimes we need to step back and get ourselves healthy before we can adequately help others? I believe this is the case for not only the church but for our government as well. I'm not suggesting isolationism, however there should be a number of years designated in which both entities significantly reduce spending outside of this country (except for emergency humanitarian situations). * Point is our country needs to focus on its own needs first rather than straining already stressed resources and depleting our ability to sustaining the helping of others. A refocus of efforts over the next seven year period would allow for the Gen Z's to begin entering their upper education period (to prepare them with specific information and access to provide their role in the effort), along with the country having a renewed focus nationally with plans on what steps to take internationally.

Along those same lines of refocusing, I communicated at the beginning of this chapter that the church has given in to the pressure of having to entertain its members/congregation while limiting the opportunity to "hear" the Word of God preached which as you've seen throughout this book is extremely important to your walk and spiritual growth with the Lord.

One of the many references in scripture on the importance for us to hear the Word of God is when Jesus said **(Luke 6:47-49)**BSB "Whosoever comes to me and hears my words and acts on them, Then he is like a man who built his house on a rock foundation, so when flood waters arose it could not be shaken, for it was built upon a rock. But he that hears and does not act, is like a man who built his house without a foundation on the soil, so that when the flood waters rose the ruin of the house was great." So not only is it important for each of us to hear the Word, so too is it important for the church to spend more time focusing on communicating it, otherwise its foundation becomes weakened in an effort to entertain over the opportunity to reveal the wisdom of God.

Additionally, not only is it important to hear the Word of God but even more important to act on it and this is covered in other areas of the book in greater detail, but I just wanted to take the opportunity with this particular scripture to point out and emphasize.

Another scripture that is relayed in a similar context is **(Romans 10:17)**KJV "So then faith comes by hearing, and hearing by the Word of God." When we hear all the stories, topics and teachings in the Bible it builds our trust in our Lord for a multitude of reasons which in turn magnifies that trust even more within us. So when combined with God's gift of faith to us, our trust and faith abounds into a powerful tool for us to possess along our journey.

In summation, there is no shortage of opinions and advice in this world today and "others" can communicate messages of insight to their hearts content, but they cannot save souls. As stated before, it boils down to the individual (to you) to choose to do something and then to act on it. Jesus is the only one who can save souls, and you have to open your heart and allow Him to enter and be the Lord of your life. I can personally attest and assure you that it will be the most positive and transformational action you will ever take in your lifetime! So begin considering this option starting now and continue to read on to get guidance on how to navigate this process and do so at a fraction of time then doing it trial by error, as well as being informed on the tremendous amount of benefits that you can claim from a grace filled relationship with the Lord.

Churches & Putting a Spin on the Word of God

In the previous subchapter, I touched on some problems that the church has been experiencing and I was going to leave this section out, but the Spirit nudged me to put it back in. Before I continue, I would like to make perfectly clear that **the church is extremely important to our spiritual journey** and have emphasized the importance of the church in my own journey by conveying it throughout this book. So this is not an attack, nor is it an opportunity to create fake news, but rather as I've noted many times that I'm just relaying the truth.

I've read a few internal newsletters of churches in which they speak of their congregation as "consumers" (I suppose "consuming," what it is they have to sell) and it's also public information of the millions of dollars some of the churches are bringing in every year. Churches today are big business and have significantly evolved, that is contrary to the perception many once held or still mistakenly hold of the role churches are supposed to play. Therefore it is important to keep an open mind in relation to these dynamics. Many pastors today have either taken it upon themselves or their church elders/assemblies have made this decision for them and that is to entertain their audience and worse to dummy down their service, sermon and messages in order to gain a larger audience. Problem is that this practice is contrary to what the Lord wants (see scriptures below). This is not the time to recite a dissertation on what a church should provide its followers, so in brevity * a church is to teach, equip, support and grow its following in every regards to the Word of God, therefore it needs to positively impact our culture and not become a part of the problem.

- A significant failure is with the churches not properly teaching on the Holy Spirit (as you've read thus far and will read in greater detail in the upcoming chapters, * the Holy Spirit and your walk with Him is crucial to your relationship with the Lord and crucial to living an abundant life).
- The Holy Spirit topic along with other topics that have been dummied down, watered down, or are diluted versions from what they truly are, leaves people confused and inept (unskilled & unproductive) by not accurately and fully understanding the wisdom and principles of God!

The following are scriptures that touch on the topic of when someone is twisting God's word or putting a spin of their own on it:
- **(1Tim 6:3-5)**ESV "If anyone teaches a different doctrine and does not agree with the sound words of our Lord Jesus Christ and the teaching that accords with godliness, he is puffed up with conceit and understands nothing. He has an unhealthy craving for controversy and for quarrels about words, which produce envy, dissension, slander, **evil**, suspicions, and **constant friction among people** who are depraved in mind and deprived of the truth, imagining that godliness is a means of gain."

57

- **(Gal. 1:9)**ESV "So now I say again, if anyone is preaching to you a gospel contrary to the one you received, let him be accursed."
- *** **(2Tim 4:3-4)**ESV "For a time is coming when people will not endure sound teaching, but having itching ears they will accumulate for themselves <u>teachers to suit their own passions</u>, and will <u>turn away from listening to the truth and drift away from God</u>." (emphasis added)

As I was writing this short piece on putting a spin on the Word of God and a few major problems related to some churches, a portion of the church body and our society as a whole, the Spirit was guiding me in the following specific revelations: after having written that people who are hearing diluted messages become inept or unproductive with regards to a full range of God's wisdom and blessings, I then pinned that people are turning to the demonic because of Hollywood for one (i.e. movies and TV) promotes it, teaches it and its power. This may be difficult for some to believe and accept but a couple of days later the Spirit brought this scripture to my attention, not only validating what I had written but bothered me a bit as well.

> **(1Tim 4:1)**ESV "Now the Spirit expressly says that in later times some will <u>depart from the faith</u> by devoting themselves to <u>deceitful spirits and teachings of demons</u>."

So, you are wondering what the big revelation is and why would it be a bother. Aren't all <u>false teachings</u> linked to the devil (i.e. demonic) and hasn't this been going on for thousands of years? Yes and yes. But what bothered me was that the Holy Spirit brought this specifically to my attention and as I believe we are in the end times (although may be hundreds of years yet to live out), it just adds another layer upon layer of problems and issues we face today. The good news is that He did bring these revelations to my attention for a number of reasons, and the one most important is to communicate it to you. And my hope, faith and Believing is such that God will assist us in correcting these ills and many more.

Jesus Saves: Lost, Lonely or Lucky

Have you ever taken a walk down the road called "Lost," although in your final analysis, you either believe you are lost, or you believe that you are not. *
Therefore the point is, you and only you will determine whether you take a step towards Jesus, or not. See it's pretty cut and dry, but then again, it's not; although it can get pretty complicated, but only if you allow it (this is what is referred to as a "paradox;" contradictory qualities or statements). That road you've walked down that you may now be denying was called "Lost" may have actually been called "Lonely," but are you going to admit it, or deny it as well. Regardless whether Lost or Lonely, often times it simply does not fit into the neatly organized

box that you view yourself in, so not many people like to admit things such as this, and that is okay. I will although cover this topic because as you read on, it's a topic matter that's a major problem in our society today.

So, if you do not believe you are lost, then great. If you don't believe you are lonely, then good for you. What I will NOT relay is that this book is not for you, or that you don't need God in your life. Because <u>this book is for everyone</u> and <u>so too is God for everyone</u>. **News flash:** I am not trying to "sell" you on anything; for one thing not everyone will "buy into" what I am disclosing; not everyone will get saved; not everyone will once they are saved, do something more about it; not everyone will...you get the picture. I'm the messenger, I'm delivering a message I was given by God, our creator. Now after I've communicated the message, the first, second, third (and so on) steps are entirely up to you and God; then beyond that it is up to your relationship with God and your relationship with your brothers and sisters of faith, the body of Christ.

Back to the topic of being lonely, keep in mind that there are numerous other ills that you may have, but lost and lonely are sufficient to convey this message. For those of you that say, "how can I be lonely and not know it?" or "I really don't feel lonely, sure there are struggles in my life but I don't have an overwhelming sense of loneliness, so in other words I'm really not sure," or for the others that know they have a void in their life but cannot understand or explain why or what it is; the answer is somewhat simplistic which is a relationship with Jesus Christ and if you allow it to become paradoxical and difficult or complex then it can be that too. Often when someone thinks they have a void in their life or knows they do (and this person can be a successful actor/actress making millions of dollars but still know there is a void), the void is: not having Jesus in their life or not building their relationship with the Lord and thus living a truly abundant life.

The naysayers would probably stop right here and say, "You're trying to convince me (or others) of being lonely. This is another way that you are attempting to manipulate me to get saved. You've probably given this extensive thought and planning, then reverse engineered your arguments to take everyone down the same path." And on and on. Isn't that our culture, full of opinions and the easiest way to shut something down is to adamantly and categorically reject it? Thing is, since this is our culture I realize that some will admit to needing Jesus in their life for this, that or another reason; and some will dance around the topic; some will be sincere in their consideration; and some will reject it; the purpose of me to continue to cover the negative viewpoint is so that I reach a broader audience but as mentioned I know for a fact not everyone will get saved and by the way so does God.

Regarding convincing someone of thinking, or feeling, or believing something, fact is: "You" are your own person. For example: you can be either lost, lonely, fearful, anxious, angry, filled with resentment or bitterness, etc. Or you are not. Point is: Nobody or nothing can make "You" feel or believe anything or anyway unless "You allow it." As examples: "they made me feel as though I'm not a part of the team;" "they hurt my feelings;" "he made me sad;" "she made me mad;" "he/she is the reason for my anger and resentment;" "I am anxious over _____;" and on and on. To reiterate, you are your own person and if you are that easily manipulated then you've got some work ahead of you. The good news is that the Lord will help you in this area, He will give you God-confidence and He will help you from **rearming** the enemy in your mind that causes you to "think this way," and He will help you in **disarming** the enemy if you backslide and open portals. (See chapters on My Lord's Prayer, Holy Spirit, Spiritual Warfare and the Mind) Briefly, due to our fallen nature and a time without God, the supernatural forces of darkness on earth have access to the mind of mankind, referred to as the devil, who uses primarily deceit and distraction as his primary tools to manipulate us. This is often referred to as a conflict (or battle) that goes on in your mind and has to do with good vs. evil, right vs. wrong, etc., and since we've all been given "free will" (the freedom and ability to choose), you have the right and ability to make any decision you want to.

(**Col. 1:21**)KJV "And you, that were some time alienated by God and with **enemies in your mind** by wicked works, but now hath He reconciled." (condensed)

Wicked works = devil / reconciled = balanced (disarmed and now made of no effect / made the devil of your mind of no effect or disarmed)

(**Col. 2:15**)NKJV "And having **disarmed** principalities and powers, He made a show of them openly, triumphing over them by the cross." (principalities and powers = devil/satan)

As per our discussion, if you want to allow others to make you feel bad then you have that power to do so, no matter how counter-productive it may be; if you want to believe that you don't need God in your life, then you have the power to do so. As to what happened with Adam and Eve, when they chose to eat from the tree that they were commanded not to, the devil then took up residence in the minds of mankind. *So when you make a decision that is contrary to God it results in a number of negative consequences, one of which has been pointed out here and that is thinking negative thoughts, then believing them and those thoughts manifesting into greater conflicts and continues to grow and perpetuate the problems in your life.

Lucky (blessed) is the man/woman who is not lonely and who feels they are not lost but the Lord determines He would pursue them anyway, get their attention and then convince them to allow Him into their hearts. I've alluded to this early in the book and that is, it would have been great if the Lord had done that with me early on in my life because it would have saved me and others a lot of heartache and pain. Don't get me wrong, I've had an incredible life full of experiences but I have no doubt whatsoever that my life would have been even more incredible and in addition to that I would be able to say it was meaningful in terms of other people and thus absolutely fulfilling. I'm getting closer to being able to relay just that, as I mature in my walk with the Lord and I think that I will accomplish it with His continued support. My point is that I just wish I would have had the opportunity to get to know Him sooner in my life because I know that so many more people would have been blessed and lives enrichened if I had. I would like to also relay, what is more important to me than being able to say that I had a meaningful and fulfilling life, rather that I was able to impact others' lives in a meaningful and blessed way and ultimately for me is to hear God say these words: "Well done, well done my good and faithful servant."

The next subchapter divulges the attributes of a Believer and illustrates what I just mentioned about a blessed and enriched life and a couple of keys to achieving them is to believe wholeheartedly, commit yourself to this renewed lifestyle thoroughly, receiving all the blessings bestowed upon you and acting on them. God bless.

Attributes of a Believer Who Walks in the Spirit: Hope, Love, Faith, Trust, Confidence, Joy

In the prior sub-chapter I referred to the enemy of your mind and how the Lord will help you, therefore the **HOPE** that you have in God is that He **will** help you from rearming the devil along with his deception and distraction tools and He will help you in disarming the enemy if you backslide and open portals (* NOT that we know that God can and we are "hoping" that He will, but our Hope is in Him that He has done this consistently in the Bible, therefore He will also do so with us; and note that this is one of His many promises to us; and He fulfills all His promises). One of the ways in which this occurs is by "the renewing of the mind" which is done daily (see this discussed in detail in My Lord's Prayer and Holy Spirit). In regards to the topic of being lonely, the HOPE that you have stems from the confidence and trust that God **will** fill that void in your heart with Himself (His Holy Spirit and His son Jesus) and with that you will be blessed with all the attributes that go along with having your heart filled with Him; note: "God is love" **(1 John 4:8)**, therefore He not only loves you, He fills your heart with love, then

61

it is your choice what you are going to do with it afterwards. Take a moment and read that verse in full context **(1 John 4:7-12)**NKJV "Beloved, let us love one another, for love is from God, and whoever loves has been born of God and knows God. Anyone who does not love does not know God, because <u>God is love</u>. In this <u>the love of God was made manifest among us</u>, that God sent his only Son into the world, so that <u>we might live through him</u>. In this is love, <u>not that we have loved God</u> **but that he loved us** and sent his Son to be the propitiation for our sins. Beloved, if God so loved us, <u>we also ought to love one another.</u> No one has ever seen God; if we love one another, <u>God abides in us</u> and <u>his love is perfected in us</u>." These are just five lines of scripture out of the hundreds that are an example **of the HOPE that we are given in God by his promises to us and by what he's done consistently and forevermore in the Bible.**

A key * word in the prior sentence is "**given.**" Hope is a **gift** from God! Hope is another dichotomy of God's kingdom in which He gives us a gift, BUT that we must cultivate it and act on it for it to come to full fruition in our lives. It seems counter-intuitive to many: God gives us hope and it's not something that we ourselves develop on our own power over time nor is it based on His performance or our performance. He gives the gift of hope, not because He has so very much to offer which would give us hope after we had figured that out, but He gives us hope and then we have the choice to utilize it (act on it) or not; this is a similar process as compared to our faith (confirmed trust) in that we are given faith and we develop our faith by developing our trust in Him and this takes time so you can utilize, or not; and there are many similar gifts/promises that it is up to us to Believe and then we are able to participate. The other Key * word in the same sentence is "**in.**" If you adjust the sentence it reveals the answer to what Hope is. It is the HOPE that we have <u>in</u> God. Meaning we hope in God to do what He has <u>promised</u> us (period). Yes, God's kingdom is overflowing with gifts, blessings, capabilities, powers, etc., so in a specific situation you can hope for this or that (but hoping for something is not what HOPE is). **HOPE is what we have "in" God and what He has promised us; it is a divine promise that we can and should stake our lives on.** Hope also has to do with our outlook on life in terms of how we perceive life. * With having received the gift of hope and us having cultivated it with trust, faith, love and confidence should result in a positive outlook on life rather than a negative one; this is a Key * to having an abundant and fulfilling life.

> **(Isaiah 40:31)**NIV "<u>Those who HOPE in the Lord <u>will</u></u> renew their strength; They will soar on wings like eagles; They will run and not grow weary; They will walk and not be faint.

(Isaiah 40:28-31)BSB "He gives power to the faint and increases the strength of the weak. Even the youths may faint and grow weary, and young men stumble and fall. But those who wait (Hebrew: expect/hope) upon the LORD will renew their strength; they will mount up with wings like eagles; they will run and not grow weary, they will walk and not faint."

LOVE is a comparison example to HOPE, it too is a gift from God. Previously in **(1 John 4:7-12)** John's passages concerning love ("NOT that we have loved Him, but that He loved us"), in other words, we don't have to love Him but He will always love us no matter what. When you take the entire Bible in context you can paraphrase by saying, "That God is love and that all love is of God." Meaning first of all that God cannot-not love and that since love is a gift to us given by God then "all love" expressed anywhere/anytime is of Him. So again with this example it's counter-intuitive, meaning: you don't have to love Him to "experience" His love (whether directly from Him or from any other person imparting His love); also there are no conditions of your performance to "receive" His unconditional love, although in order to "receive" it and then "release" it to others, you do have to do so through being saved by His son Jesus Christ. * You can know "of" His love, but to receive it and its power and glory you have to be in relationship with Him (e.g. "to know God is to love God"). To further that, to "receive" God's grace and blessings to the fullest extent (a product of His love/giving) then you have to be "in proper relationship" with Him. Note: this love is what is referred to as agape love (supernatural; unconditional) which translated means "giving" love not a "romantic" love (you know what romantic love is, or at least you think you do; I'll save that for another chapter). Hopefully I did not get too far off the path of hope by giving you a comparison example of love. The purpose was to convey that love and hope have a relationship that are intertwined.

As I've said in relation to most topics, I could write an individual book on Hope and there are numerous in print. There is a trend today of pastors who primarily focus on specific biblical topics such as Hope and Grace which are the two most popular. But our purposes for now are to illustrate the meaning of Hope in relation to the topic of being lonely. In reading this book from cover to cover, you will see the relationships between God's gift of hope: and how it allows us to experience joy in our lives; also hope allows us to experience abundant living; the hope that He is always there for us with the promise that He will never forsake us gives us security and comfort; when our lives do a 180 degree turn and it no longer resembles what we had dreamed it would be, we have hope in Him to help figure it all out; that He relates to our struggles and storms of life and is "an ever present help in time of trouble" **(Psalm 46:1)**; in other words, * we have hope in Him and

63

we can therefore have faith in Him (trust) and count on Him (confidence); the hope of having a brighter day today and tomorrow (joy); the list goes on and on. All of these, factor into us having a positive life, a positive experiential spiritual life journey on earth so that He can live through us and us through Him. This should begin to start adding up and making sense to you and with that puts you on the correct path of understanding which leads to abundant living.

FAITH too is a gift from God. This gift is often misunderstood because a) people don't know that faith has been given to us by Jesus, therefore b) they are confused about it because they are "working" at figuring it out and trying to develop their faith and trust and then trying to increase their faith. For example, the passage **(Eph. 2:8-9)**NKJV "For it is by grace you have been saved, through faith—and this is not from yourselves, it is the gift of God—not by works;" when this passage is shortened it confuses even more "By grace, through faith have you been saved." Here Paul is referring to salvation (to be saved) as the gift (not faith); and that we receive it by the grace of God; and that it is through our faith (trust) in God and all the variables involved in His kingdom that makes salvation not only possible but promised. So faith is another counter-intuitive gift that God gives us then it is up to us to use it, act on it and develop it in part by trusting in God and His Word. What throws many is that often people say that you did not get _____ because your faith is not strong enough. For one thing, only God knows whether it is strong enough or not and He will let you know it as long as you are in tune to Him; also if you listen and believe others opinions of what is wrong with you then that is a problem in and of itself; * faith is intertwined into your relationship with the Holy Trinity (Father, Son and Holy Spirit) which determines its "strength;" etc. So, we have faith when we are saved, and it involves a trusting relationship with God and that faith is an integral part of God's kingdom.

I wanted to get that explanation made first, as well as illustrate to you how things can be easily confused. Faith itself is not confusing; all it is, is having the already confirmed trust in God and in relation to your relationship with Him. Most of the confusion stems from faith's connection to God's kingdom and how faith operates/functions within the kingdom. With all that said, you should be prepared for the next step and that is defining what faith is. Note: I've used 3 different translations (that illustrate why you should use different Bible translations) to illustrate to you how this topic continues to get confusing for people. Paul states it succinctly in **(Hebrews 11:1 KJV)** "Now faith is the substance of things hoped for, the evidence of things not seen." (NIV) "Now faith is confidence in what we hope for and assurance about what we do not see." (AMP) "Now faith is the assurance (title deed, confirmation) of things hoped for (divinely promised), and the evidence of things not seen [the conviction of their reality—faith comprehends as fact what cannot be experienced by the physical senses]." As you can see the Amplified version is more detailed in its explanation assisting in the comprehension of the message being relayed. The New International Version is the easiest to understand but not as explanatory as the AMP. **FAITH is an already confirmed (by God) trust that we have, in what God has promised us; even though we have no physical proofs, and yet we choose to believe in Him (true faith occurs when we incorporate a wholehearted belief).** We have to **trust** that God (is what He said He is and does what He says He will do) has confirmed/substantiated/validated His power and authority throughout the kingdom and the world, and that we can trust in His guaranteed Word (Bible) even without any physical proof. So the example of not having enough faith or it not being strong enough becomes clearer here that it is entirely between Jesus and that individual to work it out via the Holy Spirit. If that leaves a gray area for you regarding the way to "strengthen" your faith then you are still struggling with the concept because in order to strengthen your faith you must ask for more faith from Jesus and He will give it out based on your conviction and trust; subsequently that conviction and trust strengthens the faith, therefore it is similar to the "full circle" concept: we're given a gift, we act on it, the Lord increases it along with increasing our blessings and the cycle continues as long as we hold up our end of the responsibilities.

   * A common thread throughout this Hope and Faith explanation is the word "**TRUST**." We trust in God's guarantees / promises (our Hope in Him) and we trust in the who and what God says and does (our Faith in Him). Next, we are commonly referred to as "**Believer's**" and that is derived from the faith and the trust and the hope and the love/giving that we have "in" God (to Believe). Next, we are not commonly referred to as "**Receiver's**", but I want you to put this into your vocabulary and your thought processes as you read this book. A Believer, who is in an obedient Spirit filled relationship with God that actively applies his/her faith, hope and trust in everything pertaining to God has the keys to God's kingdom. Meaning, God's full grace is filled with His glory and infinitely abundant blessings and He shovels those blessings continuously from heaven to us but the key is to be a believer who is in an obedient Spirit filled relationship with God that actively applies his/hers faith, hope and trust in everything pertaining to God, then you have the access to now "receive" those blessing and "act" on them. I've referred to the "processes" of God probably a couple dozen times already in this book leading up to this most significant process in His kingdom if you are going to experience and live an abundant life.

   * To relay the prior paragraph more succinctly: you must be saved by Jesus; you should do your best to maintain an obedient relationship with the Father, the

Son and the Holy Spirit which requires a "daily walk/communication" with the Holy Spirit; you need to practice your faith, trust, hope, love/giving as a **Believe**-r; you need to **Receive**-r all the messages, gifts, blessings that God is raining down upon you (you receive by believing it is so [Mark 11:24NKJV Therefore I say to you, whatever things you ask when you pray, believe that you receive *them*, and you will have *them*.]); and since you received it by believing it is so you must "**ACT**" on it whether a continued act of believing until it happens or act on whatever variables needed to make it manifest into being. Now listen up, this is the optimum goal: to achieve this abundant favor from God. But I wanted to let you know so you don't get frustrated, that as a Believer you will be blessed by His grace as I had pointed out previously by the same measure that you put into it. As an example, when I was a "babe" in Christ and on my early learning journey my blessings and rewards were still significant and it was also abundant living, but I lacked in so much understanding which in turn hindered my growth (but such is life). I didn't grasp the concepts of faith and hope or understand how to receive let alone know what I was receiving; nor did I understand the "act" of believing it is so and acting on it; etc. But as my walk matured via the Holy Spirit so did my understandings and execution which resulted in even improving my already abundant life.

CONFIDENCE, trust and believing are three attributes of a Believer that the Lord does not give to us as a gift, rather these three are entirely our responsibility to choose to utilize, grow and apply and are essential components in our relationship with God. Primarily because these are the components in which we solely choose to do, versus being given gifts of love, hope, faith, etc. which in the final analysis we still have to choose to participate, and if we do so, these gifts provide us with an advantage *because it originated as a gift that has power behind it. The entire Bible and specifically the Gospel is designed to give us assurance that God will do what He promises He will do. That assurance really takes root for us when we've chosen to believe and then believe wholeheartedly. *With believing in God, then combining that with Jesus's assurance and the gift of faith, gives us the ease and ability to trust and have confidence in God which in turn begins to solidify our relationship and puts it on a path to success. This is another illustration in how trust and confidence are so closely related and how they strengthen each other.

Do not confuse confidence with self-confidence (which is confidence in self). Remember that in your relationship with the Lord you are to die of self and make him the Lord of your life. This confidence I speak of is something we develop in unison with developing our trust in the Lord. Therefore in this example we have confidence in the Lord, but I did want to take a moment to explain another term I refer to as "God Confidence." This made such a positive impact on my life that I wanted to share it with you. In brief, I am extremely uncomfortable in having to speak in public for a number of reasons I've already mentioned in the book. I already know that practice helps to reduce the anxiety and gain confidence. The problem is that you can't always practice if for example you are in a corporate meeting or interactive seminar, etc. in which your presentation is impromptu. As I matured in my walk I found that I could * unleash my God-Confidence in my morning prayer in which I anticipate having to give a talk and it's worked every time (note: that the Holy Spirit will actually present you with topic matter to prepare you; that is if you are using your tools of discernment that the Holy Spirit has provided you). I believe that it's primarily worked because as I've matured in my walk, and therefore I am more contented, less anxious, more confident and trusting in the Lord, etc. and they all combine to provide me with the God Confidence that is always with me and always accessible. The topic of God Confidence is very important to me and important for me to relay to others. It made such a positive impact on my life and is ongoing. Try incorporating it into your prayers and try cultivating it to work for you. One important suggestion is to take the term self-confidence completely out of your vocabulary and always say, or think of it, or have the mind set of: God-confidence. Note, that it is not just a matter of semantics (using one term rather than another) and it is not a mind or thought altering technique. I've communicated to first pray for God-confidence regularly, then receive it and believe it is so and act on it by utilizing your God given talents, gifts and blessings to successfully handle the situation. In the example of public speaking, you should prepare and practice when applicable or be prepared by anticipating what may be presented that day (point: God-confidence is not blessing you with the ability to "wing-it"). ** Another extremely important aspect of God-confidence is in realizing that your walk with the Holy Spirit is all day and night and the true basis for your God-confidence is that He is beside you step by step (as in this example) in assisting you in your clarity of thought, focus of mind, accessing your memory and communicating topics clear and concisely. For those of you who can't relate to problems with public speaking there are a multitude of examples in which the Holy Spirit is always by your side and giving you the God-confidence you need to hurdle various roadblocks in life.

JOY is also a gift from God. And it too falls into the same category of being counter-intuitive in that God gives us the gift of Joy, but it is up to us to grow it and incorporate it into our lives, preferably on a consistent and daily basis. The definition of Joy is that it is a positive state of mind and an orientation of the heart, an ongoing anticipation of happiness. If you did not pick up on it, the reference to the mind and heart is directly relating to our soul. And our soul is our fleshly nature, our feelings and emotions, often negative if not being renewed regularly in your walk with the Spirit, the part of us which can allow portals to open and allow the devil to manipulate and influence, etc. The key here is your daily walk with the Spirit and a continued effort to grow spiritually in wisdom while developing your relationship with God. If this is taking place, I assure you that you will have joy exceedingly abundantly in your daily life. This is obviously a contributing factor of leading an abundant life. It is also a reward that many will pursue that are lost and lonely. Often times the first stage that you achieve is having a positive outlook, secondly it is achieving a state of daily contentment and inner peace and thirdly is the ongoing process of building the gift of joy to dominate your state of being day in and day out. A quick note, happiness by definition is from the root word happening which means that to be happy is a state that is due to something that has happened, and therefore is temporary to the extent of the happening ending. So joy is related more closely to contentment and a positive attitude than it is to happiness, although can at times involve all four components.

Even if you think you have everything that this life could possibly offer, but you don't have Jesus, then you don't have everything. Because what you don't have is the promise of eternal life that is beyond this life, and the only way to receive it is by salvation (getting saved) through Jesus Christ. If you are **lost** (meaning not saved) then you need to decide whether to open your heart and accept Jesus as your Savior and Lord of your life; if you are saved but you are lost on what to do (or very recently got saved) then if you * focus on building your relationship with God via the Holy Spirit and the Bible then you'll receive an abundance of gifts such as hope, faith, love, etc.; so in turn if you are **lonely**, angry, unforgiving, bitter, etc., you will have the hope, the faith, the love, the grace, the blessings, the guidance to wash those negative things from your being and move towards an abundant life with your Lord.

On a personal note, I've experienced severe depression before I was saved; I've experienced being lonely a number of times; obviously before I was saved, I was lost but to expound on that I was lost in a number of different ways with various contributing factors before I was saved; but I can relay to you with honesty and firm conviction that after being saved along with some time to develop a greater understanding of the kingdom of God and his Word, from that day forward I have never since felt lost, lonely, depressed, etc. and even having some valley lows and wilderness experiences that afterwards I knew were trials I needed to experience, that because of my relationship with Him and my daily walk with the Spirit I have always stayed on an even keel and have continuously had a state of contentment during those lowest of times that I can only thank God for. *So what's significant to mention is that I have very few trials overall which leaves the remainder of my life filled with joy, love, faith, trust, hope, confidence, etc., thanks be to God! And this is what I hope that you can aspire towards and achieve yourself because I know beyond a shadow of doubt that it is available for you, if you so choose and desire to pursue. Please note: some of these topics are scaled down in order to cover the topic and stay in context with being lonely (or lost) and that you can find significantly more information on these topics throughout this book.

Wisdom

Please see God's Guidebook on life and abundant living, His living Word, **the Bible**. But only do so with your personal trainer, **the Holy Spirit**, to lead, guide and direct you through it and through your experiential spiritual life journey on earth. And utilize "A Fathers Wisdom for a Lost Generation" as a reference guide and to broaden your understandings of the Bible.

Wisdom continued

I did not leave a portion of the Wisdom page blank for no reason. It was for the effects, to grab your attention and drive home an extremely important life or death message. Yes, I'm serious about that statement. The **Father's Wisdom** is as crucial to you and your life as the air you breathe. He created his Guidebook for man's/woman's lives, just as He created the air they breathe to sustain that life. So if the Guidebook is that crucial for each and every individual, then why doesn't everybody know it by heart and study it daily? Well, I'm answering that question as you are reading because it is one of the overarching messages of this book from cover to cover, but to briefly relay, everyone has free will to choose to follow God, or not, and to live their lives selfishly on their own, or * as a collective for His purpose driven goals designed to optimize each and every individuals lives on earth and optimize their spirit/soul in preparation for their eternal life.

We all know the Bible is definitely not a step-by-step manual and I wanted to point out that it is NOT a manual whatsoever. It truly is His "Guidebook" for life and abundant living. And He gave us an incredible gift, His Holy Spirit as our personal guide to help us navigate the Guidebook and apply it to our daily lives in order to navigate our experiential spiritual life journey on earth. A manual implies that one size fits all, thus all you have to do is follow it step-by-step to accomplish what? Manuals are static and one size are supposed to fit all, so then are the final goals yours or His? Rather, God gave us another incredible gift which is free will, also would you agree that you are different than your brother or sister to the point that **you are extremely unique (as in uniquely designed and made) and that being so then what you require is a personal guide (Holy Spirit) to lead, guide and direct you through God's Guidebook (Living Bible) that is referred to as living because although the words are the same in every book for everybody, with the help of the Holy Spirit those same words jump off the page at each of us differently (in revelation) and fortunately so, because we have the free will to change our decisions at will and doing so the words change that are jumping off the page at you; this in turn guides all of His children through this maze called life while we are accomplishing His predestined goals for us to optimize our lives abundantly on earth in preparation for life eternal and so that He can live through our lives.

I just relayed a lot of information, so feel free to reread it a couple of times over, because it is a brief synopsis of why we are here, what we are supposed to be doing and how to do so. Obviously, I'm conveying all of that and more in greater detail throughout this book. Be sure to always be in the Word daily in your walk with the Spirit and be sure to be validating and justifying what you read and hear concerning scripture and other matters. I myself do that and require the Holy Spirit as my guide in doing so as well as rely on qualified teachers (pastors) to hear the Word and to receive additional revelation from. Hopefully you find these writings informative, inspirational and revealing God's Word and messages to you. Just as with the Bible, you should read this book and reread whenever you get the opportunity. Also as with the Bible and due to the amount of scripture that I've conveyed, you can read today and get "A" revelation, read again next week and get "B" as a revelation, read again next month and get "C" as the revelation, in other words <u>a different revelation each time</u>. That occurrence is what is taking place and by definition what is meant by the "living" Bible, and every Believer knows this is the case.

You may have thought this book was going to be a sequential list of phrases of wisdom and the supporting stories as examples of how that wisdom plays out but is not the case. I did although utilize some personal stories and other stories to deliver messages but with supporting lines of scripture that provides the wisdom. * I want to communicate an important point, I purposely tried not to relay any of man's wisdom and if I did it was to show that *man's wisdom HAS NO POWER. Man's wisdom has either a close resemblance to scripture or just the opposite, therefore can have little impact or none whatsoever on other people and primarily consists of man's logic and rationale, often his ignorance, sometimes common sense, accumulated knowledge even if it is false, etc. <u>Only God's wisdom has power</u>, via His supernatural almighty power that can significantly impact us and everything around us.

The apostle Paul spoke on the wisdom of man and of God. In **(1Cor. 2:4-5)**KJV "And my speech and my preaching was not with enticing words of man's wisdom, but in demonstration of the Spirit and of power, so that your faith would not rest on men's wisdom, but on God's power."
(1Cor. 1:17)KJV "For Christ did not send me to baptize, but to preach the gospel, not with words of wisdom (men's), lest the cross of Christ be emptied of its power."
(2Cor. 11:19)KJV "For you suffer fools gladly, seeing you yourselves are wise." Translated: "You gladly put up with fools, since you are so wise."
(1Cor. 3:19)KJV "For the wisdom of this world is foolishness in God's sight."
(1Cor. 3:20)KJV "And again, the Lord knows the reasoning's of the wise, that they are useless."
(1Cor. 1:24)KJV "Christ is the power of God and the wisdom of God."
(1Cor. 1:30)KJV "But of him are you in Christ Jesus, who of God is made to us wisdom, and righteousness and sanctification and redemption."

The apostle Paul basically conveyed that God gifted us with his Son, thus giving us a wisdom from the source of all wisdom, which surpasses any wisdom we could have derived from nature or from man. *So in relation to this book, "A Father's Wisdom for a Lost Generation" has nothing to do with my wisdom but has everything to do with God's wisdom which He sent to us and we have full access to in the form of his Son Christ Jesus, who is revealed throughout all of the pages of the Bible and of this book along with His wisdom.

Please note that the topic of wisdom is, as just mentioned, throughout the entire book but more specifically there is a section pertaining to it in Ch3 * My Lord's Prayer and also Ch5 The Holy Spirit. And by the way, I can use the same analogy as I had before but with more clarity, "The **Father's Wisdom (Jesus and the Holy Spirit)** is as crucial to you and your life as the air you breathe," and this should become crystal clear to you in the upcoming chapters.

God's Formula 'My Theorem' (Wisdom cont.)

After having previously touched on the subchapter Power of Hope, Love, Faith, Trust, Confidence, Joy and Believing, now would be as good a time as any to give a synopsis of these powers by means of an easier to remember formula.

Wisdom = Knowledge and Understanding

Early on in my walk with the Holy Spirit, He instructed me on the importance of God's wisdom and that it consisted of all of God's truths as per what's written in the Bible. Whereas man's wisdom is only a culmination of past experiences whether accurately recalled or not and is a wisdom that is fallible and has no power. In addition to that man values his importance on his own knowledge and intellect well over that of his wisdom. If we used man's example as a babe in our spiritual journey we would be searching for "knowledge from God and acquiring it based on our self-inflated intellect" and by the formula's illustration it would be a wrong path to take. God's wisdom on the other hand is loaded with power and benefits for us. To clarify how it works the Holy Spirit instilled in me this statement (which quantifies and verifies the formula): * * * "Wisdom gives us knowledge and understandings of God's kingdom and of the things of this world." Therefore, you must first seek God's wisdom in all of your endeavors and this is done via your prayers and your daily walk in the Spirit along with him directing you to the proper and appropriate scriptures (whether during your reading or your hearing of the Word) and he assisting you in your discernment of the Word and of the things of this world in order for you to make informed decisions which are in alignment with God's will and purpose for your life. His vast wisdom gives you the knowledge that you need while at the same time helps you understand that particular knowledge and wisdom that was revealed and received. Well that was a mouthful and a lot of information packed into a succinct statement. Thing is, that says it all. This is truly God's formula from my perspective because the revelation was presented to me by his Holy Spirit, but since because it is not directly stated in the Bible (although relayed in context with Jesus's teachings and Paul's) I will refer to it as "my theorem" (an idea or proposition proved by a chain of reasoning or truths; a truth established by means of accepted truths).

If I were to attempt to put the full explanation in a formula it may read like:

God's Wisdom = Knowledge + Understanding (of God's kingdom & the ways of the world)

=> Informed choices & decisions (to reduce negative consequences) and remain in alignment with God's will and purpose for you

(Note: => reads "yields") Well I did that not to see if it could be done but as a prelude to relay additional messages in formula form for the previous "attributes" of a Believer. For some it will be helpful but for others who cannot relate, you should probably stick to the explanations throughout the book rather than the equations.

God's Wisdom + Gift of **Hope** = Knowledge + Understanding (coupled with your choice to believe, have trust and confidence) +action => **unleashing the POWER of HOPE in your lives**.

God's Wisdom + Gift of **Faith** = Knowledge + Understanding (coupled with your choice to believe, have trust and confidence)+action=> **unleashing the POWER of FAITH in your lives**.

God's Wisdom + Gift of **Love** = Knowledge + Understanding (coupled with your choice to believe, have trust and confidence) +action => **unleashing the POWER of LOVE in your lives**.

God's Wisdom + Gift of **Joy** = Knowledge + Understanding (coupled with your choice to believe, have trust and confidence) +action => **unleashing the POWER of JOY in your lives**.

Signs of the Times

In terms of the "Lost Generation," I conveyed the meaning of what a lost generation meant; the various characteristics of our present generations some good and some not so good and in explaining them I exposed some cultural issues we're having to endure. These are all "signs of the times" in which Jesus warned about, that we should be diligent and discerning to be able to identify, then evaluate and then do something constructive to resolve the issues. In **(Matt 16:3-4)**BSB Jesus said, "And in the morning, 'Today it will be stormy, for the sky is red and overcast.' You know how to interpret the appearance of the sky, but you cannot interpret the signs of the times. A wicked and adulterous generation looks for a sign, but none will be given it." He was relaying that even back then people figured out ways of forecasting the weather although they acted naïve, or ignorant, or simply apathetic towards discerning the things that were happening right in front of their eyes, and thus not doing anything to resolve the problems of that age. Next, He was saying that those same people are stereotypically defined as a "wicked and adulterous generation" that looks (and asks) for a sign from above before they would <u>believe and then maybe act</u>. He's saying that if they ask, that no sign will be given because of the disregard for anything but themselves. Additionally, Jesus knows that people who are purposefully ignorant, lazy, apathetic, has wicked evil ways and are adulterous typically possess more than one of these detriments because they are all bedfellows, where you see one you typically see them all (that also means each individual that fits the stereotype of that generation has most or typically all those characteristics).

Note, Rather than I convey my thoughts, I'll allow you to determine the following: concerning the scripture I just mentioned prior **(Matt 16:3-4)**, do you think what Jesus was communicating thousands of years ago applies to us today?

I won't put you through a plethora of examples for the signs of our times. You already know about the natural disasters, wars, threats of wars and possibly another world war; terrorism; Islamic extremists; worldwide poverty; the division of our government; the division of race and social injustices; but are you keying in on all of our cultural issues: violence: crime; drug addictions; corruption; pornography; overall decline of morality; dishonor of others and betrayal; divorce and the further breakdown of the family; the disappearing middle class (division of wealth, the haves and the have nots); just to name a few. Come up with your own list, then contemplate whether any effort of value is actually being done to fix/resolve the problems.

On a side note, I personally experienced an organization in which it was fractured and divided. I expressed my concerns on a number of occasions and paraphrased this scripture **(Matt 12:25-28)**NKJV "But Jesus knew their thoughts, and said to them: "Every kingdom divided against itself is brought to desolation, and every city or <u>house divided against itself will not stand</u>." To be politically correct and not relay religious beliefs in the workplace, I paraphrased: "a divided house will fall, and this company has been split way too long, with nobody addressing the diseases (people) that are causing it." For me it got to the point that I no longer wanted to be a part of it, so I left. Now, I had no intention of prophesying the ending of that company, but it was a few years later that it did fail, $100M+ in annual volume, filed bankruptcy and closed down.

I hope that you are beginning to see that <u>the Bible</u> is truly a <u>living document, meaning that its information is ageless,</u> even 2000+ years later it is pertinent to the issues we face today. I didn't purposely find scripture that applied to today and paired it up with issues and events, as mentioned its teachings apply to everything we face. These examples should also illustrate what I meant in the introduction chapter when I communicated that the Bible is the "guidebook to life and living." With having said that, your daily walk with the Holy Spirit will give you the power of discernment. As with most words **discernment** has a number of meanings: a) to perceive, grasp, or understand spiritual meanings and teachings, without passing judgement; b) the ability or skill to interpret a broad range of things we encounter daily with extreme accuracy via the help of the Holy Spirit c) to have sharp perceptions and good judgement, typically involving psychological or moral issues. Therefore in the case of the signs of our times, the Holy Spirit would bring things to your attention and then assist you in interpreting with accuracy what is taking place and the possible solutions. Don't confuse the next example with intuition because discernment is not at all like intuition. Say for example you arrive home at your front door and the welcome mat is slightly off to the side of center of the door. The Holy Spirit will bring it to your attention rather than ignore it especially since you keep a spare key under it and the Holy Spirit again will lead you to be super aware and cautious. I wanted to point out that discernment and walking with the Spirit even has to do with everyday things not just saving the world. Another way of explaining it is it heightens your awareness, senses or radar all day long and assists you in passing judgment or making decisions for small and great things. It is something everyone should pray for daily and praise regularly. I can attest to its benefits and I could give hundreds of examples of discernment that has positively impacted my life. (See additional information chapters: My Lord's Prayer, Holy Spirit)

I hope that you realize (as I do) that <u>this book is not about me</u>. **It is about you.** It is about helping you and everyone I can in understanding the importance of a spirit filled relationship with God through Jesus Christ, as well as the blessings, benefits, and the overall improvement in the quality of life when you live the abundant life Jesus promised all who believe!

Another thing I hope you realize is that this is a process and that it doesn't happen overnight. It's not an instant gratification thing in any way shape or form; not a, "I have God now and I'm all fixed." The excerpt from the song <u>Amazing Grace</u> "I was once lost, but now I am found" is referring to being saved and now being established as a son/daughter of the almighty and loving God. The saving part happened instantaneously but the building of the relationship with the Lord is a gradual process. I was saved 20yrs ago and started benefiting from it immediately except I didn't realize it until a couple of years had passed and then only in retrospect, I could tell how it was transforming my life. I can confidently say though that within 3-4yrs I had the past behind me to evaluate the progress and while in the present I was seeing immediate benefits whether daily, weekly or otherwise. It was a gradual process and I could see that by whatever measure that I put into it, I would get out of it; **(Matt. 7:2)**KJV "With whatever measure you measure it will be measured to you." There is never enough time in our busy lives so when other things took precedent over my focus on growing in the Word then the growth would seem to go into a holding pattern although the relationship, the guidance, the protection, the blessings, etc., continue as normal. A common analogy, is when you plant a grape seed in <u>good</u> soil it requires water, sunlight and (food) fertilizer to germinate and grow; then it requires that same continued support along with eliminating weeds, insects, rodents; then after the first year of growth the same continued support and a post winter pruning; eventually with commitment and perseverance you will reap the harvest from your efforts.

(Luke 6:38)NIV "Give and it will be given unto you. A good measure, pressed down, shaken together and running over, will be poured into your lap. For with the measure you use, it will be measured to you." The prior scripture and **(Matt. 7:2)** fulfills a number of messages for me to relay. First, you can tell with my response "It was a gradual process and whatever measure I put into it, I would get out of it," was that I was taking baby steps early in my journey and as I matured I understood that the more I put into my spiritual journey I would get exponentially more out of it. So these two scriptures help to reveal that. But what I also wanted to point out is that in Matt. 7:2 the true context was if we judge others, we would be judged the same; and with Luke 6:38 this context was in regard to giving. This is an example of taking scripture out of context which I have warned against doing, so always take the time to determine whether it really applies accurately or not whether from me or from anyone else. In this case no harm was done due to the topic matter, but the scripture Luke 6:38 has been abused for years and done so consistently with what is referred to as the "prosperity gospel" which conveys a message that if you give monetarily that this is God's message to man that He will multiply those monies. *Note: if you encounter this message turn and run from the pastor delivering it. Jesus warned on numerous occasions (primarily with the religious Pharisees/elite of that time) not to manipulate scripture for personal gain and/or to mislead others. The so-called prosperity gospel is another such example of just that. Granted, when we give of ourselves to others in whatever form that may be, God does bless us far beyond what we gave, but as a "concept" of God that is specifically concerning money and a greater return on that money, that is a false teaching. To finalize and clarify, *God's process is that we "get" from Him so that we can "give" to others thus glorifying Him and the process can be perpetual as long as your intent and motives are a product of your humility and just so you know it, God knows this of you.

For practical purposes, if you want to excel in your "walk with the Lord" then it requires <u>time, effort and commitment</u> on your part, so if you devote yourself along with these requirements you will see significant gains with respect to your life. But if after a while you back off of the time, effort and commitment in your relationship with God it is like most things and go into a cruise control mode where there's no noticeable gains although the Holy Spirit is there as you need Him. And of course, if you turn your back on God (whether intentionally or not) and pretty much pay Him zero attention then you'll reap nothing in return (remember though that He is an awesome God and when you come back to Him with "sincerity" He will take it up right where it was left off). To combine the two prior explanations, when you are putting in the time, effort and commitment so too is God. God has planted his seed "inside" of you, His son Jesus who is supplying you internally with the "living water" and the "bread of life" and externally supplying you with more (via His teachings), while the Father prunes the bad leaves (dead or diseased issues, evil or problems) from you, and if need be, cut off any un-producing branches (from your life that conflict with Him and your goals for abundant life) while the Holy Spirit does his comprehensive work so your crop yield (fruits of your life) is optimized and abundant. So, <u>transformation is a gradual process which requires your commitment, patience and perseverance.</u> Note: there are transformations of the miraculous nature that, just as with most <u>miracles,</u> are rare and a uniquely separate occurrence in God's kingdom (than from your daily walk) and most often are instantaneous or comparatively rapid happenings. Whereas to reiterate, your transformation that takes place with your walk with the Lord is a gradual process which requires your commitment, patience and perseverance.

Since I've been referring to gifts from God, Salvation is another of His free gifts to us. When you are saved (the act of asking Jesus into your life <u>and receiving</u> Him; the giving up of the old person and the "birth" of the new person with having Jesus enter into us) is a <u>miracle</u> and it takes place instantaneously and then the gradual process begins that I've been mentioning. Also note that many people get caught up in the "emotions" of getting saved and after a couple of days those emotions calm down and they allow the excitement and the enthusiasm to diminish and they don't act on anything, or they do act but they are not getting the proper help and information to advance in their journey. Don't allow this to happen to you!!! The good news is this shouldn't happen to you because you are reading this book. One of the primary reasons for this book is that it will cut down on the "learning curve" of trial by error approaches by giving you advice on how to further your relationship with God through Jesus Christ and via the Holy Spirit. After just a couple of chapters and in what you've already learned, optimistically you are seeing this beginning to occur, also that you are seeing, feeling and believing in its broad benefits. But if not yet, the more you read the greater the possibility of success of this happening.

Walking with God

Walking with God is an extremely important thing for us to do. Throughout this book I have emphasized to "walk in the Spirit daily," because it is an essential aspect of our relationship with God and with maturing in our spiritual journey. Did you know that the Bible refers to walking and walks over 300 times and 50 of those times it is referring to doing it daily? The context is primarily in relation to the following 3 things: a) in making progress towards a destination, b) interacting with another, c) in referencing a passage of time (i.e. daily). God is relaying that in order for you to make certain your progress towards your sanctification, your destination of eternal life, your experiential spiritual life journey on earth, your abundant living, etc. that you must #1) walk (take action) and #2) walk with God (Holy Spirit) to receive His favor and blessings and #3) so that you make progress towards your sought after destinations and what He has predestined and purposed for you. Obviously, there is so much more to it, but you get where I am going with making that statement.

To paraphrase **(Amos 3:3)** can two go walking together and not be in agreement? He is establishing that to "walk together" means to be in agreement with each other. In regards to God, when we walk with Him, we are in agreement with Him. The flipside of that statement is that, if we are in disagreement with God, we could not walk with Him (e.g. non-believers walk according to their own evil lusts and fleshly nature, which is in enmity [opposed] to God). * In walking with God, we understand Him and He us; We know what He expects of us and we do our best to deliver; He always delivers on His promises and He lets us know that as we deepen our discussion while on our walk; He knows our desires and our needs because of the daily walk and have intimate conversations with Him to reveal these things and more. I've stated elsewhere in the book that too many people treat their relationship with God similar to a phone call, once they relay their laundry list of wants they hang up the phone and go about their days and nights as they please and without giving Him any other consideration (unless of course something happens in which they need to call Him again). Is this how you handle your relationships with loved ones as well? I think not. There is a saying, "To know God, is to love God," and this was derived primarily because He is love and all love is of God, therefore to walk with Him and to know Him intimately is to truly love God. So if you truly love God, why would you only spend a couple

78

of minutes a week on the phone with Him asking for His blessings? Because He is a father figure and that is what we do in society today, is go to dad to get things? Just food for thought. * To get to my point, if you walk with Him daily, spending time communicating your thoughts to Him throughout your hectic day rather than all the self-talk you do, and you are open to receiving His messages and discernment of the things around you, then your life will be a spirit-filled one and in turn realizing the benefits thereof and living a truly abundant life.

As pointed out, throughout the Bible there are detailed accounts of people who walk with the Lord: David, Job, Noah, Moses, Abraham, Joseph, Elijah, Enoch, etc. So what I just disclosed sheds a different light on those stories and gives you the opportunity when reading those accounts to glean much more out of them with the understanding to evaluate the importance of each one of their "walks" with God. I've conveyed the concept of shadows and types in the OT elsewhere in the book and in order to illustrate foreshadowing is to review the story of Enoch **(Gen. 5:24 & Heb. 11:5)**. Throughout the entire genealogy of Genesis 5 each generation would finish with "and he died, and he died, etc." until you get to Enoch, "who walked with God" but instead of it saying that he died it conveyed that "and he was not, for God took him." As previously mentioned, there are multiple examples and rich stories of people walking with God, but the Holy Spirit had me relay this one. I even contemplated not using this particular example because it is hard for most to comprehend but this is a good example of the unseen supernatural aspect of God as well as revealing one of His mysteries and allows you to research on your own the other rich stories mentioned. The story of Enoch is still highly debated as to whether God translated him to heaven, or rather God translated him miraculously to another place on earth because he was facing a horrific death due to his beliefs and preaching's (this interpretation is the one most widely accepted among scholars). Really there is no reason to determine an answer because it cannot be proven due to its supernatural nature and in trying to it just gets into a legalistic argument that wastes everyone's time. * The key message here is that Enoch walked with God and the result in doing so: he is pleasing to God, he is glorifying God and he is in God's unique and powerful favor (to the extent of being saved from certain death). God recorded and revealed this in the Bible so that for millennia man would understand the importance of walking with God for himself (thus the foreshadowing of what we need to do ourselves). By the way, *I suggest reading the stories of David's and Joseph's lives which are rich in the trials and tribulations of life, the losses and successes of life, how it all relates to the importance of walking with God and the benefits thereof. Now would also be a good time to relay that in the OT the Spirit of God was only available to man as per God's designation and it was usually temporary, therefore most accounts in the OT was referring to walking with God rather than the Spirit. Now it's completely different, remember that when Jesus ascended, the good news (gospel) was that we would receive a helper the Holy Spirit of God. This is the incredible gift we were given and who we have the opportunity (if we so choose) to walk with daily and in turn get rewarded. Question is, why wouldn't you choose to do so and take advantage of such an incredible life changing, life improving opportunity?

> Note: Paul's brief 2 lines of scripture in the explanation of Enoch, he points out that Enoch had to of had faith because **(Heb. 11:6)**NKJV "But without FAITH it is impossible to please God; for he that comes to God must BELIEVE that He is, and that He is a **rewarder** of them that diligently seek Him (walk with Him)."
>
> **(Gal. 5:16)**KJV "This I say then, Walk in the Spirit!" Here Paul is stressing the importance of walking in the Spirit of God, meaning to take direction from God himself. Note that he capitalized the W in Walk attempting to get the attention of the readers to its importance. Also note, the context in which he is relaying this important message: it has two references a) if you walk in the Spirit you'll be released from the lusts and evil appetites of your flesh and b) if you walk in the Spirit you'll be released from the dominion of the Law. Regarding the law, Jesus revealed that with his new covenant with God we are no longer under the law and its burdens but rather we are under God's grace. This is just a different way that Paul chose to relay the same thing and it is interesting how he does that. *He's pointing out that the flesh is known for its long list of sins and that the Spirit is known for its even longer list of God's graces and also that the law has no power over either of these two heavyweights. Also Paul is implying that God's grace (if we give it the opportunity) will beat out the flesh and its sinful nature and how we could accomplish that would be to "Walk in the Spirit daily" as he so emphatically instructed!

Good News: God's Grace

Let's begin with some background information and foundation:

> Genesis 1 is an account, a record of God creating everything; and He did so by his spoken word as was relayed "And God said..."

He also blessed everything he created, as was relayed "And God blessed them..." *Man having been given this blessing, will always have a longing (emptiness) deep inside his spirit and soul to be blessed continuously by God and only God can fill that emptiness and void. One of man's problems is that he/she looks outward (to other people and things) to fill the void but this lasts only temporarily if at all; or they look inward as directed by self-help motivators/therapists, or by false religions, etc. to fill the void, again this too is only temporary; but the answer

80

lies in who created us, therefore we should be looking upward to God to fill the emptiness and void that is within us and the key is that it would be done for an eternity.

* God never intended or desired that we should be anything other than blessed! But evil entered the world and due to God's just and legal nature man was forced to either be sinless in order to have a relationship with God, or to sin, therefore not be in relationship with Him. The Law was enacted so that man could <u>identify sin,</u> but man could never live up to the Law's standards, no not even one man. So sacrificial offerings were made to appease God and it was only a select few high priests, a select few prophets and select few men that were allowed a conditional relationship with Him. *It was not until His son Jesus chose to come to earth as fully God and fully man and eventually choose to die on the cross for the full redemption of man's sins all past, present and future, then resurrected to heaven to sit at the right hand of God was man then justified and able to have a relationship with God through his Son Christ Jesus (this is a significant portion of the Gospel of Christ, although relayed in a nutshell).

This was a much-abbreviated explanation leaving out a significant amount of details which obviously can be sourced in the Bible, but this was done so that I could fast forward to the topic of grace. Now God has a renewed opportunity to bless mankind continuously but due to man's free will it is up to man to first accept His Son Jesus (the sacrificial lamb who made this all possible) as his Lord and Savior, then to allow Jesus into their heart to be the Lord of their life which then allows them to have a relationship with the Father. Many of you understand what I just relayed and have followed through with the process, but many probably do not realize that God is now blessing you continuously via his grace (this is an important * key point to remember).

Allow me to elaborate. Let's begin with the topic of love previously covered in this same chapter. I communicated that God is love...also that all love is of God, therefore there is nothing we can do to earn his love or nothing we can do to deserve his love, because He loves us unconditionally regardless. Again, many do not understand that God loves the sinner but hates the sin. Also, even more do not understand that God loves us more than we could ever imagine or comprehend. In that same manner, God is grace...and all grace is of God, therefore there is nothing we can do to earn his amazing grace (* unmerited divine favor). Note: God's grace is a manifestation of his glory and his blessings are a manifestation of his grace. In other words, His blessings are a direct product of his grace and because his grace is a continuous outpouring, so too are his blessings which are freely given by God, on the basis of His grace only, BUT must be received by us

81

(His Believer's) in order to benefit by them. To further, Jesus is God, and therefore He too is grace, although at times Jesus refers to his Father's grace, nonetheless He too is grace (*Jesus is grace personified) and having this mental picture will help you in understanding this process of God. This is where it can get a little tricky due to it being counter-intuitive and leaning towards appearing to be contradictory but be patient with my explanations and do your best to look at the big picture rather than dissecting the details. Note: after you understand the overall concept then you can dissect all you want as long as you don't turn into a legalist in doing so. If you recall legalists spend the majority of their time dissecting details and arguing their position or stance to the point in which they lose out on experiencing Jesus and having life in abundance.

Speaking of legalism, this is perfect timing to briefly cover something highly debated (the ultimate form of legalism) that I do not want to ignore in case you come across it, but I must caution that this argument is a distraction designed to confuse and distract (via the devil) and please don't allow it to. * Grace is one of the foundational precepts of God's Plan for mankind, therefore it is key that you understand its processes. Having said that, * grace therefore plays an integral role in the **Gospel of Christ** (good news of Jesus) but their intent is to relay the significance of grace, thus some pastors have coined the phrase "the Gospel of Grace," which by some is considered a misnomer (an inaccurate designation). But is it? Paul relayed one time in scripture the phrase "the gospel of grace" (**Acts 20:24**) and with that I'm sure that those pastors took the liberty to refer to it likewise (note: so will I, but will use the two interchangeably). Even though the following are variations of the same thing, what I will NOT do is confuse matters by using these other scriptural references of the gospel:

- **(Eph. 1:13)**KJV "the gospel of your salvation"
- **(Eph.6:15)**KJV "The gospel of peace"
- **(1 Tim 1:11)**KJV "The glorious gospel of the blessed God"
- **(Rev. 14:6)**BSB "Eternal gospel" (glad tidings) as proclaimed by an angel
- **(Matt 4:23; 24:14)**KJV "The gospel of the kingdom" note: as communicated by Jesus (the 12 disciples preached of this one; but only Paul was given revelation from God about the good news of His grace)
- **(Rom. 2:16; 16:25; 2 Tim 2:8)**KJV "My gospel"... (Paul) The 12 disciples all learned of the gospel of the Kingdom together from Jesus; only Paul was able to refer to his as "my" because he was given a revelation from God about His grace as an offer of salvation without works which was in addition to the gospel messages the others were conveying.

- **(Acts 20:24)**BSB "I consider my life worth nothing to me, if only I may finish the race and complete the task the Lord Jesus has given me, the task of testifying to the gospel of God's grace."
- Contemporary pastors have coined these: Gospel of Hope; Gospel of Grace; Gospel of Faith; Gospel of Love; etc. as though any of the components of the gospel of Jesus Christ can be inserted into a focused preaching or specialized doctrine that they preach day in and day out.
- In another chapter I disclosed that there are gospel false teachings that are dicey (potentially dangerous). They seem as though they might be applicable but the intentions or motivations of the person(s) communicating them are self-centered or greed driven. Also keep in mind you will always be able to validate whether something is the truth or whether it's false by researching the Bible. In this case I'm referring specifically to "the prosperity gospel" and be aware that there are others out there.
- Final note: Paul warns **(Gal 1:6-7)**KJV "Anything which adds to or detracts from the good news of God's grace, is a distortion or perversion of the gospel of Christ." One thing he is alluding to is that by adding, subtracting or trivializing the gospel falls under the category of false teaching and is a desecration which often results in confusion and doubt among Believers or worse!

Key point: there are no conflicts or contradictions between any of the gospels mentioned! Except of course the prosperity one (See the sub-chapter on the Gospel in Ch.7 for additional information regarding the prosperity gospel and the confusion it's linked with). The writers simply wanted to emphasize specific areas of discussion at that particular time and chose to refer to the gospel in the same manner of emphasis. So now the only question is: "What's in a name?"

As mentioned previously in this book, there is only one gospel, the **Gospel of Christ**, but I would like to take the liberty to also refer to it as the **Gospel of Grace** for emphasis of God's powerful and amazing grace which Jesus personifies! Having revealed that keep in mind that just about everything is somehow interconnected, interlinked or intertwined in God's kingdom. With that said, the following attributes all fall into the gospel category: love, hope, faith (believing, trust, confidence), grace, blessings and so on… And since we've covered most of the attributes that leaves us with grace and its blessings.

So with that background and foundational information, let's continue:

Apart from God man is on his own to do as he pleases or so he thinks. The earth is Satan's domain, so if you are not of God then you are of Satan (there is NO in between). In other words, you have "given your-self over" to Satan in controlling you and emphasizing the lusts of your fleshly nature, allowing the ebbs and flows of your life to be dramatic highs and the lowest of lows, taking on all aspects of a broken spirit, soul and body, and on and on; but you are doing what you want to do, to do as you please, maybe some flat out wickedness or just some mischief but for sure having your worldly fun because that is what is most important to you. On the other hand, when you are seeking a relationship with Jesus but doing so intermittently then the following will apply: apart from God's grace, I do not want to obey God. But when we are in an intimate relationship with Him, walking in the Spirit, receiving His blessings, giving of yourself to others, walking in obedience to Him, etc. we are able to freely receive God's grace (think of it as a conduit from you to God in heaven and His grace flows through it). God's grace gives us the heart to be **faith**-full (to sustain our faith) and to obey Him. This is yet another example of a "full-circle" event in which the more grace we receive the more blessings we have to bless others with, so the more we glorify God in doing so and in turn God pours out more grace and the cycle perpetuates. * I promise you that you'll wind up living in obedience to God accidentally, then you ever have on purpose. It is only when we ourselves pinch the conduit closed, by departing from or not including God in our daily lives; or that we shut off the spigot completely, in order to do as we please, the result is that we are turning our backs on God entirely. This is the reality for many a Christian who for whatever reason gets sucked back into the lusts of the world. Also tragically, either the gospel or grace are not properly preached and as a result the sincere Believer gets confused about their standing with God and in that confusion they may abandon God's grace for other false teachings (whether other religions or even misguided Christian based false teachings) or worldly inferior alternatives or just give up altogether.

* The "amazing grace" of our incredible God even has a stopgap (temporary) measure in place to counter us from doing that, if it is not enough for us to lose His grace and His blessings so we can go out sinning as we please then He will cause His grace to "abound" in other words increase dramatically to counter our sinning in order to get us back onto His correct path (the Bible uses the term: dunamis which in the Greek means dynamite; and used primarily to exemplify and reveal God's power, God's strength, not ours). But as mentioned, it is only temporary because man has free will and can choose not to go back and this is where I must alert you of a danger and that is God will then "give you up" meaning give you over to your desires and He actually boosts those sinful blessings for you (again temporarily) in kind of a farewell gift (saying goodbye to His favor and His fellowship with you). **(Romans 1:24; 26; 28)**

This is a good point in this NASCAR race of life to take a pit stop to refuel, change tires and pull the tear off from the windshield to give clarity to the drivers sight (you); in other words I think it's time to interject some principles so that you understand where I am going with the prior and the upcoming statements. Just about every person in this country and many around the world have heard of God's "mercy" and maybe a few less have heard about his "grace" and I want to clarify what both are in a boiled nutshell.

- To name a few of God's primary attributes: God is merciful, loving, compassionate, faithful, forgiving and giving (gracious), etc. Wouldn't you agree with me that these are typically the most common foundational attributes that we associate with God? With Mercy and Grace being regarded as the primary, then with love, compassion, faithfulness and forgiveness as direct products of the two. To elaborate,

Mercy

- o **Mercy**: the definition is, withholding punishment that is deserved; which involves forgiveness and compassion; another way of saying, the withholding of due punishment, is to "give" in an unmerited fashion; God's hands were tied so to speak before Jesus gave up his life so that we can have a relationship with the Father, but now God can legally show us His mercy, grace, favor, etc.

  - Forgiveness: overcoming anger and resentment; **(John 16:33)** remember that Jesus said that He overcame the world. Overcame means victor, therefore when you forgive you are a victor over your anger and/or your resentment.
  - Compassion: sympathy for the suffering of others.
  - **(Psalm 86:15)**KJV "O Lord, you are a God full of compassion, grace, patience, tolerance, with plenty of mercy and truth."
  - Unmerited: NOT deserved and NOT earned.
  - Favor: God's approval of and demonstrated delight, in us, (His admiration and subsequent action on his part)
  - Unmerited favor: not deserved and not earned approval by God and in how He demonstrates giving His gifts to us.

Grace

- o **Grace**: is difficult to define because it is all encompassing, therefore a multitude of characteristics, for now though we'll focus on the context at hand: God's grace is **God freely giving unmerited favor**; note the emphasis on freely and on giving,

85

meaning that freely is without restraint, thus His favor is in continuous abundance; blessings are the subsequent action that He releases as a result of his favor for us; and this is done even though we do not deserve it and have not earned it (i.e. unmerited).

- Reminder, God is Love, therefore all love is of God; and God is Grace, therefore all grace is of God; both love and grace being a gift from God. **(Rom. 11:6)** If it were by our works and earned/deserved it would be a reward and not a gift.
  - * Jesus being the "Unspeakable Gift" of God to us, dying a sacrificial death for us and was subsequently resurrected so that we can be a) spiritually alive with God, b) be in relationship with Him and c) live for an eternity with Him; we therefore did not earn or deserve a, b, or c! In addition to that, you could say that all of God's gift to us are unmerited (not earned and not deserved).
  - * * BUT with Jesus's works we have been <u>justified</u>, set free to be called the adopted sons and daughters of God and reap the full benefits and blessings thereof.
    - o Justification is the "root" of God's legal system; a 1-time act of God that removes our guilt and penalty of sin via his Son's works on the cross.
    - o Before Jesus's works, God could not randomly select who gets what and after Jesus's works His abundance of grace was released to all. So it is either all or nothing. **(Rom. 2:11)**NKJV "There is no partiality with God."
  - Therefore, in God's eyes we now have merit and have earned and deserve His full grace. "I am the righteousness of Jesus in God's eyes," and this is due to Jesus's works on the cross.
- Why did I go to that elaborate an explanation? So that it is clear and no room for misunderstanding. Because with what so many pastors are preaching it is easy to get confused and misconstrue what they are saying versus what God's truth truly is. They will use unmerited favor and grace interchangeably while always reminding you the definition of unmerited. Did you know the word unmerited is never used in the Bible? Thing is, unmerited

favor is an accurate description of God's grace, * but do we need to focus on the fact that we cannot earn and do not deserve His gifts or do we need to focus on the endless ways God's grace can impact and improve our lives! To lessen the confusion, it would be nice to create a compound word such as mercy-grace because most everybody would understand and remember the definition of each and thus not get confused, but that's not even a word, so since unmerited favor has been in use for so long I'll use it and explain what is meant by it in detail. So I'm not yet finished,

- In another chapter in this book, I relay the importance and significance of you having the right frame of mind and a positive mind set. I am very concerned about this because due to recent surveys * <u>so many Believers have disclosed that they are unsure of where they stand with God,</u> and that this could be one of the contributing factors. For example, I'm not receiving the punishment that I deserve because of my sins (His mercy); I'm can't earn God's love or grace or other "gifts" that He gives me because if I was able to "work" to earn them they would be rewards and not gifts; additionally I don't deserve the gifts either, all because of my sins (unmerited favor/grace). So I'm told this and reminded of this over and over again, so I question as to whether I am worthy or not, from one sin, incident, or moment to another. You cannot doubt or waver on the truth of God or your faith. I can give endless examples, but you see where I am going with this.

- * * * You MUST BELIEVE! You must do so whole-heartedly, you do call yourself a Believer don't you, also you know God relays over and over again that you must believe! So now BELIEVE, do not doubt, do not waver, do not question, just believe, trust, have faith, have confidence in God, His Son and His Holy Spirit and His word the Bible (the <u>guidebook</u> for life and abundant living) and "rest" assured in Jesus and what He did for you, and in God believe in His: mercy, grace, favor, forgiveness, legal process and justification, etc. The following is one of the reasons why Jesus is our Savior and why He should be the Lord of your life and why we should honor God 24/7! Jesus had compassion for sinful man/woman and therefore left his state of blessedness with God in heaven and voluntarily underwent the hardships and miseries of human life and by his sufferings and death procured salvation for mankind. Thus man was forgiven all his past, present and future sins and therefore now has merit in God's eyes and can now receive the fullness of all of His gifts (grace, favor, love, faith, etc.). Therefore BELIEVE! Trust in Him, have faith in Him, have confidence in Him, what He reveals to you via the Holy Spirit and in what you know of the Bible, And know exactly where you stand with God!

- **(John 15:5)**KJV Jesus said, "For without me you can do nothing." Are you getting a better appreciation of that statement?
- **(James 1:6)**KJV "But let him ask in faith, nothing wavering (no doubt). For he that wavers is like a wave of the sea driven with the wind and tossed."

Let's back up and cover something that you might now have a question about. Back when I relayed: God is grace…and all grace is of God, consequently there is nothing we can do to earn his amazing grace (unmerited divine favor). Earn is referring to your works; you cannot perform works to earn His grace. But wait a minute, I also relayed that you have to be saved, and that it must only be through Jesus (the Way) is how you can have a relationship with God. Yes, that is true and also in having an ongoing intimate relationship you are continually blessed by His amazing grace. So you do have to do something? The reason this is difficult to answer is because there is two parts to it. On the one hand the answer is "Yes, somewhat." Meaning that God always expects you to act/do something, although that is an expectation and not necessarily a prerequisite. On the other hand the answer is "No, not exactly," * I communicated that God's grace is available for all; including those who choose not to accept Jesus or those who choose to turn their backs on God after being saved, and in both those scenarios God will "give you over" to your desires and his grace will abound and bless you in the direction that you have chosen, with regards to those particular matters of your heart. Just as stated in a couple of prior paragraphs, God will, in a temporary and one-time fashion, as kind of a farewell gift say goodbye to His favor and His fellowship with you. **(See Romans 1:24; 26; 28)** So, that should answer any question because in actuality the concern had to do with the measure or proportion of grace rather than if we can earn it or not. Hopefully you heard that loud and clear, so we don't have to labor on that aspect of the grace equation. Therefore His grace is not only available for all, it is given to all and the important take away for you is that if you walk with Him daily, renewing your mind, His grace and blessings are continuous!

Before I continue, I wanted to point out that this section on Grace is very important for you to read as well as the next "A Discourse on our soul and spirit." Rather than going into great detail on the following and subsequently losing some of you swiping pages forward to the next chapter, I'll instead do a rapid fire bullet point explanation on some attributes and just a few of the multitude of benefits that we receive from God's amazing grace:

- Sin consciousness **(Heb. 10:2; 22)** vs Grace consciousness. If your focus is primarily on not sinning then you will ultimately sin and do so with regularity; but if you focus on Jesus and receiving his abundance of blessings, most will not even consider thinking about sinning!
    o Grace is said to be the glue that bonds a Believer to God's will over their self-will.
    o The Law forces one to be introspective (i.e. why am I this or that?) and that pulls us away from God.
- The Law is demand minded vs Grace is supply minded
    o God will supply all of our needs; therefore stay contented and rest/trust in Jesus
    o The law will demand of us and creates a stressful environment; and stress kills! Also as previously mentioned, the law kills because we cannot fulfill its standards; therefore, we would be set apart from God, in which we experience spiritual death.
    o *Also keep in mind that when grace abounds, sin diminishes. We choose not to sin due to His abounding grace that fills and consumes our lives.
- The Law is the ministry of death **(Paul 2 Cor. 3:7)**; Under the Law, man cannot fulfill it, therefore He is separated from God and experienced spiritual death. God understood the danger hid the 10 commandments under a blood-stained mercy seat in the Ark of the Covenant, but people still want to hang them on the refrigerator, on the wall, etc.??? Yes, they're still a model/standard for men to follow but the value that grace brings to man is so much more important and vital to convey that message over the law.
- Jesus did not come to destroy the law but to fulfill it by choosing to be the sacrificial lamb to end the Law's bondage.
    o We still live in a fallen world that bares the effects of the curse (and so does the planet) **(Rom 8:22)**. Although those effects

89

remain, the good news is that man is redeemed from the curse of the Law. Thanks to God and Jesus.

- And thanks to the Holy Spirit and his awesome help. Due to His guidance and direction He was primarily responsible for replacing the Law. He assisted man in communicating to God in prayer and then assisting man in receiving God's blessings.
  - o Put another way, Jesus revealed God's grace to us (the replacement of the law via the Holy Spirit) and the Holy Spirit facilitates grace/blessings between God and man/woman.
- The New Covenant is between Jesus and God; and not God and man as it was in the Old Covenant. Therefore Jesus is "the Way" to the Father; He is "the Truth" made into flesh; and He is "the Life" due to his works (sacrifice) on the cross which allowed us a relationship with the Father so that we would have spiritual life, abundant life while on earth, and eternal life after our bodily death on earth.
- * **(Rom. 1:16)**KJV "The gospel is the power of God." Power in the Greek is dunamis, in which we get our word: dynamite.
- * **(Rom. 5:20)**KJV "Where sin abounded (increased), grace did much more abound." In the Greek the word used to more abound is hyperperisseuo which means "ultra-super" abounding (Grace)! You could also refer to it as hyper-grace.
  - o *Another way of wording that is: where grace abounds...sin diminishes; we choose not to sin due to His abounding grace that fills our lives.
- *Jesus always blesses first, then He says, "Go and sin no more." This is the process of grace! Not the opposite (but many people think, stop sinning in order to be blessed; but it's impossible to stop sinning to be perfect [i.e. why Jesus works on the cross].
  - o *Blessings often come before repentance. As an example, Peter caught a boat load of fish during a time that there had been a fishing drought, and while he was bringing the catch in he turned to Jesus and said, I should not be in your presence, for I am a sinner. (he received the catch blessing and admitted he was a sinner and not worthy!)
- When we fail a "test/trial" God has us take the test over and over and over again until we learn from our mistakes and poor choices. He desires for us to succeed and fulfill our purpose. If you find yourself in the same spot over and over again, then this is the process that is taking place and you need to pray for guidance and receive His grace and then act on that guidance even if it is something that you don't really want to do.

* The benefits of Grace are innumerable! A few additional key benefits I feel are important to relay: Peace; that surpasses all understanding! And contentment; no anxiousness, just resting in the assurance that Jesus promises. And Joy; the Joy that most all people aspire towards, but few actually experience! This is the even keel lifestyle I now experience, appreciate, give thanks for and praise Him for daily!

- **(1 Peter 4:10)**KJV "As every man has received the gift, even so minister the same, one to another, as good stewards of the <u>manifold grace of God</u>." (manifold means innumerable)
  - o *Giving is what we do. Here Peter is communicating the importance that we glorify God by being vigilant and steward the countless blessings from His grace to all others that we can, and in doing so it perpetuates over and over and over, full circle!
  - o Imagine if we (the full body of Christ) as a collective, lived our lives in this manner by focusing on the important things of God, what this world would be like! We would move mountains!

* God's grace enrichens our lives, which in turn allows us to be fruitful (giving, loving, goodness, etc.), complete (purposed filled and abundant life), and filled with glory and joy.

We've been blessed so that we can be a blessing to others! As Jesus is, so am I, and in this instance as Jesus did, so am I to do.

- Thus becoming more like His "image" every day.

*Grace should be a foundational principle that you live your life by! Even though it is continuously raining down from God, <u>it is up to us</u> to be diligent in receiving the blessings and living in accordance with His will, walking always with Him, and on and on as I've emphasized throughout this book.

- If it is to be, it is up to me.
- **(John 1:14; 16-17)**NLT "<u>Jesus, full of grace and truth</u>...**<u>from the fullness of his grace we have all received one blessing after another</u>**. For the law was given through Moses; grace and truth came through Jesus Christ."

To summarize "The Gospel of Christ/Grace," is difficult to do but here goes. The Gospel consists of many things but can somewhat be relayed in a short and concise statement, "That Jesus died on the cross <u>for us</u> (<u>you</u>), so that our (your) sins would be forgiven all past, present and future, and the Father raised Him after he had finished ALL the work that would benefit us (you). We now can choose to have a relationship with the Father through Jesus and via the Holy Spirit of God, and those relationships result in us having an abundant life and experiential spiritual life on earth. Note also that the Bible is all for us and about us cover to cover, that **is** what God intended it for, and it's all about being a guidebook for us on how to live this life abundantly, if we choose to read it and believe in it wholeheartedly and allow the triune God to help us with it and through it. It is all about God giving to us and us giving to others."

It cannot be said that there are end results of the Gospel because it never ends, it's everlasting and it is "All-in-All" (everything in God's kingdom), but rather it can be said that one of the most significant and beneficial consequences of it is: Be sure to always remember this, that anything and everything **we** have in this world that has value and is good…is because of Jesus. Therefore, anything and everything **you** have in this world that has value and is good…is because of Jesus…and due to the works, He finished during his lifetime and on the cross! Without Him and without what He did, we probably wouldn't be here or the life we have would be completely different (negative, dark, evil, heavily burdened slaves) from how we currently know it. Because of Him we have a relationship with God and favored in His eyes and get to experience a relationship and an abundant life with Him, his Son and his Holy Spirit! In addition we are given power and authority in this world to be able to live life to the fullest and to be in positive relationships with our fellow man.

A Discourse on our soul and our spirit
Which of the following would you prefer to have win out in your life? The fruits of what your soul by itself can produce i.e. attempting to achieve selfish, self-driven desires; or the fruits of what your spirit in conjunction with the Holy Spirit can produce, i.e. abundant living and eternal life.

In the subchapter on Glorifying God we covered an extensive amount of material and included in it was the following scripture **(1 Cor. 6:20)NKJV "For you were bought at a price; therefore 'glorify God' in your body and in your spirit, which are God's," as previously emphasized, this scripture leaves no doubt that we can in fact glorify God.

**Note: the spirit is a lower case "s," therefore it is not the Spirit of God, rather it is our spirit that knew God before the beginning of time.
(1 Thes. 5:23)KJV "And the very God of peace sanctify you wholly; and I pray God your whole spirit and soul and body be preserved blameless unto the coming of our Lord Jesus Christ,"

The following is a discussion on what we are comprised of: our spirit, soul and body, and for most Believers this is a given, it's easily understood or better yet it's easier to not do a deep dive on the topic and just take it for granted. That is exactly what Satan wants and how he wants you to handle it. I, on the other end of the spectrum, am here to relay to you that this topic is foundational to your spiritual success and subsequently to your abundant living and even to the extent of impacting your eternal future. It's a topic that is generally accepted and is a building block out of the many that make up the kingdom of God and thus can be easily overlooked and on the most part it is overlooked by most Believers today. It's important to point out that during these times this topic was a given or common knowledge thus Jesus conveyed this within His messages and his disciples did the same concerning this topic. Therefore, * there are plenty of dots to connect in order to conclude an answer (which I will do here) and I would like to point out that this is a key example of where the Holy Spirit plays such an important role in guiding and directing you accurately and onto the correct path.

I could have taken the path of least resistance here as have most Believers and concluded that the soul and spirit are one in the same and it would have cut down on probably eight pages of explanation, rather than concluding that the spirit is separate from the soul. But what is interesting is that both scenarios end up taking you down the same path in regard to the analysis and begin to differ significantly only with regards to the end results, which I will begin to point out. There are those who say that the soul and spirit are one in the same? Remember that the Bible never contradicts itself, so back up to (1Thes. 5:23) that I relayed prior, it is clear that the two are separate entities. Although separate, they are so intimately intertwined that only the Word of God can separate them.

> **(Heb. 4:12)**KJV "For the <u>Word of God</u> is <u>living</u> and powerful and sharper than any two edged sword, piercing even to the **dividing asunder of soul and spirit** and of the joints and marrow and is a <u>discerner</u> <u>of the thoughts and intents of the heart</u>."

So why does there need to be teachings and clarification on the soul and the spirit? In order to eliminate confusion and misunderstandings which <u>will</u> lead to adopting false teachings; which <u>will</u> lead to more confusion and misunderstandings; which <u>will</u> lead to participating in and trying to execute those false teachings to no avail; which is exactly what the devil wants you to do by taking you off of the proper path and onto a lost path into the wilderness. *The proper path leads to abundant living and the lost path leads to you as a Believer struggling in many different aspects of your life and at the same time wondering what is wrong and why.

To begin with, in order to do a deeper dive into this topic, we can start with a falsehood that generation upon generation has passed down to its subsequent generation and that is (in very general terms): body bad and soul good. I will expose in this explanation that this is not only a falsehood but body bad is absolutely wrong and soul good is not totally accurate! This misconception is rooted primarily in the misunderstanding of the term "fleshly" where it has been taken as meaning our flesh/skin, therefore our body. Then some of the most quoted scriptures are culprits of being taken out of context and misinterpreted because they are only quoted as message blurbs and not elaborated on in accurate context. Research a Bible concordance and look up flesh and fleshly and fleshly nature and see how many numerous times it's referred to in scripture and then read a group of those scriptures to reveal the context in which they were conveyed. * Primarily the flesh is referring to our <u>fallen nature</u> and NOT ever referring to our bodies and get this, consequently our fallen nature is referring to that portion of our soul! So, can you surmise body good and soul bad? NO! As Paul would say, "God forbid." Allow me to continue, Paul confirmed what I just relayed about the body in **(1 Cor. 6:18)**KJV "Flee fornication (sexual immorality). **Every sin** that a man commits is **outside the body**, but he that commits fornication **sins <u>against his own body</u>**." The last I checked, every means all (not some or most), therefore all sin a man commits is outside the body which means that our body (which for a Believer is God's, for He bought it for a price) is only a mechanism for all things that we do (as in works, good and bad; and as in sex, good and bad; and etc.), not only that Paul then relays that sexual sins are a sin against man's own body! Not that the body is bad, but that which makes the decision to DO the sinning (that portion of our soul). To further confirming the body is good, the very next statement clarifies two of my above messages **(1 Cor. 6:19-20)**BSB "Do you not know that <u>your body is a temple of the Holy Spirit who is in you</u>, whom you have received from God? You are not your own; you were bought at a price. Therefore, <u>glorify God</u> with your body, and in your spirit, which are God's." So, the body is good and shame on those generations who communicated otherwise out of ignorance, or due to religious doctrine, or due to false teachings, or out of trying to control the behaviors of others, etc. Now do you realize my point on how negatively impactful confusion and misunderstandings towards scripture can be for the Believer in his quest for abundant life?

For the moment let's skip the discussion of the soul to cover our spirit, which is in line with the body and is itself good as well. First of all, God is spirit. Secondly, we are spirit, soul, body (take note, it is revealed in order of importance). Additionally, our spirit knew God in spirit before the beginning of time and our spirit is good. Unfortunately as you know man fell from God's grace in the Garden with Adam and Eve thus allowing evil to enter into man/woman and taking up residence in the <u>soul</u>. The following scriptures support the message of our spirit that I am underscoring:

94

(1 Cor. 2:10)KJV "What God has prepared for those who love Him, has been revealed to us by the Holy Spirit. The Holy Spirit searches all things (and brings things to remembrance), even the deep things of God."

(1 Cor. 2:11)BSB "For who among men knows the thoughts of man except his own spirit within him? So too, no one knows the thoughts of God except the Spirit of God."

(Proverbs 20:27)BSB "The spirit of a man is the lamp of the Lord, searching out his inmost being."

(1 Cor. 6:17)BSB "He who unites himself with the Lord is one with Him in spirit."

(1 Cor. 6:20)KJV "For you were bought at a price; therefore 'glorify God' in your body and in your spirit, which are God's."

So again, our spirit is good and remains good and thus is the impetus (inspiration) for us to seek out God and seek out his Son Jesus Christ who gives us the Holy Spirit to bring all things to our remembrance (since before the beginning of time and everything relevant afterwards) and will assist us in gaining control of our lost lives and lead us on the path of righteousness, holiness (sanctification), love, hope, faith, etc., so that we may have life and have it abundantly while on this experiential spiritual life journey on earth and for an eternity.

  * **(John 6:63)**NKJV "The Holy Spirit gives life (in conjunction with our spirit); the body is of no profit (in and of itself). The spirit imparts life to the body." *The spirit imparts life to the body and not the other way around, thus placing emphasis on what I mentioned previously regarding the importance of order: spirit, soul, and then body. Another important aspect to understand is that the word spirit and the word Spirit are the exact same word in the Bible in both the Hebrew and Greek and the only difference is the designation of the lower case being of our spirit and the capital "S" is of the Holy Spirit and that by adding the word Holy (holy means sinless; 100% righteous) designates its "sinless" nature in other words God's Sinless Spirit. The additional point to that is that our spirit that knew God before the beginning of time is of the same spirit as His.

That's all good, easy to understand and everything should be a piece of cake moving forward, right? Well, now comes the difficult for most to understand and thus causes problems in their journey moving forward. This is in regard to their soul. * To this point I have only relayed that our spirit and body are absolutely good and have alluded to our soul as having a portion of it as having fallen (meaning evil now resides in that portion) and thus being referred to as having a "fleshly nature." Up until you are saved, this fleshly/fallen nature dominates your life by dominating your soul, which in turn dominates your spirit and dominates your body by utilizing it to carry out acts of sinning (all things that are contrary to God's nature and holiness). That sums it up in a nutshell, although I'm going to elaborate in detail so that you can validate it.

> * **(Matt. 26:41)**KJV "Watch and pray, so that you won't enter into temptation. The spirit indeed is willing, but the flesh (soul) is weak."
> **(John 3:6-7)**KJV "That which is born of the flesh is flesh; that which is born of the Spirit is spirit. Marvel not that I said this unto you; for you must be born again."

* In Matt. 26:41 above, this is a perfect example of what I was referring to regarding how people can take the word flesh out of context and assume it is referring to the body. As a matter of fact a few Bible <u>translations</u> disclose that "the body is weak," but that is a contradiction to practically everything I've already relayed and as I pointed out, the Bible has no contradictions. I'm not going to knock the various translations because from a wider perspective they are very helpful, but it is so very important that you know what-is-what and validate the things you read and hear. I could state the exact same thing concerning pastors that I just did about translations but again, from a wider perspective many have good intentions, but they just simply miss the mark when not focusing on being more specific and relaying accurate messages. I also wanted to point out that in this passage Jesus says that our spirit is indeed willing to do what is right as it always does, but He then follows that with "BUT the soul is weak" (alluding that it can enter easily into temptation). This is a very accurate statement and I'll be expounding on that in a moment.

* In John 3:6-7 above, Jesus is stating that we are all born of the flesh, and thus are fleshly in nature (i.e. fallen nature), in that our souls are corrupted with evil. Until such time that we are "born again" and thus born of the Holy Spirit and should now be spirit dominant. The problem here is that an extremely large percentage of those who have just been born again (or many who have been born again for years and years and years; and some take it to the grave) do not die of selfish self immediately rather very gradually over time, and are therefore not spirit dominant. They are sitting on the sidelines so to speak and waiting to get into the game but afraid to commit and give up all their sins and what they falsely believe are their freedoms and for another false belief and that is of having to commit to a constricted religious life with Jesus. *They divulge in one sentence that they are a Christian and relaying in another sentence that nothing has really

changed in their lives and continue to experience trials and tribulations on an increasing scale and at the same time wonder why this is. That is deluded thinking and it takes place on a grand scale in this world. This is a BIG problem in limiting the success of your spiritual journey and can often lead to derailing it!

Additional misconceptions from scripture concerning the soul. Jesus said **(Mark 8:36)**KJV "For what does it profit a man, if he shall gain the whole world and lose his own soul?

- There are more than one messages here.
- * Jesus is underscoring the importance of our soul. That it isn't just corrupted and bad, rather with Him it is truly who we are, and we would never want to lose our soul. Additionally for another time and discussion, this illustrates that unless you have died of selfish self and allowed your spirit to dominate your life then "you are not who you think you are."
- To get to the point, this is where people misinterpret this passage. They allow it to imprint in their minds that their soul is good, and it must be the body that is bad. Well obviously by now I've communicated which is which and what is accurate, but beyond that it is important to point out the flaw that people have in misinterpreting scripture. Here the context is not whether the soul is good or not, rather * Jesus is emphasizing that your soul is ruined by your sinning and He goes on to relay that He is the way to heal your soul. Then in doing so allows you to have life and have it abundantly. Also many believe that if they gain material things and live as they please by sinning regularly that by gaining more of the world they are compensating for their souls being in ruins, rather than giving in or surrendering to their creator.

** Your soul will always be present and will never be totally isolated, or totally separated, or totally minimized from your spirit and body, because your soul is very essentially YOU, therefore you would never want to lose your soul. The key is to have your soul in harmony with your dominant spirit.

The soul is foundational to God's plan and its principles are key to understanding a wide breadth of wisdom that pertains to it. Not to throw you off but let's start with a paradox associated with it and get it out of the way.

To die, as with Adam, to die means that you sinned against God which cut you off from having a relationship with Him. A non-believer who has yet to be saved is suffering from this death and separation from God.

To die, in regards to a Believer's soul, means that you voluntarily chose (as Jesus also chose to die) but for you to die of selfish self and be resurrected (as Jesus was) as a new man in Christ, thus allowing your spirit to dominate your soul via your walk with the Holy Spirit.

Well, I just let the cat out of the bag so to speak by the latter explanation, but you will require much more information to understand what it means, and the process involved. *First you must understand the basics of the soul. In prior discussion we established that our spirit knew God before the beginning of time in spirit. Next, **(Gen. 2:7)**KJV "Then the Lord God formed man from the dust of the ground and breathed the breath of life into his nostrils and the man became a living soul." Then next, **(Psalm 139:13)**NIV "For you created my inmost being, you knit me together in my mother's womb. I will praise you, for I am fearfully and wonderfully made." * And next, this is extremely important for you to understand that being comprised of a spirit, soul and body **(1Thes. 5:23)**, our spirit and soul are so intimately intertwined that they appear to be one entity but are definitely two separate entities. For the non-believer, their soul is dominant almost to the point that their spirit is practically non-existent. The reason for the soul's dominance is due to the fall of Adam and Eve and evil taking up residence in the soul of every human being. To further that, the earth is Satan's domain for the unbeliever (although for the Believer Satan was defeated at Calvary by Jesus; note, the Believer has to believe this, receive it and act accordingly to overcome the residual effects of the devil in his mind that was there from before being saved). * For the unbeliever (and the Believer prior to being saved) Satan imprints his negativity onto each and every soul (mind) and has his henchmen the devil (and if allowed his demons) protecting his stake, in order to battle against God; this imprinting supernaturally rules the individual's life (unless they get saved, are reborn again **and** die of self, then become a new man/woman in Christ, along with a renewing of their mind daily, this allows their spirit to rule over their life and potentially eliminates the residual effects of Satan and the devil; "potentially" is for those who do not act). I know this is a lot of information and to some almost impossible to believe but hang in there and hear me out, for the balance of this subchapter and also for the balance of the book because this is covered in greater detail in the chapters "Spiritual Warfare" and "The Mind."

(Matt. 11:28)BSB "Come to Me, all those who are weary and burdened and I will give you rest. Take My yoke upon you and learn from me, for I am gentle and humble of heart and you will find rest for your souls. For my yoke is easy and my burden is light." * What Jesus is revealing here is that His yoke is lighter and easier than the yoke of Satan's! Because as a non-believer whether you want to believe it or not Satan is your keeper and you are wearing his yoke and it weighs heavy on your shoulders and on your daily grind of life. * Jesus is also revealing that his rest is not to rest as in sleepy rest, but that we can be "rest assured" of His promises will come to fruition exactly how He conveys them, but that you MUST COME TO HIM then take His yoke and LEARN from Him (He loves each and every one of us and desires us to have life and have it abundantly and He alone can teach us how to accomplish this)! Also that His heart is gentle and humble just as our heart should be (our heart being our spirit) and in allowing Him to strengthen our heart to dominate our lives allows our soul to rest assured that its responsibilities have immediately become light and less burdensome.

* As mentioned, this is a real struggle and battle for Believer's to give up their selfish self and hand their lives over to Jesus. I'm telling you to STOP this insanity. You are killing you with the stresses that this world is imposing on you. And start listening to the Holy Spirit and do what Jesus is telling you to do for your sake and the sake of your family and future generations. **Jesus is revealing, "Rest assured in Me and I will show you how to live but you must die of self and then have Me be the Lord of your life, allowing My yoke to guide you (the yoke is connected to both you and Him / Holy Spirit). He is also relaying that you can never rid yourself of your soul and you would never want to because your soul is the real you that you are, but that you must die of self and resurrect a new man in which you allow your spirit to dominate and your soul to be subordinate to your spirit which is led, guided and directed by the Holy Spirit of God to accomplish the will of God and the intentions Jesus has for your abundant life!!! While on this experiential spiritual life journey on earth.

Another thing that Jesus is saying, is to follow Him (as He modeled) and you must drag your kicking and screaming soul to the foot of His cross and crucify it once and for all thus defeating Satan's snare that he has on your soul, and then as Jesus modeled and as He promises you to be resurrected a new man in Christ; allowing the Holy Spirit to empower your spirit to **take the reins of your life by dominating the former position your soul once held. *This is extremely difficult for most Believers to do; therefore most are so reluctant and hesitant that it is either never done or done so but spanning so many years as a gradual process with them not benefiting over that span of time. The problem with this is that until you do, you are **destined to struggle** throughout the times that you don't do it and that is in every aspect of your life from finances to relationships, etc., all the while experiencing trials and tribulations and wondering why this is so???

** The fleshly or fallen aspect of your soul was so strong and dominant in your life and for so long, that this is the reason why this process is so difficult for most Believers. Our souls are comprised of a) our mind, b) our will and c) our emotions (and as mentioned prior our spirit is comprised of our heart). So our mind makes decisions and you can imagine if they are influenced by the devil as a non-believer;

99

and our will is our desires and you know how strong they are; and our emotions, many people actually make most of their decisions based on emotions which is influencing their will and their mind. Even with that said in brevity, it is still very easy to understand how difficult it is to "**Let go and let God.**"

I find it difficult to strongly suggest or especially to tell you to drag your fleshly soul to the grave, where in reality for myself it was a journey, a long and gradual process before I "got it" and let go. I not so proudly admit that I have a couple of wild stories (big deal), and in reality I suffered during those years upon years as compared to the dramatic difference my abundant life has been since I let go and let God. * I wanted to add that <u>**the Holy Spirit chisels away at you** during those years by bringing to light your issues by having you experience and re-experience related events until you had better get it and change your ways by dying off that part of your soul.</u> **Have you ever wondered why some things just seem to keep replaying in your life?** This is what is taking place, the Holy Spirit is trying desperately to bring it to light and to get you to change the way you've always done things except you aren't listening or receptive to His voice, but He will someday get your attention when you can't take your-"self" anymore.

***Okay, so I wanted you to read paragraph after paragraph of arguments and explanations of what comprises our souls and why we must dies of selfish self, meaning to die off the fleshly part of our soul, or put another way, to drag that fleshly part of our soul to the grave and with Jesus be resurrected a new man/woman with our true soul and dominant spirit. So here's a BIG revelation that many overlook, or misunderstand, or are misled by improper or inadequate teaching:

(Rom. 12:2-3)BSB "Do **NOT** be conformed to this world, but you will be <u>transformed</u> by the **renewing of your <u>mind</u>**. Then you will be <u>able to discern</u> what is the good, pleasing and perfect will of God. For by the <u>grace</u> given me, to every man that is among you, not to think of himself more highly than he ought to think, but rather to think as with sound judgement, as God has <u>allotted</u> to each a measure of faith."

1) Those who are conformed to the world are allowing their fleshly soul to dominate their lives!
2) A Believer's life on the other hand is "transformed" by the daily renewing of your "mind."
3) Remember that your "<u>mind</u>" is your <u>soul</u>!!! And it must be renewed in God's Word (wisdom) to keep the fleshly nature suppressed (which is an ongoing battle) so that the true you is exposed.

100

4) The Holy Spirit facilitates this process with you and during the process you are given "discernment" to determine God's perfect will for you!

5) Paul then reveals, "that by the 'grace' given me (actually means that by the 'wisdom and authority' given him; the same as it is given to all of us!), for you not to continue to think in a fleshly nature (highly of self), but rather in sound judgement (righteousness) that God has "given" (gifted) to each, his portion/measure of faith.

That is the BIG revelation! That passage of Paul's summarizes and confirms everything I've relayed to this point regarding our soul (mind) having a fleshly nature side that needs to be cut off, in order to allow God's portion to shine through! Where it complements our now dominant spirit (rather than battling it). How many hundreds of times have you heard that passage preached, but was it ever conveyed in this manner? I hope that you are beginning to connect the dots and understand not only the principles but what you need to be focusing on during your journey.

I think I need to take a moment and give a brief and simplistic overview, so that you have the right perspective and then we can continue on. The soul is the mind & the spirit is the heart; BUT even with everything going through the heart gateway, the mind leads the heart (important note: your spirit will follow a dominant soul; this is the case for all unbelievers and for many Believers)...BUT renewing your mind daily in the Word will give you dominant thoughts of the Holy Spirit in conjunction with your spirit (this will transform your spirit into now being dominant) and thus will direct (you) your heart (thoughts, words and actions) and mind (true you/real you/now minimized soul) towards the things of God!

***An extremely important scripture for you to apply here is **(Rom 8:16)**KJV **"The Spirit itself bears witness with our spirit"**. The Holy Spirit works hand in hand, shoulder to shoulder with our spirit, so that our spirit dominates our lives (which means that we are obedient and have Jesus and the center of our lives). With being spirit dominant, overcompensates for the imperfections of our soul and also and very importantly minimizes the devil in our mind to insignificance! This allows for us to have a **spiritually dominant heart and a spiritually dominant mind**, which now allows the conduit to God to be wide open fully to receive everything we are meant to have! I may have jumped ahead of the topic matter with this paragraph, but felt it so important a message to get relayed now before you continue reading. See the illustration at the end of this Volume 1 book with the same title as this subchapter.

I don't believe in various tactics of preaching like: shock and awe; shame and guilt; threats; other manipulations; etc. but you do need to heed warnings that God has placed in the Bible. Paul disclosed in **(1 Cor. 10:6)**BSB "Nevertheless God was not pleased with most of them, for they were struck down (died) in the wilderness. These things took place as examples to keep us from craving evil things, as they did." This passage is in direct context to sinning and having our fleshly souls rule our lives. He's referring to the Followers of God who were a part of the Exodus from Egypt, who although were Followers they would not give up their sinful and lustful ways, therefore God took their souls/lives from them during their struggles being **lost** in the wilderness. A warning of my own is that the world can only be enjoyed for a season, however your soul is just as important as your spirit and they continue forever with Jesus for an eternity; whereas the souls of those who remained of this world and enjoyed various lusts for a season are ultimately lost and destined to live in eternal torment. Paul in another context does also communicate (with added emphasis) **(1 Cor. 9:27)** "Those (Believers) who (continue to) pursue the lusts of the flesh must **prepare for combat** (with the devil within, or worse with Satan)." (se also 2 Peter 2:18) Basically, this is relaying what I mentioned in the last paragraph, that you are going to encounter real problems and issues when you are claiming to be a Christian but living the life as a non-believer pursuing lusts and idols. Do you not know that light cannot occupy darkness at the same time and in the same place? Do you not know that you cannot serve two masters? **(Job 27:8)**NKJV "For what is the hope of the hypocrite, though he has gained much, what good is it when God takes away his soul?" Jesus preached this parable of the rich fool: For a man whose greed consumed him and he ignored everything else to build more riches, that once he felt he had an opportunity to rest and be merry **(Luke 12:20)**KJV "But God said to him, 'You fool, this night your soul will be required of you. Then who will own what you have accumulated, which I have provided?" This is how it will be for anyone who stores up treasure for himself but is not rich toward God." * Again not tactics, rather we must heed the warnings God has explicitly laid out for our viewing and understanding.

> **(Heb. 4:12)**KJV "For the Word of God is quick, and powerful, and sharper than any two edged sword, piercing even to the dividing asunder of soul and spirit and of the joints and marrow, and is a discerner of the thoughts and intents of the heart.

The Word of God is described as a sword on a number of occasions in the Bible, and here Paul is saying that the Word is so precise and accurate that it can slice between and divide the marrow from the bone. It's also disclosing that the Word can divide our spirit from our soul. Paul found it important to relay information that supported his statements, therefore if our spirit was one in the same with the soul then you wouldn't be able to divide it and if that were the case then there wouldn't be much more to say, but because they are two separate entities, although <u>intimately intertwined</u> with each other, the Word can divide the two. Why is this important? Because you have got to start <u>focusing on discerning</u> between the "voice of your soul" and the "voice of your spirit," so that you <u>focus your attention</u> on your spirit and <u>not</u> your soul. To understand the point I'm expressing here let's begin with this, before you were saved you used to exclusively think and base your decisions on your physical senses and emotions (both being aspects of your soul). So worded another way but with the same meaning, that prior to being saved your soul was the origin of all of your thoughts and decisions (because your soul is in part comprised of your physical senses, your mind, your will and your emotions). * As you have gathered throughout this subchapter, you must die of the fallen aspect of your soul (die of selfish self) and allow the Holy Spirit to guide you in allowing your spirit to dominate your life and decision making. <u>This can only be done with the Word of God because it is the only tool (sword) that can separate the spirit from the soul.</u> Allowing for the conversion from soul dominance to spirit dominance and in doing so putting you on the path of life and abundant living.

Initially in this subchapter I disclosed that we are comprised of spirit, soul and body, **(1Thes. 5:23)**KJV "And the very God of peace sanctify you wholly; and I pray God your whole <u>spirit and soul and body</u> be preserved blameless unto the coming of our Lord Jesus Christ," yet in the scripture mentioned above Paul stipulated "your body" and "your spirit" but did not mention "<u>your soul</u>," in regard to glorifying God. That is in context with glorifying God so don't let that confuse you within this context because we are definitely comprised of a spirit, soul and body and the reason why Paul did not mention "your soul" in respect to glorifying God is because Paul harped on the topic of our soul, even to the point of attacking it, in numerous scriptures that he did not want to possibly mislead anybody to thinking that our souls could contribute to the spirit and the body in glorifying God. Why doesn't he just say that and then elaborate?

Because the topic Paul was discussing, was about glorifying God, therefore he is not going to change topics midstream to discuss the soul or go into any detail on it, which as mentioned, he has a number of scriptures that specifically address the soul. I on the other hand having just discussed glorifying God in the prior subchapter and now transitioned to discussing the soul, therefore I will first touch on why he doesn't want to mislead anyone into believing the soul could contribute to glorifying God and come back to connect all the dots in summary. * Paul on a number of occasions relayed that we must die of self (or as I've stated, "Die of selfish-self") which means that our fleshly soul must die! And this should happen hopefully when we are saved but the reality of it is most of us only allow our soul to die off gradually and somewhat grudgingly throughout our lifetime (which he says is wrong also), because we cannot be fully free until we do so. And this wastes our time for this short-lived opportunity we've been blessed with and that is to have an experiential spiritual life journey on earth that glorifies God in the process. To further the topic that our fleshly soul must die, just as Jesus "chose" to be crucified and did so (He is our model), we must also choose to drag our soul to the foot of the cross and crucify it (not grudgingly and gradually have this portion of our soul burnt off and then another a few months later, or tribulation later another portion, then another and so on), rather you need to read the Guidebook (Bible) and read this book and understand what exactly is meant by **(Gal. 2:20)**KJV "I am crucified 'with' Christ; nevertheless I live; yet NOT I, but Christ lives in me; and the life which I now live in the flesh I live by faith of the Son of God, who loved me and gave himself for me."

- "I am crucified 'with' Christ;" * as stated before you must choose to die of selfish-self and therefore choose to drag your soul to the foot of the cross to be crucified in order that you truly die of selfish-self, thus giving your spirit an opportunity to take over!
- "Nevertheless I live;" * * so you die but you live? How? Again, Jesus modeled it, He was resurrected, and He has promised that so will we! We are resurrected with a dominant spirit linked to the Holy Spirit who is linked with Jesus and a soul that should be "in check" with our spirit. This is key, you die of your fleshly selfish self-centered ways that are separate from God and distances you from "loving" others as yourself; in other words you isolate the evil that resides in your soul by "minimizing" that aspect of your soul to an insignificant speck when it comes to your thoughts and your decisions and "maximize" your spirit via walking with the Holy Spirit in order to take control of your life.
- "Yet NOT I, but Christ lives in me;" *** I only used a partial quote here to analyze it in steps, now that the evil aspects of the soul is insignificant (minimized) it thus allows for the Holy Spirit to facilitate Jesus taking control of my life, "I was crucified and

104

died, now I live; yet not I, but Christ lives in me" <u>as long as I have faith in Him and allow Him to be the Lord of my life</u> (and not allow my self/soul to enter back into the mix) then I will have and experience an abundant spirit filled life journey on earth!

My friend, this is how it all is supposed to work, but if you are reluctant or hesitant and therefore not "all-in," you will continue to have struggles and you will not have the abundant life that your Lord desires for you!

Paul sums it up very succinctly **(Rom. 6:11)**BSB "The death He died, He died to sin once and for all, but the life He lives, He lives to God. So you too must count yourselves <u>dead to the power of sin</u>, <u>but alive to God in Christ Jesus</u>. Therefore do not allow sin to control your mortal body so that you obey its desires."

- This is getting plenty of repetition, but that is a way in which we learn things. You must die of selfish self and therefore be dead to the power of sin; and instantaneously be (resurrected) alive to God via Jesus; and with that we do not allow sin to control our lives but Jesus to control our lives via the Holy Spirit.

I hope that helps you to understand what Paul is conveying with both books: Galatians and Romans. Please note that you have heard countless pastors preach on this with many of them missing the mark or their doctrine skews their message so dramatically and is out of line with the explanation I gave, which leaves you never really grasping what "exactly" it meant and in turn missing out on years of potential abundant living due to misunderstandings, not being able to act on the right process and getting thoroughly frustrated and disenfranchised (being deprived of a right or privilege). In other words, not being able to live the abundant life Jesus wants you to live and God has designed and purposed for everyone, that is, everyone who Believes and loves Him and knows how to receive His grace and act on it. **(1 Cor. 2:10)**KJV "What God has prepared for those who love Him."

Let me take a moment to give some advice. If that explanation was spot on for you and you "got it" the first time you read it and can tell God "I Believe it" then that's great. But for others you may have to read it more than a couple of times, validate it in reading the Bible and walking in the Spirit and it may take you time to accept and Believe it, then that is what works for you but I'm sure it is faster than waiting for it to come across to you some other way. **(Heb. 4:12)** NLT "For the Word of God is living and powerful." One of the bits of advice I wanted to relay is the Bible is known as the living Bible because for example you can read just one of the sixty six books hundreds of times and each time your takeaways can be different, meaning that one time you take away how you should treat others, the next time how a process of God works and plays out, and next a different takeaway. I'm not saying that it will ever contradict itself because that will never happen, but I'm saying the wisdom it reveals is endless. Point is, that is a lot of information to take in, absorb and assimilate into your daily life. Where do you start and what are the logical steps? Then you add what you hear contained in the sermons at church that are often watered down to be politically correct or just the opposite skewed to accommodate a doctrine, or whatever other way that can cause you to misunderstand; then the topic matter that the pastor has neatly packaged into a 5 to 8 week "series," and is that particular series what you need right at this moment in your life. Sure, it's all good but are you growing and maturing spiritually at the rate that you are satisfied with and at a rate that can get you to optimize living an abundant life today, or this month or this year?

This book is designed to fill in any voids that are keeping you from an abundant purpose filled life and a truly fulfilling relationship with the Lord. Highlight or earmark or take journal notes with reference to page numbers, whatever it takes to start understanding the BIG picture as quickly as possible. One thing that I've done is attempt to simplify your understanding of the Bible, which in turn takes "data dumping" a ton of information in this book, albeit worded and conveyed in an easier to understand format than most any other sources. Most pastors whether in their sermons or in their books believe in focusing on only a few basic points and relaying it in very basic terms; again this is going to have a tendency to confuse you with the big picture and it is going to take you forever to get all the information you need and you'll be lucky to buy the right books and hear the right sermons all in succession to give you a solid foundation to work from. But this is what is commonly practiced today because they believe that people can only take and understand and maybe assimilate bits and pieces at a time. Whereas I believe that you are able to take a significant amount of information and maybe it takes you rereading it a few or numerous times but it's all in one compact book for you to go for additional wisdom beyond what you are currently getting from sermons and in conjunction with what the Holy Spirit is revealing to you.

Additionally as I've pointed out in my experience, the walk with the Holy Spirit can itself be a slow and gradual process. This is primarily due to the degree of your personal conviction towards making things happen and the previously mentioned issues of communicating false teachings or teachings that are not well presented, therefore misunderstood. In addition, the tendency is to relay bits and pieces, commonly done by pastors with their sermons. * If you do not ask or if you are not persistent in the volume of questions that you are posing to the Holy Spirit, then He will reciprocate in like manner by giving and exposing you to incremental amounts of wisdom. In other words this process is slow and very similar to what I described as my long trial by error journey. So you need to persist in actively pursuing wisdom in your daily prayer life. An additional point is, what I'm disclosing in this book are topics that are either foundational or at a minimum, of key importance, therefore you should do your best in connecting the dots between what I have relayed, with those of what the Holy Spirit is revealing to you via the Bible and via sermons, by asking for guidance and instruction with the intent of assimilating the wisdom, knowledge and understanding into your daily spiritual life. As previously mentioned, many pastors will communicate their teachings at a slow pace primarily because they feel that people are slow to learn and therefore must slow the transfer of information and do so to reduce potential misunderstandings. I on the other hand believe that most people can take a large amount of information (such as, what I've relayed in this book) and understand and implement it without too much difficulty and that if they do encounter problems understanding then they have other avenues to receive information from. I'm hoping that with this book you are able to cut what took me 20yrs down to a fraction of that time. Why did I stop midstream to relay this advice? Because the information I am covering here is deep and is very commonly misunderstood and so it is very important that you take the time to understand it and act on it.

To summarize first in general terms, the spirit is not bad, the soul is not bad (if the portion of evil has been properly dealt with by you and the Holy Spirit and you are able to suppress and contain your soul to allow your spirit to dominate your decisions), and the body is not bad. The "good news" we have in Jesus is that He can compensate and overcome (in victory) our fallen nature with the gifts He's freely provided us including righteousness, holiness which means we are becoming sinless (via sanctification), love, hope, faith to name a few of the foundational ones and accessing them and acting on them with the help of the Holy Spirit. Conversely, without Jesus we are left to our own devices desperately trying to achieve abundant living which the consequences, trials and tribulations very quickly reveal that it is only a futile effort taking considerable more time, energy, and resources that devours what you had mistakenly and originally thought was your freedom to enjoy life on your terms. In other words and put succinctly, ** our spirit is supposed to govern our soul with Jesus as our Lord; so conversely, our soul governs our spirit when we do not have Jesus in our lives. So before it is too late for you to get the most out of life and do so abundantly, seek Jesus and have Him be the Lord of your life via the Holy Spirit, while with the true intent of dying of self and controlling your soul by allowing your spirit to dominate your thoughts and decisions, so that your choices have positive consequences which puts you on the path of life and abundant living while you are on this experiential spiritual life journey on earth.

107

(Prov. 20:5)KJV "Counsel in the heart of man is like deep waters, but a man of understanding will draw it out."

(Illustration of "Our spirit and our soul" please flip back now to final pages of Ch6; and see www.afatherswisdom.org for a color illustration)

When God Gives You Over to Your Sinful Desires

In a previous subchapter "Good News: God's Grace" if you're bouncing from one topic to another, I'm suggesting you read that subchapter in full in order to get a better idea of its complete context. It is too important a topic to overlook but did not want to take away from the other important topics in that subchapter with this explanation. This is the subchapter excerpt from "Good News: God's Grace" that is most important in knowing prior to reading this subchapter:

> * The "amazing grace" of our incredible God even has a stopgap (temporary) measure in place to counter us from doing that, if it is not enough for us to lose His grace and His blessings so we can go out sinning as we please then He will cause His grace to "abound" in other words increase dramatically to counter our sinning in order to get us back onto His correct path (the Bible uses the term: dunamis which in the Greek means dynamite; and used primarily to represent God's power, God's strength, not ours). But as mentioned, it is only temporary because man has free will and can choose not to go back and this is where I must alert you of a **danger** and that is God will then "give you up" meaning "give you over" to your desires and He actually boosts those sinful blessings for you (again temporarily) in kind of a farewell gift (saying goodbye to His favor and His fellowship with you). **(Romans 1:24; 26; 28)**

The last sentence is conveying that God will bless you in the desires of your heart and mind, even if it is sending you down the wrong path and away from Him. What's your take on that excerpt? The former being the topic of His amazing abounding grace. Those who understand this aspect of God, praise Him for what He's done in their lives in this respect. The latter being the topic of God giving a person over due to them consistently doing as they please (in disobedience to God) with regards to their selfish desires. Do you know anybody that the latter applies to, or should I reference that question another way, how many people do you know fit that description? That at one time they had considered themselves Christians or maybe are in self-denial and still believe they are. Yet from your perspective looking from outside-in it appears God has given them up to their selfish desires and appear to be blessed for the time being, or that time has passed, and their better days are far behind them? Maybe you see yourself when reading that description, or maybe you do not think it applies to you. If you are uncertain then maybe you should first meditate on it.

The chances are of a high percentage that God may be "giving over" pseudo-Christians especially between the ages of 28-45yrs old. Why do I think that? Because I've witnessed the most disobedient of behaviors within this age group. A few of their common traits: many have their career path set; they've had children for a while now, so that path is set; their income path is for the most part set; they're busy with their children's commitments whether sports, dance, arts, etc.; most of what they once considered as "fun" has been over for some time, or they never had the opportunity in or just out of school, so now the only fun they can muster up is on the edge and is sinful; they've either started hopping from one divorce to another or they are close to doing it; they pray on occasion; go to church only on occasion or only during holidays or maybe not at all because they're just too busy; when conflict, trials, problems, tragedy, tribulations hit they run to God for help, comfort and/or guidance; forget tithing, also they don't attempt to give or donate, etc.; they are "Christians" for now, but they are especially not Believers.

Do you agree with this being some of the characteristics of today's norm, or not?
What do you expect God to bless them in, obedience?
Or do you expect God to bless them in, disobedience? Meaning to give them up to their selfish desires.

* For those of you who this may apply to: My friend, please read/hear this loud & clear: STOP "drifting" away from God! Before it is too late. Not that He will forsake you, because He will never forsake (leave) you. But you are the one who is negatively impacting your own life and everyone that is connected to you. It is by your choice to turn your back on God. And don't self-deceive yourself into believing that you are not, otherwise you will not only experience a rude awakening but rather possible devastation.

* Point: I myself thought that to surrender my life to God meant what most of you think, and that is life and fun is over from this point on; that to live a committed Believers life is restricting and I'd be wearing out the knees in my pants from kneeling in prayer; and there goes my weekend because I have to factor in going to church and that is an event in and of itself for the entire family to execute; I'll lose all of my current friends; and here comes all the shame and guilt for what I've been doing wrong/sinful for all these years and I'll be pressured to change; and on and on and on...

You can believe me or not on this one, I'm telling you it's NOT at all that demanding or dreary and remember this is coming from someone who purposely stayed single till 30yrs old and knows how to party and have fun. As a matter of fact, the process of surrendering to God is "progressive" in nature, therefore a progressive process to becoming free! And that is not hype, neither an attempt to manipulate, I mean it from my heart to all of you who are not secure in their relationship with the Lord. I can relay it but I don't know if you'll receive it or even believe it, that being the freedom, the contentment, the peace (that surpasses all understanding), the love, your outlook and attitude towards everything changes for the better, etc. and I know that some of you are thinking that sounds like some stereotypical religious propaganda but it is not. It is the truth that I am conveying, and it is the truth that God reveals in His word and is just one aspect out of many that make up what Jesus meant by life and having life abundantly.

Oh and by the way, I am not taking any meds whatsoever, I don't drink alcohol or smoke anything (since after my conversion) just in case you're thinking that I might be medicated☺. Let's tackle a couple of the so-called negatives or restrictions to life as mentioned. You may or may not experience friend changes, and that some will fall by the wayside, however that is for the better and some relationships will strengthen and that too is for the better. Experiencing guilt and shame may not or it may come, but it will occur up front and be short lived which is part of the cleansing and renewal process that you should welcome. It does definitely change your path, but that too is for the better in that it can reduce stress and give you peace by getting you on track and going to church and getting into the Word and walking with the Spirit (all of which is bettering the quality of your life and your future). Will it cut all the fun out of my life? That depends on what you deem is fun. If it is on the fringe, meaning sinful behavior then God's grace you receive will influence you to <u>not to desire</u> to do that. And when it comes to fun, when you have your freedom from the burdens of the world and of the devil then life is fun in general and you have no idea what you have been missing out on. And guess what, you can now afford to give 10% of your income because He will give you control over your finances and your new found life will allow you to have more disposable income. So was it the wrong impression that a life with the Lord is restrictive? Yes restrictive is the wrong impression, you and I were both dead wrong and I've lived it and now I have revealed that it was completely opposite for me. I truly feel free and it transformed my life significantly for the better.

I wanted to get everything said in the order and flow that I just did, now let's revisit the "society's norms" that I had previously mentioned. I've got numerous stories and examples of these characteristics playing out in real life. Note: I've got a number of additional examples but here I'm using a group of three people that eerily have similarly close personalities and self-destructive behaviors (although they could not see it if you rubbed their face in it). In just the recent past I've had three mid-level managers, 33-45yrs old, two male and one female, earning $100K/yr., each married (although on the fringe) with kids; financially unstable (always in emergency mode and probably little to no savings); claim they are Christians (one non-denominational and attends church sporadically; one Catholic and attends church occasionally; one Jehovah Witness and attends meetings and conventions somewhat regularly; or so they say); inflated egos; persons of questionable character; rumors rampant of affair(s); attractive; living the life (or living the lie); fair at hitting sales goals but poor at leadership/coaching, rather has tendency to be dictatorial in their management approach by being overly friendly one minute then criticizing/condemning the next; extremely manipulative to all (employees, customers, upper management, spouse); habitual liars (pathological, lying even when they don't need to); tardy to work is no problem and skips out of work throughout entire day like kids skip classes in high school (absentee parent/manager although present in office and at home); in mentioning high school, quite often their behavior mimics that of a teenager with throwing fiery darts, back talking, backstabbing others, frowns and stare downs, etc.; always on their cell phone (sounds more like an entry level employee than a mid to upper level manager); much of what was mentioned leads to very dysfunctional work teams (either having characteristics of abused spouse syndrome who won't speak up, or they got fed up and forced a mutiny) and I could go on and on but you get the idea.

I mentioned the word eerily in describing their behaviors and here a few examples. I did everything in my power to help them and they briefly at first accommodated/patronized me, then each eventually and again eerily said to me "I got this." In other words, they don't need me anymore (especially my presence at the business) and I thought the exact same thing with each of them which was: no you don't, as a matter of fact, you don't have a clue. They weren't about to change, whatever little they did change, was a temporary act. Again, I could go on and write a book but rather to get to my point, * this is a microcosm of their lives and I believe they subconsciously told Jesus "Hey, I got this" and "I don't need you anymore" because their guilty conscious desires that He not be involved in their dysfunctional lie filled life (although they deny this to themselves; i.e. self-denial). And this is exactly one of the type of examples in which God's grace abounds to get them to repent (change their ways) yet they have free will and they choose to continue down the path that is leading them to destruction or maybe not that severe, but what word is more appropriate for what happens to the children of a broken marriage?

    I'll switch gears for a moment and directly quote what a past work associate said (at 35yrs old), when announcing it was over between her and her husband, while backing it up with shallow supportive advice, "All of our kids friends at school have divorced parents and they're fine, it's commonplace and our kids will be fine too." It still echoes in my head and that was 25yrs ago, because she was dead wrong and it did lead to a form of destruction that to this day still has its deeply impacted repercussions on everybody but her (in one sentence you can see the lies, manipulation and self-denial). It may seem to you that I'm being a bit overly subjective here but wanted to relay that I'm being objective and simply stating facts, which are in context with and coincide with the topic at hand.

Now back to the example, those three no matter what I said couldn't and wouldn't do it, see it, or try to change it or do anything for that matter, but rather remained in the same self-denial, self-centered, narcissistic behaviors that my friend also exhibited. Note, with all four of them you wouldn't be able to tell by looking at them or talking to them that they are so dysfunctional, on a crash course, and/or misled. They are all extremely social and personable, attractive, outgoing, nice, intelligent, etc. but those are just a few of the aspects that comprise the many and contribute to the deception that manifests itself to such a great extent. I could do a deeper dive into this topic but would require writing a book. Although the topic does not end here because there is one very important outstanding point that needs to be communicated.

So yes, I will say it. Exactly what should be said because it is the truth. What happens to men/women when they "drift away" and turn their backs on God? God gives them over! **(Romans 1:24; 26; 28)** He gives them over to the sinning desires of their hearts. Meaning they are now taken over by Satan/devil because this is his domain for those who are not Believers. I realize that some of you do not agree with this, although you may agree with everything else I have said in this subchapter. But I have to tell you that this is stated specifically in God's word (the Bible). Important note, it is not God that is initiating this. I am simply covering the process God takes, whereas it is the individuals doing the sinning against Him that are "giving themselves over" because they chose to take the sinful route.

    (Eph. 4:18-19)BSB "They are darkened in their understanding and alienated from the life of God because of the ignorance that is in them due

to the hardness of their hearts. Having lost all sense of shame, <u>they have given themselves over</u> to sensuality for the practice of every kind of impurity with a craving of greed."
(Phil. 3:19)BSB "<u>Their end is destruction, their **god** is their belly and their glory is their shame</u>, **their minds are set on earthly things**." (Unbelievers/non-believers/pseudo-christians)

Additionally, He will never forsake you (abandon, leave) but He can give you over, which means He will bless you one more time regardless if it is in your sinful endeavor which in turn happens to be with the devil, as your new lord. Also, keep in mind that <u>He did not forsake you</u>, so what that means is He will be waiting for you to return just as the father did in the Parable of the Prodigal Son **(Luke 15:11-32)**. So, those of you that are on the other end of the divorce (or whatever similar issue) may be saying that is not fair that they can be forgiven and allowed back into God's graces after what they did. But that is God's amazing grace! And you and every Believer should be constantly thanking Him for that. So also see the Parable of the Workers **(Matt 20:9)**, two of the numerous messages conveyed in that parable is to not hold grudges or envy others. In other words, be happy for them and if you can't be, at least let go of any bitterness and go about your own life with no thought for theirs and focusing on your relationship with the Lord and with others (<u>constantly moving forward</u>).

If you are wanting a truly abundant life in the present and thus provide a secure foundation for your family's future…He is the WAY! For He is the TRUTH (wisdom)! And He is the abundant LIFE! He is your life on earth and your life eternal!!!

Grace vs. the Covenant of the Law (The 10 Commandments)
(2 Tim 3:16) imparts to us that <u>all</u> scripture is useful for teaching, rebuking, correcting and training in righteousness. The covenant of the Law (10 Commandments) had its purpose and it was perfect **(Psalm 19:7)**. God found fault with the Law not because there was anything wrong with it but because there was something wrong with man which then required a new covenant to counter man's fallen nature **(Heb. 8:6)**. In addition, Jesus said, **(Matt 5:17)**KJV "Do not think that I have come to abolish the Law or the Prophets; I have not come to abolish them but fulfill them." (Jesus was the sacrificial lamb that took away all the sins of the world and thus fulfilled the law). He goes on to say that anyone who practices and teaches these lesser and greater commands will be called great in the kingdom of heaven. He was referring to practicing and teaching; He did not say fulfilling it to the letter, because He already fulfilled it for us all! Also when He made this statement in **(Matt. 5:19)**, it was no coincidence that He

communicated this at the beginning of a long dissertation emphasizing the role of lesser and greater commandments as well as emphasizing the importance that man understand how to behave and once they had heard all of the commandments be able to relay these messages moving forward. * The dissertation begins at Matthew 5 continuing up to Matthew 8 and please make note that this is the foundation of Jesus's doctrine (teachings/instruction).

Paul stated, **(Gal. 3:24)**NKJV "The law is a tutor to lead us to Christ." What he is conveying in Gal. 3:22-28 is very revealing and I suggest you study this in context to grace, the law, our faith and believing. It first covers that those who Believe will receive (by Faith) the promise of Jesus Christ and points out that man was "kept" under the law (held up in custody and forced to obey perfectly a law that no one could fulfill perfectly, thus perpetuating the bondage and especially under the curse), until faith is come (this supports what I've mentioned on the section of faith, that when Jesus came he is the personification of faith having modeled it for us with his Father, therefore Jesus gifted man with it (i.e. faith is a gift). Also contained in **(Gal. 3:13)**KJV "Christ has redeemed us from the curse of the law." Keeping in mind that the law no longer keeps us under bondage as it once did, but rather is written in our hearts and minds so that we have a moral foundation along with moral precepts (as an internal guide only) for our lives **(see Jer. 31:33; Heb. 10:16)**.

To clarify, the 10 Commandments are a perfect set of laws that lay the groundwork for mankind to build upon a jurisprudence (i.e. American jurisprudence; legal system), but we are now not held in bondage if we do not obey the law perfectly, that is if we sin. Now in relation to man sinning, Jesus atoned for our sins with his works on the cross. So as the sacrificial Lamb of God, He atoned for all of mankind's sins including all past, all present and all future sins! That is an example of God's amazing and powerful grace. This is a common area for argument, so please note: * Grace does not give us a free pass to sin! **(Rom. 6:15)**KJV "What then, shall we sin because we are not under the law but under grace? God forbid (certainly not)!" * God's grace is an outpouring of blessings for us to receive and then release to others, thus glorifying God in the process and perpetuating it "full circle," from glory to glory. That means that if you are a faith filled Believer, walking daily in the Spirit and obedient to God then grace actually removes the desire to sin because now you realize your life is so much better along this path rather than the path that you used to take while you were sinning.

There is so much confusion when it comes to grace and the law. Let me make something perfectly clear, if you don't get this foundational precept of God correct, you will struggle immensely and the confusion and frustration can actually lead to one's fall from God (note: a precept is a general rule, in this case foundational; intended to regulate behavior). On the other hand if you get it correct, understood and apply the wisdom by **act**ing on it, your journey will be fulfilling, and you will live life in abundance.

The analogy of leaven with respect to the law is very accurate. Put just a pinch of leaven (yeast) into your pizza dough and it goes from a thin foundational crust to thick and chewy crust. If you put just a pinch of the law into grace it degenerates it (diminishing a property previously present). * ** GRACE IS FOUNDATIONAL to the gospel of Christ and for us its incredible dynamite power is at our disposal. In order to access and maintain that power you must understand the specifics: that man is no longer under the <u>condemnation and death</u> of the <u>law</u> (death from God); Jesus (grace personified) <u>set us free</u> from that happening; now there is no longer a granite tablet etched and held over our head ready to fall upon us, but rather that God then wrote his laws onto our hearts and placed them into our minds so that we have an innate knowledge of the difference between right and wrong, therefore know what sin is **(see Jer. 31:33; Heb. 10:16)**. Do NOT allow grace and law to combat each other! The law as it was received by man through Moses is the same law but it no longer has its sting of death, it no longer is executed as it was in the Old Covenant. **(Eph. 2:15)**BSB "By abolishing in His flesh the Law of commandments and decrees." (definition of abolish: officially put an <u>end</u> to a practice; as an end of the Law's bondage but remains a moral compass) Whereas Jesus is the administrator of the New Covenant so now it is in effect for man, thus setting us free! How? Note the following: Jesus at the Last Supper and holding the challis up towards the Father said, "This is the New Covenant in my blood," pointing out that the New Covenant is between Him and the Father and no longer between God and man, rather that man MUST go through the sacrificial lamb Jesus (grace personified) in order to have a relationship with the Father; thus defeating not just the covenant between man and God which could never be fulfilled, but also defeating man's spiritual death that separated him from God, again by not being able to ever fulfill the Old Covenant. This is what Paul was referring to regarding the law as the "<u>ministry of death</u>." Then conversely the new covenant of grace is the "<u>ministry of life</u>."

* Extremely important, the devil loves it when we argue about this, because within our spirit and soul it creates confusion and doubt (his 2 most favorite ways to steal our lives away)! So initially, don't try too hard to understand this, because it will come to you in your walk with the Holy Spirit and the renewing of your mind. So, rest assured in Jesus and "take it easy," don't let the sound of your own wheels drive you crazy (☺ Glenn Frey/Jackson Browne). Pray to gain wisdom

from the Holy Spirit and to validate everything I've relayed to you by reading and hearing the Word of God. To summarize, Jesus is the grace of God that saved us from the curse of the Law. Now that God tattooed the law on our hearts and written it in our minds we now know innately the difference between right and wrong, but due to our fleshly nature we need guidance and instruction and we accomplish that by focusing on Jesus, living by His grace through faith and receiving the blessings thereof, renewing our minds in the Word and walking with the Holy Spirit daily, and when we act on releasing those blessings to others while glorifying God in the process, we will live life to the fullest and have life abundantly while on this experiential spiritual life journey on earth and forevermore! In the precious name of Jesus and by His power! Amen and amen.

GPS God's Positioning System

To begin, this is an important message. Yes, the title is a play on words, but this is NOT a token chapter to add pages to the book.

**Why is God's Positioning System GPS relevant and important?

First allow me to state that in God's kingdom there are definitely <u>absolutes</u> but a good part of His commands, declarations, directives, instructions, etc., have <u>flexibility built into them</u>. Most non-believers have the opinion (if they even share an opinion at all) and many Believers have the opinion and misconception that God is mean, punishing, full of wrath, etc., but I am here providing evidence throughout this book that our God (Yahweh, the Great I Am, our creator) is loving, giving, compassionate, understanding, flexible (applicable to this context), etc. Regarding my opinions expressed in this book, they are rarely absolutes due to the infinite range of variables that are involved, and my opinions are just that, my opinions, and thus how often could they be expressed in absolutes. Having communicated God's absolutes vs. His flexibility for this topic and others; and that I relay very few opinions of my own in the book, but when I do, they are definitely not absolute. The following is one of my opinions and yes it is not an absolute, I think a significantly large portion of men/women have veered off of not only their personal goals in their life, but as a Believer has veered off of what God had originally planned for them (which I refer to as His <u>predestined purposes)</u>, or it's not a factor of veering off course, rather it is quite often Believers have never searched what their predestined purpose(s) is, therefore never knew and never pursued it. And friend, please understand that God has got a purpose for every single child of His and this is another of those topics in which you need to really believe that this is true.

A short excerpt of my version of the Prayer of Jabez which I pray regularly is as follows (See Ch4 Prayers for complete prayer): "Bless me Father, Bless me indeed...Please continue to expand my territories and horizons and continue to mold me and shape me into that person you have predestined and purposed me to be..."

A couple of key points here, this is a prayer of petition asking for blessings of importance for my everyday life. It is not just a prayer that I came up with but is a variation of a prayer in the Bible in which God did answer with blessings and is available to you rather than you having to come up with your own format. It is well aligned with what we are discussing although in general terms where we are going, acknowledging the significant role the Lord plays in it, and it implies that if I were to get off of His chosen path to let me know. So rather than implying something, you can choose to be specific and you can easily alter this prayer to accommodate that, you can also alter it or create a new one in which you specifically ask what He wants for you to do this month or year, or what your grand purpose is during your lifetime, etc. Obviously this is not that type of prayer and that's because I've already in the past asked in prayer for direction and answers regarding my purpose, so having received the answers, then this prayer is confirming that I understand where I am at in my journey and for him to watch over me, bless me and notify me of any potential problems. I strongly suggest that you ask for guidance on what your purpose is, 1) so that you know, 2) so that you're living a purpose driven life which is very important for you and your loved ones, 3) "if you don't have a target, you will surely hit 'nothing'," which means you should have a target to shoot for, otherwise you are in a sense lost and wondering in regard to what your purpose in life is, 4) also that you don't obsess over it, it will happen in due time (God's perfect timing) so what's expected of you is to pursue it rather than being slothful, idle, lazy, apathetic.

So yes, the God of all creation with all the complexities and who knew you before the beginning of time, can easily pre-designate and track 1 or more predestined purpose(s) for each and every one of us!

Whether in the business world, professional sports world or in this game we call life, you manage the things involved in the enterprise and you lead, mentor, coach people by setting goals (standards of achievement) and tracking (measuring, evaluating) performance to hit or surpass those goals. I'm often quoted as saying, "You (team or individual) are in control of your own destiny." Now what is included in that, is I will give them all the tools they need to succeed and they must "CHOOSE" how, when and where they will apply those tools in association with their natural gifts and talents along with the trained skills we've provided or that they're bringing with them from prior experiences, so that they can draw from all of those resources. Also, I approach many aspects of my life from a coach's perspective, therefore I also coach them based on their strengths (God's gifts and talents and acquired skills) and their weaknesses. I focus on optimizing the utilization of their strengths, whereas I will work on developing their weaknesses if needed for the position. In other words, I do NOT set them up for failure, nor do I position them for mediocrity but rather I position them for success. With having relayed that, they are truly in control of their own destiny with respect to their "job," and as one prominent football coach would say "Just do your job" and I like to add, "And give 150% wholehearted effort!" If you are a Believer you can relate to everything I just mentioned, because on the most part it's been taken directly out of God's Guidebook to life and abundant living (Bible). Maybe He will have me write a business book next?

One key to success is the measuring of the performance with the subsequent coaching and feedback of tips, suggestions, and teachings to assist in the prospering of the individual, team or organization. This business / sports analogy is not at all spot on perfect to the way God's kingdom functions and how its processes work, but it will provide a background of comparisons along with some contrasts.

Let's begin with a contrast and a dichotomy to get this kicked off and then I'll shift to the comparisons. God wants the best for you (as a Believer you need to believe and trust this is so), and we can in relationship receive the guidance and instruction directly through His Holy Spirit. Now we have all been given the gift of free will to "CHOOSE" if we want to follow this path, or not. If not, contrary to the analogy of business which if you do not follow directions you'll be asked to leave and probably not ever reconsidered, God on the other hand will empower you in the different routes you choose. And yes, He will even do so if it is 180degrees in the opposite direction of His predestined purposes that He's designated for you, and even if you choose to redirect your life in the opposite direction of Him (as previously mentioned in this chapter; God's Grace & When God gives you over). Note, if this is the case, He will not bless you for very long but as a parting gift He will bless you in abundance in the direction you are wanting to go. I needed to relay that but hopefully this doesn't apply to you. Now the point I am making is that you are truly in control of your own destiny. "Whoa!" You say. Doesn't that contradict the phrase you hear so many people say? Which is "God is in control." Well I can't speak for anybody else, so what I will do is relay to you that God is in control of His kingdom and there is no doubt whatsoever about that! As one example, read the New Testament concerning the life, death, resurrection of Jesus with emphasis focusing on his life and what He did, which is more than adequate evidence that God is in control. Regarding man/woman specifically, God purposely designed us to have free will, therefore we have freedom to make choices. Because He wanted us to choose to be in relationship with Him, or not. And remember that we were created so that He could "live" through us (via an experiential spiritual life) and He purposely did not want us to be His robotic slaves. Having said that, you are in control of your own destiny and that is how He designed it to be. Note, for non-believers there is consideration given and especially for Believers that, not if, but when you screw up, he will come to your rescue! You can trust Him for that and believe that He is in control! He is a loving, giving, compassionate God and with that said, when "life happens" (world, devil, etc.) and it takes you down the wrong paths, He will do His best to get your attention and offer you a "life preserver" with options, that depend on the various choices you make, and He will give you assistance on getting back onto His "right" path. Keep in mind that with His Guidebook He relays clear messages on numerous topics on what to expect, BUT you have to be in the Word to get these messages. One such that applies here is "whatever you sow, you will reap," meaning that "whatever you put into something, you will get the same measure out of it." Also note, with respect to the 180degree prior example or other similar instances, that this is not an absolute because God loves you so much that He yearns that you have the best, so whether He is attempting to get you turned around, or coming to your rescue, or trying to adjust your steps from one path to another, He will consistently attempt to get your attention (even when you are unresponsive).

Previously in the business analogy, I touched on strengths and weaknesses and wanted to underscore that a person's ultimate strength is their relationship with God, hands down. How can anyone disagree? For He is a giving God and we share in His power, authority and glory just to name a few attributes. So for those boldly receiving His power and blessings, then acting on them throughout their daily lives, nothing in this world can top that. Regarding one specific weakness (not to be confused with any other weaknesses) is sin. I just wanted to relay a brief message concerning sin. It is a weakness that all men/women have to deal with to varying degrees, but it should not be as influencing a factor to a Believer who is confident in their relationship with the Lord. Those that are insecure often allow sin/weakness to take over their lives or at least significantly and negatively impact their lives. * The key takeaway here is for the ones that lack confidence to **not** be paralyzed by it, rather take command of the situation (as others have) with God confidence, by approaching it confidently with hope, trust and faith in God! This encompasses a broad range of teachings, so see Ch7 for additional information.

Are you on the "right" path? What is your GPS communicating? Let me get you started off in the right direction on this topic, your GPS is the Holy Spirit. Rather than "walking" in the Spirit, think of it as taking a journey with the Spirit. So what is your GPS communicating? Some GPS's announce "recalculating" and others announce "repositioning" both are referring to when you go off the designated path. Do me a favor and think about how often in the past 3 years and the past year how often your GPS announced "repositioning?" If it is numerous "repositioning, repositioning, repositioning, repositioning," then the Holy Spirit is trying to get your attention by raising a "red flag," which for 98% of Believers this is an indication of some real issues. Whereas 2% may be, by design, intended to live in the repositioning mode. Also the case may be that at this stage in your life you are repositioning often and either trying to actively pursue direction or just the opposite and allowing life and the world to lead you (often down wrong paths). Obviously, the GPS is a metaphor for what to look out for and may help some identify and relate to better than they would to Biblical instruction. So the balance of this discussion will consist of both the GPS examples and the spiritual instruction.

How do you utilize your GPS (Holy Spirit)? 1st see Ch5 which specifically pertains to the Holy Spirit, or Ch3 has a significant portion dedicated to the Holy Spirit. A brief synopsis: It begins with your relationship with God through Jesus via the Holy Spirit who dwells in you and you renewing your mind daily in the Word walking with the Holy Spirit in praying and petition in relation to what your purpose is, along with Him assisting you in making significant life decisions as well as not so significant decisions, to petition (ask) for advice before making decisions on your own which in turn assists you in learning how to hear the answers…this my friend is God's system and this is how He leads, guides and directs our paths in life (and always within the parameters of abundant living). Similar to the GPS (on your cellphone), you enter a destination (maybe what you have aspired to do or to go; or maybe it is a dream goal that you've had for some time) and it searches and calculates in order to provide you with the fastest and safest route; maybe it will deter you from going a certain route; or once on that route maybe it determines that another route is much better or that the route that you are on that something has changed or occurred and suggests/prompts a change of route. These examples are very closely related to what the Holy Spirit does in your walk, however you must learn how to access the information He's trying to relay.

This will probably end up being a controversial statement especially if taken out of context but here goes, "All paths lead to God for those Believers who believe, hope, have faith and trust in Him and are committed to their relationship with Him." One point here is, I have experienced this myself on more than one occasion because remember that I wasn't saved until my mid-thirties so I was lost for some time and after my conversion I still made some poor choices which sent me down paths He definitely did not want me to take, but with all the paths I've been on He's finally got me zeroed in and focused on what, when, where and how to go now. Note, regarding the statement about "all paths lead to," please excuse this brief disclaimer: I am NOT conveying that all religions have a path to God. Okay nuff said.

Back to what I had touched on concerning a "dream" goal, if it is from God meaning that God put the dream in you, then He will let you know it and when He lets you know, ask Him for help in having it come to fruition. Much of this is subjective and unique to the individual so keep that in mind and you should receive this in very general terms. When it comes to asking for direction, please do your best to leave your logic, your rationale, and especially your emotions out of the picture and focus on the messages the Holy Spirit is communicating to you via the Word, sermons and other random occurrences that stand out (even ones that seem like odd coincidences, these need to be meditated on). Your walk in the Spirit takes time to develop but you have to trust and have faith and act on things which will help you to know that you are making progress hearing His still small voice. * Also remember that the part of your soul that used to give you problems are related to your wants, desires and lusts and are seated in your will, emotions and unfortunately your mind. So that does not make this process easy in attempting to drown out the noise of the world that the devil has caused you to focus on but try to make it a conscious effort to do so. Are you listening for and to what God/Jesus/Holy Spirit is telling you?

- Are you reading the Guidebook for life and abundant living, the Bible, and looking and listening for guidance?
- Are you listening to your pastor with the intent to understand? And are you taking notes? Are you validating what He is relaying? You know many a time it's those nudges for me to get something validated that turns out to be the message He wanted to relay to me. This is one of the forms of communication He uses.
- The same goes for taking notes or keeping a journal. You may at first think that you jotted down the note as you used to in school because you think you need to know X, but the key is when the Holy Spirit brings you back to that note or exposes you to related readings or teachings that the dots then become connected, thus He is communicating to you. It's really an amazing process once you get some experience with it.
- * Are you "receiving" God's blessings? This is a process in and of itself and it too takes time to figure it out and then to just do it. This is highlighted in other parts of the book and what is important to know is that many people are not even aware of this, or familiar with the process, and miss out on so much of what God is pouring out to His children.

121

- Are you "acting" on the blessings you receive? This is a process in and of itself and it too takes time to figure it out and then to just do it. Our God is not passive when it comes to doing things and when it comes time for us to "**do**" things.   * He expects action and nothing will transpire until you put your **faith into motion!!!**
- Tip: The Lord is always in continuous motion and He is always moving forward.
- Is the path you are on God's way? Or is it your way? (Or the highway? ☺ time for a little humor). Seriously though, if you trust and have faith in His way, then He will do more than just help you get there! That is my Godly advice and it doesn't have a direct scripture but there are numerous related scriptures (Abraham comes to mind and how God told Him to pack up and leave everything and trust in Him); I should add a word of caution regarding that example: there are a number of passages in the Bible that warn against doing things to the extreme, such as packing your bags and leaving whether leaving a family or straight out of college leaving to another country or across the US; make sure this is God's plan and God's way for you to go and note that if it is extreme then that is a red flag that needs much prayer and meditation. For myself, I've had a few similar situations one being when I was in the Cayman Islands and wanting to move back to the states and the Big Recession was still impacting cities, states, jobs, etc. and out of intense frustration in having had already put off time and time again returning back home, there were numerous other hurdles and uncertainties, not to mention that I also wanted to make sure that where I moved was where He was directing me to go. He spoke to me and I clearly heard Him say, "I will bless you wherever you go." And He did!!! I can't express the emotions that just came over me in writing this…Yes He did bless me and yes He did keep His promise and yes, I too have done my best to glorify Him in return for His amazing grace and blessings!
- God knows how it all began and He knows how it will end on earth for each of His children, therefore trust and have faith in Him and have Him guide you along His victorious journey He's planned for you.
- (**Matt 7:14**)BSB "But small is the gate and narrow is the path that leads to **life**, and there are **few** who find it.

- **(Matt 7:13)**BSB "Enter through the small gate. For wide is the gate and broad is the <u>path that leads to</u> **destruction** and **many** enter through it."

I've taken a number of significantly different paths in my life, so I can verify that God will "reposition" the path or the directions to get you onto a better path than the one you were misled or foolishly took. In other words, He will direct you back into His direction. The point is this journey we are on, ideally we were meant to be aligned with God which means for us to be in line with His will and His ways and in line with the purpose He has planned for us and in line with the paths in life that He wants us to take…well this is definitely not a perfect world and it certainly is not the ideal world. Therefore similar to the process for our sanctification, as we mature spiritually, we will step by step get more aligned with God, where sanctification takes a lifetime and often longer, we need to do our best to become aligned with Him as soon as possible. As we are accomplishing that, the sooner we will be able to walk on that proper path that God has designated and repositioned us to and the sooner we can start living the abundant life that both He and we desire.

(See diagram in final pages of Ch6) for an illustration of what it looks like when someone like me takes wrong turns, make poor decisions, goes backwards, sideways, gets lazy and does not make any forward progress.

Possible arguments posed against my explanation in the prior paragraph:

- If God is going to "reposition" to accommodate me getting off track in my life, then why would I even worry or be concerned about anything I do?
  - o To begin, if you are happy with your life which involves much sin and see no need for improvement, then go for it and continue down that path. But if you do not like where that path is taking you and/or your conscious is speaking to you and alerting you that this or that is wrong and you agree, or for whatever reason you desire a change and that change is to have God participate in your life then read on.
  - o Because this is analogous to what is now and has been taking place between God and man for 2000yrs now. He's already repositioning to accommodate us and as mentioned previously in this chapter, He's built into this process some flexibility. Now if they are a non-believer or a pseudo-believer (claims they are to others but in reality, simply lying to others) then this discussion does not pertain to them. But if they are a Believer who has been struggling for some time or maybe a very long time, <u>God knows their heart</u> and He knows that they are on the cusp so to speak and

if one of these times they actually <u>earnestly commit a portion of their time, energy and attention</u> then He will almost assuredly win over that soul. Can you disagree that this is what's been taking place since Christ's resurrection?

o   To further the discussion, if you'll read the subchapter on Grace you'll have a better understanding: <u>reposition 1)</u> we were forgiven <u>all</u> our sins past, present and future; <u>next reposition 2)</u> Believers that are faced with or experiencing sinning, then God's grace goes into hyper mode to us and it abounds meaning our cup runnith over with blessings to keep us from sinning (Paul uses the example, "Should we sin so that we receive more grace?" And he responded to his own question, "God forbid") no, because of this; <u>next reposition 3)</u> that when we "Let go and Let God" and truly desire to change our ways and are willing to have the Lord work in our lives then we can rest assured that He will take over and once the process is occurring with some consistency we begin to change inside and no longer have those desires to sin, and that change inside is also attributed to us desiring to become more and more aligned with God which in turn is another factor that reduces our sin, all because God was flexible, understanding with compassion and love and also utilized His hyper-grace component during this transition. I myself would say that there's quite a bit of flexibility built into that model. Read God's Guidebook to life and abundant living specifically what Paul taught regarding grace and you'll see it is spot on to what I just communicated, minus the GPS repositioning.

In the Prayer of Jabez paragraph at the beginning of this chapter, I lined out a number of suggestions for you on how to and why to search out the purpose that God has predestined for your life and now I'm wanting to relay what transpired in my life. Even long before I was saved, beginning in high school and especially in college I was wondering what my purpose in life was and at times I thought I may have figured it out only to have this or that dream come to an end and me figuring well that wasn't it. I was lost, although you couldn't have convinced me of that, and when somebody is living life with no sense of direction, let alone some sort of a compass to use as a guide, they are going to either bounce all over the place and having all the wrong influences directing them here and there. Or in my case I would attempt to emulate (copy) a popular society figure's life that I supposed was first real and second applicable to "society's norm" and when that didn't work I attempted to model the character of someone I knew personally that I highly respected and who was successful and that only got me so far because once I was making good income the lusts of the world would always come into play (literally) and send me off onto another path. Keep in mind that by choice I remained single up to the age of thirty (so to get all the fun out of my system) and then having children really changed my entire outlook and approach to life, but let me say that I now know that without God in a person's life no matter how "responsible" they think they are being, that they will continue to either bounce, drift or whatever and make decisions with no true direction and it will come back on them sooner or later, as it did with me.

Right around forty years old I was saved and eventually after having an understanding of what was what as it pertained to God's kingdom, I was well beyond the point to ask what I want to do when I grow up or what should I do. So I prayed and followed the same advice I disclosed to you at the beginning of this subchapter. Only I never received a definitive response and that is important for you to know for your own search. The way the Holy Spirit led me to determine it, was another long process of revelations from scripture, to pastor's sermons and especially from what I had experienced in my past, also what I knew deep inside. So if you caught that, it was primarily in retrospect in looking back on my life and seeing a common thread that ran consistently through the patchwork quilt of my life. Obviously if you are young then it would be difficult for you to utilize this method but don't discount it and ignore it either. As I mentioned, it was a number of things and sources that contributed to me finding my purpose and the Holy Spirit played a pivotal role in guiding me and in accomplishing it.

The following is an excerpt I pulled from Ch7 Jesus, subchapter Giving, this is one of the examples that the Holy Spirit brought to my remembrance in retrospect: * **"GIVE, it's what we do!"** I know it's what I've done my entire life, way before I was saved. At 28yrs old, my mother asked me, "When are you going to stop doing things for everyone else and start living life for DW?" This was still long before I was saved, and I paused only about 2 seconds and said, "Never! I like my life the way it is, I have most everything I want, and I enjoy doing things for others."

My purpose is so general that some might laugh or say, "isn't that a purpose that we all share?" Yes, in those terms it is. But for me I don't discount it, I take it seriously and it is a passion that energizes me. My purpose in life is to help others. It's what I do. It's what I've always done. And it is the impetus (drive, force) in everything I do. The difference between before I was saved was that it was sporadic, haphazardly accomplished and done discriminately upon my choosing, whereas now after being saved and understanding why I am here and what I am to do, I help others in need to better their lives and I do it to glorify my

God who gifted me with the abilities to do so, by blessing all the works of my hands! I can only speculate but this may be one of the reasons He's tasking me to pen this book. Just food for thought and something to think about, asking in prayer as to what your life purpose is, to the God of all creation who knew you before the beginning of time and now has filled you with His Spirit to bring all things to your remembrance and He reveals to you the predestined purpose He predetermined possibly before the beginning of time, or thousands of years ago, or hundreds of years ago, or as He formed you in your mother's womb, whichever it happens to be, to me that is incredible! So I discovered it in retrospect and remembrance and now carrying it forward in all that I do!

Side note: **The Lord is always moving FORWARD**. I should probably devote a separate subchapter for this (see Ch6), but it coincides with this topic matter so treat this like a "wisdom" commercial interruption. As the title states, the Lord is always moving forward. He is our model, and therefore we too should always be moving forward.

**This is a key and important composite teaching of Jesus: Do not dwell in the past, do not be fearful or anxious of the future, nor be fearful or anxious in the present, but to live in the present and have life and have it abundantly, today!

(Note: this does not mean to live it up today and forget about tomorrow; this is not carpe diem) It's an incredible golden nugget of wisdom for us all and especially in today's world. What's important to add to this is that God is always moving forward in all that He does. All means all, and again from our perspective He is our model and we desire to glorify Him, so we should model that behavior as well in every applicable aspect of our lives.

For example, if you have a problem (trial or tribulation) and it's got you and you are trying to work through it,

a) * "Walk" it forward…walk in the Spirit, walk in the Word, walk in sermons; you must renew your mind (spirit & soul) from the world and all of its twisted views.

b) Warning: there is no such thing in God's universe as standing still, you are either moving forward, or you're moving backward!

c) * Note, that the Holy Spirit does not operate like a TV or a video game meaning that you should not just think that you can flip the switch when you need Him. As mentioned numerous times, it is an intimate relationship you have with Him, therefore it is an ongoing (always on), ever advancing (always moving forward), always present, always present help in times of trouble, etc. Now that description conveys that He is always present, but not so that you can flip the switch on and off, rather that He is always present which allows you to always turn to Him for all things and in doing so you are in tune with each other and to receiving His guidance and instruction with confidence. (see Step into His Presence, Ch6)

d) So face your problems head on with God confidence! And whether it is your problem, or you are advising someone concerning theirs, have this mindset: "Okay, now let's figure out what we need to do, moving forward." **

   1. Not dwell in the past; not dwell on it and everything associated with it; what good would that accomplish.

   2. Not be fearful or anxious for what the future holds because of repercussions from this problem, rather work it out now with future considerations factored in so that you can move forward with God confidence; and utilize the Holy Spirit to accomplish this along with seeking only Godly advice from others which is sound biblically based support. (see God Confidence, Ch6; and Positive Future Faith)

e) For subsequent mornings for however long it requires be sure to key in and focus on this topic in prayer to the Lord and He will give you strength, confidence and guidance.

   1. * This is likened to an Olympian workout regime, the conditioning of a super achiever to rise early in the morning and receive your instruction for the day and face the day with God confidence and the Holy Spirit's supernatural support. This is certainly a way in which you can glorify God.

Back to the illustrated GPS map. The shortest distance between two points is a straight line, according to the natural world. But we serve a supernatural God whose Spirit dwells in us and we share in His power and in His authority, so with regards to the wrong paths that we take whether misled by other, poor choices, or otherwise, He has given us the power and authority to impact anything and everything associated with changing direction and paths. Also keep in mind that He is a supernatural God that works in the supernatural realm which supersedes the natural realm and natural world. And this you must BELIEVE!

As you can see on the illustrated GPS map how it actually goes in retrograde (backwards) for a while and recovers and begins to move forward. This is a benefit for Believers, again our God is always moving forward, and His children will not be going backwards for any length of time if they trust in and have faith in Him. He will not allow this to continue, also He will pull you out of any pit you get into. Okay, so what if you did take 5 steps forward and 10 steps backwards, as previously stated, walk it forward and always keep moving forward in all that you do. Remember that trials and tribulations are either designed to get your attention or is a learning experience you are to endure and recover from because God designed it as part of your journey and note that it is part of the abundant living process. Very important to remember and if need be relay in prayer that you know of this promise and that is, He promised that He would never give us a temptation, trial or tribulation that we are not capable of handling WITH Him! Failure is only a problem, if you give up trying. So never give up, always persevere, always move forward, always keep your eyes focused on Jesus (Peter sank from on top of the water when he took his eyes off Jesus and started looking at the rough waves surrounding him), Believe and have God confidence every day!

(1Cor. 10:12-13)NKJV "Therefore, let him that **thinks** he stands firm (on his own), be careful not to fall. There has no temptation taken you but such as is common to man: but God is faithful, who will not allow you to be tempted (trials) above that you are able; but will with the temptation also make a way to escape, that you may be able to bear it.

The Wilderness Experience (an insert)

Wilderness in the Bible is often referring to being: LOST. So when the Bible mentions the wilderness, most often being lost is one aspect of being in the wilderness. The Israelites who were in the exodus from Egypt were lost for "forty years in the wilderness," it should have taken them 60days to make that trek but because of their disobedience to God He had them sojourn for forty years, a time in which they had much to learn from conflict and strife, to wars, to how to worship, etc. and pass on to the next generation who by the way were the only ones that would enter the Promised Land. Not even Moses. An incredible story with much wisdom and insight, but keep in mind that it is under the Law and the Old Testament (made between God and man via Moses) and their life was full of rules that now to us are strange and their relationship with God was significantly different than what we benefit in having.

There are numerous instances in the Bible in which people were lost in the wilderness and many not realizing at the time they were lost just that they were struggling with problem after problem after reoccurring problem and not knowing or understanding why but accepting it as a part of life. Whereas if they had allowed the Lord into their life and walked in the Spirit, life would have been significantly different.

What's the old adage, "time flies when you are having fun?" So, does time slow down when you are in trials and tribulations? Time does not speed up or slow down. It really has to do with your focus. When Peter focused on the waves and everything other than Jesus, he could no longer walk on water. It was only when he was focused on Jesus that he could. * If you are focusing on your problems, then you are missing out on your blessings. If all you do is sulk and worry and be fearful and focus on your problems and not the solutions, then you can end up in a deep wilderness experience. The distraction(s) can make it seem in retrospect that time has just flown by because problems and depression can cause you to live your life in a fog (partial darkness), so then you must earnestly seek out Jesus who will bring you into the light and give you the proper focus. Once you are out of the fog, it likely will appear that you've lost time (and for a number of different reasons you have; specifically you've lost precious time from your life). Years can pass you by if you allow it and that is exactly the problem, if you allow it to continue and during the process not seek Jesus and His ever-present help in times of trouble. Conversely, Jesus should be your immediate reaction to seek Him out and ask for His help.

I can certainly relate to how problems, trials and tribulations can send you into a tailspin and knock you onto a completely different path in life, in unknown territories and totally lost in the wilderness. I've felt lost a few times in my life, but two times specifically I traveled deep into a chasm in the wilderness. The first time I started hanging with the wrong crowd and was easily influenced with sex, drugs and the rock & roll partying environment. This was when I was a non-believer and the deeper I traveled into the dark wilderness even though it was for just one year, the more I began to wonder if I'd ever make it out and be able to resume the life that I once lived (the past was obviously better than that hell, but I had no idea that the past life in itself was not much of a life especially compared to one with Jesus). But practically every other night something bad or messed up happened to somebody and if not that frequent then at least once a week. Looking back in retrospect I could see God's initial fingerprints and after time Him being the hand that pulled me out of the fire. It was no specific single shocking event or set of "hitting the bottom" events that made me decide to depart from everybody associated with it, but I just left and also went cold turkey. I could write a novel about the craziness of those dark times. There is no doubt in my mind and heart looking back on it that it was God who saved me from that Hell on earth and helped me to get right back (almost overnight) onto the same track I was on before that craziness and I didn't even know who He was, therefore didn't know to thank Him. My career took off immediately, ten years went by and during that time I was slowly getting introduced to Him by listening to sermons on Christian radio, then started watching some on TV, then anytime I was traveling over the weekend for work, on Sunday I'd find a church near the hotel regardless of the denomination and attend and take it all in. After witnessing the births of my daughters along with a strengthened curiosity regarding God, combined with a couple of trials and tribulations, I was soon on the path of getting saved. This is quite different from many testimonies you'll hear in which similar to the situation I was in with drugs, alcohol and wild living most people would have said that God saved them both from that corrupt life and in doing so saved their soul as well. Ultimately, He did the same for me although in the manner and sequence in which I am relaying.

So He saved me from throwing my life away ten years prior to saving my soul and then He saved me again from being lost deep in the wilderness, this time within the same year of saving my soul. I had a failed marriage, I was torn with the realization that I was going to be a part time weekend only father and I lost a CEO position among other things; I will not bother you with the details. Long story short I went into deep depression to the point of contemplating ending my life and...He saved me again. This was a longer road to recovery than the first occurrence mentioned that He saved me from, but He was by my side through it all until I got back on my feet and resumed my new life.

It's difficult to expose these things of my past but they are my unique testimony and my experience of having witnessed God in action. I also realize it is my responsibility to relay this to others so that it may help them in time of need and/or to consider allowing God into their heart. Also, I've been blessed beyond anything I could ever imagine and what is incredible for me to be able to do is share one Godly occurrence after another with you, as pertaining to my relationship and my journey with Him (and not referring to my testimony) which is also my evidence of and witnessing God in action and I'm writing them all down in this book, for all to read and benefit by.

Please note that the aforementioned Wilderness Experience is the commonly understood meaning of being in the Wilderness and how falling that low can result in positive outcomes with God's help. I purposely covered it in this manner so that you can better understand the deeper meaning of the Wilderness Experience, one that will transform your life, however it is very important that you understand it and how to execute it. If you would please turn to Chapter 8 and read "**<u>A Wilderness Experience that is Transformational</u>**." I placed it further into the book because it pulls from many principles that I have yet to cover. Therefore you will probably also question a few of the principles mentioned, which is good because it will give you the opportunity to search them out in the upcoming chapters. So, you will benefit by reading it now and again when you've read to that point.

This subchapter began asking whether God's Positioning System (GPS) is relevant and important. Hopefully what I've written answers those questions, but if not, there is no question that God is active in our lives prior to and especially after we are saved. So it's definitely relevant to relay, as it does apply to the context of this book. Of course the GPS is an analogy, but it is a very appropriate one that I believe plays an important role in conveying a variety of messages. Just a few of which are listed here: **

- Do search for your purpose, in your walk with the Spirit.
- Don't get frustrated if you are not provided a "clear" and distinct answer. As the Bible underscores, on numerous occasions: "be patient;" this process will develop for you and with you over time.
- Don't obsess over your purpose, take things in stride.
- Don't do things in the extreme.
- Do give it a wholehearted effort, as you should with everything in your life (family, friends, career/job, etc.).
- Don't ever believe that the path you are on cannot be corrected.
- Don't ever give up. Always race to win but know that even though you may not come into 1st place, your effort and enthusiasm is evidence that you are a winner.
- Do believe that God will either reposition your path or He will alter your destiny in order to accommodate His son/daughter that He so loves.
- Do live your life with intention and focus; and live life to its fullest!

This list is endless so could go on forever. **Focus on gaining as much Godly wisdom as you can on a daily basis. Convert that wisdom to current day applicable knowledge with understandings; Pray and believe it is so; Receive all the tools God has for you and Act on what you know and what you are given with a wholehearted effort and you will succeed beyond all expectations in living an abundant life while on your experiential spiritual life journey on earth that God has created for you, gifted you with and facilitated His GPS to guide you along the way!!! **(Please see the GPS diagram in final pages of Ch6)**

Chapter 3 My Lord's Prayer & In the Spirit

My Lord's Prayer & In the Spirit

I walk, talk, pray and do everything <u>in the Spirit</u>. Now that might sound odd to you, or it might sound extreme to you, or you may understand it because it's what you do, regardless it is simply what I have developed over the years and I want to relay how you too can accomplish this and how fulfilling it is when you do. I mentioned elsewhere in the book that praying should not be like carrying on a cell phone conversation and hanging up when it's time to do something else. Prayer should be focused and direct, also primarily while in your "secret place" **(*Mat 6:6)** but the communication should continue throughout your waking hours, it's a continuous relationship, you just don't "hang up" on God to go do something else; it is written, **(John 15:5)**KJV "for without Me, you can do nothing;" so why not do everything with him. It is also written **(Phil 4:13)**KJV "I can do all things <u>through</u> Christ who strengthens me;" please note: "all" means "all;" also whatever you do through Him, he strengthens every aspect of the circumstances. In other words where you thought you were good at something, include Him and you'll excel). So much like prayer, your relationship with the Holy Spirit should also continue throughout your waking hours, with practice over a period of time you will be doing everything in the Spirit. *Also keep in mind that Jesus promised his Father's Spirit (Holy Spirit; referred to as the Advocate, the Comforter, and the POWER from heaven) will dwell in you as my replacement when I physically leave earth **(as it is written, John 16:7-8)**. Jesus even touted the additional virtues of an indwelling Holy Spirit over having Jesus in person!

I've already given numerous examples of occurrences in how the Spirit has led me in my life/spiritual journey; from Him telling me to do this (green light) or don't do that (red light), to Him answering within just a matter of days and sometimes hours a spiritual (or scriptural) question I posed, to Him comforting me with respect to a loss of a loved one, to Him helping me with my personal struggles so that I can find peace and contentment and have it prevail in my life, to guiding me through God's Word, as well as navigating others false teachings, and the list is endless.

I truly revere the Holy Spirit of God that dwells in me and cherish my relationship with Him. I think, I talk, and I do things through Him, and He through me; this is what I mean by walking in the Spirit daily. He has "peeled the scales back from my eyes and ears" so many numerous times throughout my walk with Him, that I couldn't begin to recount the occurrences. One such specific occurrence that I would like to share with you is called "My Lord's Prayer," but before I do, I first should give you some background which requires a bit of explanation regarding the how's and why's. It's important that I take this deep dive for you, because it should exemplify what you yourself are capable of achieving with the Holy Spirit.

The Spirit worked with me on "My Lord's Prayer" for well beyond 1 year divulging an idea, thought or at times just a single word that was meant to enlighten me. Obviously, it would be at God's perfect timing for when He felt the time was right to reveal another aspect of truth to me and thus the reason for the overall length of time it took. In saying that, I wholeheartedly believe these are truths that were revealed to me for the purpose of my spiritual growth and also that He always had the intent that these truths would be shared with others. I tell you; you cannot fathom <u>the importance of this prayer in your prayer life or how essential it is in releasing God's power and Grace into your life</u>.

Do you perceive a bit of hesitation on my part with how I'm approaching this topic? I don't know if hesitation (or reluctance) is the appropriate word to use in this situation, but what I am going to eventually relay in this chapter may be controversial to some, so I am just trying to cover all my bases. I am the first to agree with the majority of non-denominational and even some of the denominational pastors who say, "Read the scripture within its context" which means that you should read a segment or an entire chapter in order understand the context in which a line or two of scripture was meant to convey. All too often, many will take one line of scripture and expound on it <u>so to suit the ends</u> to <u>their means</u> within the <u>confines of their context</u>, not the context in which it was meant in the Bible. Another way to put it, is when a person who is putting together topic matter for a discussion, study or sermon that seems to relate or be similar in nature to a passage in scripture, that scripture should not be translated or communicated as a "disguised interpretation" to accommodate an agenda by taking it out of its original context in which it was meant/designed for (there is consensus among

133

most contemporary pastors with regards to NOT participating in this form of manipulation; manipulation of God's Word and/or the manipulation of man).

I've meditated and prayed on this and have determined that I know beyond a shadow of doubt that I have not interpreted or translated, nor have I come up with the following to express an agenda of my own. When the Holy Spirit first started to teach me on this topic and divulge new truths to me (new to me but always having been present in the Word) and divulge one or a couple of words, I had no idea that this would be a progressive teaching spanning a period of over a year and a half. Another aspect I wanted to mention was that I am not writing or rewriting scripture, actually it is a prayer and as you know many of us say thousands of prayers over a lifetime some ritual while others are improvised as we think and speak them and are typically unique to the situation at hand.

So there, I wanted to get that stated first before proceeding, because I'm sure more than one person is going to take me out of context and try to accuse me of false teachings or even blasphemy. Nonetheless be patient with me and read all the way through "The Lord's Prayer" and "My Lord's Prayer" as well as with the complete analysis/explanation that follows…it is POWER PACKED!

* (Note "power" in the Greek [exousia] is translated as both power as in "force," and authority as in "mastery and privileged; delegated influence." There are times in which power means force, or it means authority as in privilege and vice versa when authority is mentioned it can denote the two meanings. Therefore, we are given incredible dynamite power and a mastery of influence in the natural realm [partially in the spiritual realm] by our Father in heaven!)

The Lord's Prayer
Came about when the disciples asked Jesus to "teach us how to pray." You can find two different references to this occurrence in (Luke 11:1-4)NKJV and (Mat 6:9-13). Upon researching the two references mentioned you will immediately note that they vary somewhat in how it is relayed in words and structure although the context pretty much remains the same. In combining the two, Jesus responds by saying:

> "Our Father which art in heaven, hallowed be your name,
> Your kingdom come, your will be done on earth as it is in heaven.

134

Give us this day our daily bread, and forgive us our sins, for we also forgive everyone who is indebted to us.
And lead us not into temptation, but deliver us from evil.
For yours is the kingdom and the power and the glory forever. Amen.

Let's begin with determining the type of prayer this is, whether ritual or improvised and whether it is a prayer of praise or petition. Does the prayer above qualify as a ritual prayer? By definition, it is a prayer that is meant to be repeated on a regular basis. So yes, the "Lord's Prayer" is a ritual prayer and in saying that it should be a ritual part of our prayer life, if not daily then weekly or monthly. Additionally, this prayer has a two-fold purpose and is also very important for you to know for your prayer life * The 1st purpose is: for The Lord's Prayer to be prayed verbatim as a group; and the 2nd purpose is: Jesus meant for you to incorporate what he said into your prayers, meaning don't just say this prayer exclusive in and of itself. He said "pray in this way" and in saying that He's instructing that you should use it as a model to structure the other improvised prayers you pray in order that your prayers are properly communicated to the Father and get effective results. Does this make rational sense, for our Lord to teach us in the proper ways of prayer because it is a function vital to our relationship with God thus promoting the means to having an abundant life? I certainly think so.

*This is a foundational principle that you need to understand and is a message that is underscored throughout the Bible and that is: God gave us free will, which means that you have a choice! From choosing to believe in Him and His Son; to choosing to worship Him (if so, when and how); to how to pray to Him; etc., etc., or to choose not to. Too many people who criticize Christianity (most having very little to no research to back up their criticisms) do so by saying Christianity is a form of slavery to a master and is binding and legalistic, which means that you must follow all of God's demands according to how He dictates, otherwise you are condemned forever or some other form of condemnation. This is so far from the truth! Skeptics or simply people with different beliefs if having done some research, like read the entire Bible, would then determine that is simply not the case and that God wants us to choose in every aspect if, when, where, what and how we go about choosing our spiritual paths, if any at all. I'm paraphrasing here, Jesus said that if the Father simply wanted slaves then "He would have made the trees bow down and worship Him." To get to my point, in all aspects of your journey and especially in reading the Bible keep the mindset that God wants to be in relationship with you and His Word/The Bible is a guide (not a manual) that covers many topics that pertain to a relationship with Him, one of which are the gives and takes and consequences of doing something your way versus His way, and it is ultimately your choice on how you want to go about carrying it out, or not. Having said that, in the example of the Lord's Prayer Jesus is recommending to "pray in this way," which I say again is a model for you to improvise (or not) and take components of it to add to your own unique prayer with its unique circumstances and needs.

Now, give this some thought and please answer the following questions (you will understand the importance and significance of answering the questions within a few paragraphs):
- What does the "Lord's Prayer" mean to you?
- What does it say/relay to you?
- What are you saying to God when you pray it?
- How does it relate to the overall teachings you've received along your journey?
- How does it relate to where you are at in your spiritual journey?
- Has your interpretation of it changed over a period of time?
- How does it relate when you pray it in context to your current wants and needs?

TAKE A MOMENT AND REREAD THE PRAYER AND ANSWER THE QUESTIONS BEFORE CONTINUEING.

Well, to some the prayer is just a series of words they have memorized and then blurt it out without any substance or an attempt to convey anything! Or they've been praying it for 20 to 40 years and it is so automatic that it's like walking from your bed to the bathroom, it's become habit and no real thought even went into it (is this true for you?) Then to some the prayer is an attempt to convey to God thanks for providing their daily needs, often times food (as in "daily bread"; which by the way this is not at all referring to baked bread or food we ingest); and/or a praise for forgiving them; or for leading them in His will and direction; which of course is better than the first meaningless example of blurting out a memorized prayer that virtually is not communicating any intent or sincerity on your part. The thing is, all the above examples significantly **miss the mark** (some, more so than others). Remember He wants you to receive His best, receive his blessings and benefit from them, thus He desires that you hit the mark as often as you can. Or as Paul put it, **(1 Cor. 9:24)**KJV "Run the race to win." If you are relaying virtually meaningless ritual prayers (or ones with no sincerity behind them) then why would you not expect Him to respond in like manner, by giving you nothing in return? That is why I am going to the extent that I am with this topic as well as throughout the book, so that you know and understand the who, what, when, where, why and how's of God's plan, His design and His desires for you.

With regards to my journey, for whatever reason and God only knows, the Holy Spirit was determined that <u>I fully understand the teaching, the meaning and the importance of the</u> **"Lord's Prayer."** He peeled back the scales from my eyes with respect to this, so that I could clearly see the length, breadth and height of this prayer. In doing this each meaning was attached to a principle teaching, and get this, if I had not yet received the teaching or misinterpreted the teaching then that aspect (or word or phrase) would not be revealed to me until I understood the true meaning. Isn't He an awesome God! So in other words, this was not only a segmented process but a lengthy one and on top of that, understanding this prayer was not the exclusive end goal of God's purpose in this endeavor. The Holy Spirit not only spent months getting me to fully understand the Lord's Prayer but he took another year in which, I don't dare use the word create (although possibly compose or pen), so for a lack of a better word, to modify the prayer into "My Lord's Prayer."

* Three key takeaways here is that the **"Lord's Prayer"** utilizes the words <u>"us and we;"</u> remember that Jesus was responding to a request from a group of his disciples to teach "us" to pray <u>together</u> and therefore this prayer is clearly designed to be communicated to the Father **as a collective group** (<u>or an individual praying for a group/family</u>). Please do not misunderstand and discount the Lord's Prayer because it is a powerful prayer for a group of Believer's whether they're babes or mature. Especially the babes (immature in the knowledge of God) because as they are new or already on the path of learning, it is a powerful example for them to participate in a group prayer in which they are not only included but also as a group petitioning to "give us our," which often delivers one of its important messages that God himself is giving us blessings. *Also keep in mind that Jesus was there with the disciples and had not yet revealed that He would be leaving them or that they would be receiving the Holy Spirit, so there is no reference (or for that matter praise) with respect to either one of them in this prayer (you'll note the importance of this in regard to "My Lord's Prayer"); *Additionally the prayer is within the context of that time in history, therefore they petitioned the Father to "forgive their sins;" whereas we now know and believe our sins are forgiven all past, present and future due to Jesus's works on the Cross. So why would we pray that and do so as a ritual whether daily or otherwise? It's delivering a confusing message especially to those who do not study the Word but who have memorized this prayer possibly years and years prior and pray it regularly. Also keeping in mind what I had alluded to before and that is many pray The Lord's Prayer with little or no substance/emotion/thought/praise behind it and lacking intent to convey anything, therefore what worth or value is it to that person; or God for that matter? Think of it this way, if someone is praying in this way how would they ever believe they are having an intimate relationship with God, as in the type that He yearns to have with them? Please don't misunderstand me with respect to the Lord's Prayer, there is no other like it when it is prayed properly as a prayer of praise and done so as a collective group.

* A couple of the key takeaways with respect to **"My Lord's Prayer"** which are in contrast to the prior paragraph. The "My" designates that this is personal and therefore **to be prayed individually**. * It also incorporates the full triune Godhead, thus allowing us to praise the Father, the Son and the Holy Spirit with one comprehensive prayer. * It is a prayer like no other, it has layers upon layers of depth incorporated into it. With that said, please review the prayer first then I will break it down into its pieces and parts. This will in turn illustrate to you the extensive length, breadth and height that is integrated into it and assist you in understanding the vast importance of it (as the Holy Spirit did with me).

My Lord's Prayer

My Father who art in heaven, hallowed be thy name, holy is your name Father, I praise you upon high and I bow in worship to you;

Your kingdom come into me, so that your will shall be done on earth as it is in heaven; I understand that I must die of selfish self, surrender to your will in

138

obedience and be reborn again in Christ Jesus today (a new man/woman); To Glorify you in the things that I think, that I say and that I do; to Honor you, Trust in you, have Faith in you and Believe in you, whole-heartedly; and to Love you! (As I always will)

So give me this day my daily bread, your Word, the bread that nourishes me spiritually, mentally and physically, your Son Lord Jesus; who is the way, the truth and the life for me; who chose to die on the cross for me; who defeated satan, the devil and death for me; and who you rose, again for me, so thank you Father; Thank you for forgiving my sins, as I forgive others who trespass upon me;

Your Holy Spirit dwells in me, comforts me, counsels me; leads me, guides me and directs me in your righteousness and your truths; fills me with your wisdom; leads me not into temptation and delivers me from evil;

For this is your kingdom Father that dwells with me; in it I share your Power, I share your Authority and I share your Glory, respectfully; today, tomorrow, forever and ever - as you promised, me! I thank you, I love you, In Jesus name I pray, hear my prayers and make them so, Amen!

I'm curious of what you think, at first glance. Too lengthy, will it be too difficult to memorize? Actually once you continue to read the balance of this chapter you'll see that by having each line broken down into its proper meaning it will help you in your clarity of the context from beginning to end and in doing so it will make it easier to memorize. In addition to that, we are to pray and praise with enthusiasm and boldness with the intent of accurately conveying our praise and love; the following guide will assist you in doing that as well. * Also, the following is very important information for you because it delves into many foundational questions you might have and answers them with scripture. As mentioned, it is powerful in many ways.

My Lord's Prayer (interpreted)

As previously mentioned, this is a personal prayer meant to be prayed between you and God (your heavenly Father). It is a praise prayer, and not at all a petition prayer (asking/requesting). So in saying that, you are giving thanks and praise for His love and all that He has done for you with an attitude of gratitude, which in turn should energize you to deliver it with enthusiasm and boldness! Also as mentioned, at first DON'T try to memorize it for memorization sake, but to first seek to understand each and every statement. In doing so you'll not only easily memorize it you will be able to say it with certainty of understanding and accurately relay the message God wants to hear from you!

My Father who art in heaven, hallowed be thy name, holy is your name Father, I praise you upon high and I bow in worship to you;

To begin, I kneel to one or both knees and with the Bible in hand, I almost always take a deep breath and smile! Because I treasure this moment every morning. If you are familiar with the term "Abba Father" then you know it is a term of admiration and endearment in relation to a child's personal intimacy with or affection towards their father (in various cultures it can be somewhat similar to papa or daddy, but in the Greek it's conveying, "I'm the son [or daughter] of the Father), and Jesus and Paul both used this term in their teaching. Although I don't say it, I think in terms of it before I begin with *"My Father who art in heaven..."* and it sets the tone of enthusiasm that I've spoke of. (By the way, the root of enthusiasm in the Greek is entheos which means "God within" or "God inspired") Hallowed means Holy; therefore I just emphasize it by repeating it *"hollowed by thy name, holy is your name Father."* God is above us in all aspects thus the *"I praise you upon high"* (for He is above me and I acknowledge it) *"and I bow"* (whether bow on my knees or bow my head; as a sign of reverence to Him) *in worship to you."*

Your kingdom come into me, so that your will shall be done on earth as it is in heaven;

His kingdom to begin with is the fullness of the triune Godhead (Trinity); it is all encompassing of the who, what, when, where, why and how of God; an infinite list that includes His mercy, grace, forgiveness, giving, blessings, love, peace, joy, power, glory, authority, etc.

Next, His kingdom is in all who are saved in Christ; so take note, again this is not a petition, it is a fact **(John 14:20)**KJV "For I am in my Father and you are in me and I am in you" and with that so is the kingdom. In addition, with regards to the phrase * **(2 Cor. 3:18)**KJV "From Glory to Glory," (see also Ch2, Grace) this means that His glory shines upon us and we reflect glory back to him (an example although a bit abstract, would be: if our spirit, soul, body had reflection properties similar to a mirror and the glory that is transcended [transferred] to us, is then returned to God [BUT NOT automatically reflected] and in reality it is only returned/reflected [to God] by how we glorify God in the things we think, in the

140

things we say and in the things we do [primarily think, say and do towards others]; this I've coined as "From glory to glory, full circle.") Thus the explanation for: *"Your kingdom come into me,"*

"so that your will shall be done on earth as it is in heaven;" As revealed in **(Isaiah 55:8-9)**KJV "For my thoughts are not your thoughts, neither are your ways my ways, declares the Lord, as the heavens are higher than the earth, so are my ways higher than your ways and my thoughts than your thoughts." So to paraphrase, His will is not our will, and this is true because our will is of a fleshly and sinful nature and His is Holy and pure. Repeating again that He is above us, therefore much of His thoughts, His will, etc., is above and beyond our comprehension. The prior explanation regarding having His kingdom in us and with that the fullness of the Godhead in us, and with that His gift of His full glory in us, empowers us (if you so choose to utilize it) to be able to discern His will via the Bible along with the Holy Spirit's guidance and direction, in order that we would/could/should be able to carry out His will on earth as it is in Heaven.

Another element and relevant factor in this is, that earth is satan's dominion, (see chapter on "Spiritual Warfare" for a greater understanding of the role this plays). For now, just as we have our fleshly and sinful nature battling against fulfilling God's will, there is a greater battle than that that we have in satan, his demons and the devil. That is what makes the statement *"so that your will shall be done on earth as it is in heaven"* so powerful and important, that you are proclaiming to the Father that you understand the breadth of this matter and that you will see to it that this gets accomplished. Jesus knew this as well and proclaimed it, **(Luke 22:42)**NLT "Father, if you are willing, please take this cup of suffering from me; yet not my will, but yours be done." With that said, this is a statement that is also communicated by you in not only praise, but in confidence and enthusiasm that this shall be done!

I understand that I must die of selfish self,

To begin with, the *"I understand"* is somewhat self-explanatory although I wanted to take a moment to relay that *the Holy Spirit fills us with God's wisdom (via His Word) so that we may have knowledge and "understanding" of His kingdom and of this world. Therefore in this context, I "understand" the breadth of what "dying of self" means. From one perspective, self refers to our ego, or our inner self (volumes and volumes of books have been written on this topic),

141

self is often conveyed in various terms as: self-identity, self-importance, self-confidence, self-improvement, selfishness, etc. Regardless of how it is commonly referred to, self is in direct conflict with God. "Self" separates us from God because self relies on itself rather than our spirit, soul, body relying on and working in conjunction with God's Holy Spirit. To further that, when God told Adam and Eve that if you eat of that tree you will surely "die," death to God means to be alive yet spiritually dead and separated from Him. Put another way, those who allow their self (ego) to rule their lives it separates them from God, therefore they are literally the walking dead on earth (this may sound like an exaggeration but it is not very far off from reality). Another topic that has been discussed previously is that you cannot be unsaved but what can definitely happen and this does happen quite often is that after being saved you can for a multitude of reasons turn away from God thus separating yourself further and further from God to the point that you are no longer in relationship or God's favor. Note: the good news is that He will welcome you back **(Luke 15:11-32)**, if you want to resume the relationship (note: you cannot be saved again, or reborn a second time, because it simply cannot be done) you must repent of your sins and with sincere intent change your ways to enter back into relationship.

From another perspective *"dying of selfish self"* is when we are saved (or put another way, a requisite of being saved) is that we must **(Rom 6:6)**KJV "die of the old man/woman" and in addition to that **(John 3:3)**KJV Jesus said, "Truly, truly, I say to you, unless one is born again he cannot see the kingdom of God." Note: "born again" in the Greek: "born from above." So in basic terms, when we are born again, we die of the old person that we once were and are born again an altogether new person in Christ. Not to complicate things but to relay additional truths, with having referred to the Romans 6:6 verse, Paul's teaching is: just as Jesus was crucified, so are we crucified to our old person; also just as Jesus was resurrected, so are we resurrected as a glorified born from above new person (note: this is not done by our own decisions or in our own power, but it is by a gift of God and by his grace have we been saved). Additionally note that God alone saves, therefore He alone deserves the glory. Again, not to confuse the context or delivery of this message but another teaching that corresponds with this topic is that with the previous explanation of "crucified and resurrected" illustrates how the Bible uses shadows and types, meaning our lives are a shadow of Jesus's experiences on earth (and in heaven). It can be somewhat difficult to grasp this concept so bear with me. A shadow is an image cast by an object and representing the form of that object. So as you know a shadow is not as well defined as the actual image that it was cast from. Therefore, we are the shadow that is cast from the image (or actuality) of Jesus, thus provides the reasoning behind the teaching of Paul on the relationship of the crucifixion and resurrection in regard to Jesus and us. FYI, the entire Old Testament is a shadow/type of the New Testament (even though the OT chronologically comes before the NT the Son was never revealed before He became flesh but His "shadow" was ever present from the beginning to the end of the OT; another way of putting it is that by our hindsight in reading the entire NT we are able to see His shadow presence throughout the OT. As mentioned, this can be confusing but with adequate explanation along with hundreds of examples in the Bible, it can be easily understood. (For more information, see Ch7, 1st subchapter).

For just 9 words ("*I understand that I must die of selfish self*") quite a bit of information was just relayed although much more could have been added as you peel back the thin layers of that particular onion. So let's not lose track and continue forward.

"surrender to your will in obedience"

We "die of selfish self" and commit to living a life continuously improving the reborn new man/woman in Christ in order to have life and have it abundantly every day. Our surrender to God's will is another requisite of this relationship although it too is not forced upon us but is our choice. In reality it is the rational next step when we die of self to then surrender to God's will and do so as obedient followers. The old man/woman is gone and so is our rebelliousness (the opposite of surrender). Note: keep in mind that what I've been describing is a process and that it is really up to the individual how quickly or how long this process takes. Think about this concerning yourself, for those who are saved, how long did it take for you to "die of selfish self" (to give up the ways of your old man/woman) and surrender fully to God? Subsequently how long did it take for you to believe you are a "new" man/woman in Christ and not only begin the journey but start reaping the blessing of an abundant life? God has revealed that when you repent of your sins and commit to change and ask Jesus to be the Lord of your life that you are surrendering the old man/woman and instantaneously becoming a new man/woman by surrendering your will to God to begin your spirit filled journey with Him! In reality, did your "mind" allow this to take place, and in reality, did you make a long-term commitment to accomplish this? You need to give some serious thought to those two questions, and I recommend that you meditate, pray, praise and worship on the questions and your responses. Keep in mind that this book was in part written to help others in improving their overall life and spiritual journey (just two of the many reasons) to better understand the processes, to understand what God expects and by what you need to do to fulfill those expectations, etc. The mere fact that you've purchased this book and are reading it illustrates that you care enough to try and hopefully make a firm commitment to do.

You probably know this but hopefully do not come across it that often and that is the universal sign of surrender is holding your hands up. This is why (especially in church) people hold their hands up in worship and praise to illustrate that they surrender their everything to Him. *If you think about the big picture, we are surrendering everything to Him and ask that He would be the center of our life. To put it another way, we surrender a self-centered life to a God-centered life (that is a foundational principle of our faith). The guidebook to life and living, His Word the Bible is all encompassing and we are surrendering to the Lord and committing to obediently following Him and His Word. This part of the prayer *"Surrender to your will in obedience"* is making a statement to God that I will be obedient to His will daily in all that is expected of me.

"and be reborn again in Christ Jesus today (a new man/woman);"

This is not a continuation of the previously discussed "must be born again" topic. It does although involve the same basic topic matter, but here it is conveying a distinctly different and specific message. Read it carefully, (*and be reborn again in Christ Jesus today a new man/woman*) this seems contradictory to the statement "you cannot be unsaved and reborn a second time," and since this is a ritual daily prayer you especially cannot be reborn daily, but that is not what is being relayed here. This message is simple and relays that I understand that I will always have a fleshly nature, therefore I need to be <u>conscious</u> of it and never return to the old man's/woman's ways. That every day is a new day and that every day I want to have Jesus as the center of my life.

(2 Cor. 4:16)KJV "Even though our outward man is perishing, yet our inward man is being <u>renewed day by day</u>."

144

(2 Cor. 5:17)KJV "If anyone is in Christ, he is a <u>new creation</u>; old things have passed away; behold, <u>all things</u> have become new."

This statement in the prayer is meant to trigger your mind to remember when your conversion took place and of when the old man/woman was put away and the new man/woman was born and the importance of renewing your mind daily in the Word via the Holy Spirit. For me, the statement does just that and triggers the thought of my conversion of when I was reborn in Christ Jesus and how my life has been transformed! Finally that I am <u>consciously doing</u> this <u>TODAY</u>!

As often as is the case there are other important teachings that are interlinked with one another and I feel it important to relay some here. Please understand that we do not necessarily have to "work" every day at <u>not</u> regressing back to the old man/woman. The "being conscious of it" that I mentioned, simply means to put it into a file in the back half of your mind. With that said there are a number of reasons why I make that statement and use the filing analogy: a) Because the good news is, now we have the Holy Spirit to correct us (red light), which means to alert us or remind us that whatever we are thinking, saying or doing is contrary to God, separating us from God, returning us to our "old man/woman" ways, etc.; then subsequently we utilize the Holy Spirit's guidance and direction (green light) in terms of thinking, saying and doing the right things. b) To further the good news, we have God's favor and grace now (See Ch2, subchapter on Grace). In our obedience and earnest pursuit of our relationship with the Lord we receive an abundance of blessings from His grace, which promotes living in His favor, which promotes not to go back to our old ways, which promotes doing the right things for God, which promotes giving to others and loving others, which promotes etc., etc. It's a positive cycle and is a product of His gift of Grace. Putting it in simple terms: we love the way we live when we are in relationship with Him in obedience, which in turn promotes a positive cycle that continues to perpetuate itself. c) Another point is that God does not want us to be preoccupied with thinking the wrong things of the past or the old man/woman of the past, therefore file it (remember this from the introduction chapter: do not dwell in the past, nor be fearful or anxious of the future but live in the present and do so abundantly); this is what the Lord wants and teaches, as in remembering the good things of the past and don't repeat the bad things, so do not dwell in the past, rather He wants you to live in the present moment and have life and have it abundantly today! Having relayed that, * it is very important for you to always think positive and to have a positive outlook, thus another reason NOT to be sin focused or "sin conscious" but rather to be positive and grace focused or "grace conscious." His grace allows us to focus on having an abundant life rather than focusing on the negatives that result from sin. In an attempt to be brief, during the times of the Old Testament people were taught and lived sin focused and sin conscious which was a life centered around "Do not ..., Do not ..., and Do not..., and if you know your history (or the Bible) you now know the results of that kind of negative oppressed lifestyle. In being grace focused/conscious our paradigm shifts entirely, in other words our "mind is renewed" and now focused on our earnest love/obedience towards God and thus focused on and receiving the blessings that God truly desires for us. Which is to have a wealth of His wisdom and practice it daily in a positive environment that promotes: "You, Can do..., Can do..., and Can do..." *So, which would you rather live, the Do not life or the Can do life? I for one am living His "Can do, life" and it's awesome because it's living an abundant life of experiences. That is one of the reasons why I desire to glorify Him daily.

To Glorify you in the things that I think, say and do; to Honor you, to Trust in you, to have Faith in you and Believe in you whole-heartedly; and to Love you! (As I always will)

In order to convey how we glorify the Father, we first must understand what is meant by God's glory.

Side note: not long after God told me to write this book, one of the teachings the Holy Spirit spent months upon months on, had to do with the topic of His glory and how we are able to return it and in turn glorify Him. I also wanted to point out that my journey has been a little different than most of my brothers and sisters in Christ in terms of my walk with the Holy Spirit and the teachings I've received. Probably what differs slightly is my earnest and whole-hearted commitment and with that an attention to detail and being able to discern common threads and teachings that link with one another. One point I'm making is the Holy Spirit did not relay to me that "over the next few months your task is" to understand God's glory and how you are to return it by glorifying Him in what you think, say and do. To the contrary, I'd work at my job 60 to 70hrs per week, devote as much quality time as I could for my family and friends, get out and relax and have fun and ride my Harley, work around the house, rollerblade and exercise daily, sleep average of 6hrs/night, go to church on Sunday, watch and listen to pastors on Christian television at night, read the guidebook on life and living (God's Word

146

the Bible), meditate, pray, praise, worship, etc. The Holy Spirit would bring scripture, topics and concepts to my discernment and to my remembrance. Most of which could take a paragraphs worth in my journal or up to five pages and spanning a couple of weeks. But this topic on glory and glorifying stood out, it weighed heavier on my heart so to speak and it was consistently coming up in every other topic being brought to my attention; so I would eventually realize the significance of that particular topic matter. Another point is, the more I prompted and/or allowed the Holy Spirit to give me more, He gave me much more. * I just wanted to take a moment and relay the process and to say that I'm not special and that you have been given the same blessings and gifts and with that are capable of taking this same path and reaping the benefits for your journey, you just have to desire it and acknowledge such to the Holy Spirit.

You might be thinking DW just went off on a rabbit trail in the middle of this chapter. No, it actually directly applies to the topic at hand, the Glory of God. First important factor, remember that I said it was not long after my conversation with God, meaning that He must have believed it important that I start my journey with this foundation. Second important factor, as mentioned the process of learning of His glory took an experiential all-encompassing tour from qualifying his existence, to volunteering and helping others in need, to traveling and living outside the U.S., to dealing with the mountain highs and the valley lows of life, to understanding His purpose and mine, to understanding the breadth and magnitude of Him and His kingdom, forgiving, giving, loving, honoring others, the collective of man and of men/women of faith, and on and on. See this is His Glory! And all of our lives matter and play a significant role in it. So if someone asked me to give them a definition of God's glory, I would first say that there is no adequate definition to explain or describe it; but in an attempt, it would consist of a similar explanation I just gave and summarizing it by saying the visible aspect of His glory begins with a blinding bright light and filters its way down to us on earth as the magnificence of the world that we see around us; next, in terms of the tangible and the intangible aspects of His glory is an all-encompassing loving kindness that permeates all life and for mankind begins at conception and involves each individuals experiential journey on earth and for those saved in Christ involves an experiential spiritual life journey on earth; this is made abundantly clear via His principles and precepts and the gift of our relationship with Him while on earth and continues for an eternity; for me anyway that's my definition of God's Glory.

As I alluded to before, there is a definition for all things in God's kingdom except for one, His Glory; it would take an infinitesimal list to define it and then that would not be adequate.

Now how do we glorify Him?

As mentioned, we reciprocate His glory to us, by glorifying Him. And we do this by our living our lives in relationship with Him. * God created us so that He could live through our lives. Since we are not puppets or robots but are a spirit, soul and body that has free will to make our own choices, thus living in relationship with Him (or not), the former allows Him and us to live abundantly according to His plan. The latter (or not), allows you to live your life as you please, or so you think (because the trade-off now involves satan taking charge). If you agree with the set of statements regarding God as the Lord of your life, then it is reasonable to say, that: * **We glorify God in all the things we think and that we glorify God in all the things we say and that we glorify God in all the things we do!** My point is that if my (or your) daily walk with the Lord is consciously carried out with that prevailing thought…Oh, what an abundant life you would have. Could you imagine the world we would live in if the majority if not all peoples would live this way? But the reality of it is mankind has had this opportunity since before and after Jesus lived on this earth, and this world is what its current state is and most of us agree on what that is and who and what got it and keeps it there. The good news is that we have a forgiving and loving God who still has this plan in place for us and as mentioned in the introduction chapter, it takes one person to start to change the world and it takes one step to begin a journey. For me, my life has been transformed by having "this" in my daily walk… "this" referring to for a lack of being able to pin it to one definition: this moral precept, this moral compass, this personal standard and rule, this personal daily and lifetime goal, this belief and creed: *"To Glorify you in the things that I think, that I say and that I do;* (see Ch8, Glorify God) *to Honor you, to Trust in you, to have Faith in you and to Believe in you, whole-heartedly; and to Love you! (As I always will)"*

"to Honor you,"

To honor the Father is to glorify Him. Well, that appears to be a redundant statement (to glorify you, to honor you). Yes in terms of how I just defined it, it is a redundant statement, but keep in mind the point here is that it is beneficial to

148

communicate your prayer and praise in very specific terms, also make sure your points have a specific meaning associated with them whether spoken or at least clearly and specifically contemplated. So having said that, to glorify includes the additional statement of think, say and do in a way that glorifies Him. But with respect to the individual definitions of "glorify" and "honor," both are very closely related. So here is the explanation for the rationale of why I believe honor is specifically mentioned even though it is somewhat redundant with the previous glorify statement.

To begin, honoring others is a big problem in our culture today and one of the ways to get everyone's attention in the hopes of changing the trend is to include it in a daily prayer to God. Since it is very important to honor God and with promoting it in this prayer, then maybe people will start honoring and "loving one another as Jesus has loved us" **(a new commandment; John 13:34)**. <u>The opposite of honor is betrayal</u> and has been an aspect of our fallen world since Adam & Eve betrayed God, then of course Judas betrayed Jesus and there are scores of examples of betrayal throughout the Bible. So does this mean we should live with it, excuse it and accept it? Of course not, we need to first honor God and then we should honor others accordingly (i.e. love one another as I have loved you; honor one another as I have honored you). But as mentioned, in today's culture betrayal trumps honor and just as with many other sins, this is reaching epidemic proportions. As an example, compare our culture today to that of the 50's, 60's, 70's, etc. with regards to: betrayal, passive aggressive behavior, blatantly aggressive behavior, bullying, two or more people forming alliances to sabotage the efforts of others in order to make themselves look good (pointing out and emphasizing others perceived mistakes or errors), withholding information, apathy, resentment then retaliation, gossip, creating conflict, attacking others, manipulating to controlling others, focusing on self, negativity... whether in our own homes between family members, or school, or the workplace, or our elected officials and government, or just about everywhere; doesn't this sound like I'm describing and defining our current "Gotcha" society in which we live? For those who do not agree with me on this and maybe believe that I am looking at our society from a half empty glass perspective then you are free to have your opinion but I would think the majority would agree that this topic is one of the many that has brought this world to an all-time low.

So when we treat each other in relation to any of the above list of behaviors, are we glorifying God and honoring Him? The answer is absolutely not. Now since 71% of the American adult population claim to be of Christian faith with just over 50% professing that they are active in their faith, then that implies that people do not practice what has been preached to them. Or has it been preached in this manner, that they are not glorifying God or honoring Him? It doesn't matter, in my opinion it is common sense, yet people are too caught up in what the world is currently doing, being and offering. As you know I could take this narrative down so many different rabbit trails but do not see the need to do so here in the context of this prayer. * So back to the point at hand, if we emphasize to God every morning that "I honor you" and one of the attached meanings is that I honor Him in my relationships with others by honoring them, then maybe just maybe this world may become a better place. Where people value glorifying their God, they in turn do the same and respect the relationships they have with others. *"To Glorify you in the things that I think, that I say and that I do; to Honor you..."*

"Trust in you, have Faith in you..."

To trust in you, have faith in you and believe in you are all three very closely related and are interconnected. Trust and faith are slightly more so interrelated than believing, so there is no need to separate the two for this explanation. The natural progression (yet can fall into place by any number of combinations) is that most people first trust, although minimally but trust enough to ask to be saved, then are born again, which at that point they are then given faith as one of the many gifts from Jesus (note: Jesus is the administrator of faith). Even though this is a gift it is counter-intuitive in that when we receive it, we must develop our understanding of its full potential. The gift of faith alone is simply a starting point from God and an encouragement for us to choose to grow in our believing in Him. Faith by definition is an already confirmed (by God) trust that we have, in what God has guaranteed (promised) us that He will do; even though we have no physical proofs, and yet we choose to believe in Him (note: true faith comes into play when we believe wholeheartedly). Most generally the mere fact that people have taken a step forward and asked Jesus to come into their life probably involved at least one component or a portion of all three. They trusted, had some faith or believed that by asking Jesus into their life, He would enter into it and give them the support mechanisms to grow their trust, faith, hope and belief. So that is typically what takes place, they are given faith and due to other positive events and/or they've studied and grown their knowledge of God's Word, kingdom and promises to them and thus strengthened each of these components.

150

Note: scripture specifically defines faith, as written by Paul in **(Heb. 11:1)**KJV "Now faith is the substance (assurance) of things hoped for, the evidence of things not seen."

* The common thread between the two definitions is that <u>faith</u> cannot be verified by sight or physical proofs, therefore requires <u>trust</u> which is the basis for their <u>hope</u> in that they <u>believe</u> that God will fulfill His vast list of promises throughout their life. That statement illustrates the point made previously regarding the progression of faith, trust, hope and believing. Trust is a critical component and God knows this and does his best to communicate that to us. It's critical because having a relationship with God is crucial to growing and maturing in your spiritual journey. Also, trust is an <u>absolute</u> must when it comes to a relationship with God as well as when it comes to a <u>successful</u> relationship with another person. Without trust you cannot maintain a relationship, period.

Do you agree with that statement? If so, why do you maintain relationships that do not involve trust and hope and think that it will work out down the road? Meaning that rather than it being a relationship, it is more so a casual relationship or a mere association.

* Very few people will blindly trust something/anything. So the impact that God (the Bible, Jesus, missionaries, etc.) has made over the millenniums supports the reason why someone would step out and trust in Him with their initial invitation for Jesus to become the Lord of their life and <u>thus triggering the Power of God</u> to respond in building their trust, faith, hope and belief.

King David, **(Psalm 2:12)**KJV "Blessed are all they that put their trust in Him."

(Psalm 118:8)KJV "It is better to trust in the Lord than to put confidence in man."

Then isn't faith simply another word for trust? In its simplest form, yes. But faith has a number of additional more complex attributes than trust. Faith involves trust and it also involves having confidence as well as assurance, your Biblical knowledge base and understanding, and also hope and Believing which culminates into the components that make up the **"STRENGTH"** of your faith. * The key differential though with faith, is its "POWER" that is derived from being intertwined into <u>your relationship with the Holy Trinity</u> (Father, Son and Holy Spirit) also in conjunction with your Biblical knowledge base and understanding. BUT please note that nobody can at any time tell you that, "You apparently do not have enough faith;" by the way do not ever allow anyone to tell you that * because faith and its strength, not to mention its power, is a matter only between you and

God (within the parameters of your intimate relationship with Him). Note also that the power of faith is released by God into your life based on His will, His predestined purpose for your life, in other words, as He sees fit. This power is no different than any other power God has, it is miraculous in nature, so when you feel the need to call upon Him to release to you His miraculous power in association with the faith you now possess requires you to petition Him in prayer and you really need to understand that His will shall be done with the event or crisis that you are going through. Put yet another way, * the power is not in our faith but in God, in whom faith relies. * Also note that the strength of your faith is based on all the factors previously mentioned and that strength of faith is what will significantly impact your life daily in a positive manner, resulting in an abundant life! And this is the area that should have your focused attention on a daily basis, keeping in mind that Jesus is the administrator of faith and you must ask Him for more (as with the disciples in Luke 17:5) and He freely gives to those who are advancing in their walk with Him. As a matter of fact man cannot increase his own faith (in and of itself), it is only increased through Jesus and generally via prayer, petition and spiritual growth; but also you MUST receive (take) the faith when Jesus imparts it to you and then you MUST act on it (do), all the while believing wholeheartedly in your relationship with God. This is the process that takes place and for many they are simply ignorant of what all it takes to accomplish. Fortunately for us we are adopted sons/daughters of an awesome God and even though we may be ignorant of what or how to do things, His system is such that He blesses us first and so our effort in simply trying, often results in us only receiving and acting on only a small portion of His blessings leaving most of it untapped or significantly underutilized (as an example: God blesses us first which leads us to repentance, not that we repent and then He blesses us for doing so).

Man learns by repetition, so would it be right of me to say to reread this section a couple times over again to understand faith? Thing is I don't know what percentage as a result would gain any more understanding of it, by doing so. Faith can be very confusing, especially since the word faith alone has been so diluted and misused in that it now has dozens of different meanings (i.e. is Christianity your faith; I am a person of faith; I have faith in my fellow man; etc.). Therefore I feel the need to spell it out for you, so having read this section at least once if not a couple of times and now hear this:

a) Man is not born with faith and cannot create faith out of his power, intelligence, etc.

b) You also <u>cannot increase</u> your faith, in and of yourself. Period!

1. Jesus said, **(John 15:5)**KJV "For without me, you can do nothing." He was referring to many things here, but this is one of them specifically.

c) Faith is a gift from Jesus and only Jesus can increase your faith (He is the administrator of faith); He hands it out freely to those who are growing in their walk and spiritual growth and hands it out as He sees fit according to His will and His plan. Faith is the gift from Jesus that truly keeps on giving...as long as #2 we grow in our wisdom, knowledge and understandings and the BIG #1 is as long as we ASK!

d) We must ask for more faith, otherwise it will NOT be given to us. And when we ask for more faith whether to deal with stresses or pressures due to our situations or just to grow in strength (Oh ye of little faith), we need to understand that we need to be growing in our overall understanding of the guidebook to life and living and the processes of God so that when we are given additional faith we'll know how to "RECEIVE it" and then how to "ACT" on it to better utilize it via the Holy Spirit's guidance.

e) Faith is a gift, but did I ever relay or imply that trust is a gift? No. Because we are not God's robots, He gave us free will and with that we have choice. He specifically desires that we <u>chose to trust</u> in Him to decide whether we want a relationship with Him. So as mentioned, we grow and strengthen our trust during our growth in the Lord with respect to our spiritual growth.

f) This next statement is a profound one that pertains to both trust and faith and is a key aspect of trust and its interrelation with faith:

    1. * I trust in you my God, therefore having received the gift of faith I now have faith in you God, in **that you will do what you say you will do** (His promises to us).

        a. *That is what faith is, trusting in God that He will do all that He says He will do. And as we grow in wisdom, knowledge and understanding of Him we are more equipped to <u>receive</u> faith and <u>act</u> on faith, to utilize the various powers that God has imparted to us.

        b. I probably shouldn't add another variable but now is as good a time as any and it may or should assist you in understanding this statement by Paul **(Eph. 2:8)**KJV "For by grace you are saved through faith and not of yourselves; it is a gift of God."

i. *Therefore, we "receive" grace (a gift) through faith (a gift) having trusted (our choice) and then believed (our choice). And God's grace, are the promises fulfilled via blessings of grace (gifts) to us that we have the faith that He would fulfill because we know in part of His wisdom and we therefore have knowledge and understanding; and this is because we first trusted and then believed in Him.

ii. Not only is that amazing, this is amazing in that His gifts and our spiritual growth work hand in hand, not like building blocks but as exponential manifestations working together; that is if we so choose to pursue growing at this rate in our walk with Him, all the while His grace is abounding in us.

iii. For myself this was the case on numerous occasions in my journey and at times I was forced to back off from my pursuit because it would become too overwhelming. You might say a good problem to have.

This explanation might just encourage you to want to praise Him for the exceedingly abundant providence and gifts He's blessed you with, such as with your faith and trust. And that is what My Lord's Prayer is designed to do daily, giving you an opportunity to spend time praising God and doing so armed with the background of information/knowledge previously stated.

"...Trust in you, have Faith in you..."

"and Believe in you, whole-heartedly,"

The process of Believing is an all-encompassing belief that we have in God. All-encompassing means just that, everything. I did want to emphasize one specific aspect which includes all of His promises He's made to us. Therefore as per the previous discussion on faith, we must "receive" all the blessings from grace that He is raining down upon us in order that we can optimize/<u>act</u> on all those blessings and desires He has for our lives, while we are on this experiential spiritual life journey on earth that He has so graciously given us an opportunity to participate in. In order to accomplish that requires a mature walk which means you have to start somewhere (with your first step and second and so on) so that you can mature and get to the place of true faith, believing whole-heartedly, and resulting in true abundant living while on this journey. To be able to Believe in this capacity requires a whole-hearted effort on our part (not only in terms of trust, faith, hope, belief, but also in servanthood, giving, loving, walking in the Spirit daily, reading the Bible and on, and on and on...)

I BELIEVE!!!

And I do so whole-heartedly!

That pretty much sums up the prior paragraph and is exactly what I communicate to my God in how firmly I believe in Him and His kingdom! Elsewhere in the book I've referenced numerous times how we are "Believer's in God" and have substantiated that by pointing out <u>how exhaustingly God relays to us that we must believe</u>. Just one example, in **(John 14:1)**NKJV Jesus said, "If you believe/trust in God and you believe/trust in Me..." Note, different translations have believe, while others have trust, which illustrate that we have to choose on our own free will to believe and to trust in Him, or not. That is to have Him, or to have Him not. A book or probably numerous books could be written emphasizing the importance of believing in God and His kingdom and realm, as well as having a relationship with Him based on believing. So although this is one of the most crucial aspects of this prayer, it will have the least disclosure and discussion in at least this particular chapter, because in this case less is more and hopefully that approach makes the biggest impact to get your attention and receive your focus!

"and to Love you! (As I always will)

How many times in this book can I keep repeating the word "all-encompassing?" The reality of God's glory is all-encompassing, so having said that it is practically impossible to define. As your walk with the Lord matures, you are able to "receive" portions of His glory (this is very similar to receiving His grace and His blessings). Our thoughts, our words and our actions when directed towards others are primarily the way in which we in turn glorify and honor Him, and even to an extent love Him back. In other words, the three are inter-related: love, honor and glorify. Can we love Him and do it honestly and sincerely, yet at the same time not honor or glorify Him? Use a spouse as an example, can you love them and do it honestly without honoring that person? Can we love others as Jesus loved us while at the same time not honoring them? All I'm doing is trying to elicit thought or introspection on your part and I'm not trying to make anyone feel guilty or force anybody into a corner. Point is, we can only try to do our best and for some they'll give their absolute best and as we know Jesus is the only one who is perfect and that we will fall short and miss the mark occasionally, or do so often; but I guarantee you this, if you do not have a target to shoot for you'll fall way short of the mark when it comes to how to "love" others. Also within the same context, since we are not a perfect being, this is not an excuse to do and act as one pleases. The target or mark to shoot for <u>must first begin with our relationship with God and filter down from there</u>, thus the purpose for the sentence in the prayer: *To Glorify you in the things that I think, that I say and that I do; to Honor you, Trust in you, have faith in you and Believe in you, whole-heartedly; and to Love you! (As I always will)* For you to truly love your Father in heaven then you must honor and glorify Him in your thoughts, your words and your actions and you do so by how you interact with other people.

I'll try to be brief with the following important and key principle about loving God. Along the same lines of the previous questions, "Can you say you love God in prayer at one moment, and despise, dislike, hold contempt or hate other person(s) at the same time or at another moment?" The majority of people do, and many do so constantly. Oh, you say that's not fair; or that you are justified in thinking, saying or acting on those types of beliefs or feelings. 1st point is: we are commanded to love others as He loves us. 2nd point is: when we turn our backs on God, he first responds by us losing His favor along with most of His blessings; next He responds by falling out of fellowship with us; but He never forsakes us and He never despises or hates us (He forever loves us; but hates the sin). And 3rd point is: *** you must first love God before you can <u>truly</u> love another being!** True love is a gift we receive from God and if we do not have that modeling experience then we only think we know what love is. I know I've opened up a can of worms here and need to expound on this but cannot adequately do so without getting off track of the current topic/prayer at hand (please see Ch8, Know the True You for additional information).

King David declared throughout the Psalms "I love you with all my heart and all my soul, with all my might." **(Ps 18:1; 9:1; 23:6; 119:34)** Jesus had two new commandments and one is **(Matt 22:37)**KJV "You shall love the Lord thy God with all of your heart and with all of your soul and with all of thy mind." It should not be because we are commanded to, but as a true desire whether it is a result of the intimate relationship we've developed with Him or due to the abundance of blessings and abundant life experiences on earth that we're having while in relationship with Him and we are thankful and grateful and love Him for it (or for whatever reason it is that you have your love for Him). * Finally, it is an affirmation and declaration that we are making daily in this prayer in order to remain focused on Him and on all others we interact with. Note: I placed in parenthesis *"As I always will,"* and did so because I truly do love Him, but did not want others to be compelled to say so unless they really believed it for themselves as well.

Note: I heard a well-known and popular pastor preach that, "It is impossible for man to fulfill Jesus's commandment to love your God with all your heart." And I have much respect for that pastor, but this statement was off the mark and just plain wrong. I just relayed a page and a half of information on how we should love God and how we should illustrate it in all of our actions and I suppose a large percentage cannot love God in that capacity, but bottom line for me is that I truly love Him (the Father, the Son and the Holy Spirit) and wanted to take this opportunity to say so. I concur with what King David said and often relay this to my Lord, "As King David said and as it is written, I love you with all of my heart, with all of my mind, to the depths of my soul and with all my might I love you; ...*as I always will.*"

So give me this day my daily bread, your Word, the bread that nourishes me spiritually, mentally and physically, your Son Lord Jesus; who is the way, the truth and the life for me; who chose to die on the cross for me; who defeated satan, the devil and death for me; and who you rose again for me, so thank you Father. Thank you for forgiving my sins, as I forgive others who trespass upon me;

So give me this day my daily bread, your Word, the bread that nourishes me spiritually, mentally and physically, your Son Lord Jesus;

157

After telling the Father I love Him, I do not petition (ask) Him for my daily bread, it is an acknowledgement that I know that He's already done this for me and praising Him for it. His Word made into flesh is His son Lord Jesus, who said, **(John 6:35 & 51)**KJV "I Am the bread of life." Its meaning is that He is the bread for people who are hungry for a relationship with Him. And that I have access to Him "daily," for He is ever present in my life and fulfills all of my needs.

One out of many definitions of nourishment is, "a substance necessary for growth and strength" and applies well to this context because what I am saying is that we rely on Jesus to provide the "sustenance" (someone or something that maintains life) and nourishment for our daily and ongoing growth. This "daily bread" is freely given to all of His children and is a supernatural bread that supplies all of our needs from: all of our spirituality needs, to all of our mental emotional needs, to all of our physical needs. You might be thinking that that is a tall order or an exaggerated statement, but not for our Lord and Savior, for He provides all of our needs via the Holy Trinity and the guidebook to life and living, the Bible. Note: there are other areas of the book in which I elaborate this point (also referred to as God's providence). For now let me also add, that you either believe this wholeheartedly or you don't believe in it at all because there really is no in between. **(John 15:5)**KJV "For apart from Me you can do nothing;" and **(Phil 4:13)**KJV "I can do all things through Christ who strengthens me." For example, He blesses "all the works of our hands," meaning that when it comes to your academics, career, athletics, etc., from choosing a partner/spouse, to the daily living of your abundant life, it is He who blessed our abilities to function and perform in this experiential spiritual life journey on earth; finally, He provides the access to living beyond that journey on earth to an eternal after life with Him in heaven. **(John 14:6)**KJV "He is the way" and **(John 10:9)**NLT "He is the gate." So I'm communicating to the Father that I understand the relationship and vital importance of His son in my life and understand that His son is **(John1:14)**KJV "The Word, was made flesh," and as mentioned, I have the Bible in hand and I raise it in corresponding acknowledgment that it is both the bread I speak of and it is His son, Lord Jesus. Note also, that I am not only holding the Word who is Jesus, but that He is in me and I in Him.

"your Son Lord Jesus; who is the way, the truth and the life for me"

* As just pointed out, He is the way and also the gate (or door) for us to have access to the Father and this is how He worded it, **(John 14:6)**KJV "I AM the way, the truth, and the life. No one can come to the Father except through me." And **(John 10:9)**KJV "I AM the door. If anyone enters by Me, he will be saved." These are a couple of the most significant foundational versus for you to understand.

To begin, allow me to first clarify what is meant by "I AM." In **(Exodus 3:14)**KJV, God said, "I AM that I AM" when Moses had asked His name; and Jesus said in **(John 8:58)** "Most assuredly, I say to you, before Abraham was, I AM." This is one of the significant confirmations that Jesus existed before Abraham **and** that He is God, **(John 1:1)**KJV "In the beginning was the Word, and the Word was with God, and the Word was God. **He** was with God in the beginning. **Through Him** all things were made; without Him nothing was made that has been made. In him was **life**, and that life was the light of all mankind. The light shines in the darkness, and the darkness has not overcome it." Then in **(John 1:14)**BSB "**The Word became flesh** and made his dwelling among us. We have seen his glory, the glory of the one and only Son, who came from the Father, **full of grace and truth.**"

* The previous 3 paragraphs covers much of the "foundational who" that Jesus is to us and the "foundational what" that He means to us (although the full breadth of Jesus can only be grasped by understanding the entire Bible and when you think you know it all, you don't): I AM is a name for God (the Father and Jesus); God's Word is God's "**Truth**" of life and of all things, it is also called the Bible, the guidebook to life and abundant living; Jesus is God's Word made into flesh and dwelt amongst us; and He is God (part of the Godhead of the Holy Trinity); He is **Life**; He is the light of mankind; we can do nothing apart from Him (anything that has been done without Him is nothing); He provides all of our needs; we can do all things through Him that strengthens us; He is the **Way** and the only way to be saved; therefore He is the door/gate for the only access to the Father; He is the glory who came from the Father; and who came full of truth because He is truth and full of Grace because He is Grace (an abundance of blessings) and believe me we are only getting started! *"your Son Lord Jesus; who is the way, the truth and the life for me"* *"who chose to die on the cross for me; who defeated satan, the devil and death for me; and who you rose, again for me."*

Jesus on earth was fully man and fully God, therefore He has free will as we do, and He had the choice to go to the cross and die for us. Let me first point out that the crucifixion and the resurrection is absolute and paramount for us to have eternal life which in turn gives us hope which in turn gives us joy; also it is the only way to have a relationship with the Heavenly Father that in turn gives us a specific role and purpose in this journey, which the Father in turn gives us His Holy Spirit to dwell in us and fulfill our spirituality and guide us (especially in relationships) and in our journey; and is the only way to have life and have it abundantly by living it through Christ Jesus, who is the Lord and center of our life. On the other hand, give it some thought as to what it would be like for mankind for the past 2000yrs to be completely and absolutely without God on just only the points previously mentioned? No hope beyond this life (no eternity in heaven) and not much hope during this life, no joy (defined as the anticipation of something great/wonderful as in blessed living, whereas happiness requires current happenings that are good) therefore little to no happiness, no guidance and direction on life in general especially not on living abundantly, no internal moral compass (and little to no morals at all), no miracles, no blessings (no one is blessed to be a blessing to others), therefore all would be strictly "self" driven with no giving to or loving others, I could go on and on and the thing is that mankind probably wouldn't have made it 1000yrs let alone 2000; and if they did, would they had ever <u>grown</u> in terms of technology, as one example? Another thought to ponder, mankind made it this far with God including at times a lackluster approach, but as we get further and further distant in relationship and in overall knowledge of God, what does society look like then? Is that where we are at now? Or what about the scenario that if the majority of this world turns its back on God, then what do you think will happen to society and mankind?

I apologize for going down that rabbit trail, but we need to consider and think about these critical issues especially since things are worsening worldwide and occurring directly in front of our eyes. The other point of taking this rabbit trail is while you are contemplating these matters (on the one hand X or on the other hand Y), I believe that for most they would choose the one hand that is of God rather than the alternative. In other words, it assisted in driving home many points.

The details of the crucifixion and resurrection is in Ch7 on Jesus. For the purpose of brevity, as mentioned Jesus <u>chose</u> to give up His life **(John 10:18)** by taking on all our past, present and future sins and dying in the process (a living sacrifice); He took on our sins and in doing so took our place in God's judicial system in order that we can stand before God's perfect justice with no sins whatsoever, and thus we are declared righteous in God's eyes (we are now the righteousness of Jesus Christ, in God's eyes); therefore we are no longer under God's Law or His wrath; so no matter how good one tries to be and no matter all the good works one may perform they could never attain God's standard of perfection unless they accept Jesus (the door/gate) as their Lord in salvation (to become saved and born again) and enter into the righteous relationship with the Father. This is why Jesus had to take on all the sins of mankind and die on the cross.

That is only part of the "good news" and there is much more to this story with the most important being that none of this would have been possible unless by proving He was God and was risen from the dead, then ascend to heaven to reign over us and to be in us. Hallelujah (a rejoicing that means: "God be praised") and amen! That is the crucifixion and resurrection in a nutshell and hopefully it gives you a greater understanding why it is incorporated in "My Lord's Prayer," *__who chose to die on the cross for me;__ who defeated satan, the devil and death for me; __and who you rose, again for me.__* The "for me" is important and I will expound on this after covering the other good news of who and what Jesus defeated for us.

"who defeated satan, the devil and death for me;"

See chapter on Spiritual Warfare for additional information. Jesus's "works" on the cross are numerous, valid and crucial to our existence, but I wanted to clear up a common misstatement and that is Jesus defeated satan while on the cross or with His works on the cross (implying that a battle took place). This is not Biblically or scripturally accurate. For one thing God is the Creator and satan was an angel and part of God's creation as we are; therefore the power of God is exponentially greater than that of satan or of an unbeliever. Which means that God does not have to battle with satan, and satan is well aware of that. So, the question is, in what way did Jesus defeat satan? By Jesus's death He defeated satan's power over Believers who feared his power and authority, one being the fear of death (both physical and spiritual). Jesus showed us that not only He would be resurrected but so will we and live for an eternity, therefore we should not even fear the physical death because it is inevitable and that after that inevitable physical death we have the promise of life eternal. Also concerning the spiritual death, God is a God of promises and He keeps and fulfills all of them, so for example **(Hebrews 13:5)**KJV "I will never leave you, nor forsake you," and remember the point made much earlier in this chapter with respect to, you cannot be unsaved although you need to keep your side of the commitment to the relationship, thus you do not have to fear a spiritual death from God. This is one of the ways and primary to this context in which Jesus defeated satan by His death and resurrection. I did want to take this moment to mention another of Jesus's defeats over satan by disarming his powers, the statement **(Isaiah 53:5)**KJV "By His stripes, we are healed" means that Jesus again became our substitute (sacrificial lamb) and by the stripes (beating) He endured it, "broke" His body so that we could be healed and made whole. Thus meaning that we are no longer subject to satan's power over disease, sickness or illness of this world; that Jesus made our bodies whole and gave us the power over disease, sickness and illness! That is, if we only believe.

"who defeated satan, the devil and death for me;" So what about the devil? I'm only going to touch on this briefly in this chapter, for one thing it is somewhat a controversial viewpoint. As mentioned, the chapter Spiritual Warfare covers this topic in greater detail, let's first define the devil: what he is not is satan; although he is still an agent of evil; see satan likes to imitate God in as many ways possible (as a mask to fool us or confuse us; confusing us is his greatest and most effective weapon) and he tries to outdo God, so in imitation he has a thrice system (as in the Trinity but not really), since satan is not omnipresent (#1 of the system, not able to be everywhere at the same time) he requires the use of demons (#2 of the system, who do not have satan's full power although they have some power and authority), he also utilizes the devil to torment and he is within us due to our fallen fleshly nature (#3 of the system, and he too has limited power and authority but due to his proximity "within" us he is very effective); he dwells not in our spirit but in our mind and for mankind there has been a constant battle taking place in our mind with him (that is until Jesus defeated him or more accurately disarmed him, for Believers). This battle going on in our mind is: against good vs. evil, against right vs. wrong, against Godly obedience vs. selfish desire, against sin-lessness vs. sin; and on and on. The keyword here is disarmed, as with Jesus disarming satan with respect to death, He has disarmed the devil with regards to having the power to manipulate our minds; and just as with the satan's death example it is only as good as our faith in the Lord is. One way of putting it is that

since the devil is a permanent fixture in our minds we can either minimize him to practically non-existent by the things we think, say and do or we can give him power (sometimes super power) over us depending on where our mindset is and our fleshly desires. Remember that he's been disarmed by Jesus, for you His Believers, but is your self-interest, ego, desires, transgressions, trespasses, etc., going to rearm the devil with ammunition to have the power over your thoughts or are you going to keep him in check (disarmed and minimized) by being obedient to God? I've got to take a moment to plug in something positive and important, note: living an obedient life for God is NOT a burdensome can't have any fun chore; one of the key messages and common thread that is woven through this book and through the Bible is that an obedient life for God is fulfilling and abundant way beyond what most of you may think; another point is that in obedience we are given an abundance of grace one of which is His hedge of protection protecting us from evil. Back to the topic, yet another way of looking at it is when we have sinful thoughts, words or actions we (Believers) open access portals for the devil and even additional demons to gain ammunition and build upon the power over us. Even the apostle Paul who wrote one-third of the New Testament could relate because he on occasion had issues in this area as well and spoke on it **(2 Cor. 12:7-9)**BSB "I was given a thorn in my flesh, <u>a messenger of Satan, to torment me</u>. Three times I pleaded with the Lord to take it away from me. But he said to me, '<u>My grace is sufficient for you</u>, for **my power is made perfect in weakness'**." So, was Paul having sexual desires or did it have to do with desires in other forms, or something other than desires (such as an infirmity, which by the way is another Greek translation of "suffering," he had thanked people for the "care" packages he was receiving; it could have been digestive problems that he perceived as a continuous thorn); this has been an ongoing topic for ages as to what the "thorn" was but I used this as an example to encourage you to think on this topic and how it may relate to you [what thorn(s) are you struggling with]. I won't further elaborate on this example of Paul's here (so to see additional information refer to the chapter Spiritual Warfare).

Back to the prayer, we are praising God for his son Lord Jesus who is the way, the truth and the life for me, who chose to die on the cross for me, *"who defeated satan, the devil and death for me;"* and I'm acknowledging my full understanding of how He defeated satan, the devil and death for me.

A Father's Wisdom

"and who you rose, again for me."

This has been previously covered in the above teaching on the resurrection. What is important is that our praise to the Father is acknowledging that we know that it was He that rose Jesus from the dead and we are giving our thanks and gratitude for His gift to us **(Romans 10:9)**NKJV "That if you confess with your mouth the Lord Jesus and believe in your heart that God has raised Him from the dead, you will be saved." To further that, His son Christ Jesus's resurrection made all things possible for us and made all things new for us who are Believers in Him.

Finally, keep in mind that this is a personal prayer from me (you) to God. In regard to the "for me" that is throughout this part of the prayer, it has not been placed there to emphasize self (me, me, me), but is meant to drive home the point that He does everything for me and with me in mind; that He wants me to live a fulfilling and abundant life because He wants to live His life through mine. Rejoice in this and give Him the praise!

"So thank you Father. Thank you for forgiving my sins, as I forgive others who trespass upon me;"

First of all, the Father gave us the "unspeakable" truth/gift **(John 3:16)**KJV "For God so loved the world that he gave his one and only Son (to die on the cross for us), that whoever believes in him shall not perish but have eternal life." The paraphrase, to die on the cross for us, was inserted to relay what is meant by the saying, unspeakable or unmentionable truth/gift, that God so loved the world that He GAVE us his Son to die for us. And because of this truth/gift all my past, present and future sins are forgiven! Hallelujah! So this passage is definitely a continuation of the prior and should be conveyed as flowing from the prior to the latter. And I am thanking the Father for Jesus and raising Him and thus for forgiving my sins!

Next, I understand that in the same manner and measure that He has forgiven my sins that I MUST forgive other who trespass upon me. This is extremely important because if I don't He will NOT forgive me of my trespasses **(Mark 11:25-26 or Matt 6:14-15)**NKJV "And whenever you stand praying, if you have anything against anyone, forgive him, that your Father in heaven may also forgive you your trespasses. But if you do not forgive, neither will your Father in heaven forgive your trespasses." Trespass in the Greek means offense, misdeed,

164

wrongdoing, infringement, annoyance, to injure, and is similar to the word transgressions meaning an offense against God. Note: the verse does NOT say "as I forgive others who SIN upon me," because only God can forgive sins, and we are commanded to forgive others their trespasses. Also note and be sure to understand this, the not forgiving us our trespasses is NOT saying that He will not forgive us our sins (remember Jesus died for us to have that and it is permanent). *Moving forward, a forgiving spirit in us is extremely beneficial, but contrary to that a bitter, resentful and unforgiving spirit separates us from God and we lose out on His blessings (among other things as well). Does this motivate you to forgive? To forgive ALL others? And do so as Jesus commanded **(Matt 18:1-22)**BSB "Then Peter came to Jesus and asked, Lord, how many times shall I forgive my brother or sister who trespasses against me? Up to seven times? Jesus answered, I tell you, not seven times, but seventy-seven times."

Concluding this passage, keep in mind that this is a personal daily affirmation and it is in accordance with His Word, all the while praising Him.

"Your Holy Spirit dwells in me, comforts me, counsels me; leads me, guides me and directs me in your righteousness and your truths; fills me with your wisdom; leads me not into temptation and delivers me from evil;"

Whether we are discussing the Father, Jesus or the Holy Spirit, each of these topics could fill volumes of books, therefore this is a condensed overview of the Holy Spirit as it pertains to this passage of the prayer (for additional information, see chapter Holy Spirit). The Holy Spirit: is one part of the thrice Godhead of the Holy Trinity; He is the Spirit of our God the Father; He is portrayed as a person (for example, God the Father is a spirit yet He is portrayed in the Bible as a person and we think of Him as "a Father to us," and of course Jesus was made flesh and dwelt among us thus a person as well) then so too is the Holy Spirit portrayed as a person in the Bible and we think of Him as a person, whose name by the way is "Holy Spirit," so when you are talking to Him refer to Him by name (Holy Spirit); also that He was sent to dwell in all Believers after Jesus ascended to heaven. Just prior to Jesus ascending He referred to Him as "the Comforter" **(John 14:16 & 26)**KJV "And I will pray the Father, and he shall give you another Comforter, that he may <u>abide with you forever</u>; But the Comforter, which is the Holy Ghost, whom the Father will send in my name, he shall <u>teach</u> you <u>all things</u>, and bring all things to your <u>remembrance</u>, whatsoever I have said unto you." As mentioned in the 16th verse, the Holy Spirit abides in us forever, another way of putting it is He dwells in us; yet another way is we have the indwelling of the Holy Spirit. An important line of scripture for a number of reasons is what Paul revealed in **(1 Cor. 6:19)**NLT "Don't you realize that your body is the temple of the Holy Spirit, who lives in you and was given to you by God? You do not belong to yourself." This not only confirms that He dwells in us, but also that our body is a temple to house God and therefore does not even belong to us but is of God's property (see Ch10, "In Charge"); yet we abuse the temple in so many different ways (please contemplate the different ways and the ramifications of how you might abuse the temple). When Jesus referred to the Holy Spirit as the Comforter, He was relaying that He would be leaving earth soon and that the Holy Spirit would provide all Believers comfort in Jesus's physical absence. Since there are so many meanings to the Greek word "parakletos" He could have also been referring to any or all of the following: comforter, encourager, helper, advocate and counselor; one "sent" to be alongside ("sent" by the Father); one who speaks in our defense; one to teach, testify and convict the world of guilt.

"Your Holy Spirit dwells in me, comforts me, counsels me; I've communicated what is meant by His indwelling us and briefly how He comforts us and now to how He counsels us. This is B-I-G big, because some Christians believe in a doctrine in which God would never talk directly to us and many Christians believe that God no longer talks to us or communicates with us and that is just not the case. As I pointed out in the introduction chapter, I've had God the Father speak to me three times and I also mentioned that after numerous requests it was revealed to me that His Holy Spirit is sufficient for me to communicate to Him, and He to me. I am here to say that the Holy Spirit is not only sufficient but awesome and He does talk to us (although not in an audible voice) but in a "still small voice" **(1 Kings 19:12)** within us and we have to be open to and train ourselves to hear. It's been made clear that He indwells us or that our bodies are a vessel that holds God's Spirit, so since that is the case why would He be in us if He did not communicate with us? What purpose would He play? Also if He didn't talk to us, how would He communicate and then how would we know how to interpret a special form of communication? As previously mentioned, one of the primary meanings of parakletos's is "counselor" and defined as "one who is trained to give guidance; a mentor, adviser, consultant, expert." As an expert consultant for us He would need to communicate to us to help us with our needs and hasn't that been a

common thread for God throughout this book and the Bible, and that is "helping us with our needs?" A very popular verse often quoted is **(Psalm 46:1)**KJV "God is our refuge and strength, a very present help in trouble." The Holy Spirit is God and is present inside us and He talks to us, comforts us, counsels us and gives us guidance. Therefore as with all the past verses, praise God for His gifts and blessings to us *"Your Holy Spirit dwells in me, comforts me, counsels me;"* and do so with great passion and enthusiasm because this is (in capital letters **B-I-G**) significant!

"leads me, guides me and directs me in your righteousness and your truths;" This is a continuation of what the Holy Spirit does for us but it's focusing in on some specific areas as in God's righteousness and His truths. There is much to relay here so let's start with: leads me, guides me and directs me. As mentioned, He talks to us in a unique way and one in which we have to train ourselves to hear and even when we've done that it is very easy to hear our "self-talk" over His voice (for additional info see chapter on Holy Spirit), yet for many they may misinterpret the origin and actually hear the devil's nudging's or dig's instead (for additional info see chapter on Spiritual Warfare). As a point of reference and to use as an example, many of you are familiar with the term "intuition." Now I'm going to warn you coming out of the gate that I am just using this as a "similar" analogy BUT whether you are hearing the Holy Spirit's voice or picking up on His signs/clues that He often relays, it is only similar in alert but very different in origin and its benefits than intuition. So, if you are familiar with intuition then you are familiar with the process you've developed on how you are alerted or pick up on your intuition such as through signs/clues, or gut feeling, or a hunch, etc. As mentioned, this is "not comparable" but only similar to how you develop your method of communicating with the Holy Spirit. Intuition is defined as an instinctive feeling rather than having to rationally deduce something. Key word here is * "feeling," because intuition has emotions attached to them and stems from your soul (which houses your fleshly nature and your emotions, feelings, self-will, etc.). Whereas communications from the Holy Spirit will not be based on emotions and feelings, rather it is based in Biblical truths or Divine direction which has to do with directing you towards your life purpose or away from distractions, etc. and quite often will require you to develop the message further that you've received from the Holy Spirit to determine an answer, whether via rational deduction or otherwise. **Why? Because life is an ongoing learning

167

experience and the Holy Spirit is our teacher from the spiritual realm who gives us guidance in the earthly realm and to a much lesser extent the future heavenly realm; also in doing so He expects our participation in order to grow in wisdom so that we have knowledge and understanding, rather than just giving us the answers to all the questions of life. To elaborate on that point, the Holy Spirit will talk to us primarily when we are in meditation and prayer, and He can talk or guide us at other times of the day as long as we are "tuned in" to Him. I had mentioned this in another chapter, much like talking on the phone or texting we either hang up or finish and go on to something else, but if we make a conscious effort to "walk in the spirit" and stay tuned in to his frequency then we can hear from Him at any given time. Note, *He also communicates to us through scripture, sermons, signs, clues, nudge or urge, a need, a supernatural force, indicators, counsel by example, cautions, warnings, etc., and once you've developed this process you will readily identify it by how it looks, sounds, acts, reacts, etc., then you'll be able to "walk, talk and discern in the spirit" with certainty, confidence and do so skillfully. These non-verbal ways of communicating is a process that I refer to as "red light, green light" because often the Holy Spirit will get our attention by using one of them first and then add other indicators to lead us along a specific path/decision which would be to either "Go"/do what you were intending or "Stop"/change direction or change what you were planning on doing.

Finally, the believer who is skillful with intuition and skillful in walking and talking in the spirit knows that the two are distinctly and significantly different and would also realize that the latter is far superior over intuition and therefore would rely on (trust) walking and talking in the spirit the majority of the time if not exclusively. In order to communicate effective messages and teachings I have to lay this groundwork first and unfortunately it can get lengthy. Having said that, these methods mentioned are the way the Holy Spirit *"leads me, guides me and directs me..."* and does so for a multitude of reasons and all for our benefit!

"...in your righteousness and your truths;" a specific goal that the Father has for the Holy Spirit is to relay to ALL of us to: lead, guide and direct us in the way of righteousness and in understanding His Biblical truths. Regarding righteousness, it's a gift we received from Jesus but it's one that's developed as a process that takes years or even take a lifetime to develop; from another chapter you also know that "we are the righteousness of Jesus in God's eyes," due to another gift but this one being the unspeakable <u>gift</u> from the Father of his Son

dying for us on the cross. With that, the Father now only sees us as righteousness and declares us righteous since we were cleansed from all our sins due to that <u>gift</u>, BUT that does not mean that we even for a moment whether in our thoughts or actions that we conduct ourselves in a moral and ethical manner while being obedient to divine truths lined out in the Bible and following divine instruction via the Holy Spirit. This is where the passage of this prayer comes in and reminds us daily of our obligation to become better overall stewards in His kingdom by growing and maturing spiritually and it is primarily accomplished via the Holy Spirit working within us. One way to put it is this is an opportunity for the inward spiritual man/woman to become the outward spiritual man/woman. Thanks to Jesus we have been "labeled" as holy and perfect, a prerequisite to entering God's kingdom in heaven when that time comes for us, but as mentioned for now <u>as we are on this experiential spiritual life journey on earth we must do our due diligence to mature and grow in divine truths and instruction and become the person that God predestined and purposed us to be.</u> The underlined is the summation of what is meant by being "led, guided and directed in the knowledge of His righteousness." Now on to covering what is meant by "truths."

* The Biblical definition of truth is: God's comprehensive message, which involves an endless list that includes his character, his beliefs, his laws, etc., etc., to all of God's utterances (His living words in the Bible) and with saying that I just disclosed a definition of the Bible. Put another way, God's truth is the living Word of God; the all-encompassing and comprehensive account of the living Word of God is called the Bible and as I've mentioned many times the Bible is the guidebook to life and abundant living. Put yet another way, when the Word became flesh and dwelt among us, the Word is God's truth and His truth became flesh (Jesus) thus our teacher who teaches God's truth for He is truth; so is the Holy Spirit (God) who leads us, guides us and directs us in all righteousness and all truths! That is one of the reasons why Paul said **(Romans 12:2)**KJV "And <u>do not be conformed to this world</u>, but **be transformed by the renewing of your mind,** that you may prove what *is* that good and <u>acceptable and perfect will</u> of God" not only does the "acceptable and perfect will of God" fit in with what I conveyed regarding righteousness but to "be transformed by the renewing of the mind" means (as often as possible) to be in God's Word (scripture) and do so with the help and counseling of the Holy Spirit and it will transform your life! The flipside of this coin has to do with false teachings and as with everything else, here

169

too the Holy Spirit leads us, guides us and directs us <u>away from false teachings</u> by leading us to the proper truths in the Bible (God's truths) and in the process renewing our minds and transforming our lives. In addition, I mentioned in a previous chapter how we must renew our minds via the Holy Spirit and the Bible which will in turn begin transforming us into **spirit dominance** over our soul's carnal nature (us no longer being led by our senses [carnal] and our feelings). This is how that inward spiritual man/woman becomes the outward spiritual man/woman as previously mentioned. *"leads me, guides me and directs me in your righteousness and your truths;"*

"fills me with your wisdom;" True wisdom only comes directly from the Bible (the guidebook to life and abundant living) and the Holy Spirit, thus this passage "fills me with God's wisdom." The following is a profound statement that was revealed to me early on in my journey: * "God gives us His wisdom that we may have knowledge and understanding of His kingdom and the things and ways of this world." <u>What wisdom is **not**</u>, is what is commonly referred to as someone who is wise or has wisdom (unless it is from God, as what was just relayed); it is not our accumulated experiences and knowledge over time that gives us this wisdom (although most believe this is so); this <u>wisdom</u> I am referring to is <u>a gift from God</u> and is available to all on an ongoing basis, but you have to <u>pursue it</u> in scripture with the help of the Holy Spirit, then you have to <u>receive it</u> as knowledge and by <u>acting on it</u>, it will provide you a greater overall understanding. As mentioned, this wisdom is from divine instruction and benefits us in the knowledge and understanding of His kingdom in its entirety, as well as benefits us on the "ways of this world" so that we can successfully navigate through it while on our journey. This is wisdom that all should be striving to attain in order to have an abundant life and is a gift from God that we should be praising Him for. Actually, I can't understand why anybody would not strive for it other than they did not know of it or how to access it. Please note that if you review the paragraph immediately prior to this sentence, I continuously refer to wisdom as "it" and did this so to not confuse anybody, but I need to point out that God gave us Jesus and Jesus is the Word made into flesh and the Word is God's wisdom, therefore <u>Jesus is wisdom</u>. * <u>So Jesus gives us wisdom from the source of all wisdom</u>, and again, I typically will refer to wisdom as "it" although I could just as accurately refer to wisdom as "Jesus." The confusion that I'm trying to avoid, as for example in my above statements, "You have to pursue it (Jesus), and receive

170

it (Jesus), etc., so I hope that you now understand the potential for misunderstanding and why I'm instead relaying it this way.

Imagine for a moment having this kind of wisdom. Seriously, take a moment and contemplate you having access to the wisdom of God. Just 2 out of His infinitesimal attributes is that He is omniscient (all knowing; totality of knowledge all past, present and future) and He is omnipotent (all power to do all things, anything is possible), He is the God of all creation! And you have access to His wisdom which gives you knowledge and understanding of His kingdom and the things and ways of this world, via the Bible (the guidebook to life and abundant living) in conjunction with the Holy Spirit.

Now as mentioned, this requires you to be an "active participant" in God's kingdom and a few requisites I'd like to reiterate is: that you are saved (born again); that you've been baptized in water and committed to a relationship with God; that you've been baptized in the Holy Spirit; that you are pursuing and receiving God's Word/Truth through scripture via communicating with the Holy Spirit while seeking and acquiring wisdom to have knowledge and understanding of God's kingdom and of this world. This in a nutshell answers the statement I made in a previous paragraph with regards to the one who did not know how to access God's wisdom. See Ch5 on The Holy Spirit and Ch2 on Wisdom for more information.

The Holy Spirit is a "filler of wisdom;" He's also a teacher, a coach, a counselor, a comforter, etc. In **(John 14:26)**KJV Jesus said, "The Comforter, which is the Holy Ghost, whom the Father will send in my name, he shall teach you all things, and bring all things to your remembrance." So He also brings all things to our remembrance. First you need to know the true definition of remembrance. Briefly, God knew us all "in spirit" before the beginning of time; the Holy Spirit knows everything from eternity past through eternity future (our lives on earth is in preparation for eternity future); **(Acts 1:8)**NKJV Jesus said, "You will receive power when the Holy Spirit has come upon you." This power we have applies to doing a multitude of things but for this context by dwelling in us the Holy Spirit provides us with the power to comprehend the teachings of God's truth in scripture and what is revealed to us by the Holy Spirit. The big picture of remembrance is our spirit has been around since eternity past and so has the Holy Spirit although before being saved we had no knowledge of it but now we not only know of it, we have the power to comprehend it and we have the Holy Spirit to teach us and counsel us as He brings it to our remembrance (note: He brings all things to our remembrance in the same proportion to the amount of energy and wholehearted effort that we put into expanding our knowledge of God. If you are not actively pursuing, then He won't either.)

Note, other translations (NIV, NLT) use the word "remind" rather than "remembrance" and this is an example that concerns me and that is: in an attempt for readers to more easily understand and have an easier read as these translations are meant for, they've "dulled down" the true meaning of what was supposed to be relayed. If you were reading the John 14:26 passage of scripture and "remind" was used, then you would very likely not question the meaning and thus not investigate further. Whereas when you come across a word like "remembrance" and you question it, then you start researching it (even Google it and read up on it that way), the thing is the Holy Spirit wants you to know more and since you are actively pursuing wisdom, knowledge and understanding it is just a matter of time that the answers are revealed to you. It's an awesome process to participate in and you have the same opportunity as I.

The full breadth of understanding remembrance was revealed to me as was the other revelation I'd recently mentioned, "God gives us His wisdom that we may have knowledge and understanding of His kingdom and the things and ways of this world." As mentioned, numerous times, * the Holy Spirit is a teacher who teaches us of God's truths in order to expand our knowledge base and forward that in understanding via everyday practical applications. Since we are not of this world and in reality our lives are preparation for eternity future, we need to have all of God's wisdom, knowledge and understanding that we possibly can in order to navigate this experiential spiritual life journey on earth. * The more wisdom base we can access the more likely that we don't have a chaotic roller coaster (up, down, fast, slow, upside down, jarring, spinning) experience with life, but rather have a life that is as grounded and balanced as possible so that we "have life and have it abundantly" on earth and in preparation for eternity future. Note: we will have ups and downs because trials and tribulations are a part of our lessons while on this journey, except they will happen significantly less and to a lesser degree due to our walk with the Spirit, our accumulated wisdom and knowledge and understanding.

* When we have the "power" of the Holy Spirit coupled with the wisdom of God creating a broad base of knowledge and understanding, it provides us with a "super" confidence to take on anything this world has to throw at us. The Holy Spirit plays a vital role in "empowering" us to achieve this super confidence, therefore I rarely use the word confidence anymore. Instead I call it like it is, I refer to it as "God Confidence." I tell you, an excellent example of this that I've painfully experienced: has to do with having had to leave my grade school classrooms and go to a speech therapy class while getting laughed at and made fun of all the way through till the fourth grade, then my OCD preoccupation with the enunciation of my words has over the years created huge stumbling blocks for me in my career growth. Up until my mid-forties I had taken a public speaking course in high school and another in college, then a couple of 16-week Dale Carnegie programs, a couple of Toastmaster programs and read numerous self-help and motivational books to improve my "self-confidence." The thing is "self-confidence" only gets you so far, I can personally affirm the validity of what "God Confidence" can do in your life! I still struggle some, but I am no longer a victim but a victor, therefore I no longer consume precious time in my life with feeling defeated and embarrassed. Another benefit to being filled with God's wisdom is the attribute of discernment. The Holy Spirit leads us and guides us in discerning the things of God versus the things that are not of God. Discernment plays an integral role in navigating this life. Both God Confidence and the techniques of discernment will be covered in other chapters. I've probably spent entirely way to long in explanation for this portion of the prayer but God's wisdom is that vital and important, including how we acquire it via the Holy Spirit. To remind you of where we're at in the prayer: *"Your Holy Spirit dwells in me, comforts me, counsels me; leads me, guides me and directs me in your righteousness and your truths; fills me with your wisdom;"*

"leads me not into temptation and delivers me from evil;" We've covered how the Holy Spirit leads, guides and directs, and here He's specifically leading us but this time it's "not into temptation." Taking charge and leading us is actually what we need for Him to do here rather than simply guiding us away or directing us away because temptation is an area that we are extremely vulnerable in for a number of reasons, one specifically is our fleshly nature. It's important to relay up front that we are not just concerned about temptation with this passage of the prayer rather we need to address the broad range of meanings of temptation which

173

will help us to realize that the Holy Spirit has his hands full if He needs to take charge in these areas and lead us from them as well.

You're probably thinking that it would be simple to define temptation, pretty much everyone believes that the contemporary definition is that it means to be tempted or heavily persuaded to do something (often concerning the things you should not be doing); another contemporary definition: being tempted by the devil. Well although correct statements they are too simplistic, not specific enough in terms of what you are doing (whether good or bad) and there are way more forms of temptation that are critical to your journey that we need to review in detail. First did you realize there are three primary categories of temptation: good, moderate (meaning borderline to evil) and bad (evil). Keep in mind that things should be kept in context, so in following that the Greek word temptation is comprised of these different meanings:

a) Regarding the good and moderate: "to experiment" (to test)
b) Regarding the bad (evil): "to experience" (sin)
c) Regarding all 3, good, moderate, bad (evil): "a trial;" "a test;" "to prove;" "adversity"

In greater detail: a) we experiment or put to test various things in our lives that may be good for us or that may be border lining bad/evil (referred to as moderate); this is the first and least focused definition of temptation with regards to the prayer. b) here we are tempted to experience sin (this fits our contemporary definition and meaning); if unsaved, you do not know (or care) to know better; but for the saved this is outright disregard for what you know is wrong (sinful) but you are allowing your selfish desires to take control of you and what you are doing, also you are ignoring the efforts of the Holy Spirit to "correct" you in an attempt to alter your course (repent of your ways and change); this is the second definition of temptation and is really pretty self-explanatory on how to deal with the how and why's to resolve, so although a very important topic to review it is secondary in emphasis in this prayer. c) This is the primary emphasis for this prayer and in reality using the word temptation is still proper because it relates from good to borderline bad, to evil and to being tested, to proving something, to having adversity, and to what the Bible's primary emphasis and focus is on for this prayer and that is our **"trials"** that we will encounter throughout this life journey.

Please take note how expressive the Greek language is here in that the word temptation covers a broad range of meanings and is a great illustration of what

I've previously attempted to relay and that is the importance of knowing the translations of texts so that you better understand the context of the message. To begin I would like for you to try to do a mind reset (paradigm reset) to clear the thought of the contemporary definition of the word "temptation" and focus on the primary context. That being, ALERT: the primary message and context here is NOT about being tempted and doing bad/evil things (although this is important and will be reviewed); the primary message is for the Holy Spirit to assist us in leading us away from potential **trials** (and tribulations)! Jesus never said that our lives would be full of happiness and no problems as Christians, bad things do happen to good people (at times with regularity); He also didn't say you "might" have trials, but rather that you "will," so count on it, prepare for it, expect it, be patient in it, and be constant in prayer because it will come, if it hasn't already; Life is full of "mountain highs and valley lows," life's ebbs and flows, so a Christian that "walks in the Spirit" is more likely to keep their life(ship) on an even keel (balanced, consistent) with a more stable and calm life (a servants provision from God), versus the alternative of a life(ship) thrashing about from side to side (unbalanced, chaotic) due to the crashing waves (trials) of life without God's relationship, guidance and provision. **** You measure your walk with Christ by how much time you devote to prayer and reading the Bible.**

Supporting passages of scripture:
(**1 Pet 4:12-14**)BSB "Do not be surprised at the fiery trial when it <u>comes upon you</u> **to test you**, as though something strange were happening to you."
(**James 1:12**)BSB "**<u>Blessed</u> is the man who remains steadfast under trial**, for when he has stood the **test** he will receive the crown of <u>(eternal) life</u>, which God has promised to those who love him."
(**Galatians 5:16, 22-23**)BSB "<u>Live by the Spirit</u>, I say, and do not gratify the desires of the flesh.... The **fruit** <u>of the Spirit</u> is love, joy, peace, patience, kindness, goodness, faithfulness, gentleness, self-control."
The apostle Paul as it pertained to his trials, including the "thorn in his side" said, (**2Cor. 12:10**)KJV "Therefore I take pleasure in infirmities, in reproaches, in necessities, in persecutions, in distresses for Christ's sake; for when I am weak, then am I strong!" Referring to Jesus's power is perfected in Paul's (our) weakness.
(**1 Cor. 10:13**)NKJV "**<u>No temptation (trial)</u> has overtaken you that is not common** to man. God is faithful, and **He will not** let you be tempted

175

(tested) beyond your ability, but with the temptation **He** will also **provide the way of escape,** that you may be **able to endure it.**"

Have you picked up the proper messages yet? a) The word temptation is used in both the "Lord's Prayer" and "My Lord's Prayer" because it covers a broad meaning; but b) the primary emphasis is on "trials" (tribulations and tests). Remember that this life is a learning opportunity for our continued journey from earth to eternity * **(this life, in and of itself, is not all there is to life; worded another way, this life is preparation for eternity).** Also that God wants to experience life through our lives and to accommodate that we need to be as obedient followers as we can be. * **Trials reveal who we are (in Christ) and who we are not.** Note, trials can often produce wisdom, comfort, good, growth, learning, maturity, put another way: we can find comfort in trials; we can get wisdom from trials; there is often good that comes from trials; we grow, learn and mature from trials.

** Another important and significant point to acknowledge is that even though trials are to be expected in our lives and that trials help us to learn, grow and mature, the Father, the Son and the Holy Spirit do NOT want us to experience trials excessively or have to experience unnecessary, redundant or needless trials that could leave you defeated, depressed or worse. Everyone is different and there is a fine line between learning, growing and maturing, and between becoming defeated, depressed or worse and God knows this (i.e. 1 Cor. 10:13 as mentioned in the prior paragraph) and if He is going to experience life through you * **He wants you to manage your life** (via the Bible the guidebook to life and abundant living and the Holy Spirit) so that you have a balanced life; that even keeled life previously mentioned. Also key: think about it, why would God want to see us falter or why would He hamper, hinder or obstruct our lives? He doesn't and this is just one of the many reasons God gave us the gift of the Holy Spirit to be our counselor, our advocate, our comforter, our coach, etc. To counsel and coach us and lead us through difficult times and struggling times. This is just one of the aspects of **the HOPE that we have in Christ.** He also gives us a **PEACE that surpasses all human understanding and guards our hearts and minds (see Phil 4:7)**

This brings us back to the point I had originally mentioned with regards to the Holy Spirit taking charge and leading us. He does take charge and He leads us in the respect of bringing things to the forefront, getting our attention and making things weigh heavily on our hearts and minds, but that is it, what He doesn't do is take charge and force us to change our ways (because we've been given free will and we have the right to choose how we want to manage our lives). So if we stray off the path and appear to be headed either into a trial, adversity or evil, the Holy Spirit will "correct" us (red light) and for some He has to take more aggressive measures and will convict. <u>Convict</u> (in the Greek) is a term that means "to expose," and also at times to expose with shame. If shame is a part of this then the shame would not come from another person (as is how we typically get shamed into doing or not doing something) but would have to come from the Holy Spirit in the form of us having to shame ourselves (i.e. heavy heart/mind) which may or may not be effective depending on the individual. Point is if we have strayed off the path and appear to be headed either into a trial, adversity or evil, the Holy Spirit will "expose" to us what we are doing wrong and it would be up to us to make the choice on what to do about it. * Here is why it is important to "walk in the Spirit," because the more participative you are in the relationship the quicker you'll receive the message and the clearer the communication, or vice versa the poorer your relationship with Him the weaker the message and the muddier the communication.

(John 16:7-8)KJV Jesus said, "I will send the Holy Spirit to you. And when He has come, **He will convict** the world of <u>sin,</u> and of righteousness, and of judgment." Briefly in regard to the temptation to do evil/bad things, don't confuse what I was mentioning previously, I was not dismissing this but was simply setting it on the back burner until I was ready to relay it to you. It is a very important issue and can easily derail you from the path of your spiritual journey with God. We know the difference between what is right and what is wrong and there may be times that you wonder if something is a sin or not although most of you generally know what is or is not a sin. As previously mentioned, being tempted to sin and then complying is a blatant disregard for the relationship you have with Christ and as just pointed out Jesus said, "that the Holy Spirit will "convict" the world of sin," meaning that not only do you have the basis of knowledge of right and wrong but also as a believer you have the Holy Spirit "correcting" you of sin and in worse scenarios (exposing) convicting you of what it is wrong and sinful in order to change direction. Keep in mind that to convict the world of sin is referring to worldly unbelievers, but as mentioned, in worse case scenarios the Holy Spirit will also convict Believers. Having said that, it reminds me of a maxim/motto (or individual standard) that I know many people ascribe to and that is in their daily life they approach issues with the intent to "do the right thing." It's a good philosophy to live by and by the way if your daily walk is with Christ and you honor Him by "glorifying Him in all that you think, say and do," then the fruit you produce will be significantly more than a person who simply has a maxim/motto to: do the right thing.

* In **Jude 1:16** he lists some of the diseased fruit that ungodly people produce: "Ungodly sinners are whiners and complainers, living only to satisfy their desires. They brag loudly about themselves, and they flatter and manipulate others to get what they want." Not always but often these are the people who at some point in their lives have a worldly sorrow and grief by expressing it in terms of regrets, unhappiness, remorse, depression, heartache, etc. for the shipwrecks they've made of their lives. Fortunately, at many times of our lives we all have the <u>choice</u> to have faith and trust in God and walk with Him daily to provide us all the tools we need to learn, grow and mature in our lives. * So that whenever storms appear on the radar we have the <u>Holy Spirit to lead us not into those trials</u>; or whether the storms appear to have come upon us beyond our control or if we made the mistake on our own free will and decide to venture into those storms, we again can trust in the Holy Spirit (and the Bible) to lead us, guide us and direct us safely through them keeping our ship intact and on a balanced and even keel (our overall lives being calmer, more stable, consistent and balanced).

Supporting passages of scripture:

(**Isaiah 43:2**)NIV "When you pass through the waters, I will be with you; and when you pass through the rivers, they will not sweep over (overwhelm) you."

(**Jere 29:11**)BSB "For I know the plans I have for you, declares the Lord, plans to prosper you and not to harm you, plans to give you hope and a future."

(**Phil 4:6-7**)BSB "Do not be anxious about anything, but in every situation, by prayer and petition, with thanks and praise, present your requests to God."

(**2Cor 1:3-4**)BSB "<u>**Praise**</u> be to the God and Father of our Lord Jesus Christ, the Father of compassion and the God of all comfort; who comforts us in all our troubles, so that we can comfort those in any trouble with the comfort we ourselves receive from God.

To summarize this in-depth explanation, in "The Lord's Prayer" and "My Lord's Prayer" God is relaying to all of us that this life has trials, but that we are to diligently use His Holy Spirit to *"lead me not into temptation"* and to rely on Him to lead, guide and direct out paths before, during and after the trials in order to keep our lives as balanced and as stress free as practical.

"and delivers me from evil;" Much of what the Holy Spirit did for trials and temptations will come into play here and then some. ***Glory be to the Father!** Because #1) He knows there are 2 very big construction hurdles that we have to deal in building this experiential spiritual life on earth and they are called trials and evil; #2) He has really provided us with the tools to deal with trials in life as well as the tools for dealing with evil. The 2 tools you'll utilize daily and that should rarely go back into the toolbox is the Holy Spirit and the Bible (the "guidebook" to life and abundant living; in this example the "blueprints" to life and abundant living).

How does the Holy Spirit deliver us from evil? Fortunately there is no mystery to unfold, no hoops to jump through, no complex maze to construct or maneuver through, it is a combined process (teamwork if you will) that includes you and the Holy Spirit (as with most things in God's kingdom). So let's break it down into its parts and then work on adequately answering this question. "Deliver" definition (Greek): to rescue; to rescue for the deliverer; it is one of those words in which you say "deliver means to deliver (from and to)," there really aren't that many meanings (in the Greek that is; in English there are numerous, but irrelevant), so let's not make this more complicated than need be. In this case we need to first establish the foundation before we can build upon it, which is that Jesus has already "defeated (disarmed)" satan, his demons and the devil (as mentioned previously in this prayer), therefore He has already <u>delivered</u> all of us from evil. Having said that, the Holy Spirit is responsible to "rescue" us for the <u>deliverer</u> (Jesus), as noted in the above Greek definition. Now this "rescue" relies on us to be fully participative so for example until we fully understand what "disarming" means then we rely on the Holy Spirit to "deliver (reveal and convey)" this information to us so that we can then properly act on it. * As previously covered, Jesus by His works on the Cross "disarmed the power" of satan, his demons and the devil over Believers, BUT that we must have faith and trust in the Lord and renew our minds daily in the Word with the help of the Holy Spirit to minimize the potential of future threat and maintain the disarmament. Remember that we can (and often do) open portals of access into our minds, our bodies, our homes, our families, our workplace, our church, etc., via sinning whether in our thoughts, our words and/or our actions and thus re-arming the power of evil over us. And so why would we ever want to do that? Well that's the million dollar question as to why we would choose to sin (for to satisfy our fleshly desires, which are only temporary and in the end not satisfying) over choosing obedience in order to have a balanced life and have it abundantly on earth and in eternity. That is why we are relaying to the Father via this prayer, that not only do we know how all this works and that He's given us all the tools to avoid it, but that we are also praising Him in making all this so. *"and delivers me from evil;"*

To further this, we've covered evil in the respect of "the evil one" (the 3 heads of evil): satan (the father of all lies), his demons (they do most of satans dirty work) and the devil (the demon in our mind; "fleshly 'rebellious against God's nature"), but this word "evil" has a broader meaning. "Evil" definition (Greek): 1) the evil one; 2) evil; bad; wickedness; malicious (intentions to do ill will); diseased; ungodliness. The effects of evil: toilsome (slavery), pain and misery, slothful (lazy, inactive), etc. Well, with all those meanings there is no real need to add to it with contemporary meanings except I will touch briefly on anger, bitterness and unforgiveness. I will not put all these meanings into context but will attempt a brief overview (see chapter Spiritual Warfare for additional information).

(Eph 6:12)KJV "For we wrestle not against flesh and blood, but against principalities, against powers, against the rulers of the darkness of this world, against spiritual wickedness in high places."

The evil one and their evil doings are real, this Ephesians 6:12 passage by Paul is very explicit about this and specific about the who, we are up against. This is of the spiritual realm, therefore we need access via the Holy Spirit to combat it. I could not realistically fit all the Bible passages regarding "evil doings" and sin into this book, because it occurs from cover to cover in the Bible. The good news is that God has made every effort to protect us but now it is up to us to turn away from sin and turn towards the Lord and the Holy Spirit to maintain this protection. The point of this section is to review some real threats. Evil for us is to sin and sin causes a separation between us and God and the more you sin the further the separation becomes (i.e. falling out of our relationship/fellowship with God and out of His favor) and can ultimately get to the point where we turn our backs on Him entirely. As defined, evil is bad (the opposite of what is good); evil is wickedness (a broad term that houses all the qualities of evil, i.e. dishonesty, immorality, corruption, perversion, promiscuity, etc.); evil is ones intent to do ill will (whether the actual occurrence or even just the intention or thought fulfills it); evil is diseased (this covers spiritual, physical, emotional, etc., and yes we are protected against it but this is for another discussion); and evil is ungodliness for people who participate. In terms of the effects of evil: evil produces slaves; evil produces pain and misery; evil produces people who are lazy and inactive (meaning no initiative to do anything about their situation; apathetic); evil produces all that is bad, etc., etc. Another area that should be mentioned is if evil cannot get us to sin, it finds other ways to separate us from God and these are primarily battles that take place in the mind: anger and bitterness/resentment and unforgiveness are the best examples of this. The Bible reveals that these are not things of God, therefore they are of the devil; also that each of these will separate you from God; often, over a period of time these types of behavior open so many portals for demons that the believer turns to other sins while getting further and further away from God; in a nutshell this is the way **we** decide to throw our lives either into perpetual chaos or throw them away entirely). * Point here is that we decide either to succumb to the enemy or we decide to keep evil disarmed and minimize threats by renewing the mind daily in the Word of God (Bible) and with the Holy Spirit.

(**Eph 3:16**)NIV "I pray that out of his glorious riches he may **strengthen you with power** through his Spirit in your inner being."

(**Galatians 6:8-9**)BSB "If you sow to your own flesh, you will reap corruption from the flesh; but if you sow to the Spirit, you will reap eternal life from the Spirit. So let us not grow weary in doing what is right, for we will reap at harvest time, if we do not give up."

(**Rom 12:2**)KJV "And be not conformed to this world: but **be ye transformed by the renewing of your mind**, that ye may prove what is the good, and acceptable, and perfect, will of God."

In saying that we need to renew our mind daily in the Word via the Holy Spirit, it coincides with what Paul communicated to the Ephesians (and to us) that we should put on the armor of God "daily" and once you read

181

through it you'll realize that it is a summation of much of what I've communicated:

(Eph 6:10-18)KJV "Finally, my brethren, be strong in the Lord, and in the power of his might.

Put on the whole armor of God that ye may be able to stand against the wiles of the devil.

For we wrestle not against flesh and blood, but against principalities, against powers, against the rulers of the darkness of this world, against spiritual wickedness in high places.

Wherefore take unto you the whole armor of God that ye may be able to withstand in the evil day, and having done all, to stand.

Stand therefore, having your loins girt about with **truth**, and having on the breastplate of **righteousness**;

And your feet shod with the preparation of the **gospel of peace**;

Above all, taking the shield of **faith**, wherewith ye shall be able to quench all the fiery darts of the wicked.

And take the helmet of **salvation**, and the **sword of the Spirit, which is the word of God**:

Praying always with all prayer and supplication in the Spirit, and watching thereunto with all **perseverance** and supplication for all saints."

The above Armor of God consists of: Salvation (saved by Jesus); the Word of God (Bible) = Truth and Righteousness, Gospel of Peace; our Faith (trust in the Lord); the Holy Spirit (His sword is the spoken Word of God for us to use as a defense; note: the only defensive weapon; all others are offensive weapons), through prayer and supplication (asking for in prayer) via the Holy Spirit (who makes things happen).

As Paul stipulated, we must be in the Word daily with the Holy Spirit to minimize the threat. The prayer he spoke of are prayers of petition (asking) "Praying always with all prayer and supplication (asking) in the Spirit." A specific prayer of petition that fits into the context of this message is to ask the Father for His "hedge of protection." This is an extremely effective prayer (see chapter on Spiritual Warfare for additional info). To add, satan is fully aware of God's hedge of protection and the power in it, and an example of this is conveyed in the story of Job.

(Job 1:9-10)NIV "Does Job fear (need) God for nothing?" Satan replied. "Have you not put a **hedge** around him and his household and everything he has?"

182

"leads me not into temptation and delivers me from evil;" To summarize this passage, with regards to trials the Holy Spirit is taking charge and leading us (navigating the storms) which leaves the majority of the actual work left up to us (to learn, grow and mature) but in the case of evil we are going to rely on Him to deliver or to rescue us from evil, but don't mistake this rescue as a passive one because we are definitely an active participant. We rely on the Holy Spirit in prayer and communication to deliver us from this dangerous threat. We are not necessarily going to learn a significant amount, or grow and mature from lessons of evil, because it is like playing with fire, never is a burn minor or short lived and it always leaves a scar (often for a lifetime). What do we all learn about fire from a very young age? Once you've been burned, you stay the heck away from fire. If you have any common sense, and God expects His sons and daughters to have common sense through what they receive daily from His Holy Spirit, then you would from the get go stay the heck away from evil and if you allowed a portal to open, then you are now skilled at operating the 2 essential and critical tools He gave you, the Holy Spirit and the Bible. Then make sure your toolbox has the instructions for renewing your mind, the details of the armor God provide you and the petition prayer of protection that forms a protective hedge first and foremost around you and then whoever else you request. You now have your complete toolbox of all the tools a Believer needs to know about and to know how to skillfully use with respect to the topics we've covered. Having said that, all those tools God has placed at our disposal are housed in a metaphorical toolbox. *The toolbox is comprised of God's POWER (lid) and AUTHORITY (box) that we reach into to access the tools previously mentioned. We must unlock the lid to access His power and the tools we are pulling from the box (in which He has given us authority to operate), must be used to effectively and successfully carry out <u>any</u> job at hand. *Many on this subject are either confused or have been given false teachings, we share in God's power and authority and the key word is <u>share</u>. (Note, in the Greek power means dynamite force and authority means master privilege; in the natural realm and to an extent in the spiritual realm) I've previously mentioned processes in other contexts and this coincides with those processes (albeit the most crucial one). <u>The process I speak of is that we must be actively pursuing and playing out our relationships, trust, faith, obedience, prayer, renewing the mind daily, forgiving, giving, loving, and on and on with God in the center of it ALL and that is the key to how we have access to unlock his power and authority.</u> An analogy of this is if you are familiar with massive power tools,

they require massive power which requires 220 volts vs. 110 volts, and requires a dedicated 10guage cord vs a 16guage extension cord, etc. otherwise at times they may function but improperly and ineffectively or they don't function at all. If you expect to have God's power and authority, <u>in which He has given all Believers</u>, to properly function then you must be an active participant in the process and do so in conjunction with how it was originally designed to operate and function successfully.

"Your Holy Spirit dwells in me, comforts me, counsels me; leads me, guides me and directs me in your righteousness and your truths; fills me with your wisdom; leads me not into temptation and delivers me from evil;"

"For this is your kingdom Father that dwells with me; in it I share your Power, I share your Authority and I share your Glory, respectfully; today, tomorrow, forever and ever - as you promised me! I thank you, I love you, In Jesus name I pray, hear my prayers and make them so, Amen!"

"For this is your Kingdom Father that dwells with me"

(See the beginning of this prayer *"Your kingdom come into me."* for additional information on the meaning of God's kingdom.) Now that we have just uncovered so many related truths and teachings, hopefully you understand what Jesus was saying when in **(John 14:19-20)**KJV He said, "Because I live, you also will live. On that day you will realize that I am in my Father, and you are in me, and I am in you." Then in **(John 3:3)**KJV Jesus said, "Truly, truly, I say to you, unless one is born again, he <u>cannot see the kingdom</u> of God." He is revealing that you would not visibly see the kingdom, but that in order for the kingdom to enter you via the Holy Spirit and the living Bible's wisdom, knowledge, understanding, principles, teachings, etc. you must be born again (born from above), and combining the "He is **in** us" statement results in the following: *"For this is your <u>Kingdom</u> Father <u>that dwells with me.</u>"* This may be controversial for some yet others will truly welcome it because they've believed this and know that it is a truth of God. For me personally, I know that I know that the Father's kingdom dwells with me and what I'm doing here is confirming it scripturally. Also note, Jesus in the Beatitudes communicated the pure in heart will "see" God, so in that instance and this one, He is referring to us clearly discerning with spiritual sight our God. Finally, this initial part of the verse we are praising Him while acknowledging that His kingdom dwells in us so that we can fully utilize the benefits there of, which leads into: *"in it I share your Power, I share your Authority and I share your Glory, respectfully;*

When we are fully active in all the various processes of God, then His kingdom is **in** us, allowing us to fully utilize and share in all that He is. (See three paragraphs prior, regarding His metaphorical toolbox comprised of power and authority), we now know exactly that based on what we have learned, that we share in His power and His authority and His glory. As pertaining to His glory, in **(John 17:1-5, 10)**NIV "After Jesus said this, he looked toward heaven and prayed: "Father, the hour has come. <u>Glorify your Son, that your Son may glorify you.</u> For you granted him <u>authority</u> over all (flesh) people that he might give eternal life to all those you have given him. Now this is eternal life that they know you, the only true God, and Jesus Christ, whom you have sent. <u>I have brought you glory on earth by finishing the work you gave me to do.</u> And now, Father, <u>glorify me</u> in your presence with **the glory I had with you before the world began.**" "<u>All I have is yours, and all you have is mine.</u> And **glory has come to me through them.**" Here Jesus is relaying much, but specifically this is the process in which God glorifies, in this example, Jesus glorifies Him back; but we as well have the ability to glorify Him back. As in "[4] I have brought you glory on earth by finishing the work you gave me to do" here it illustrates that we glorify the Father in what we do such as satisfactorily finishing the work that was assigned; also in respect to this passage "glory has come to me through them" Jesus is saying His "Believers" glorified Him in much the same way. As I have mentioned prior, I conclude that we glorify our Father in heaven in the things that we think, in the things that we say and in the things that we do, those things that honor Him. This lends itself to the other phrase I came up with and have previously mentioned, "from Glory to Glory, full circle" meaning that God first glorifies us so that we too can then glorify Him back full circle. So in this prayer we are acknowledging that we understand the breadth of gifts God has given us, His power, authority and glory, therefore we receive this "respectfully" with the utmost of honor. *"For this is your kingdom Father that dwells with me; in it I share your Power, I share your Authority and I share your Glory, respectfully."*

"today, tomorrow, forever and ever - as you promised me!" In the same passage as we reviewed before **(John 17:1-3)**NIV "Glorify your Son, that your Son may glorify you. For you granted him authority over all (flesh) people that he might **give eternal life** to all those you have given him. <u>Now this is eternal life that they know you,</u> the only true God, and Jesus Christ, whom you have sent." Jesus's primary emphasis is on eternal life, that He gives His Believers eternal life and that His Believers know the Father because He sent Jesus in order that we may have eternal life and that it is the Father's gift to us. So in the prayer passage, we are saying that His kingdom dwells in us and that we share in his power, authority and glory and do so respectfully; and with the knowledge of eternal life we relay it by saying *"today, tomorrow, forever and ever"* and finish it with *"as you*

*promised **me**!"* because eternal life is a promise He makes to us. Our God is a God of promises and He yearns to and He loves to fulfill His promises to us. * He also enjoys hearing us affirm our knowledge and understanding of His promises, so get into the habit of #1 knowing all of His promises and #2 when relaying one or two of them incorporated in your prayer, finish it with "as you promised me." This is just one of the "mechanisms or triggers" in God's kingdom that initiates things to happen.

"I thank you, I love you, In Jesus name I pray, hear my prayers and make them so, Amen!" We of course in closing thank Him and proclaim that we love Him (as unconditionally as we are capable of). * Then another "mechanism or trigger" that initiates things to happen in God's kingdom is when you say, **"In Jesus name I pray," because there is power in His name**! To refer for a third time the scripture **(John 17:11-12)**BSB Jesus said, "Holy Father, protect them by the power of your name, <u>the name you gave me</u>, so that they may be one as we are one. While I was with them, I protected them and kept them safe <u>by that name you gave me</u>;" this is an illustration of how Jesus knows how it works and the power that is in His name. * Also Paul wrote in **(Col 3:17)**NKJV "And whatever you do, whether in word or deed, <u>do it all in the name of the Lord Jesus, giving thanks to God the Father through him</u>;" so by saying in prayer "in the name of Jesus" this not only releases power but it at the same time is giving thanks to God, as in the previous passage points out that by acknowledging "that name the Father gave Him" it is a praise to Him that did this. Throughout the New Testament they did things in Jesus's name: baptized in His name; salvation comes in His name; we are justified in His name; we cast out demons in His name; we heal in His name; etc. We are praying in His authority, submitting to His will and leaving any indication of our name out of it and I am confessing He is mine and I will represent His best interests. In **(John 14:13-14)**BSB " <u>And I will do whatever you ask in my name</u>, so that the <u>Father may be glorified in the Son</u>. You may ask me for anything in my name, and I will do it." And **(John 16:23-24)**NIV "In that day you will no longer ask me anything. Very truly I tell you, my Father will give you whatever you ask in my name. Until now you have not asked for anything in my name. Ask and you will receive, and <u>your joy will be complete</u>." Those passages should convince you to always conclude in prayer: *"In Jesus name I pray."* Finally, we complete the prayer in saying *"hear my prayers and make them so, Amen!"* and Amen!

This is a prayer of praise to our Father in heaven and is a ritual prayer and prayed individually. The prayer ends in "hear my prayers and make them so, Amen!" not only for the purpose of this prayer but can be an introduction to any improvised prayers you may say after this and you are asking now for Him to hear all the prayers you are to pray. For me this prayer does and says so much. My mind races as I'm praying this with the thoughts of how each word or statement impacts our relationship or has had a specific occurrence attached to the day or evening before. I had stipulated for you to say this prayer enthusiastically, but that just comes normal for me because it means so much to me and my relationship with Him. It's hard to describe and to get the true emphasis across but it is as though I have all the attention of the Godhead, I am praying in the Spirit as well as referring to the Spirit and I'm referring to Jesus in a praise offering to my heavenly Father. To say the least, it gets my day moving in the right direction every day in and day out. By the way, not a day goes by that I don't give Him the respect by making time to give Him my <u>first thoughts</u> and my time first thing in the morning. Does your creator deserve anything less? Please take the opportunity to read "My Lord's Prayer" again, with the intent of knowing it intimately and being able to communicate it intimately as well.

My Lord's Prayer

My Father who art in heaven, hallowed be thy name, holy is your name Father, I praise you upon high and I bow in worship to you;

Your kingdom come into me, so that your will shall be done on earth as it is in heaven; I understand that I must die of selfish self, surrender to your will in obedience and be reborn again in Christ Jesus today (a new man/woman); To Glorify you in the things that I think, that I say and that I do; to Honor you, to Trust in you, to have Faith in you and Believe in you, whole-heartedly; and to Love you! (As I always will)

So give me this day my daily bread, your Word, the bread that nourishes me spiritually, mentally and physically, your Son Lord Jesus; who is the way, the truth and the life for me; who chose to die on the cross for me; who defeated satan, the devil and death for me; and who you rose, again for me. So thank you Father. Thank you for forgiving my sins, as I forgive others who trespass upon me;

Your Holy Spirit dwells in me, comforts me, counsels me; leads me, guides me and directs me in your righteousness and your truths; fills me with your wisdom; leads me not into temptation and delivers me from evil;

For this is your kingdom Father that dwells with me; in it I share your Power, I share your Authority and I share your Glory, respectfully; today, tomorrow, forever and ever - as you promised me! I thank you, I love you, In Jesus name I pray, hear my prayers and make them so, Amen!

187

*** If you are on the fence as an unbeliever or have recently been saved the following statement does not apply to you because you are unable to act on it with the Holy Spirit. For those of you who are Believer's whether babe or mature you've covered a lot of information to this point, so before you go any further in this book it is important to do the following: <u>pray and meditate on My Lord's Prayer along with the first two chapters in mind in asking the Holy Spirit to</u> **<u>validate</u>** and **<u>justify</u>** that it is **scripturally accurate** <u>and right in terms of what the Lord desires to be relayed and revealed to you, from Him.</u> If it is so and you receive His blessings to continue then by all means do so. If not, I suggest that you ask why and continue your prayer and supplication (petitioning) in an effort to validate this source. I'm confident that it is scripturally accurate and biblically sound but desired to show you my sincerity in wanting the best for you and for you to always whether with this book or anything else (and can't stress this point enough) that you are to do this daily in your walk in the Spirit, with regards to any scriptural message you hear or read outside of the Bible itself.

Chapter 4 Prayer

Prayer

You just read the previous chapter on the "Lord's Prayer" and "My Lord's Prayer" and in it I covered many aspects of prayers of either praise or petition, and prayers that are either ritual or improvised and how to structure the improvised prayer by Jesus's model.

For any of you who were confused with the previous chapter concerning a ritual praise prayer, when your habit for years has been to ask God for things regardless if it is ritual or improvised. If this is the case then maybe I need to delve deeper into this subject to clarify the different types of prayer and give you guidance on how, to quote Jesus, "pray this way." So we'll use the teachings I relayed in the "Lord's Prayer" and "My Lord's Prayer" chapter and you can refer back to it and utilize that information in relation to the following expanded teachings.

If your confusion is due to a habit of always asking for a list of needs during your prayers, then I can just hear the murmurings among you, with the majority of you in disbelief and very possibly on the edge of your seat to ask this question: "Now wait a minute, why would I not "ask" God or as you say "petition" God during the Lord's Prayer? It is what I do whenever I pray, I ask for 1, 2, or maybe more of my list of needs." To begin with, My Lord's Prayer is a ritual **prayer of praise** (not petition). Much of it at a glance may look like things you would request, but that is not the case. Secondly, man is an intelligent being BUT...I better be careful so I don't offend anybody...but if you believe that you have to analyze the process and determine what you believe would be best to do...YOU ARE GOING TO OVERTHINK IT AND MESS IT UP! God is "higher" than all and in all respects, His thoughts are not our thoughts and His ways our not our ways, so that is just one of the reasons why He inspired the writing of the "guidebook to life and living" The Bible. *Please hear this and understand, we are to do things the way He instructs and we are to **pray, and believe** "it" already **is;** and praise Him that "it" is already done (it is finished; and already provided/given) and praise Him continuously for it (not just in 1 or 2 prayers). Jesus said,

> **(Mark 11:24)**KJV "Therefore I tell you, whatever you desire and ask in prayer, believe that you have received it, and it will be yours."
> a parallel accounting:
> **(Matt 21:22)**KJV "And all things, whatsoever you shall ask for in prayer, believing, you shall receive."

Also, we are to relay to Him that we know what He wants us to know, He knows all and there is nothing that we are telling Him in this or any prayer that He doesn't already know. *We learn, we pray, then we embed it into our heart and mind by our own repetitiousness of thought and we give thanks for this and for His amazing Grace and all the Blessings that flow from it. * The key here is that we know it (understand and believe in it) and that is what we relay to Him in praise while doing so!

Yes, most believe this process is counterintuitive which makes them uncomfortable at first (or longer, and sometimes indefinitely primarily due to a lack of faith to believe in the process). Unfortunately some are a product of either a) lack of understanding due to a passive approach to their faith over the years, or b) false teachings. Or as mentioned, they overthink it and do it how they believe God should accept their prayers.

    *If any of this applies to you, then a red light should have come on because typically a "root" problem with this is that you are not walking in the Spirit, being guided in the Word (essentially guiding yourself without the "helper" God has gifted us with) and if that is the case for you then * you need to be sure you are baptized in the Holy Spirit (not referring to water baptism) and you would petition His help then ask for specific guidance, such as to answer a specific query in scripture then listen for His still small voice while in scripture, meditation, prayer and praise; *a vital "tip" in training yourself to "hear" His voice, is to keep a journal in your secret place with your Bible and write down what you think He is telling you, now sometimes the answers are immediate but often it is within a day or a week and it's typically in conjunction with reading scripture or hearing a sermon or hearing Godly advice from a Godly person (or rather than asking a question of scripture, ask a question that has been weighing heavily on your heart and He often guides us with "red lights or green lights," so when you get that nudge it is Him communicating to you. Ask Him is that you and is that your answer and again listen for His still small voice and write down what you think He is communicating with you), then continue to develop the relationship and you'll initially begin to understand how He communicates, then you'll get to the point that you no longer need the nudges or the journal, and you get this transfer of communication that you know beyond a reasonable doubt that it is the Holy Spirit. Hopefully by that point the guiding principles that I'm conveying begin to make sense and then become effortless in their execution because now the Holy Spirit is guiding you in Truth and in your purposed experiential spiritual journey.

190

So if you desire His Grace with His abundance of Blessings and you expect to receive them, then I've laid the groundwork for you and now you need to "choose" how you are going to approach it: **pray in petition, declare in Jesus's name, receive/acknowledge the blessings, and believe it is so, then praise Him for it.** Or you can call Him up whenever the urge comes over you and ask Him for your laundry list of wants if that is what you think the process should consist of.

Since I am on a roll and this is "good stuff" I would like to shift gears slightly from prayers of praise and relay additional teachings on **prayers of petition** (typically improvised and asked due to a need or want). There are two important points that I have yet to focus on, a) declaration, b) receive. Regarding declaration, it is a key component in the process and has to do with declaring in the name of Jesus the thing(s) you prayed for, that you are declaring your right to petition it, declaring the power given to you by Jesus, to declare it into existence and take ownership. Then this is very important, you must "receive" the blessings! Acknowledge that you have received it, and as I've pointed out elsewhere that God knows these things, but it is your responsibility to speak it (just as God spoke things into being in Genesis). Also, get ready for a curve ball backed up with a fast ball. For the curve ball, God has already given you exceedingly abundantly above all you could ever utilize, desire, need or dream of (Jehovah Jireh, the God of Providence) and He has done so back when He predestined you according to His will, and get this, to fulfill your petitions according to His will. So the blessings are there for the taking, so to speak. Well actually that is the fast ball, "receive" in the Greek and in that day means "to take!" So the blessings are there for the taking. Get this, Jesus wants us "to take" those bucket loads of blessings! This not only applies to prayer, but a significant portion of what Jesus has for us, He wants us to take! Again, another paradigm shift and one that leaves Believers who have been given poor instruction or false teachings much confusion on what is correct and what am I to do, and it's going to take some time to work all this out. I'm not finished, did you know that when you ask for something (petition) God in prayer, declare in Jesus's name and receive the blessings, and believe it is so and praise Him for it, you are to also "ACT" on it? The laundry list comment I made in the last paragraph brought this to mind. Many believe that they can just text Him or call Him up anytime, anywhere, under any circumstances and ask Him to do this or that and that He's going to answer by blessing them with His Grace and abundance of blessings and gifts that are at His disposal. *My point is, He expects you to ACT on it. Not only that, he will "strengthen" you in it, so you can accomplish it; That is also why you continuously pray and praise on it because it is a process (not something that is just handed to you because you are just sooo special; remember the church lady skit on SNL "isn't that special"). The Bible is crammed full of examples of God expecting us to ACT on our prayers and needs. Try this, research some of those examples on your own and see if you can come up with a few. A common reference used is when Moses and some 2 million people needed God to part the Red Sea. Why do you think Moses had to lift his staff above his head and why do you think the people needed to step into the Red Sea first before God would perform a miracle? He wanted them to #1 have faith and to #2 show their faith and He wanted them to #3 ACT on their faith!

* Get ready for another curve ball, <u>we pray, declare and receive, and believe, and praise that it is so and we ACT on it while we "rest" in Him, so that He "strengthens" us to accomplish it; and that is how He blesses us and gifts us our prayer/needs</u>. A pretty incredible paradox, wouldn't you say? I'll bet you're asking, "Where did the "rest" in Him come in at?"

> **(Phil 4:6-7)**NKJV "Be anxious for nothing, but in everything, by prayer and petition, with thanksgiving, present your requests to God. And the peace of God, which surpasses all understanding, will guard your hearts and your minds in Christ Jesus."
> **(Matt 11:28-29)**BSB "Come to Me, all you who are weary and burdened, and I will give you rest. Take my yoke upon you and learn from Me, for I am gentle and humble in heart, and you will find rest for your souls."

Jesus pleads (or often emphasizes) for us to rest in Him, not only to relieve our stress and turn our burdens over to Him, but also, He gives us perfect peace (or rest). Also His **power** rests on us when we rest (our power) in Him. So it's another form of an <u>act</u> (action) that we do to receive benefits when we do it, although it sounds counterintuitive to rest and act at the same time. Although it may seem counterintuitive, don't allow that to confuse you or to stop you from doing it. Rest is referring primarily in us "resting assured" in Jesus and His promises to us. What it is not is the rest that we associate with resting, relaxing or sleeping (See Ch2, Discourse on soul/spirit for additional details). Regarding the "He strengthens us" to accomplish the petition

> * **(Eph. 3:16-19)**BSB "I pray that out of the riches of His glory, He may **strengthen** <u>you with power through His Spirit in your inner being</u>, so that Christ may dwell in your hearts through faith. Then you, being <u>rooted and grounded in love</u>, will have **power**, together with all the saints, to comprehend the length and width and height and depth of His love, and to know the love of Christ that surpasses knowledge that you may be <u>filled with all **the fullness of God**</u>."

(2 Cor. 12:9)KJV "And He said unto me, My grace is sufficient for you. For my strength is made perfect in weakness. Most gladly therefore will I rather glory in my infirmities, that the power of Christ may rest upon me."

If you recall the explanation of "free will" which allows us "choices," I relayed a *warning with it in that He will "strengthen" us in whichever choices we make. In other words, if we choose to believe in Him or if we choose not to, He will strengthen us if we go to Him! Or He will strengthen us if we turn away from Him! Additionally, He strengthens us in our weakness (another paradoxical statement). Or maybe not paradoxical if you think of it in this way: He loves us and He wants us to have an abundant life so where we are weak in our fleshly nature and we repent and sincerely act on changing our ways, He blesses us with strengthening in that area (*remember if your intention is to act on positive change then He will bless).

Having outlined the processes and hopefully you are not confused and if you are just reread from the beginning of this chapter to here (although reading the entire book and taking it in comprehensively will help you out the most). So now, I'm going to interject some current events, my observations, identification of potential changes that need to take place, or general helpful information for the reader, in following suit with what I've done in all the other chapters to assist you in grasping these Godcepts more easily and/or connecting the dots easier with some explanations. Let me begin by saying that there is a movement in parts of the church today that claims that most everything you've learned concerning prayer is either outdated or wrong (from false teachings) and you will continue wasting your time and effort if you continue doing the same thing from false teachings, and the way to get your prayers answered is with praying by declaration in Jesus's name. Well those people making this claim have coincidentally written books on how to correct your prayer life with a "how-to guide" in declaring your prayers and is quite frankly a good way to promote book sales with subsequent profits. Let me set this record straight, it is primarily a marketing ploy and sales pitch. Although I will give them this credit, in that **we are to call out our declaration of our rights given to us by Jesus and should be stated with conviction and followed up by stating "in Jesus's powerful name,"** but that everything else that is stated "in the Bible" as it has to do with prayer is accurate and applicable and please do not discard those practices. Those practices in conjunction with declarations are vital to "receiving" grace and blessings (that have already been given). The key word is receiving, that is what takes all the components stated in the Bible in order to come to fruition. Please note the following partial list of critical key factors that make up a successful prayer life:

Jesus; the Holy Spirit and walking with Him; the Bible and reading scripture daily; maintain an intimate relationship with the Father, Son and Holy Spirit; worship; praise; prayers of praise and petition that include <u>declarations</u> and declaring them in Jesus's name and "believing" that your prayers are answered, receiving/taking what Jesus wants you to have, and "acting" on them as though they are, along with having and expressing positive future faith and knowing that it will fuel your positive present, believing that the Lord desires for you to have an abundant life and experiential spiritual life journey on earth, resting in and trusting in the assurance that Jesus and the Father will do what they say they will do while maintaining your Faith in them, Trusting in the Hope the Father has given us with His promises and what you've witnessed to date; Believing in God and loving Him with all your heart; and living in obedience to the Lord always; giving of yourself to others and those in need; and you feel free to keep this going by filling in the rest in what you "believe" applies…

There is no silver bullet, no secret sauce, no 7 steps to _____, when it comes to prayer or for that matter when it comes to any aspect of this spiritual relationship with our Lord (note, I covered a portion of the topic of Faith in much the same manner). Everything just mentioned is a <u>component</u> that plays a role in making things happen in God's kingdom, sure there are integral (essential, fundamental) components but they are a given and they make up the BIG wheels, while the lesser components make up the smaller wheels in this machine, nonetheless all the cogs must interlink with each other and do so with precision since the mechanism is in constant motion and always moving forward; you benefit when you (in obedience) have the wisdom of each component which gives you knowledge and understanding of God's kingdom and of this world, and you prosper more as you take on more and more of the wisdom of each component (in the machine)! To dismiss any of it, and also to do so to focus on a specific agenda is blasphemous (an action against God). Having just used the analogy of interlinked wheels on a machine, gives me the opportunity to relay: please do NOT get all caught up on the "mechanism" of prayer or any other system/process of God! Sure in this case it is very important to know what makes the clock tick, but with the foundational knowledge you will be led to how to actualize it, and thus your focus is on the relationships with Jesus, with the Holy Spirit and with the Heavenly Father first and foremost! There are some people who get so caught up on the process, they miss out on the results and life altogether; don't let this be you. I had previously remarked that for a pastor to focus on a specific agenda that puts the wrong spin on God's Word is blasphemous, I wanted to point out that on the other hand, to enhance the teachings by focusing on a specific area is a great approach to take, also a benefit to all associated with it. For example, a pastor that focuses on Hope and another that focuses on Grace has got their hands full because the breadth of the topic is so large, they can spend a lifetime teaching it but they also know that it is interlinked with all the other component topics, therefore they need to be taught as well. Declaration of prayer is important, as with other components, but I'm sorry but it is not critical and does not take a priority over other similar components. Do not misunderstand, it is still a very important component of your prayer life.

Having said that, I also wanted to mention that a Believer does not have to know everything before they can participate in the benefits of God's kingdom. As you've picked up on regarding the workings of my personal journey after being saved, I had mentioned that after a couple of years I was able to look back on my progress and then after five year and after eight years and so on, I was benefiting more and more and on an increasing scale (primarily due to my passion for my Lord and wanting to learn more). In short, you don't have to know everything to receive blessings, but due to the intimate relationships with the Father, Jesus and the Holy Spirit, you cannot hide it if your attempts are half-hearted and one sided (benefiting you only; pseudo-christian) and it will catch up to you.

Many people today live in their comfort bubble and either have zero to do with God or have attended church for selfish reasons or did so with good intentions, but the effort quickly wanes due to their "so-called busy" life that is poorly time managed in respect to God. Many people want to leapfrog to the meat of how this or that works, without having to put in the time, energy or effort it should normally take. Often it is those same people who are looking for a silver bullet, that there must be some trick to this system, so just let me know the basics and the tricks and I'll be good to go. But is that a good premise for a deep and long-lasting relationship? Of course not, and if attempted it would fail with a person and especially with your Lord! The church is to blame for a portion of the illiteracy today and if that is not bad enough, there are those who perpetuate it while taking advantage of the situation by selling 125page books on how to prosper at prayer or otherwise, to those people who are thoroughly confused and are looking for help or those who are looking for the silver bullet.

The topic of declaration in prayer and its recent new emphasis, or might I say the reviving of it, segues well into how the church is evolving for the worse rather than the better, and its subsequent style of teaching and narrow subject matter. I've touched on this topic elsewhere in which I mentioned that sermons are watered down and/or dummied down and are often more focused to entertain than telling specifically about the truth, and relaying in truth (even if it hurts). The following sums up what Jesus expected out of His disciples, when He relayed the Great Commission...and we've fallen way short and continuing to go in that direction with this generation.

> **(Matt 28:18-20)**BSB Then Jesus came to them and said, "All authority in heaven and on earth has been given to Me. Therefore **go and make disciples of all nations**, baptizing them in the name of the Father, and of the Son, and of the Holy Spirit, **and teaching them to obey all that I have commanded you**. And surely I am with you always, even to the end of the age."

Concise version: Jesus delivered this message, "Go and make disciples of all nations and teaching them to obey all that I have commanded you." My point is: we are to teach ALL precepts and principles of the Bible. The problem is: the majority of teachings focus on the alpha (the beginning) and dabble in between with then moving to the death and resurrection, with a few of the predominant stories sprinkled in between. Most Believers today are illiterate and their knowledge base all boils down to the following that you have been taught or will be taught: just random hits and misses of the Bible outside of the following; Jesus: bits and pieces of His ministry, His death on the cross (although very little with regards to the details of His works on the cross), His resurrection (although very few specifics concerning it; during and after with His role in heaven and current status); maybe bits of the Holy Spirit or an overly simplistic representation of Him; God with his relationship to our beginnings but very little about the importance of how to have a relationship with Him; and that about sums it up, and relays my point well enough for now. God specifically said that (His people) "we are destroyed for a lack of knowledge," and that is exactly where we are headed unless something changes dramatically in how and what we teach and deliver in our messages from the church (house). We are on the most part Bible illiterate and that has got to change. I hope and pray that this book will make a difference with the current situation and that it is a benefit to a large number of people in opening their hearts to the Lord and to Believers ranging from babes to mature.

Your prayer life is extremely important to your entire spiritual journey and relationship with God. Please take these teachings to heart and follow the Holy Spirit's guidance. Be sure when reading this book to take a moment and seek to understand the full context of the various prayers that I've included in it.

Meditation / Contemplation

Regarding meditation / contemplation, please note that I'm referring to simply concentrating and focusing intensely on your prayer and what feedback you are receiving from the Holy Spirit. What I am NOT referring to is eastern culture forms of meditation such as in Hinduism and Buddhism, including practices of mindfulness, or chants during yoga exercises. Do not practice these forms of meditation (or an altered form), because you can easily and <u>unknowingly</u> open portals for the devil. These are not in accordance with our faith, thus the reason I reject its practice.

> Jesus warned against praying repetitiously, **(Matthew 6:7)**KJV "When you pray, do not use vain repetitions <u>as the heathen do</u>. They think their prayers are answered merely by repeating their words again and again."
> (So note, do not pray in vain repetition and in chants like the Islamic Muslims do)
> (Also note that this does not at all apply to our ritual prayers because you do not repeat them over and over and over again in the same sitting; also they are not chants; finally <u>they are of rich content of praise and love</u>)

So please understand, **meditation in prayer** is extremely important and beneficial. I've used the phrase **"fervent prayer"** a number of times, meaning to pray with intensity and wholeheartedness and by doing so it is a form of meditation. As a matter of fact, when you do this with that kind of intensity for prolonged periods of time it has rejuvenating, revitalizing, refreshing, re-energizing benefits for your inner-being and your outward-being. It can expand your experience in prayer and with the Holy Spirit, also it can intensify things like your enthusiasm, outlook, passion, health, energy, strength, vigor, etc. I strongly encourage you to practice meditation in prayer but only do it within the parameters of God's kingdom and Bible scripture.

Key Prayers

I am the adopted son of the Great I AM,
Therefore I am Spirit, I am forgiving, I am giving, I am loving, I am compassionate, I am tolerant, I am peaceful, I am persevering, I am enduring, I am everlasting,
I am the adopted son of the Great I AM,
Therefore I am Spirit, I am healthy, I am strong, I am mighty, I am successful, I am significant, I am intelligent, I am gifted, I am blessed and I am uncommon,
And I am the adopted son of the Great I AM!
Therefore I am Spirit...

197

Heavenly Father, Lord Jesus and Holy Spirit,
I love you with all of my heart,
With all of my mind,
To the depths of my soul,
With all my might, I love you!
This is surely a day the Lord hath made,
And I will rejoice in Him and in it!

Lord Jesus,
I love you with all of my heart,
You are my King of Kings, my Lord of Lords, my Savior, my teacher, my brother and my friend!
And I thank you for everything, and I love you!

Lord Jesus,
Direct my path,
Via the Holy Spirit,
As you instructed me,
Not to dwell in the past,
Not to be fearful or anxious of the future,
Nor be fearful or anxious in the present,
But rather to have life and have it abundantly today, in the present!
(Optional continuation)
And that I have a Godly day today. For a Godly day is one that is filled with glorifying you with all that I think, with all that I say and with all that I do, may it all glorify you, each and every minute of each and every day! In Jesus name I pray, hear my prayers and make them so, Amen.

Or a separate prayer,
I am truly grateful and thankful for this experiential spiritual life journey on earth that you have blessed me with and the mere opportunity of it. May I glorify you in return with all that I think, with all that I say and with all that I do, may it all glorify you, each and every minute of each and every day! In Jesus name I pray, hear my prayers and make them so, Amen.

May the angels in heaven sing glorious songs of my love and my praise for You,
May it echo through the heavens, so that all may know that I am Your good and faithful servant.

Heavenly Father, I am your warrior, your foot soldier, and your good and faithful servant;
Please tell me Your will you have for me, that I may carry it out, that you may be well pleased with me.

The Lord's Prayer

"Our Father which art in heaven, hallowed be your name,
Your kingdom come, your will be done on earth as it is in heaven.
Give us this day our daily bread, and forgive us our sins, for we also forgive everyone who is indebted to us.
And lead us not into temptation, but deliver us from evil.
For yours is the kingdom and the power and the glory forever and ever. Amen.

My Lord's Prayer

My Father who art in heaven, hallowed be thy name, holy is your name Father, I praise you upon high and I bow in worship to you;

Your kingdom come into me, so that your will shall be done on earth as it is in heaven; I understand that I must die of selfish self, surrender to your will in obedience and be reborn again in Christ Jesus today (a new man/woman); To Glorify you in the things that I think, that I say and that I do; to Honor you, to Trust in you, to have Faith in you and Believe in you, whole-heartedly; and to Love you! (As I always will)

So give me this day my daily bread, your Word, the bread that nourishes me spiritually, mentally and physically, your Son Lord Jesus; who is the way, the truth and the life for me; who chose to die on the cross for me; who defeated satan, the devil and death for me; and who you rose… again for me. So thank you Father. Thank you for forgiving my sins, as I forgive others who trespass upon me;

Your Holy Spirit dwells in me, comforts me, counsels me; leads me, guides me and directs me in your righteousness and your truths; fills me with your wisdom; leads me not into temptation and delivers me from evil;

For this is your kingdom Father that dwells with me; in it I share your Power, I share your Authority and I share your Glory, respectfully; today, tomorrow, forever and ever… as you promised me! I thank you, I love you, In Jesus name I pray, hear my prayers and make them so, Amen!

Prayer of Jabez (my version)

"Bless me Father, Bless me indeed,
Always be with me and never forsake me, as you have done and as you shall always do;
Continue to expand my territories and my horizons,
And continue to mold me and shape me into that person you have predestined and purposed me to be..."

Additional (as applicable), And
"Protect me Father, protect me indeed,
Protect me with your hedge of protection,
As You have done and as You shall always do,
Protecting me from evil, evil doers, evil ways,
Satan, his demons and the devil;
And keep me healthy, wealthy and wise,
In You and through You, in me and through me, Full Circle
(As it is written) from Glory to Glory..."

Additional (as applicable),
Please protect my mother _____ and my aunt _____,
And protect my daughters' ___ ___ and my son _____,
With your hedge of protection;
Please protect my immediate family and their families,
Protect my friend's ____ ____ and their families,
And protect them with your hedge of protection,
As You have done and as You will always do,
Protecting them from evil, evil doers, evil ways,
Satan, his demons and the devil;
And keep them healthy, wealthy and wise,
In You and through You, in them and through them, Full Circle
(As it is written) from Glory to Glory,
And may they all open their hearts to you and get to know you as I have and love you as I do,
In Jesus name I pray, please hear my prayers and make them so, Amen."

Last Supper; Holy Communion

Heavenly Father, Lord Jesus and Holy Spirit, please join me in partaking of the Last Supper, in Holy Communion with me. Please welcome me into your presence, from the natural to the supernatural.

(Holding the bread and the cup to the sky give thanks to the Father) Heavenly Father, please bless this bread that represents your Son's flesh and this cup filled with the fruit of the vine that represents your Son's blood. I give you thanks for your blessings.

This bread represents Jesus's flesh and Jesus said, "As often as you do this, do it in remembrance of Me," relaying that as often as you "break bread" (even with others) that we should do it in remembrance of Him (and He illustrated this in the Last Supper with his disciples).

Jesus also said that I must eat of His flesh and drink of His blood and to do this in remembrance of Him. (So hold the bread up to the sky and say) Jesus is the bread of life, born in the city of bread (Bethlehem); Jesus is my daily bread. This bread represents Jesus's flesh and He said that I must eat of His flesh and drink of His blood, and eating of His flesh is not literal rather it means that I must "<u>hunger</u>" for <u>His wisdom</u>, because ultimately His wisdom is what will prosper my life on this experiential spiritual life journey on earth. Therefore, <u>I must hunger for His wisdom</u> by eating of His flesh and I do this in remembrance of what He did for me on the cross.

(Speaking to Jesus), You **chose** to have your body broken because you knew that when it was beaten and broken that at that exact moment instantaneously and supernaturally, I would be made whole (now break the bread) so you became my substitute and was broken so that I am made whole again in You and through You. (For You are in me and I am in You and I am no longer broken but made whole through Christ)

This grape juice / this fruit of the vine represents Your life-giving blood and Your water that cleanses my soul. Again, You chose to die on the cross for the redemption of my sins (all past, present and future), so when the Roman soldier pierced Your side with his spear, blood and water came gushing out; Your life giving blood and Your cleansing water for our soul. That is what this cup represents (holding the cup up to the sky) Heavenly Father, as Jesus did and said during the Last Supper, "This is the New Covenant in my blood." And I am so thankful and grateful that you Jesus have made the New Covenant with God rather than between God and man, because when it was between God and man, man failed miserably and could never attain the standards of the Law. Now, the covenant is between You and Him and I understand that I have access to it and to Him through you Lord Jesus via the Holy Spirit. Jesus, you said that I must eat of your flesh and drink of your blood and to do this in remembrance of You. And Your blood, this fruit of the vine, is representative for me to "<u>thirst</u>" for the abundant life on earth and eternal life in heaven (drink of the cup) and I do so and do it in remembrance of what you have done for me on the cross.

I thank you Heavenly Father, Lord Jesus and Holy Spirit for joining me in Holy Communion and would like to ask for (insert petition prayer) knowing that You are my provider of all things and that you love me and want the best for me and I thank you for granting me these prayers and I receive it and declare it in the name of Jesus. In Jesus name I pray, hear my prayers and make them so. Amen.

God's promises of providence (at meals)

Thank you heavenly Father, for blessing all the works of my hands.
Thank you for blessing my storehouse.
That I may provide for my family and be a blessing to others.
Thank you for your promises of providence and fulfilling all of your promises,
For you provide exceedingly abundantly above all I could ever utilize, desire, need, or dream of,
And with the exceedingly abundant providence, comes your surplus for me, to be a blessing to others,
May I return those blessings to you one hundred thousand-fold, in those that I bless with your surplus.
I thank you, I love you, In Jesus name I pray hear my prayers and make them so, Amen.

(Optional insert)
Thank you for always blessing my food,
For my consumption and my health;
May you bless that it provides me with nourishment, vitamins, minerals and protein to all the cells in my body (from head to toe) (your Holy Temple), and that my cells convert it to your pure energy which provides me with strength, vitality, vigor and energy!
This I pray in Jesus name, hear my prayers and make them so, Amen.

Chapter 5 The Holy Spirit

The Holy Spirit

You've heard me relay this before that my writing styles and approaches are a bit unconventional and this chapter is an example of that statement. Have you heard of "data dumping" or it could just as easily be called info dumping? It's a process in which a significant or at times an overwhelming amount of facts, information, details and messages are communicated in a brief and hopefully concise manner in order to relay to others information to achieve a desired result. In the case of selling an item or service it can work to your advantage or to your disadvantage depending on the individual you are discussing the matter with. In this case, I am covering the ever so broad topics of the Holy Spirit from the who and why along with the activities, responsibilities, goals, background, etc. And yes, depending on how you read and learn will determine whether this writing style and approach works for you or not. Keep in mind that all the rest of the chapters of this book support this chapter and often takes deeper dives into specific topic matter. For example, there are 14 pages devoted to the Holy Spirit in Ch.3 "My Lord's Prayer" and numerous other mentioning's throughout the balance of that chapter. Having said that, please note that in an effort to reduce redundancies you will need to read both of these chapters and the entire book to get the comprehensive information regarding the Holy Spirit. It should go without saying, but keep in mind that the Bible is the original source for this information, and I've provided much of the scripture source references to give you the opportunity to follow up, validate and expand your knowledge.

Jesus taught in parables. Why? For a number of reasons but one specifically is that people learn things in a variety of ways and the easiest and most fundamental is via storytelling. His parables were primarily true to life stories that were easy to remember and understand, whereas some were metaphorical in nature (using an object or action that is abstract but to be symbolic of something else), and some were relayed by using analogies (the comparison of two things for explanation or clarification of a topic). All are similar in nature and parables are what He deemed best for man and of course He knows us best, He is our God. Throughout the book I've primarily used mine and others testimonies which are true to life current day stories that directly relate to a topic matter of the Bible. I did my best not to overdo the storytelling and leave it open so that you could research scripture and have those parables as your guide.

On the other hand, Jesus did not data dump his principles, precepts, rules/laws, commandments, etc. that people would probably have difficulty understanding and especially remembering, and thus His messages getting lost in the dumping of information and subsequently losing their interest and losing them following Him. He came to save the lost, not keep them in that lost and confused state. Previously mentioned in another chapter is that Jesus's religion if you even want to call it that is one of relationships first and foremost above anything else because with having a good and positive relationship with our God reduces the need for rules, laws, governments, etc. and reduces man's desire to sin in the first place.

* Please keep in mind one of the primary objectives of this book: to relay clear and concise messages of the foundational wisdom of God and the processes involved and how it impacts our lives daily throughout our entire life on this earth and beyond. And relay this information so that you can cut through all the years of learning and years of trial by error occurrences which is what I had to go through, and it was not necessary. In other words, get to living the abundant life sooner in your life than halfway through it, near the end of your life or sadly never. Note also that another objective of this book is to cut out the unnecessary information that is preached by pastors, or should I say the "church." Now don't get me wrong or take this out of context, everything in the Bible is relevant but there is a time and place for covering all the stories in the Bible. What I'm relaying in this book are all of the foundational principles and key topics that you need for the basis of your experiential spiritual life journey on earth and nothing more (except a few of the bits of wisdom in Ch6). For those who are babes, you may not realize what I am communicating here but you will, and for those who are mature Believers you know exactly what I am conveying because it is what you get a large portion of at church, or podcasts, or TV, or radio, and you're wondering why you've devoted this time to what you feel are irrelevant topics or topics that have catchy phrases and funny anecdotal stories designed to entertain more so than to inform and educate.

Now let's delve into the who's and the what's of the Holy Spirit and how important and essential a relationship is between you and Him. Due to the endless amount of information pertaining to the Holy Spirit the format of the chapter is unconventional in that it is primarily bullet point details with some explanations and to an extent it is in an order in which the topics flow in somewhat of a concise manner. As previously mentioned, utilize the other chapters for deeper dives of information and much more importantly * utilize the Holy Spirit by asking Him to assist you (and He will!) in revealing the wisdom, knowledge and understandings in your initial read and especially when you return and take one bullet point topic at a time and having Him teach, counsel and guide you into a deeper understanding of each of those topics.

Two of God's infinitesimal attributes is that He is omniscient (all knowing; totality of knowledge all past, present and future) and He is omnipotent (all power to do all things, anything is possible), the God of all creation! YOU are given access to not just these two attributes but many more, including all of God's ₁wisdom which gives you ₂knowledge and ₃understanding of ₄His kingdom and the ₅things and ways of this world via the ₆Bible, the guidebook to life and abundant living and this is all accomplished via your walk with the ₇Holy Spirit.

- ₁Wisdom
- ₂Knowledge
- ₃Understanding (for practical application)
- ₄God's kingdom
- ₅The things and ways of this world
- ₆The Bible (the guidebook to life and abundant living); God's truths; the Word in the flesh is Jesus.
- ₇Holy Spirit
  - o One of the three persons of the triune Godhead (the Father, the Word, and the Holy Ghost); note: the Word being Jesus and the Holy Ghost is another term for the Holy Spirit; as is the Spirit of God and God's Holy Spirit.
  - o In the Old Testament the Holy Spirit was not accessible by man, rather only via the direction of God the Father was the Holy Spirit given to specific individuals for specific time frames.
  - o That changed in the New Testament: **(John 14:15-17)**NKJV "If you love Me, keep My commandments. And I will pray the Father, and He will give you **another Helper**, that He may abide with you forever— the Spirit of truth, whom the world cannot receive, because it neither sees Him nor knows Him; but you know Him, for He dwells with you and will be in you. **(John 14:25-26)**NKJV "These things I have spoken to you while being present with you. But the Helper, the Holy Spirit, whom the Father will send in My name, He will teach you all things, and bring to your remembrance all things that I said to you.
  - o **Baptism of the Holy Spirit** (not water baptism); (John 3:5)KJV Jesus answered, "Truly, truly, I say to you, unless one is born of water AND the Spirit he cannot enter into the kingdom of God" **(Acts 1:4-5 & Acts 11:16)**NKJV Jesus said, "Wait for the promise of the Father, which I told you. For John baptized with water, but you will be baptized with the Holy Spirit." **(Acts 1:8)**KJV Jesus said, "You will **receive power** when the Holy Spirit has come upon you." **(Luke 21:15)**BSB Jesus said, "For I

205

will give you **speech and wisdom** that none of your adversaries will be able to resist or contradict;" **(Luke 12:12)**BSB "For at that time the Holy Spirit will **teach you what you should say**." **(Acts 19:4-6)**NKJV Paul came across some men who John the Baptist had water baptized and said, "John baptized with a baptism of repentance, telling the people that they should believe in the One who would come after him, that is, Jesus. When they **heard** this, they were baptized in the name of the Lord Jesus. And when Paul had **laid his hands** upon them, the Holy Spirit came on them, and they began speaking with **tongues** and prophesying; **(Acts 2:4)**KJV ...as the Spirit was giving them **utterance**." After we have been saved and baptized in the Spirit, we now have the indwelling of the Holy Spirit, meaning He dwells inside of us.

- **(1 Cor. 6:19)**NKJV "Do you not know that your body is a temple of the Holy Spirit within you, whom you have from God?"

o He counsels us with a still small voice (also communicates to us with non-verbal cues); **(Counselor)**

o **Comforter**; Jesus said, "Let not you heart be troubled, believe/trust in God and believe/trust in Me;" and "I will pray the Father and he shall give you another Comforter, that He may abide in you forever." **(John 14:16)**KJV

o Remembrance (**Teacher**) He brings all things to your spirit's remembrance, from since the beginning of time. Because since we are now flesh, the things that we once knew as spirit has been hidden (lost) from us until we choose to have Jesus as the Lord of our lives, thus liberating us from bondage and allowing the Holy Spirit to bring all those hidden things to our remembrance.

- I was once lost but now am found.
- When the student is ready, the teacher will appear. This applies to both Jesus and the Holy Spirit and typically under different circumstances.
- **(John 16:13)**KJV "When he, the Spirit of Truth comes, he will **guide you** into all truth; for he shall not speak of himself; but whatsoever he shall hear, that shall he speak; **and He will show you things to come.**"
  - * It is important to point out that the Holy Spirit does not "give or gift" you with truth and especially if you did not ask for it. He guides us (points out the way) into the fullness of God's truths; for us to glean (extract) what we may from it. So we must at least

206

pursue truth (if not specifically ask for it in prayer); then the Holy Spirit guides us along our journey in the pursuit of truth; and we **must act** on every stage of that pursuit otherwise that particular pursuit ends; whether we have achieved the fullness of the wisdom resulting in knowledge and the understanding of that particular topic. Note, we have the confidence in the Holy Spirit and assurance already given to us by Jesus that what we ask for will be provided. **(as relayed in John 16:23; John 14:13)**

- That entire prior bullet point statement is exactly what I've been relaying has happened to me throughout my journey; and specifically with the 1.5+year journey with regards to "My Lord's Prayer," I quickly realized that I must continue the pursuit and continue to act on what I learned and if I took a break from it which I often did, the conduit of information would temporarily close off and fortunately I could pick back up where I left off and continue moving forward on my search and journey.
  - (1Cor. 2:9-12)BSB "As it is written, no eye has seen, no ear has heard, no heart has imagined, what God has prepared for those who love Him. But God has revealed it to us by the Spirit. The Spirit searches all things even the deep things of God. For who among men knows the thoughts of man except his own spirit within him? So too, no one knows the thoughts of God except the Spirit of God. We have not received the spirit of the world, but the Spirit who is from God, that we may understand what God has freely given us."
- Our **Advocate (John 14:26)**KJV "But the Advocate, the Holy Spirit, whom the Father will send in My name, He will teach you all things and will bring to your remembrance, whatsoever I have said unto you."
  - He is our Advocate in our relationship with God.
  - He is our Teacher and **Minister** in the blessed process of taking all the things of Christ: showing them to us, imparting them to us and testifying to us.
- * I could have begun or ended this chapter with this critical information, but instead felt placing it in between would assist you in having a greater understanding. ** We can NOT pray to

<u>God without the Holy Spirit, and He will NOT pray to God for us when we are not in Him!</u>

o   The following passage often relates to other topics, but do not miss the message as it relates to the Holy Spirit, **(Matt 12:25-32)** Jesus teaches that a divided house will fall, and in the mainstream is often associated with the family, or with business, or government, etc., but His context is regarding the Holy Spirit. So if we call ourselves Believer's yet we do not have anything much to do with the Holy Spirit, then we WILL fail. Jesus takes it a step further to point out that all of your sins are forgiven except if you (disrespect) "blasphemy" against the Holy Spirit (considered the unpardonable sin).

o   **The Power of Discernment** (The Holy Spirit our **Coach and Interpreter**)

   ▪   **One of the gifts He gives us is discernment; a powerful tool that we use in our daily interactions with our fellow man (as in discerning the thoughts and intentions of the heart; Heb. 4:12); the ability of having a sharp perception that allows you to make nuanced judgements to accommodate God's kingdom over the things of this world. * And of greater importance is having the ability to discern messages from God via the Holy Spirit; meaning that when you hear a sermon you are able to pick out (discern) key words and topics in which the Lord is specifically delivering to you and/or you are then able to supernaturally go to specific areas of scripture to further your wisdom, knowledge and understanding.

   ▪   Discernment is often instantaneous for a mature Believer but can still be a delayed revelation so to better fit into God's perfect timing. Also discernment is quite common <u>a product of **prayer**</u>, meaning that prayer in petition for something such as a revelation of what to do about employment opportunities, <u>triggers</u> the power of discernment (the Holy Spirit is ever present and listening) which opens doors that were previously closed or unnoticed by you; or leads, guides and directs you in the way you are to go; or reveals things that were not apparent previously that will assist you in making the right decision; etc.

      •   Prayer definitely triggers the Holy Spirit into discernment action. But also when you are pondering a question about just about anything/everything, the Holy Spirit will spark your attention to something related and you consciously know that was Him and when you direct those thoughts towards Him in pursuing an answer he really kicks in. It's the same for when you are searching for something. Especially when it has to do with a query pertaining to God's kingdom and His truths, the Holy Spirit works double time and it is amazing how the dots start connecting from so many different sources, what transpires in reading scripture, listening to sermons, influences of others and then what conclusion is achieved.

- Morning "**First Thoughts**" is another area that the Holy Spirit triggers. Similar to as just commented on, if your 1st thoughts are of God the Holy Spirit can often cause your mind to race in trying to keep up with the information being presented; if your 1st thoughts are about what you have a passion for, the Holy Spirit will provide you with discernment of insight so to help you in your endeavors; and if your 1st thoughts are worrisome, fearful or fleshly/sinful in nature you'll actually minimize the Spirit, that is if you do not heed His prompting to not worry or be fearful, or His warnings of correction of sin, and if that is the case then you can choose to freely ponder those things.

- We can now discern truth from error (the error of our ways).

- *** Discernment is a gifting of spiritual wisdom.**

- Discernment is an amazing skill that the Holy Spirit guides and directs you in first identifying, then learning, and honing it to a talent. It is incredibly beneficial not only in your walk with the Spirit, but with achieving and maintaining an abundant life. What is discernment? A general definition is, a power of the mind by which it distinguishes one thing from another, as a truth versus a falsehood, a virtue from vice; the power of perception in terms of the differences of things or ideas or how things relate; a connecting of the dots is a common tool used when discerning; acuteness of judgement (not judging others because only One does that; rather the ability to come to right and correct decision making and actions).

A definition from my personal experience is difficult to put into words, at least a congruent statement in which others can grasp the importance and depth to what it is, but here goes: it is having this special connection to the Holy Spirit of God and your mind has now expanded exponentially and you are able to pick up on so much that you had never even thought possible or even attempted; it's a heightened awareness of everything and yes it takes a lot of time to get to that point and yes it takes a concerted effort but it is not something you are obsessing over, it comes hand in hand with your walk with Him and the non-verbal communication that you share; at the very least it is very special. The numerous times in the book in which I made the comment, "this is just another example of the Holy Spirit coming to my assistance," here I'm referring to the process in which He gave me the discernment to identify those things that He wants to bring to my attention and those things He wants to bring to my remembrance.

- Paul said in **(1Cor 2:13-15)**BSB "And this is what we speak, not in words taught us by human wisdom, but in words taught by the Spirit, expressing spiritual truths in spiritual words. The natural man (unbeliever) does not accept the things that come from the Spirit of God. For they are foolishness to him, and he cannot understand them, because they are spiritually discerned. The spiritual man judges all things, but he himself is not subject to anyone's judgment. "For who has known the mind of the Lord, so as to instruct Him?" But we have the mind of Christ.

- Jeremiah said in **(1Kings 3:9)**BSB "Therefore give Your servant an understanding heart to judge Your people and to discern between good and evil. For who is able to govern this great people of Yours?"

- *Don't just gloss over this, it is a significant revelation. In that, it relays <u>that a "Believer" is one who walks in the Spirit and therefore receives discernment to understand the spiritual things of God</u>. Often you will encounter people who disclose that they do not understand or comprehend what they've heard with respect to the Bible and this is typically the reason for it. It is often an immediate giveaway that they are an unbeliever, a pseudo-Christian, or possibly a babe in Christ (regardless of how many years they've been in the church) who hasn't matured in their walks and receiving communication and discernment from the Holy Spirit.

- So yes, I have a gift of discernment. Is it the same as the gift of prophecy? No, there is a close parallel, but I wouldn't go as far to say there is a fine line between them. Both involve your walk with the Holy Spirit, and both are messages from the Holy Spirit, but prophecy could be described as discernment multiplied by ten. Much of my discernment in retrospect was prophetic, but that is one example that illustrates that the two are different. A person with a gift of the prophetic, knows up front that they have insight that few others if any would know and that they receive a message and are prompted to relay a message of prophesy to someone else. For me, I am too humble to ever tell someone that what I am going to tell them is a prophetic message, rather I will just tell them I think, or I believe this or that, relayed as Godly advice. As I mentioned, I cannot tell you the number of times that my discernment and statements eventually did come to fruition, but I just do not believe that I have the spiritual gift of prophecy.

- In summary, this is very important for you to know, for your walk and for your abundant life. Additionally, in 1Cor. 12 Paul lists the "gifts of the Spirit," and prophecy is one of them, but as you'll notice that discernment is not listed. So, jump to joy that it is NOT allocated to a special few, and my point being that it is available to all. Therefore, it is imperative that you work on developing this skill at first and then master it as a talent. As mentioned, it takes your walk with the Spirit, with Jesus and with the Father to an entirely different level, and thus propelling your maturity and securing your accomplishing and maintaining an abundant life!

- On a side note, the Godly advice I just spoke of, I can't tell you the number of times I've had people come back to me and say, "You were right." And I always respond in this same way, "It was NEVER about being right, all I

211

was trying to do was to help you." Also I've got to add that most of the time when I was responding my eyes were watering up from the outpouring of the Holy Spirit. He tells me to respond that way, out of truth, because it was never about me and it was never about being right, but it was all about the message that God wanted relayed. So take to heart what is told to you by someone who has told you that they are giving you the Godly advice that you seek and/or when that advice is coming from a person who you know is a person of discernment, or finally a person who you know has the gift of the prophetic and you know that it is truly out of their giving nature and not selfish intent. In your development and walk with the Spirit, you can ask Him for the legitimacy of the individual and of the message they are relaying and He will confirm it.

- o **Wisdom, (James 1:5-6)**KJV "If any of you lack wisdom, let him ask of God who gives to all men liberally and without finding fault, it shall be given unto him. But let him ask in faith, nothing wavering (doubt not). For he that wavers is like a wave of the sea driven with the wind and tossed."
  - Relaying and imparting God's Wisdom is one of the primary purposes of the Holy Spirit. As stated at the beginning of this chapter: God's $_1$wisdom which gives you $_2$knowledge and $_3$understanding of $_4$His kingdom and the $_5$things and ways of this world via the $_6$Bible, the guidebook to life and abundant living and this is all accomplished via your walk with the $_7$Holy Spirit.
- o The unforgivable sin **(Luke 12:10)**KJV Jesus said, "And everyone who speaks a word against the Son of Man will be forgiven, but whoever blasphemes against the Holy Spirit it will not be forgiven."
  - To blaspheme is to show contempt towards; to be insulting towards; to show a lack of reverence towards (reverence is a more significant form of the term: respect).
  - This showing of contempt is accomplished by: after having been witnessed to, you reject God; reject His offer of forgiveness and therefore reject a new life in Jesus Christ; in doing this you are calling the witness of the Holy Spirit a lie; another way is to mock God. This is

212

also the case for those who are saved but then decide afterwards at some point to reject God.

- o Speaking in tongues. He gives us utterance when we do not know exactly what to say to God in prayer. A gift from the Holy Spirit to speak supernaturally to God while at the same time edifying (building up, improving) oneself spiritually. He assists us in building a mansion out of our shack that we once lived.
  - Tongues will be covered in greater detail in this chapter and throughout the book.
  - Along those same lines, the Holy Spirit provides intercession for us with the Father and the Son by communicating prayers on our behalf that we cannot think of, nor utter in tongues, or cannot formulate clearly.
- o * He is the **Spirit of truth**, therefore He brings the "Living" Bible to LIFE for us! Also He is continuously filling us with the truth of God so that we conduct ourselves in a righteous manner and also in order to maximize our lives: to have life and have it abundantly.
  - He "bears witness" to us by the Word of God and what its proper context is! For example, when we hear a false teaching He intercedes by His witness and supersedes what is false with revealing to us what is right (the Truth). Of course, this takes our commitment and dedication to walking in the Spirit daily.
  - *We all self-talk, meaning we talk to ourselves. Without the Holy Spirit unrestrained self-talk leads to negativity, temptation and sinning, etc. He replaces the self-talk of our old man (old woman) with an inner-speak which is a direct line to God and to the Word. It really boils down to what we want most out of life whether to "choose" to focus on the inner-speak of God or to focus on our mind's wondering thoughts and self-talk that can get us into trouble.
    - * If you are familiar with fishing line, it is typically monofilament which means one continuous line (or single thread). I referenced a direct line to God which strongly influences our inner-speak, this is similar to that single continuous thread and it runs from our spirit directly to God. That single continuous thread is the Holy Spirit!

213

- In **(2 Cor. 4:13)** Paul refers to the self-same spirit that we as Believer's share in common and have within us; that same spirit that I've previously referred to as having known God before the beginning of time and the same that makes up what we are comprised of: spirit, soul and body.
  - The Spirit of God (our single thread to God) works mightily with our spirit so that we grow in the sanctification process and continue striving to become the person that God has predestined and purposed us to be.
- Along similar lines as self-talk, we also <u>self-limit</u>. You're probably thinking, "no kidding." Ask any elite professional athlete, actor, actress, entertainer, etc. and just because they may be one in a billion, they're still going to tell you they battle the self-limiting, <u>negative stinkin-thinkin</u> thoughts on a regular and frequent basis. Just as all of us common people have on probably a much more frequent basis. I cannot stress the importance of the role the Holy Spirit plays in significantly reducing our self-talk and our self-limiting thoughts (from our faith, to negative thinking, to wrongful thoughts as per our carnal nature, to every topic under the sun). That is one of the things Paul was referring to in the importance of our daily walk in the Spirit and the renewing of the mind daily in the Word. *The Holy Spirit is a powerful tool (or often a weapon to use in battle) to repair your mind and thoughts to thinking the way that God meant for you to and subsequently living the abundant life. For more on this topic see Chapters 9 & 10 "Spiritual Warfare and The Mind."
- "Computer Reset" is when you have a significant problem and you have to reset a computer to a previously established reference point of information or format, or if that doesn't fix the problem you now have a major one and have to wipe the memory clean to reformat and start fresh with new instructions (software). The good news for us is that He will never forsake us, and therefore we are never broken beyond repair (that is if we so choose to be "repaired"). Who are you associating with and who are you listening to? As mentioned, are you listening to

214

your self-talk; the voices of others (see Job's so called friends and their advice); or listening to the collective voices of this world (media as in TV shows whether reality or other, news whether accurate or fake, etc.)? When you listen to things that stand in opposition to God and you end up acting on those things, it can significantly corrupt your spirit, soul and body. If you're a Believer, you know you have the opportunity to "reset" by repenting and fellowshipping with God via our Lord Jesus and the Holy Spirit. Under these circumstances the Holy Spirit is our saving grace and an integral part helping us get back on track.

- **(1 Cor. 15:33)**NIV "Do not be misled, bad company corrupts good character."
- **(Prov. 13:20)**KJV "He that walks with wise men shall be wise; but a companion of fools shall be destroyed!"
- **(Prov. 4:14-19)**BSB "Enter not into the path of the wicked and do not in the way of evil men. Avoid it, do not travel on it; turn from it and go on your way. For they cannot rest until they do evil; they are robbed of sleep till they make someone stumble. They eat the bread of wickedness and drink the wine of violence. The path of righteousness is like the morning sun, shining ever brighter till the full light of day. But the way of the wicked is like deep darkness; they do not know what makes them stumble."
- **(Prov. 18:21)**NKJV "Death and life are in the power of the tongue, and those who love it will eat its fruit."

o He **Leads, Guides and Directs** us in our paths while on this experiential spiritual life journey on earth. (see Ch.3 for additional info)

o The Holy Spirit replaced the Law.
   ▪ The Law could only relay God's will to man.
   ▪ The Holy Spirit assists man to **fulfill** God's will.
   ▪ That is why it is said that "the Holy Spirit replaced the Law." Jesus's works on the cross initiated the process but it wasn't until we are saved and filled with the Holy Spirit that He assists us in fulfilling God's will, that is, if we are walking in the Spirit daily.

- Note: The Law is now our moral compass to assist us in understanding what the Holy Spirit is having us fulfill.
  - Research the following to better understand what is meant by the Holy Spirit replacing the Law: Jesus's role in abolishing the punishment and bondage of the law / written on stone vs. on our hearts/ the letter kills **(as Paul conveyed in 2Cor. 3:6)**.
  - Without the punishment and bondage of the law, a couple of the Holy Spirit's critical responsibilities to a Believer is:
    - **Corrects** us of sin
    - **Convinces** us not to sin and of the importance of righteousness and judgment
      - For detailed information on correcting and convincing see Ch10 subchapter/enemy "Condemners" this is a <u>must read</u> due to the importance. The following bullet point is an excerpt of the 4pgs of information:
      - * You must be walking in the Spirit daily and communicating, otherwise you cannot receive the correction and He will default to convicting. You do not want to be convicted like unbelievers, because next He is condemning you of sin, rather than what He does for Believers: correcting and convincing us to do what is right (and not to sin in the first place), which is a BIG difference.
    - Instill "God Confidence" by the dramatic results of the Holy Spirit's works in our lives!
  - **(2 Cor. 3:18)**NKJV "But we all with unveiled face, beholding as in a mirror the glory of the Lord, are being transformed into the same image **from glory to glory**, just as **by the Spirit** of the Lord."
    - Just as the Holy Spirit is our "single thread" connecting us to God, here Paul relays that the Holy Spirit plays the integral role in the transformation of our entire being to becoming the same image of Jesus (sanctification process).
  - * When the Spirit of God comes upon a man/woman He creates a new nature with vigor and purity. The mere fact that this new nature does indeed exist in Believer's is <u>evidence</u> that the Gospel

216

is true. That evidence is appropriate since Jesus's religion is one of truth, love, purity, holiness, grace, meekness and relationships to name a few. No other religion makes men new creatures, no other religion even pretends to do so. At best other religions may attempt to improve the existing nature of a man/woman, but again none of them can say "Behold I make all things new, <u>again</u>!" **(Rev. 21:5 & Eph. 4:24)KJV**

- *Tell me, those of you who are saved, you are conscious that you are not what you used to be; you are conscious of a new life within your soul; you are conscious of the fact that God himself dwells inside of you (as the Holy Spirit of God) and He comforts, guides and directs you; that you know that you are born again (which by the Greek means **born of God** from above) and that this is your <u>evidence</u> that the Gospel is the truth of God. Whereas you can read the Bible and the Holy Spirit can show you insurmountable evidence, BUT it could never measure up to your personal experience, in that you know that you know beyond a shadow of doubt that you are a new man/woman in Christ!

  - * **(1 John 5:4)KJV "Whatsoever is <u>born of God</u>, overcomes the world."** Overcomes means victor or victory.

o He who rests in Jesus, **honors** <u>the Spirit of God</u>; and he who values his inner life **believes** in the Spirit of God.

  - **The Spirit of God is Almighty and * <u>the complete master over the realm of the mind</u>**.

    - One example of our internal battles is in **(James 4:1)BLB** "What is the source of the quarrels and conflicts among you? Is not the source your own lusts that wage war in your members (incl. mind)?" This is just one example of how exceedingly important the Holy Spirit is to us, for He is the master over the realm of our minds. See chapters on the mind and spiritual warfare for additional information.

  - *The Holy Spirit has the <u>power</u> to illuminate the intellect, to win the affections (to win over by persuasion), to curb the will, and change the entire nature of man **(Eph. 1:11)BSB** "He works all things for His own pleasure."

    - It is in the record that He converted three thousand in one day!

217

- **(1 John 5:6)**KJV "Jesus Christ came by water and by blood. And it is the Spirit who bears witness, because the Spirit is truth."
- **(1 John 5:7)**KJV "For there are three that bear witness in heaven: The Father, The Word and the Holy Spirit; and these three are one.
- **(1 John 5:8)**KJV "And there are three that bear witness on earth: The Spirit, the water, and the blood; and these three agree as one.
  - Note, the Holy Spirit is also represented by oil; and Jesus is represented also by water and blood.
  - In the OT the rite of passage for a priest to enter into the tabernacle of God required a ritual involving oil, water and blood. Today we have access to all three: the water and blood (Jesus) and the oil (Holy Spirit) and with that we have our rite of passage to God.
    - This record is stated in **(1 John 5:10)**KJV "He that believes on the Son of God has the witness in himself." Meaning that by you BELIEVING in Jesus as the Son of God who was raised from the dead for the forgiveness of your sins, now also has the Holy Spirit (witness) indwelling you. This is what I was just referring to that we now have the rite of passage to the Father.
  - God has directed man to make a record of these events and truths (Bible) and is also witnessed by the three that are in agreement on earth with the three that agree as one in heaven.
  - Note: The Holy Spirit bore witness to Jesus while on earth from birth to throughout His life and after His ascension. For example in **(Mat. 3:16-17)**NIV "As soon as Jesus was baptized, he went up out of the water. At that time heaven was opened and he saw the Spirit of God descending like a dove and alighting on him. And a voice from heaven said, 'This is my Son, whom I love, with him I am well pleased."
- Jesus communicated that the Holy Spirit is **likened** to the wind **(John 3:8)** KJV "The wind blows where it wishes, and you hear its sound, but you do not know where it comes from or where it goes. So this is the case with everyone who is born of the Spirit." Here Jesus is

illustrating the "essence" of the Holy Spirit, although not seen by human eyes, we can see His effect on the Believer's life, just like the invisible wind and its definite effects on the environment. Even though we don't know where He is at any given time, we still know He is there and we've trained ourselves to hear His still small voice and we can see the definite impact and results that He has on our lives and is evidence that we are God's own child.

- **(John 3:6-7)**NKJV "That which is born of flesh is flesh, and that which is 'born of the Spirit' is spirit. Do not marvel that I said to you, 'you must be born again." In addition, the point should be made that everyone is born of the flesh, BUT only those who are God's are born of the Spirit!

- **(Gal. 6:8)**KJV "For he that sows to the flesh shall of the flesh reap corruption; but he that sows to the Spirit shall of the Spirit reap life everlasting." And to continue that, those who sow their time and energies in walking with the Spirit to renew daily will reap the abundant life that God desires for them and to fulfill the reason Jesus came to earth that they may have life and have it abundantly.

o This is an interesting discussion concerning the Holy Spirit, there are 2 schools of thought, but you decide based on your research, understandings and relationship with Him; a portion of Believers think of the Holy Spirit:

- As a person of God that goes by the name of Holy Spirit, who is there for us to talk to intimately, walk with Him daily and call Him by name. Since He is part of the triune, and is THE "Spirit of God," and as Jesus put it "He is another comforter and Spirit of truth who takes my place," basically Jesus's double (or icon if you will) here on earth. The Holy Spirit represents the entire triune when we are "in our walk with Him."

- As Spirit; in the form of anonymity; and who testifies of Jesus and is His double (or icon if you will) here on earth; and who witnesses to us and a witness for us; and in which we should be in "agreement" with **(1 John 5:8)** as we walk in the journey together **(Amos 3:3)**.

I'm not saying you have to choose, just relaying the prevailing two schools of thought. For me, He has been an incredible part of this journey and I combine the 2 thoughts for the best of both worlds. As you can see by what I've conveyed in this book, I love and cherish the relationship I have with the Holy Spirit, as I do with the Father and the Son.

○ We have the offer from the Lord to be One with Him! Please note, that the only way to become One with Him is by being In the Spirit!

○ The Holy Spirit provides clarity. Clarity is POWER! The Holy Spirit brings forth that which is out of focus.

Water Baptism & The Baptism of the Holy Spirit

There is some controversy over these two baptisms, and I use the word controversy because it is more than just a disagreement. My intent is NOT to validate any specific denominations doctrine, rather it is to relay exactly what it says in God's Word, the truth as it is written. You should read the scriptures on John the Baptist and how he approached baptizing with water and specifically when he baptized Jesus **(Matt 3)** to give you a foundation from which this can build upon. Jesus was fully immersed in the water and it states specifically that when He "came out" of the water, the Heavens opened up... This is an example and model for us in that when we are immersed in the water baptism it symbolizes our death of the old man/woman in conjunction with Jesus's death and then we "come out" a new man/woman as Jesus did when He was resurrected into a new life. In other parts of this book it is pointed out that we die with Jesus and we are resurrected with Jesus into a new life.

Now is water baptism a requisite for your salvation. No, your salvation is available due to Jesus's works on the cross and salvation takes place as a one-time gift when you commit in faith your life to Jesus in prayer. If your salvation was dependent on you getting baptized, then that is by your works and Jesus made it clear that there is nothing you can do to earn your salvation. Now is water baptism important to your walk and relationship with the Lord? Yes, for a number of reasons. First, it is your public acknowledgement that you have been saved by Jesus, and that you have had a conversion from your sinful past to following Christ in obedience, and your life is now transformed and thus you are a new man/woman in Christ, etc. Second, with acknowledging this to all, it also becomes your very personal acknowledgement directed towards God the Father, Jesus Christ and the Holy Spirit that you are the adopted son and brother of God. There is power in this act for those who are committed and take it seriously. And I can vouch for my experience, it didn't seem to impact my devotion or my enthusiasm although maybe briefly, but over time it did impact my relationship with Him, it solidified and strengthened and even enhanced it by making it a more intimate experience which has continued to build upon year after year. For me, it was as though we entered into a covenant (or just on my part a personal pledge) and understanding which caused the relationship to flourish over time and I believe it to this day.

One way of looking at this is, can a child commit to Him and a baptism by desiring a public acknowledgement? So why the rush to get a baby or a child baptized? Typically misunderstandings, false teachings, the parent is playing on the safe side (children are safe anyway, if they happen to lose their life they are immediately present with the Lord; this is a stop-gap measure since they hadn't an opportunity to "choose" to be saved); or their particular church doctrine requires a baptism takes place; or it's again the entertainment side of the church in that it's memorable and it creates loyalties out of possibly two generations. The child example should be sufficient an explanation although there are many more. Is it a requisite? No. Is it important? Yes very much so. And I recommend you make every effort to follow through with participating in a water baptism that has an experienced pastor properly praying over you.

In relation to the baptism of the Holy Spirit, is this a requisite of "receiving" the Holy Spirit? This is where the arguments between denominations get more intense. Some believe that you receive the Holy Spirit when you are saved; others when you are water baptized; and yet others believe you must have hands laid upon you in prayer as you are asking for the Holy Spirit to dwell in you. There are numerous teachings referring to this from Acts to many of Paul's epistles, therefore much of your decision to be baptized in the Spirit, or not, will rely on your discernment of these teachings/truths and hopefully not on what man is trying to convince you to do. Note that Baptism of the Holy Spirit and speaking in tongues typically go hand-in-hand but not always, so we will cover both topics here consecutively.

Peter and John **(Acts 8:17-19)** and Paul relay **(Acts 19:6)** ***that by the laying of hands specifically by him and the other disciples of Jesus along with prayer and declaration of Jesus's name, as well as the asking in prayer by the recipient is how an individual receives the Holy Spirit. Similar to the argument with water baptism in which it is strongly recommended but not absolutely necessary, to not be baptized in the Spirit will not keep the Holy Spirit from working inside of you, but having said that, it is strongly advised that you do indeed get baptized in the Spirit as an acknowledgement that you desire a relationship with Him and to gain His help. For me personally, I chose to be baptized in the Holy Spirit because I understood it to be similar to the water baptism results and it was just that. Even though I know that the Holy Spirit was with me since the day I was saved, it was not until I went through the process of the baptism of the Holy Spirit that I then felt a greater connection and closer more intimate relationship. It's just been

221

amazing the discernment He provides me and how we are able to work in tandem, me posing questions and thoughts and He reveals the answers to me in our walk. Throughout this book I have praised the relationship I have with Him, it is invaluable and would not have it any other way, and I would like for everyone else to have this same experience. Please note that I have baptized a few people in the Holy Spirit and would like to add an important point, as I had mentioned in water baptism, be sure that the person baptizing you is experienced at it and prays over you properly.

Speaking in Tongues

In addition to someone receiving the Spirit, from that point forward they have the ability to speak in tongues (a form of unidentifiable utterance from your spirit/soul in prayer to God). Speaking in tongues is merely an "utterance." What that means is, we'll get a nudge from the Holy Spirit to pray, but there are times in which you do not really know what to say, so we can give utterance to God instead by speaking in tongues. You say, "I don't understand?" That's right, because if you try to figure it out you will mess it up. I'm not joking, that is the case. Have faith. Actually I've told you all that you need to know as a babe with speaking in tongues, because you need to "Just Do It," and after a while I would have given you the advanced instruction and you would be more apt to continue, to accept and to understand, and then the Holy Spirit would guide you in accomplishing the process. You say, "That's not a good enough of an explanation." Well, let me say it in a different way but I'm telling you that we'll come to the same conclusion and this is one of those things that you will have to step out in faith and trust in it, then down the road look back at whether it is working for you. So this will be a bonus section because this is out of Volume 3 of this book for the advanced study. Okay, first of all rather than referring to it as utterance, let's call it jabbering. Similar to a one year old baby learning to speak and just jabbering away. That's actually a good analogy because you may be mature in your walk, but a babe when it comes to speaking in tongues, and because this is a process. I came up with the word "jabber" because my personality is such that I just tell it like it is. Although I do not want that word to mislead you! Initially I misled myself into believing it was just jabber and some supernatural mystical thing that I did not understand was taking place, but that was until the Holy Spirit stepped in and revealed the truth to me. Jabber is only partly accurate, in that what you are saying is jabber to you (and to others) but the key and the part that makes this fully accurate is that ** you are to intensely focus and center your thoughts that are based in your spiritual heart and spiritual mind that you are petitioning or are praising and release them by allowing those thoughts to travel through your jabber (utterance) to God. I know, I know, that from a logical rational view it does not make any sense, but this is a supernatural process, so again have faith and trust in this process and it will not take long for the Holy Spirit to <u>validate it</u> for you and assist you in accomplishing it! * Another important aspect of speaking in tongues that should help you to understand the process, is that you are to "let go" from your **soul** <u>"controlling" the process</u> and <u>the content of the prayer</u>. Having said that, as you let go and speak in tongues, be sure to focus all of your thoughts on Jesus or a specific topic matter of God and not just go on a senseless jabbering spree. This letting go of the soul's control and <u>allowing your spirit and the Holy Spirit to take over</u>, is yet another step in <u>your maturing</u> in the Lord. Another key point that should connect the dots for you is, * **(Genesis 1)** In the beginning <u>God...thought</u> and <u>created</u>, then <u>He spoke</u> things into existence and then <u>He saw</u> that it was good, and not along those same lines BUT rather in the exact same way, we think and create and we speak things into existence and in those times that it doesn't make sense to us, or it is too complicated to us, or you cannot put your thoughts into words, is when you speak in tongues...you jabber/give utterance to God by intensely focusing on your thoughts in your spiritual heart and your spiritual mind and the Holy Spirit will see to it that it gets delivered! Also keep in mind that the Bible relays that the Holy Spirit also intercedes for us in speaking to God those things that <u>cannot be uttered</u>. **(Rom. 8:26)**KJV "Likewise the Spirit also helps with our weaknesses: for we know not what we should pray for as we ought: but the <u>Spirit itself makes intercession for us with groanings which cannot be uttered</u>."

Speaking in tongues is a controversial subject so do not get caught up like many do in thinking it is foolish or it's demonic because it is definitely neither. Please research the numerous mentioning's of this in scriptures of speaking in tongues and again this is one in which <u>you must be the decision maker</u>. I personally have embraced speaking in tongues but have to admit have never been consistent in doing so. There have been times in my journey in which I did it regularly but at other times I went for a year with only having done it once or twice. I can't put my finger on why I do not speak in tongues as often as I probably should. There is although one instance that may have been the perfect situation and setting to do so, therefore I took advantage of the prompting and encouraging me to do so and believe it was due to the environment I was in. This took place when I was on the island of Bermuda for a couple of years and I lived close to a park in which I enjoyed going there to relax and read God's Word. I also got my exercise by walking the wooded trails that overlooked the expanse of the ocean. It was there I found a patch of large mature Bermudian pine trees on the edge of a cliff also overlooking the ocean, it was very picturesque and serene. When the wind would pick up it made unique sounds as it rushed through the pine needles and definitely got my attention. This is a perfect example of when nature serves as a channel to get closer to God and in this case, nature also acted as a facilitator in making it easier for me to speak in tongues to God. Before that experience I felt it important to <u>not</u> just randomly and senselessly speak which is easy to do when you don't even know what you are saying, but I would always focus my thoughts on topics that I wanted relayed to God only I was speaking in tongues (incomprehensible jabber; *but with focused thoughts of the spiritual mind and of the spiritual heart). In retrospect (looking back on it), I understand now that it was the Holy Spirit revealing and instructing me to utilize this process of focused thought of the spiritual heart and mind, because there was no explanation or teaching of this in the mainstream. Yet another example of how your walk with the Holy Spirit bears tremendous fruit, especially when there is no other source to obtain the information from. Therefore, I still adhere to that practice and was doing so while I was amongst the pine trees and that was the first time in years that I really felt I was accomplishing, releasing pertinent thoughts to God in an unknown language that relayed the information better than I could in English.

Also, speaking in tongues is supposed to edify the person doing it (that is uplift them in terms of spiritual development; of their spiritual heart and mind) and this too was accomplished, especially in improving my outlook, next my awareness and my discernment, which factored in to improving my overall relationship with the Father, the Son and the Holy Spirit (i.e. spiritual development). In other words it worked, but it took this incredible opportunity (that most would never have as an option) after years of perseverance with little to show for it and with little progress towards understanding it and any benefits, for me to finally let go on a daily basis and speak in tongues to the Lord and experience the true fruits of what I was doing. I wanted to add that the years prior to Bermuda I would speak in tongues in very short blurbs maybe 1 – 2 minutes at the very most, but while amongst the pine trees I found myself speaking for 10, 15, 20 minutes at a time, similar to what I do when I am praying, 5 – 15 minutes is average but can be upwards to 30 – 40min. Having just penned this explanation on paper, I believe that if you practice with an intense focus and mindset to accomplish relaying your thoughts to God in tongues then you do not need the picturesque environment to set the focus, rather do it in your mind as you would during meditation. That experience has afforded me the opportunity now to currently relay my thoughts in tongues without consideration to my environment and remains an uplifting process for me. Although as mentioned, I do not utilize it as much as I should in my journey. I've heard pastors suggest doing it while driving but even though I'm a proficient multi-tasker, I can't imagine trying to focus my thoughts, speak in tongues and pay attention to driving, but that's me. You've seen all the ads that distracted drivers cause accidents, therefore do not text and drive. For me, I would say do not speak in tongues and drive☺. Save it for when you are in your quiet place where you pray, meditate and can focus on effectively speaking in tongues to God and realize the true benefits in doing so.

Fasting

I'm going to shift gears for a moment and touch on the subject of fasting and yes, Jesus wants us and expects us to fast. Jesus is our model that we desire to become more like each day by day. He led by example and He taught on what we are to do, say, think, act, etc. Fasting was one thing that He made clear that we are to do, both for spiritual reasons and for health reasons.

During the entire time in the wilderness and His battle with Satan, Jesus was fasting. So He was in the wilderness for forty days and during that time He was battling a common temptation to eat food, but fasted, and continued to do so as He was in a spiritual battle with Satan. "Jesus having <u>refused each temptation</u>, Satan then departed, and Jesus returned to Galilee to begin his ministry."

> **(Matt 6:16-18)**BSB "When you fast, do not look somber as the hypocrites do, for they disfigure their faces to show others they are fasting. Truly I tell you, they have received their reward in full. But when you fast, put oil on your head and wash your face, so that it will not be obvious to others that you are fasting, but only to your Father, who is unseen; and your Father, who sees what is done in secret, will reward you.

Fasting is a <u>willing abstinence</u> or <u>reduction from</u> certain <u>or all</u> food, drink, or both, for a period of time, depending on a person's strength. And not just food or drink but also includes any and all temptations, from watching TV to going shopping, etc. Jesus' own words reveal that the <u>purpose of His fasting was to draw near to God</u> whether for His love and attention or for His help.

Previously in this chapter, I've spoken on discernment and the Holy Spirit and fasting heightens all of your senses and heightens the ability to "hear" the Holy Spirit's small quiet voice and in turns magnifies your discernment of all things, also search for the Holy Spirit's guidance by going to your "quiet place" and pray. That is one reason why it is important to fast during times of troubles and needing God's help (esp. during spiritual battles; see also Ch6 "Covid19" and the benefit of fasting during an illness).

Everything I just relayed about fasting, I've experienced and would like to say that I strongly suggest you take up the practice for the reasons previously mentioned. Sure at first it is difficult, and it takes routine disciplined practice and after your first year of fasting one three day weekend every other month it should become habit and you will have noticed the many benefits associated with fasting.

225

Whenever I feel I am coming down with a cold or flu, if I do not wait too late and catch it early, I will fast and almost always dodge the bullet of a prolonged illness. More importantly, fasting does heighten my senses significantly and Jesus said that its primary reason for Him was to draw near God. For me, I always <u>draw near</u> to the Holy Spirit when I fast and that is the greatest benefit, next to the <u>improved communication</u> that takes place. Whenever I plan a fasting weekend, I never dread it but rather look forward to it, because I plan the weekend around spending it with Jesus, the Holy Spirit and the Father and always finding myself giving thanks for the opportunity to spend time with them. For some people that will be hard for them to understand and they'll write me off as a fanatic, but I am not a fanatic. I just know that 5-6 times in a year I plan to spend significant time with my God, otherwise it would never get done. Also, people who spend hours in meditation may be able to relate better, because the process of fasting, spending time with them and having heightened communication, it becomes a truly powerful, energizing and fulfilling time. So please do not overlook the power and benefits of fasting and walking in the Spirit.

<u>Walk in the Spirit & To Be "In the Spirit 24/7"</u> **

As stated in another part of the book, sanctification for a Believer is an ongoing process of becoming holy which is taking place on earth and then continues into heaven. Another ongoing process that is associated with sanctification is to "Walk in the Spirit" then to mature in that walk to being "In the Spirit 24/7." By now you've also read that only one is perfect (Jesus) and to be in the Spirit 24/7 is impossible for man, however I wanted to relay that there is nothing wrong with doing your best to achieve it. To begin, we are to be born again (born from above) and at that time we are given the Holy Spirit to dwell inside of us. Note, the prior subchapter had to do with being baptized in the Holy Spirit in order to secure that it has taken place. The Holy Spirit plays a crucial role <u>in every aspect</u> of our life with the Lord and as a Believer you should understand that, embrace it and execute that relationship to the best of your ability. The Holy Spirit (as conveyed in My Lord's Prayer) leads us, guides us and directs us in all righteousness and in all truths, fills us with God's wisdom, leads us not into temptation and delivers us from evil. But that is just the beginning of the innumerable ways the Holy Spirit helps us and by the way He is known as our "helper."

We are instructed to "walk in the Spirit" daily which assists us in the renewing of our mind, which means that we are to communicate constantly and allow Him to lead us and to help us in discerning God's kingdom and the ways of the world. *The relationship we should have with the Holy Spirit is an intimate one in which we walk shoulder to shoulder with Him day and night (that is what is meant by walking in the Spirit). As you mature, it is not that you will rely less and less on

Him, rather you will <u>rely more and more on Him</u>, to the point in which hopefully you achieve communicating with Him 24/7, thus the term: In the Spirit. Therefore, your experiential spiritual life journey on earth should eventually be comprised of being "in the Spirit" or at least "walking in the Spirit" daily as He is helping you renew your mind daily in the Word of God; in other words He is our personal guide on this journey! Accordingly, whatever you put into it, you will get out of it (by whatever measure you sow, you will reap much more in this life and store up in heaven for your eternal life).

* Now that you've read an overview of walking in the Spirit and also being In the Spirit, and having read the "My Lord's Prayer" chapter about the Holy Spirit, you should have a very good idea of who the Holy Spirit is, what He does, how we access His power and how important He is to the success of our journey. So, there is much, much, more information as it pertains to the Holy Spirit because as I've mentioned, what He does for us is innumerable, therefore the balance of the book continues to provide additional information on Him. In Chapter 9, the Holy Spirit is mentioned 33 times and in the subchapter "Anatomy of a Temptation," it contains an important foundational principle, (excerpt) "When you are **saved** (a Believer) the devil has then been **a)** disarmed and minimized in your mind, also he does not have any power over you <u>unless you give it to him,</u> **b) the Holy Spirit dominates your inner spirit and mind** (therefore minimizing the devil and fleshly nature), also He has power and authority over the devil, **c)** the devil may be cunning but is no match for the Holy Spirit of God and the power of the Word of God (Bible) that renews your mind." ** The important foundational principle is that you must make a concerted effort to become "**Spirit Dominant**" and the above excerpt was a brief explanation of what is meant by that and the role the Holy Spirit plays in achieving it. Thus the progression is once you are saved to begin walking in the Spirit and as you are doing that you are simultaneously working on becoming Spirit Dominant, which leads you to being able to be In the Spirit 24/7 and this is obviously a process and often takes many years to achieve. So a brief overview may be needed here to clarify what's just been communicated, so that you understand the process because it can easily get confusing: the soul is the mind & the spirit is the heart; BUT the mind leads the heart (your spirit will follow a dominant soul)...BUT renewing your mind daily in the Word will give you dominant thoughts of the Holy Spirit in conjunction with your spirit, and thus will direct (you) your heart and mind (true you/real you/minimized soul) towards the things of God! (see additional information on this in Ch2 and illustration in Ch6 "Discourse on our soul and our spirit").

Many people are either confused or simply question what it means to be Spirit-Filled (a popular term used in the church today). The minute we are saved we are "filled" with the Holy Spirit and as the previous subchapter pointed out that sometimes it takes a dedication such as the baptism of the Holy Spirit to actualize it, causing you to be more aware of Him. Point is, once you are saved you are Spirit-Filled but as a babe you do not know how to utilize Him and over time hopefully you get more and more acquainted with Him and this is often what people are referring to as being Spirit-Filled, because He is our <u>servant leader</u> and anxious to work with us on everything. * Additional point, remember the key mentioned previously, it is imperative that you just don't get more acquainted with Him rather you walk in the Spirit, renew your mind and work on becoming Spirit Dominant. This is just another teaching that has been either forgotten, ignored, poorly preached or whatever you want to attribute it to and in turn has been detrimental to the Believer and detrimental to their ability to achieve an abundant life due to being ignorant of this principle.

You just read a couple of pages back the following excerpt but it bares mentioning again due to the following context: Jesus communicated that <u>the Holy Spirit is **likened** to the wind</u> (**John 3:8**)NKJV "The wind blows where it wishes, and you hear its sound, but you do not know where it comes from or where it goes. So this is the case with everyone who is born of the Spirit." Here Jesus is illustrating the "essence" of the Holy Spirit, although not seen by human eyes, we can see His effect on the Believer's life, just like the invisible wind and its definite effects on the environment. Even though we don't know where He is at any given time, we still know He is there and we've trained ourselves to hear His still small voice and we can see the definite impact and results that He has on our lives and is evidence that we are God's own child. So whether (**John 3:8**) or (**Acts 2:2**) I've listened to pastors who have preached that the Holy Spirit is like that of the wind. As in (**Acts 2:2**) which relayed that the Holy Spirit came into the upper room of the house the disciples were in (during Pentecost) and it "sounded like a mighty rushing wind that came from heaven." Note, it does not say the He is wind or that He is a mighty wind. Then the pastors use the example of how a Believer who tries to "walk" against the wind experiences resistance, versus "walking" with the wind experiences an ease or even a propulsion from it. So their conclusion is that if you are doing something in which you experience resistance then stop and change whatever you need to in order to find ease with what you are doing. This is all good, from the scripture references, to the analogy, to the experience description, but as I've pointed out with other topics it is too simplistic a message and thus misses the mark. The thing is, if they only just went into greater detail and took a deeper dive into the topic, they would have hit the mark. What I am referring to is to elaborate on what "walking in the Spirit" entails, from how we are to ask Him to play a role daily in our lives and then to pray and listen for His "still small voice" and allow Him to guide us through scripture and discernment

228

of all things and remembrance of all things, and with that when we experience resistance it is His nudging or even pulling that we are experiencing. Now is the time that we are to pray and ask for His guidance and He will answer and often in a wide range of ways, which will assist us in "changing" our direction and yes, we do then experience ease and even propulsion (or doors will open for us, etc.).

I've always been a very driven person (self-driven), so for me before my conversion, I would either experience resistance or had to jump over hurdles and even jump through hoops and continue until whatever I was trying to achieve finally succeeded or fell apart. Then I would move on to the next project and I've got to say that very few fell apart, therefore most (by the world's standards) were successful. Thing is, I never reacted to the resistance, but instead kept going full steam ahead. Believe me it was a paradigm shift and quite the learning experience to "walk in the Spirit" and learn how to have Him lead, guide and direct my paths, and to specifically take my foot off the gas, or to realize that I needed to change direction, or stop pursuing something completely, because I've always been so driven. Point here, is that you can continue to be self-driven...no that is incorrect, you can still be driven but no longer operating in self (or operating in your own strength = works), rather become a partner with the Holy Spirit by walking with Him daily and allowing Him to lead, guide and direct your paths on a daily basis and utilize God's power instead (God's power = abundant grace/blessings; i.e. abundant living). I'm here to say that it works, and boy does it ever. It also reduces the stress of what comes with being driven and/or a type "A" personality or otherwise.

So stop beating your head against the wall. Remember what the definition of insanity is, doing the same thing over and over again, but expecting different results. The same applies when you do not listen to the Holy Spirit and relying on your past experiences or some "inner feeling" to make decisions that have a high percentage chance to fail. If you are a Believer and have been or plan on doing the things I've suggested in this book, it is really not that difficult to take the time to pray and ask for guidance, to listen and receive and act accordingly. For many it will transform their life. Keep in mind that the natural progression from walking in the Spirit is to become closer and closer to the Holy Spirit in becoming Spirit Dominant, therefore to mature into being "In the Spirit 24/7" or as close as you can come to achieving it. Keep up the good race and continue to strive for this and it will definitely pay off in your relationship with the Lord and with living the abundant life.

Chapter 6 Bits of Wisdom / Diagrams***

Bits of Wisdom

Another unconventional approach, a sixth inning stretch so to speak in the middle of the two volumes. That is, it's time to take a break from the intense chapter topics, messages and teachings and read through some bullet point experiential topics, universal maxims, anecdotal stories, and then some very, very important intro topics of Jesus that continue into Volume II, and please see the 3 key diagrams that apply to other subchapter topics. Initially there is a mix of topics with some background of scripture attached to it and even though shorter in length they still have BIG messages (so please do not ignore this chapter). As a matter of fact, some of the most profound topics in this book are at the midpoint and latter half of this chapter, so be sure to read this chapter in its entirety because it has so many hidden gems that will benefit you.

Nothing is a replacement for God's wisdom (Jesus/the Bible from cover to cover), it is true wisdom through and through to its core (Jesus/God's Word in the flesh/the Truth). Nothing should replace or substitute God's wisdom, although experiential wisdom is a complement of God's wisdom because it involves a mix of scripture and teachings and has a big dose of what the world has to offer mixed in. The first part of this chapter has some "experiential wisdom" which I want to point out is NOT man's wisdom, although it may have some slight remnant sprinkled in, but the majority has a scriptural background and validity. The reason is because, principles are at times more easily understood in context to current day experiences rather than having to interpret non-related stories from thousands of years ago. Keep this in mind when reading through it and I hope that it is beneficial to you in your journey. Very importantly, also keep in mind to validate in prayer and in scripture and via the Holy Spirit all that I have relayed in this chapter and book.

Fear, Worry, Afraid (trap) vs. Focus

Don't get caught in the trap of saying to yourself or others, "Do not worry about…" Rather your statement should be, "You should focus on…" Example: Do not worry about your bills; Rather, You should focus on budgeting your expenses; focus on not spending money on non-essential goods; focus on what you can do at your job to earn a raise or make additional money; etc.

The same goes for do not fear or do not be afraid of ____, rather focus on what is related and important to correcting the situation. Some other examples of focus: focus on achieving; focus on doing; focus your energies on the task at hand; focus on the positive outcome.

Don't Feed Fear but rather Power your Faith

Do not feed your fear, it is fed by you focusing on your fear in relation to the situation. On the other hand, your FAITH is powered by you believing in God, trusting in God, having confidence in God and focusing on all these fronts, along with an intense focus on Jesus!

*Fear and Faith both work in the same manner and we process both the same way. Meaning: the more intense your focus is on fearing something, the more FEAR you will possess; likewise, the more intense your focus is on all the contributors to your faith, the more FAITH you will possess! Therefore, this allows you to be able to apply your power of faith (that Jesus administrated and gifted you with and helped you to grow and mature in).

"What do you have to lose"

This is an important point, you will never hear me relay to another person that you can be "saved" in terms of the following approaches "what do you have to lose" or "you have nothing to lose by trying." I just do not believe in this approach, primarily because if their "trying it out" is done with a lackluster approach then very likely it will be very short lived, therefore that approach is very misleading. Remember that the only one that can save is God, and that we are simply messengers who are at best trying to get the individual to open their heart to the idea of allowing Jesus to enter it and become Lord of their life. That is a BIG commitment and should be taken seriously, therefore we need to relay it in those terms, such as "If you are serious and believe that you could commit to an abundant life with Jesus as Lord of your life then this is how you go about it initially..." Also, "This is what you pray; also do so with conviction and enthusiasm...etc."

Never blame God

In my example of having to close a business I owned up until the Great Recession, it appeared that there were times that I was very distraught by what I had described. That is true and those times in which I repeatedly said that I was wanting answers from God, I want to make perfectly clear that never once did I blame Him in any way responsible for any event(s) related to that time of my life. As a matter of fact, never in my life have I blamed Him for anything. For example, when I lost my cousin Missy (who was my best friend) to ovarian cancer, I did not blame him for the disease or for allowing it or for not stepping in and healing her of it. For one thing, I know that in no way is God responsible for disease, untimely death or anything for that matter that is related to death because those events are a result of this world and not of His doing. I also do not believe that He allowed this to happen (as what took place in Job), because this was not a trial, test or

231

tribulation designed to benefit, grow or change her or anyone associated with her (although indirectly it impacted many others). Finally, He had his reason for not miraculously healing her. I would like to add this though, He definitely had His hand in giving her an extra year beyond what the doctors believed she had.

So I do not blame God for anything negative that happens to me, rather I praise him and believe that He is in control to the extent that He has willed for my life and that all things work together for good **(Romans 8:28)**KJV "And we know that all things work together for good to them that love God, to them who are the called according to his purpose."

Work/Life Harmony

A very common and talked about concept today is work/life balance. There are articles and articles and now books written about the topic. Briefly, it is practically impossible for many to balance the scales when it comes to work and family. Even though most people would love to spend more time with the family, they have demands and responsibilities that are essential in providing for their family which takes away from that precious time to spend with their family. Spending quality time with the family should be a priority in your journey with God and the Holy Spirit will guide you to achieve work-family **harmony**, that is if you are listening. Harmony is achievable whereas balance is probably impossible, so why add more stress to your life with something that you cannot accomplish? Focus on achieving harmony in this area and do so via the Spirit in prayer and supplication (requesting).

Love God 1st

There are a couple of places in this book about knowing the real you, also how you should love (God and others). In those discussions I communicated that you must love God before you can truly love another. In conveying that message I did not want to take too many other rabbit trails and possibly dilute the messages; therefore I am taking the time here to relay another message. Recently I have come across this principle of God a number of times and I too had to experience it firsthand a number of years ago, so I wanted to express it. I was talking to a friend who had put his wife on a pedestal (idol) and loved her above all else and unfortunately, they are going through a divorce and he is devastated. What I had done years ago before being born again was to put my daughters on a pedestal and I loved them more than anything on this earth. Well, God is not of this earth but regardless, *we are to love Him more than anything else 1st and let me make this clear, once you have done that then and only then you can love others as you love him and as you love yourself. The problem is when you love something else 1st or others or other things more than you love God. If you are a Believer, He will trip you up in order to correct it; or if you are a non-believer as I was, He tripped

232

me up over a number of things to get my attention so that I might give Him my consideration for Him to help me with the problems I had developed in my life. Also keep in mind that we are NOT under the burden of the Law, HOWEVER we continue to use it as a moral compass. Therefore we are not to have any idols before God. I hope this helps those who are upside down, as many are, who do not understand how this principle needs to be applied and to get right side up (right thinking and right actions, i.e. righteous w/God).

God wants you to Dream BIG

Whatever you can dream, you can do…
So tackle it with the boldness of your Spirit,
For then it has genius, power, authority, creativity/creation and God's glory linked to it!

Cafarellism

I lost a best friend to a massive heart attack way before his time, leaving behind a wife and two young sons; he was a doctor by profession and he was not only highly intelligent, he had common sense (often the two do not go together); This is a great bit of wisdom he shared with me, whenever applicable he was quoted as saying the following: "These guys always hang out together; where you find one, you will find the other: Stupid, greedy, lazy and dishonest."

(Job 4:8)BSB "As I have observed, those who plow iniquity and those who sow trouble, reap the same."

Evil parts

Envy is the eye of evil
Greed is the heart of evil
Lying is the tongue of evil
Deceit is the mouth of evil
Stupidity is the mind of evil
Lust is in the members of evil
Gluttony is the stomach of evil
Slothfulness/Laziness is the ass of evil (this is how the term "lazy ass" was derived)
Selfishness is the soul of evil
Wickedness is just plain evil.
(BTW, God has a sense of humor; please don't allow my humor to take away from the message)

233

Pride

Pride increases before a fall (as in what happened to Lucifer/Satan).

(Prov. 16:18)NKJV "Pride goes before destruction and an arrogant spirit before a fall."

Pride rejects God, but humility makes a home for God.

(James 4:6)KJV "God resists the proud, but gives grace unto the humble."

1 liners & short topics

- Operating in our strength = our works; Operating in God's power = results in the abundance of fruits from His grace.
    - Operating in our strength and not in God's power is damning to us (self-condemning) **(See Romans 13:2)**
- I will build my life on your rock which is my solid foundation; I will put my trust into your foundational principles to properly navigate my experiential journey.
- A five year old girl had misquoted her designated line of scripture and I found much irony in what she said, due to the state of Christianity and society today, "For God so loved the world, that He gave His one and only forgotten son." **(John 3:16)**
    - Did she misquote? Contemplate that and develop your own opinion.
- An eleven year old girl was recounting her after life experience from a terrible car accident in which she talked to Jesus prior to being resuscitated back to life. She said that He told her to tell everyone she could about her experience and not to worry because some will not believe.
    - That statement parallels what God knows all too well, and that is that not everyone will believe in Jesus.
    - But for those who do Believe, will receive His love, grace, mercy, peace, contentment, abundant life on earth and eternal life in heaven, just to name a few of His gifts He rewards us with.

Parent's Godly responsibility to their children

- To assist and help them to know God and how to have a relationship with Him.
- To help them hold God's hand and reach out to Him and trust in Him.
- To know the length, width, height and breadth of God's love for them and His other attributes.

2 liners & short topics

- There is no Gospel of Suffering, yet some church doctrines teach it. There is no question that we will suffer during our lifetime, as Jesus had to. Although never to the degree that Jesus did and as a Believer who is "in the Spirit," their suffering will be minimized and abbreviated compared to others who are not in the Spirit, and this is a truth. We must accept our trials, tribulations and sufferings for their term, but with our faith and trust, along with our walk in the Spirit and relationship with the Lord, it will be short lived and we will overcome and rise above it to continue in our abundant life.

- All of the choices we make have consequences and follow us throughout our journey on this planet. Unfortunately it is the poor choices that stand out in our minds. Point being, we need to make a conscious effort to reflect on the good choices and be positive minded. Also to thank God for his mercy, his grace, and his love for us that compensated for those poor consequences and in turn made such a positive difference in our lives.

- I am a product of the consequences of my choices.
    - o As for the unbeliever this statement really hits home, because their choices are influenced by everything outside of God (think about all the various sources that consists of, and the numerous consequences that could result).
    - o All choices have consequences (positive or neutral or negative), therefore it is imperative that we walk in the Spirit and renew our minds daily which in turn will guide our choice making along a positive path.

- Your mind can keep you from your miracle. (See Ch10)

- People get divorced for trivial things because they met under trivial circumstances and because their relationship began and was built on trivial conditions.

- * ** There is a variation of religion on every street corner…and the devil is loving it.
    - o Taking this a bit deeper, there is a variation of all religions on every street corner.
    - o Variations of Christianity, of Judaism, of Hinduism, of Buddhism, of Islam, etc.
    - o Regarding Christianity, it is imperative that you **focus on the gifts God gave you** primarily the gift of the * Holy Spirit to lead, guide and direct you in all remembrance and in all of God's wisdom by walking in the Spirit and renewing your mind in the Word daily

and focus on those things of God first, so that you can <u>verify</u> <u>"truth"</u> and validate <u>"truth"</u> in what you are hearing in the church house and elsewhere. Trust in God and He will direct your path to abundant living while on the experiential spiritual life journey on earth and then in heaven for an eternity.

- * The fruits of religion: are just shallow words and nothing more; whereas the fruits of God's wisdom: is abundant living for the individual and for the collective it results in a better quality of life for all.
- * The devil wants you to be focused on yourself; God wants you to be focused on His Son and His Holy Spirit!
- Only those who Believe…obey; And only those who obey…Believe.
  - o Does this describe you?
- We must 1st develop our relationship with God, before we can have positive, impactful, trusting, mutually satisfying relationships with each other.
- We must 1st love God, before we can truly love others.
- You cannot have a relationship with God if you do not trust in Him. The same holds true for other people, if you do not or cannot trust them, then there is no true relationship, period.
- Trust is the glue of life, holding all relationships together. It is a foundational principle of God, also NOT a gift from Him, but rather our choice to trust Him and others while on this journey, or not.
  - o A relationship without trust, does not have any glue to bind it together and will fall apart.
  - o Trust is a process.
- You cannot truly know yourself until you <u>fully</u> know God.
- The Holy Spirit will expose the real you; and show you the truth about you. (For the Holy Spirit knows the real you and only knows truth and has no lies in Him)
- Your grumblings towards others are actually grumblings towards God. **(See Exodus 16:8)**
- I teach people how to treat me, by what I will allow.
- People speak of leaving a legacy…
  - o Thing is, leaving a legacy is NOT about the person, nor is it what they did, or how much money was spent,
  - o Rather it is all about who it impacted and how.
- Pastor Dietrich Bonhoeffer:
  - o "Silence in the face of evil is itself evil: God will **not** hold us guiltless."
  - o "**Not to speak** is to speak. **Not to act** is to act."

236

- o ** He often spoke relaying, it matters not how this generation heroically delivers itself from the mess they created, rather **"How the coming generation shall continue to live."**
- o * "No man in the whole world can change the truth. One can only look for the truth, find it and serve it. The truth is in all places."

The truth is in all places

God uses other people especially Godly people as a part of discernment to answer questions; in other words **"The truth is in all places."**

You should already be familiar with the Godcept "From glory to glory, full circle," that I've referred to numerous times in this book so far. I had been struggling for a month on coming up with a descriptive complement to "from glory to glory. The term full circle is not one that I've ever really used but I came across it when I was talking to my Aunt BJ about some of God's principles and relating to our family stories, she used the term "full circle." BAM, the Holy Spirit nudged me and I knew immediately that it was what I had been looking for. We were talking about an entirely different topic, but I knew when I heard her say it how perfect it fit for that need. Keep in mind that it is not only from hearing the Word of God and not only from reading the Word of God that the Holy Spirit will utilize to answer your questions, dilemmas or perplexities. Answers to your questions can come from discussions with Godly people and especially those who are giving Godly advice; in other words, truth is in all places.

3 liners & short topics

- Beware of ideas, advice or opinions that do not have a scriptural background, they can easily result in negative consequences.
- Our job is not to get everyone to "like us." Our job is to fulfill God's purpose and plan He has for us.
  - o God and the enemy will put people into your life that do not like you. But you need to maintain your integrity, keep your cool, continue to remain focused on the prize that He has planned and purposed for you.
- Believers do not allow others to poison their day with their garbage. Some people are like a garbage truck: they fill up with bitterness, with anger, with negativity, etc. until their garbage truck is full; and then they have to dump it onto others. When that happens to you, just smile and go about your business, your Godly business, and keep your joy and keep God 1st in your life.
- Forgiveness is a decision.

- One "lost" aspect of this generation is that it is either in the process or has evolved into believing in a "safe" culture. Meaning they lean towards making choices based on what is safe. Ironically, Christianity is not perceived as safe with a negative, damning and attacking media, also there is a problem with its false teachings being widespread and confusing a significant proportion of Believers, and finally, Jesus is not perceived as safe either, which is just showing people's ignorance. Regardless of ignorant or not, society as a whole is paying a big price and has significant ramifications by turning away from Jesus.
- The gospel of Christ vs. the (mainstream/politically correct) social gospel of today.
    - Christ gives life and gives it abundantly and eternally.
    - vs.
    - Making the world a better place...to go to hell from.
    - Point is, the mainstream gospel is either so diluted or does not even mention Jesus and what it sells is to make the world a better place to live, BUT the problem with that philosophy is that without Jesus regardless of what you do, you are going to hell.
- You can be in the midst of evil and not be a victim of evil.
- Paul often spoke on "Walking in the Spirit" in his epistles (Greek) which was communicating to "conduct yourselves" in the Spirit. It corresponds with a shoulder to shoulder walk that takes place in the supernatural (Spirit) and natural realms (man's spirit) and conducting oneself under the direction of the Holy Spirit.
- To walk in the Spirit means to rely on the Holy Spirit for your guidance daily.
    - Let me clarify, to be "In the Spirit" means to graduate from walking in the Spirit to being Spirit Dominant and doing so 24/7 without giving it a second thought.
    - Your goal should be, to be In the Spirit 24/7. This way you truly have the Holy Spirit working in you constantly in helping you discern and make righteous choices while you are enjoying abundant living.
    - * Problem with Believers is that they do not understand this; also many people today are **OVER-WORDED and UNDER-SPIRITED** and therefore paralyzed.
        - Bigger problem, the majority are both under-worded and under-spirited.
        - **(Hosea 4:6)**KJV "My people are destroyed, for lack of knowledge of Me."

- We need the right balance of the Word of God with emphasis on Jesus's teachings, along with a mature walk in the Spirit.
  - TOMA is an acronym for the buzz phrase "Top of mind awareness;" if there is anything that you should have as TOMA is that you are spirit; known by God in spirit before the beginning of time and formed in your mother's womb, and now as a Believer your spirit is One with the Holy Spirit of God which gives you tremendous power and authority and the opportunity to live an abundant life on earth; and keep in mind that Jesus desires for you become One with Him.
  - We have the offer from the Lord to be One with Him! Please note, that the only way to become One with Him is by being In the Spirit!
  - The Holy Spirit provides clarity. **Clarity is POWER!** The Holy Spirit brings forth that which is out of focus.
- **The clearer the focus, the greater the impact!**
- **(1Cor 2:9-12)**NKJV "As it is written, no eye has seen, no ear has heard, no heart has imagined, what God has prepared for those who love Him. But God has revealed it to us by the Spirit. <u>The Spirit searches all things even the deep things of God.</u> For who among men knows the thoughts of man except <u>his own</u> spirit within him? So too, <u>no one knows the thoughts of God except the Spirit of God.</u> We have not received the spirit of the world, but the Spirit who is from God, <u>that we may understand what God has freely given us.</u>"
- **The greater the sacrifice, the greater is your reward!**
- The Law could only <u>relay</u> God's will to man.
  - The Holy Spirit assists man to **<u>fulfill</u>** God's will.
  - That is why it is said that "the Holy Spirit replaced the Law." Jesus's works on the cross initiated the process but it wasn't until we are saved and filled with the Holy Spirit that He assists us in fulfilling God's will, if we are walking in the Spirit daily.
- **Hunger** for the WISDOM of Jesus; and **Thirst** for the LIFE Jesus has to offer.
  - That is what Jesus meant by, "You must eat of my flesh and drink of my blood."
  - Eat as in "hunger daily;" His flesh has a number of times been represented as bread (I am the bread of life) and Jesus is the wisdom of God that we are to hunger for. Drink as in "thirst daily" for His blood that gives life (represented as wine; the fruit

239

of the vine) and it is the abundant life that He has for us and desires us to have.

- o Utilize the power of the Last Supper and take Holy Communion regularly.
- *** **The Gospel** of Christ (the good news of Jesus Christ)
  - o Paul (an <u>intellectual</u> man) **(2Cor. 5:21)**NKJV "He <u>knew</u> no sin."
  - o John (a man of <u>love</u>) **(1John 3:5)**KJV "In Him <u>is</u> no sin."
  - o Peter (a man of <u>devotion</u>) **(1Peter 2:22)**KJV "He <u>did</u> no sin."
  - o Having just relayed that Jesus was sinless and perfect, He took on all of mankind's sin while on the cross, so in turn the Father forsake Him and put all His curses, judgements and punishments on Him. Now we and our sins are covered in His blood and thus forgiven by God, we are now righteous in God's eyes, redeemed and justified, and now can have a relationship with God the Father and receive His favor, blessings, goodness, mercy, grace...
    - Because in reality man did not do anything right and Jesus did nothing wrong (He knew <u>no sin</u>; In Him is <u>no</u> sin; He did <u>no sin</u>); but He redeemed us and the outcome of it all shows how much God loves us and desires that we prosper with Him, in Him and through Him.
    - This is the "Good News" of Christ, **the Gospel**.
- Jesus is the wisdom of God revealed. In the OT Jesus was concealed and in the NT He is revealed.
- **(Matt. 6:33)**NKJV "But seek first the kingdom of God and His righteousness and all these things will be added unto you. Therefore do not worry about tomorrow for tomorrow will worry about itself. Today has enough trouble of its own."
- People today are:
  - o Trapped due to continuously dwelling on the past
  - o Because they are fearful and anxious of the what the future may hold
  - o Therefore they are paralyzed in the present.
- ** A composite teaching of Jesus: Do not dwell in the past, do not be fearful or anxious of the future, nor be fearful or anxious in the present, but <u>live</u> in the present and have life and have it abundantly, today!
- Put a period on the events of the past, then turn the page to a new chapter in your life.
- Allow Jesus to be the author of your life.
- **(James 4:14)**KJV "What are our lives except a vapor that appears for a little while and vanishes."

- o Life is short. Do not waste one day of it. Believe in Jesus and have life abundantly.
- * How often does God speak a word to your destiny, but you speak words to contradict it! Neutralizing it and making it of no effect.
- * When you rest...God works. When you work...God rests.
  - o 1st allow God to do the things He needs to do in your life by receiving His blessings and acting on them. Remember that we "rest" assured in the Lord, so if we take matters into our own hands and our works are self-driven (regardless of the situation), God rests and allows us to do all the work (typically in vain, although not readily apparent). So, do not fall into making that mistake.
- (Zech. 4:6)KJV "Not by might, nor by power, but by my Spirit, said the LORD."
  - o God was relaying that what He wanted done would be accomplished not by man's hands, strength or power but done through man via His Spirit.
- We must give thanks for the closed doors we encounter as much as we pray for doors to open.
- Stop the stinkin-thinkin with all the things you've done wrong, and start proclaiming everything that God is doing right in your life.
  - o What you think is powerful and what you say can be powerful and explosive.
  - o If you require explosive power, "declare it in Jesus name!"
  - o What you speak to: lives. So make sure it is what you want to live.
  - o Therefore always speak positive of everything.
- (Prov. 18:21)BSB "Life and death are in the power of the tongue..."
- Don't pray in desperation, rather pray from a place of victory.
  - o You know where that is; that you love Him and thank Him for _____ and He will give it unto you in like manner.
  - o Note: here I am referring to daily prayers. Regarding praying in desperation, if it is urgent and you are desperate then relay exactly that with passion and emotion so that He understands the place you are at.
- You will never rise above where you see yourself. Therefore DREAM BIG and PRAY BIG! God desires for you to do it and accomplish it.

When is the beginning of time?
I'm referring to that time that only God knew <u>you</u>.

Is it before all creation?

Is it at conception? Or is it at your birth? Or is it at the time you were saved, born again?

Is it before time began?

- Note, all creation was before time began. Remember that time began when Adam and Eve sinned against God. That is when the clock started ticking for man.

It is when God formed you in your mother's womb, at conception. God knew you before the beginning of your time. He is spirit and He knew you in spirit. He formed you in your mother's womb and breathed into you a living soul.

(Gen. 2:7)KJV "And the LORD God formed man of the dust of the ground, and breathed into his nostrils the breath of life; and man became a <u>living soul</u>."

(Jer. 1:5)NKJV "<u>Before I formed you in the womb</u>, **I knew you**, And before you were born I consecrated you (set you apart and declared you for His purpose; i.e. His uncommon purpose)"

(Rom. 8:28-30)NKJV "And we know that God works all things together for the good of those who love Him, who are called according to His purpose. For those God **foreknew**, He also <u>predestined to be conformed to the **image** of His Son</u>, so that <u>He would be the **firstborn**</u> among many brothers and sisters. And those He predestined, He also called; those He called, He also justified; those He justified, He also glorified...."

- God foreknew us (He knew us beforehand; before the beginning of time); note this does not relay or imply that there are a special few, rather He knew us all and we all have an equal opportunity to participate in a relationship and glorify Him.
- Predestinated means: "set apart" beforehand, along with preordaining (prescribing a predetermined set path in His glory)
- Jesus (the <u>exact image of God</u>) is the <u>firstborn</u> of all His brothers and sisters.

(1Cor. 15:48-50)BSB "<u>As was the earthly man, so also are those who are of the earth; and as is the heavenly man, so also are those who are of heaven</u>. And just as we have borne the likeness of the earthly man, so also shall we bear the likeness of the heavenly man. Now I declare to you, brothers, that flesh and blood cannot inherit the kingdom of God, nor does the perishable inherit the imperishable."

(2Cor 3:18)KJV "But we all, with open face beholding as in a glass the glory of the Lord, are changed into the <u>same image</u> **from glory to glory**, even as by the Spirit of the Lord."

242

Paul said, **(Gal 1:14-16)**BSB "I was advancing in Judaism beyond many of my contemporaries and was <u>extremely zealous for the traditions of my fathers</u>. But when God, <u>who set me apart</u> from my mother's womb and <u>called me</u> by His grace, was pleased <u>to reveal His Son in me</u> so that I might <u>preach Him among the Gentiles</u>, <u>I did not rush to consult with flesh and blood</u>..."

The following passage **does not** relay or imply that He **knew you** before the foundation of the world, but that He chose and predestinated **us**... **(Eph. 1:3-5)**BSB "Blessed be the God and Father of our Lord Jesus Christ, who has blessed us in Christ with every spiritual blessing in the heavenly realms. For He **chose us** <u>in Him before the foundation of the world to be holy and blameless in His presence</u>. In love He **predestined us** for adoption as His sons and daughters through Jesus Christ, according to the good pleasure of His will..."

Learn from historical accounts
A blend of OT and NT:

(Psalm 78:8)KJV "**A stubborn and rebellious generation**; a generation whose **heart** was not loyal, and whose **spirit** was not steadfast with God (not faithful to God)."

(Psalm 95:10) "For forty years I was angry with that generation, and I said, "They are a people whose hearts go astray, and they have not known My ways."

(Heb. 3:10-12)BSB Paul quoting Psalm 95:10 "Therefore **I was angry with that generation**, and I said, 'Their hearts are always going astray, and they have not known My ways.' So I swore on oath in My anger, 'They shall never enter My rest.'" See to it, brothers, that none of you has a wicked heart of unbelief that turns away from the living God." God spoke this concerning the generation of His peoples who He released from Pharaoh's bondage. "Rest" means the strength and power of His works.

***(Heb. 4:1-3/6-16)**BSB "Therefore, while the promise of entering His rest still stands, let us be careful that none of you be deemed to have fallen short of it. For we also received the good news, just as they did; but the message they heard was of no value to them, <u>since they did not share the faith of those who comprehended it</u>. Now **we who have believed enter that rest**. As for the others, it is just as God has said: "So I swore on oath in My anger, 'They shall never enter My rest.'" And yet <u>His works have been finished since the foundation of the world</u>." "those who formerly heard the good news <u>did not enter because of their disobedience</u>." "So there remains a Sabbath rest for the people of God. For whoever enters God's rest also rests from his own work, just as God did from His." "Let us, therefore, **make every effort to enter that rest**, so that no one will fall by following the same pattern of disobedience. **For the word of God is living and active.** Sharper than any double-edged sword, it pierces even to dividing soul and spirit, joints and marrow. **It judges the thoughts and intentions of the heart.** Nothing in all creation is hidden from God's sight; everything is uncovered and exposed before the eyes of Him to whom we must give account." "Let us then approach the throne of grace **with confidence,** so that we may **receive** mercy and find grace **to help us in our time of need.**

We must have trust, faith and believe in God and His works (and not in ours) and He will strengthen and prosper us.

Guard your Heart

You are instructed to "guard your heart." King Solomon said it best, **(Proverbs 4:23)**NKJV "Above all else, guard your heart, for it is the wellspring of life." (wellspring: issues of life)

Guard your heart from:

- Evil, evil doers and evil ways
- Satan, his demons and the devil
- Profane thoughts, profane speech and profane actions
- From it becoming hardened from other men's/women's opinions or actions

Guard your heart by:

- Knowing the word of God (renewing your mind daily)
- Praying and a relationship with the Lord
- Righteous and holy daily lifestyle
- To "live according to the Spirit and set their minds on the things of the Spirit; and to set their minds on the Spirit regarding life and peace." **(Rom. 8:5-6)**KJV
- **(Isa. 26:3)** "A mind and heart set on God is a peaceful, trusting heart."
- **(Phil. 4:7)**KJV "And the peace of God, which surpasses all understanding, **will guard your hearts and your minds through Christ Jesus**.
    - Therefore you must "rest" in Him (in His strength, not yours) so that you receive His peace. (the heart and mind is referring to your spiritual heart/mind, via Jesus)

But never are you to isolate yourself (that is NOT what it means to guard your heart). You are to live life to the fullest and experience an abundant life, and an important aspect of achieving that is by guarding your heart against evil but opening your heart to abundant Godly living.

Headlines: Religion by the Stats

Just a few business related topics to think about. When churches and Christian TV stations are quoting metrics in the news and they are not shy to do so on prime time TV, are they utilizing those statistics to find the best approaches to "help fellow Believers? To give you an idea of what I am referring to, the metrics they are using are the same type of metrics I use in a $60M small business distributorship, such as search engine results, SEO and social media metrics. I took note of it during the Covid19 crisis and what they were relaying was that Google searches for 'prayer" skyrocketed as the pandemic took hold. 70% of religious inquires had to do with how to pray. The #1 search was Covid19 and the #2 search was prayer/God. A Texas megachurch announced that it had been experiencing record-breaking viewing numbers ever since the coronavirus outbreak went global. "We saw 4.51 million people tune in throughout the weekend across platforms." The columnist who wrote the article about the megachurch had also interviewed a representative who stated, "We pray to cope with adversity." Take a moment and think about that statement. The columnist herself commented that the surge in prayer may also be as a result of large-scale church closures.

Sorry for pushing all that out there, but other than mentioning it, I'm not interested in taking a deep dive and chasing the rabbit down that hole. It was more for you to read, then to contemplate and then to think as you may. I will although comment on the statement the columnist mentioned regarding the surge in prayer may be due to church closures. Is she saying that the people who go to church rely so heavily on the church that they don't know how to pray? Or was it that those who don't go to church regularly, now have an urgency to seek Jesus but without being able to go to church that they are lost and lack the knowledge to know what to do? I think you can read between the lines of my questioning. Throughout the book I've mentioned various topics (i.e. a movement in regard to declaration of prayer not so coincidentally coming out during this same time and discounting past teachings and confusing people even more than they already are; Christians and their Bible illiteracy; to referring to the duration of sermons versus the balance of the "entertainment" taking place in many churches; to the watering down or dummying down of sermons; etc.) that you can either attempt to connect the dots, or not. As I conveyed those topics in the book, I also vehemently expressed that the church is crucial to a Believer's walk with the Lord, and also one of the avenues to "hear" the Word of God (in which "faith comes by hearing, and hearing by the Word of God"), and the importance of fellowship with like-minded Believers and the list goes on and on. As mentioned elsewhere, there are so many things wrong in so many different areas of this world, but one of the first focuses must be on the church (made up of the body of Christ; not a brick and mortar building), teaching, approaches, etc. because when something is requiring an overhaul you always start at the foundation and in this case the root causes for the dysfunction and work your way up from there. A good portion of my career was spent troubleshooting problematic businesses and I learned quickly that you must start at the root causes otherwise you are wasting your time, energy and efforts. Because the **toxins begin in the roots of the tree and band-aids don't stick very long to the bark.** This is true for relationships and most all things under the Sun.

Like-minded and equally yoked

News flash: there are hypocrites and pseudo-Christians in the church. Obviously, it varies from church to church, but I would estimate that an average is 15-20% leaving the balance of 80% like-minded and equally yoked people to fellowship with. This is no surprise because satan doesn't want his followers to be drunks and heroin addicts, but rather to be productive in society, to have a family, to attend church (for all the wrong reasons), etc. so this should be of no surprise. This is not an attack from me, read on to see what this brief topic matter is about. As in the prior topic and throughout the book **I've stressed the importance of church**, the teachings you receive while attending, the fellowship opportunities, the charitable opportunities that are available, etc.... So, having relayed that information, are you taking full advantage of the opportunities the church provides? Or have you made the conscious decision not to attend and instead take your chances with whatever the world provides?

As far as the world is concerned, you are assured to be exposed to worse than hypocrites. Again, I would estimate that there is a likelihood of about 15% having the opportunity to associate with like-minded and equally yoked people. If I were a betting man, I would take the 80% better odds over the 15% odds. Now anyone can challenge these estimates based on their personal experience, but this happens to be my personal experience. So, who would you rather fellowship with on a personal level and have you made a conscious effort to make that happen?

As I have generally done is give my personal examples, so just wanted to say that my most valued relationships are with people who are equally yoked and like-minded Believers. And long before I got saved, I unfortunately knew nothing about this, and I have too numerous to mention failed relationships that I know were directly related to this topic. The most unfortunate and perfect example was with the mother of my children (discussed elsewhere in the book).

We are **to evangelize/minister to everyone** especially worldly unbelievers. But remember that Jesus has specifically instructed us **to fellowship by** developing personal relationships with like-minded and equally yoked people of faith!

The Clearer the Focus (on Your Purpose) The Greater the Impact

How are you impacting others in society?

Or should I ask how are you planning impacting others in society?

All of us should be making a concerted effort to positively IMPACT other people, which in turn makes a positive impact on our society. Find your **purpose**, the one that God predestined for you!

Question is, are you contented with your life as it is and is it fulfilling and satisfying? Many of us have been blessed from God to the extent that we become complacent and live each day by day, by day. Meaning that we opt to taking the path of least resistance, which is human nature. Obviously, this is easier to relay than to be acted upon. It seems as though all the benefits of finding your purpose and executing it are common sense but taking the path of least resistance trumps common sense, as well as anything that takes you out of your comfort zone. Because the benefits are common sense, I won't take up you time lining out all of the benefits to you and to others.

My intent in bringing this topic to your attention is to relay something that doesn't get taught much but I assure you is very important to your life on earth as well as your eternal life. Not acting on your Godly purpose will not keep you out of heaven, but it also won't prepare you properly for when you step into heaven. I've mentioned this topic before and maybe you remember it or maybe not. Point: God predestined a purpose for all of His children; one reason is to contribute to the collective on earth in a positive way, while contributing to our abundant and fulfilling lives; another reason is that it directly impacts our development for when we step into heaven. Have you ever had a job in which you were not properly trained? How did you feel and how did you manage at performing the responsibilities? As I said, ****I assure you that God wants all of us trained and having well executed our specific purpose which is part of our development while on this experiential spiritual life journey on earth.** I cannot stress the importance of this enough, but it is solely up to you to pray on it and follow through with action, or not.

Keep in mind that with everything in life and as noted here, your purpose in life, that the clearer the focus you have, the greater the impact you will have on others. It is also the way that we will all contribute to changing the world in which we live!!!

247

The relationship of Fate and Faith

Leave your life up to fate and see where that gets you. When we choose our own paths in life, fate at its best only brings us only the possibilities, often with short term successes and subsequent failures. Whereas, if you choose to follow your faith (rather than self-will), faith will guide you to discern the instructions of the Spirit and choose the correct path to true long-lasting success, achievement and significance, in association with a fulfilling and abundant life!

A Father's 'Wisdom'

(1Cor 2:7)NLT "The **WISDOM** we now speak is from the mysteries of God—his plan that was previously hidden (kept secret) from before the world began, as He had decreed and destined for our glory." Remember that the Holy Spirit will bring all things to our remembrance if we give Him the opportunity.

Wisdom as per the Bible, has a number of meanings and one of which is, "skilled at making sound decisions in life." Thus in order to be skilled at making sound decisions in life which results in abundant living and a truly experiential spiritual life journey on earth, we must ascertain God's wisdom via walking with the Holy Spirit in the Word (Jesus).

Life is like a box of Hard Knocks & Round Rocks

I'm paraphrasing the popular quote with regards to the box of chocolates…you never know what you are going to get. But this is a very different take on that saying and ultimately in God's Kingdom as a Believer you actually do have a very good idea of what you are going to get, because God designed it and prefers to be transparent with us and the more we know the better it is for all parties. The Bible might speak of the mysteries of God as it pertains to those things that He has never revealed to man up until the Holy Spirit has been made responsible for bringing some of it to the remembrance of those He has deemed should know such things. So, when you are in relationship with Him, the Holy Spirit brings ALL things to your remembrance and reveals the things to assist you in achieving an abundant life that is a complete experiential spiritual life journey on earth. Hard Knocks for the Believer do not occur that often because one of the benefits you have as a Believer is that your journey is NOT like riding a roller coaster that's going up and down and knocking you into the side of the car you are in. The Believer's life journey is designed to be more even keeled, with its share of hard knocks along with its share of blessings although in a greater proportion.

So, by definition hard knocks are just what they sound like, they are those times in life in which you struggle, make poor decisions and choices, get knocked around by life and others around you, your wilderness experiences and trials and tribulations, and those tough times you may encounter that can set you back on some or all of your goals, etc. Most often hard knocks are "created" by our "self's." Meaning our ego/self, or our self that has been manipulated by the devil and in extreme cases by demons. We are very talented at doing this to ourselves, it is part of our fleshly nature to have an ego dominant outlook on life, that is, until we allow Jesus and the Holy Spirit to take charge and dominate our lives for the better. One way to determine whether our ego is getting in the way of our spiritual journey is to analyze the problems and our actions in the following (4P) categories: Pleasure, Passion, Possession, and Person. These areas are leading indicators that our ego is in charge, running our lives and resulting in an increased volume of hard knocks. It is easy to get caught in a rut, as mentioned it is not only our fleshly nature to wreak havoc in our own lives, but society as a whole is hell-bent on taking the low road (the devil's path to destruction). Not to mention the multitude of bad influences in the world (see Chapter 10 for a dissertation on the mind and related "devil influenced" topics). For one example, there is a psychological term "perseverative," which means to continuously think negative thoughts of the past, present or future that contributes to excessive worry and fear, mind wondering, and thus drifting away from God.

God has made it clear that the Believer will encounter setbacks, trials and tribulations and have wilderness experiences, because it is an aspect of our spiritual growth and life journey. The point though is, that they will not consume us nor be more than the ebb and flow of our God centered lives would require, but definitely not be the dramatic and devastating fails a non-believer is prone to have. This subchapter though is not about reviewing the principles behind both sides of all of this, because that is what the entirety of this book does. Instead, I needed to set up this topic matter by giving a generalized explanation of hard knocks so that I could then lead into a commonly missed opportunity by Believers that I've represented as "round rocks." To be more descriptive, a round rock are those smooth polished rocks you find near a rivers edge, or an entire river bed, or in bodies of water in which the flow of water over time has tumbled and smoothed the edges and sometimes even polishes the now round rocks.

What do "Round Rocks" have to do with God, not to mention "Hard Knocks?"

Well, I'll begin my explanation by using the illustration of a classroom setting in which the teacher holds a discussion regarding various examples of everyone's recent hard knocks experiences. On the 1st day the students began communicating their stories; then on the 2nd day upon arriving to their desk they each had a round rock on their desktop; the teacher conveyed that the round rocks were to relay a sign of hope for their hard knocks and to be sure to bring it back with them for the next follow-up classes. On the 3rd day there were 3 more round rocks and on the 4th day there were 27 more round rocks and were given a bag to carry them; then on the 5th day there were 19,683 round rocks and were continuing to grow by a multiple of the 3rd power. Obviously by now it had gotten out of hand and it was time for the teacher to reveal the true meaning of the round rocks:

The Round Rocks represents spiritual blessings that God has provided for us to deal with problems (hard knocks); or to simply utilize for common daily needs; or on the opposite end of the spectrum to be used to prosper our lives; or it is a form of hope (that gift of supernatural hope that God gives and instills in everyone) and in this case it is hope that has manifested into a tangible form as an after product of solving problems or from your prospering, so that now you have evidence of his blessings and his hope, so that you can increase the trust you have in Him, secure your wholehearted belief in Him, and gain in your overall God Confidence.

Thing is, many a Believer go into their quiet place to pray to God not realizing that the entire room has filled up with unused/unreceived spiritual blessings from God. Yet they are still praying their prayers of petition and asking for things that He has already provided for based on the purpose He has for their life. A number of factors contribute to this ignorance, first being they do not understand that God is Jehovah Jireh (the Provider) and He provides exceedingly abundantly above what we can utilize, desire, need or even dream of! His supernatural spiritual blessings are in the same abundance and all you need to do is "receive" them AND do something with them; and it is in walking with the Holy Spirit daily that you know beyond a reasonable doubt that God is going to provide that particular blessing and it is up to you to receive it **(Mark 11:24)**BSB Jesus said, "Therefore I tell you, whatever you ask in prayer, believe that you have received it, and it will be yours." A caveat here is that some people do not believe they are worthy to receive some blessings, while there are others that believe they deserve everything under the sun. So as mentioned, the Holy Spirit will guide and direct your path and relay what blessings to expect, that is if you are renewing your mind daily and in relationship with the Holy Spirit, Jesus and the Father. Also, more often than not, the blessings are to benefit others in need that you can directly impact, while benefiting yourself simultaneously. (see subchapter "We Get to Give"). Point is, don't miss out on the bucket loads of blessings (round rocks) that God has provided you and blessed you with.

What does 30 years, 3 years and 3 days have in common?

*It is one of the many plans of God and has to do with redemption and a new outlook on life for mankind (as only He could have planned it). See, God so loved the world that he gave his only begotten Son:

- First, to have an experiential spiritual life journey on earth for **30 years**…
  - o In the flesh (although He remained sinless),
  - o While being led by God via his Holy Spirit (the same Holy Spirit and process that He's given us an opportunity at).
- Second, to teach and relay principle messages from the Father to his disciples and to the world for **3 years**…
  - o Teach by way of relationship building, and via instruction, discussion, warning, motivation, quoting the Father, role playing, leading by example, demonstrating by helping and giving to others and by healing…
- Third, to **choose** to die on the cross as a loving sacrifice for all mankind, while paving the road of redemption and the Father's forgiveness of sin, that we may now have a relationship with the Father through Jesus via the Holy Spirit (as the New Covenant in His blood) and then God the Father resurrected Jesus from the dead on the **3rd day**…

> (John 3:16-17)BSB "For God so loved the world that He gave His only begotten Son, that everyone who believes in Him shall not perish but have eternal life. For God did not send His Son into the world to condemn the world, but to save the world through Him."

> (John 15:12-14)NKJV "This is My commandment, that you love one another as I have loved you. Greater love has no one than this, that he lay down his life for his friends. You are My friends if you do what I command you."

> (1 John 2:1-3)BSB "I am writing these things to you so that you will not sin. But if anyone does sin, we have an advocate before the Father—Jesus Christ, the Righteous One. He Himself is the atoning sacrifice for our sins, and not only for ours but also for the sins of the whole world. By this we can be sure that we have

come to know Him: if we keep His commandments." (Jesus is truly our advocate, He experienced 33yrs of life on earth in the flesh, just as we have experienced and often times more so).

(Luke 22:19-20)BSB "And He took the bread, gave thanks and broke it, and gave it to them, saying, "This is My body, given for you; do this in remembrance of Me." In the same way, after supper He took the cup, saying, "This cup is the new covenant in My blood, which is poured out for you."
(Mat 26:27-28)BSB "Then He took the cup, gave thanks, and gave it to them, saying, "Drink from it, all of you. This is My blood of the covenant, which is poured out for many for the forgiveness of sins."
(1 Cor 15:3-4)BSB "For what I received I passed on to you as of first importance: that Christ died for our sins according to the Scriptures, that He was buried, that He was raised on the third day according to the Scriptures."

The Father <u>chose</u> to raise Jesus from death, to the glory of heaven, at His right side...on the 3rd day. Note: and it was NOT because Jesus was his Son, He did it because Jesus finished the work!

Hebrews and John, assists you in connecting the dots
* These excerpts are <u>in agreement</u> with many of the topics covered to this point in the book:

*Drifting (away from God)
(Heb. 2:1)BSB "We must pay closer attention, therefore, to what we have heard, so that we do not **drift away**."

Salvation: announced, confirmed and affirmed; Signs, wonders, miracles and gifts of the Holy Spirit (distributed according to God's will)
(Heb. 2:3-4)BSB "**Salvation** was first <u>announced by the Lord</u>, was <u>confirmed to us</u> by those who heard Him, and was <u>affirmed by God</u> through **signs, wonders, various miracles, and gifts of the Holy Spirit **distributed according to His will**.

You are Jesus's brother and His friend
(Heb. 2:10-12)BSB "In bringing many sons to glory, it was fitting for God, for whom and through whom all things exist, to make **(Jesus)** the **Author/Leader of <u>our</u> salvation** <u>perfect through</u>

252

suffering. For both the One who sanctifies and those who are sanctified are **of the same family**. So Jesus is not ashamed to call them brothers. He says: "I will proclaim Your name to My **brothers**; I will <u>sing Your praises</u> in the assembly." (Jesus is saying that He will sing God's praises to us, who are His brothers). (Jesus as our Author/Leader is also in **Heb. 12:2, Acts 3:15, and Acts5:31**; He is "**Leading the way**" for all of us in everything He experienced, learned, was subjected to, and ultimately accomplished for us as well).

(John 15:13-15)NKJV Jesus said, "<u>Greater love has no one than this, that he lay down his life for his friends. You are My</u> **friends** *<u>if you do what I command you</u>. No longer do I call you servants, for a servant does not understand what his master is doing. But I have called you **friends**, *<u>because</u> <u>everything</u> **I have learned** <u>from My Father, I have made known to you.</u>

<u>Love one another; You are not of the world; Equally yoked vs. worldly people; No excuse for sin; the Holy Spirit is our Advocate, who Jesus sent to us from the Father</u>

(John 15:16-27)BSB "You did not choose Me, but I chose you. And I appointed you to go and bear fruit—fruit that will remain— so that whatever you ask the Father in My name, He will give you. **This is My command to you: Love one another**. If the world hates you, understand that it hated Me first. If you were of the world, it would love you as its own. Instead, the world hates you, because you are not of the world, but **I have chosen you out of the world**. Remember the word that I spoke to you: 'No servant is greater than his master.' If they persecuted Me, they will persecute you as well; if they kept My word, they will keep yours as well. But they will treat you like this on account of My name, because they do not know the One who sent Me. If I had not come and spoken to them, they would not be guilty of sin. *Now, however, they have no excuse for their sin**. Whoever hates Me hates My Father as well. If I had not done among them the works that no one else did, they would not be guilty of sin; but now they have seen and hated both Me and My Father. But <u>this is to fulfill what is written</u> in **their Law**: 'They hated Me without reason.' When the *<u>**Advocate**</u> comes, whom <u>I will send to</u> **you** <u>from the Father</u>— the Spirit of truth who goes out from the Father— He will testify about Me. And you also must testify, because **you have been with Me from the beginning**."

253

Ask the Holy Spirit in prayer: "Is this the truth? Please help me to **connect the dots** which correlate with what DW has outlined and with what has been established in the Word of God / Bible."

Therefore if this is the truth, God's truth, then you must **trust** in it and **believe** in it with all of your heart, all of your soul, and with all of your might! In order that you may receive the blessings He has released, which will elevate you to the abundant living you are striving for!

The BIG Picture: for Believers to Reign in Life

(John 10:10)KJV "I have come that they may have life, and that they may have it more abundantly."

God did not intend to save Believers "from" the world, but rather to save Believers "**for**" the world. To live life abundantly and experientially as He had originally planned for Adam and Eve. Having said that, now **God rescues and restores Believers** for His renewed intention which is to restore creation itself to reign "in life" while on earth * (i.e. experiential spiritual life journey on earth). Early into my being saved (a babe) I was guilty of thinking that "the world is not my home, but rather heaven is," so due to my ignorance of scripture or might I say my misinterpretation of it, I started to mock things of the world, pass judgement, become negative with my surroundings, etc. I had gotten this from pastors, Christian music, and in part from the following scriptures:

(John 17:16)KJV "They are not of the world, just as I am not of the world."
(1 John 2:15-16)NKJV "Do not love the world or anything in the world. If anyone loves the world, the love of the Father is not in him. For all that is in the world—the desires of the flesh, the desires of the eyes, and the pride of life—is not from the Father but from the world."
(Rom 12:2)NKJV "Do not be conformed to this world, but be transformed by the renewing of your mind. Then you will be able to discern what is the good, pleasing, and perfect will of God."

Reread the above scripture to pinpoint how I had misinterpreted this. For one, keep in mind that "the world" is different from the earth. The world has to do with the peoples who populate the earth and more specifically those people who are NOT Believers of Jesus. In addition, our time on this earth is temporary and as a Believer, we will leave our bodies on earth and then spend eternity with Jesus. Therefore I thought for some time that I didn't belong here, and this was only temporary, furthermore my goal was to glorify God during the time I was here, but my focus was to invest here in order to reign in heaven. WRONG and stinkin-thinkin!

Fortunately the Holy Spirit helped me to understand and clear this up. It was almost a 180degree turnabout for me and with that came a flow of wisdom (knowledge and understanding of God's Kingdom and the things of this world). I now understand and believe that God wants me to reign "in life" while on earth, and not to fall into the temptations of this world or to be of the world. To reign in life means to live life to its fullest via the abundant living Jesus preached and one of the reasons He came in the first place. It's difficult to put into words the multitude of factors that go into what it means to have and live an abundant life, because this entire book references what that is.

From a big picture perspective God wants each of us to have an abundant life while on earth and to have an eternal life in heaven. As I've mentioned countless times, He wants us to have an experiential spiritual life journey on earth, and one of my primary purposes is to (love) give to others and help all to understand God's Word, His principles and his Son Christ Jesus so that for one, they get the most out of this journey while on earth. We are all to be conformed to the image of his Son, meaning we are to become like Jesus and his attributes: goodness, forgiving, giving, loving, compassionate, tolerant, etc. Remember that it is our choice to do this, or not. If we so choose, we glorify God in the things we think, say and do, and with that comes an unspoken assurance from us to Him that we are doing our best to be obedient to Him. We are to rest in Him and be assured that He fulfills all his promises He's made to us and glorifies us by already having done the work and we need to receive it via the Holy Spirit and Jesus, according to our purpose.

"Jesus did not come to make bad people good; He came to make dead people alive." As previously mentioned, the Father wants us to be alive and to reign in life and to have an abundant life while on earth (experiential spiritual life journey on earth).

Social Injustice, Racism & the Perfect Storm

Social justice has been a prevailing topic throughout headlines not only for years and years but has been a topic of concern throughout the millennia. Now with the pandemic death scare of Covid-19, social distancing and forced isolation, overnight job losses and high unemployment, rent evictions or housing foreclosures, strapped finances and having to spend all their years of savings, and on and on, throw in the death by suffocation of George Floyd by the knee of a police officer and it sparked an all-encompassing perfect storm to bring to light for the umpteenth time social injustice with the subsequent protests, stone throwing and senseless rioting. Does anyone recall the Rodney King beating in 1991? Most do, but my point is, history continues to repeat itself as it has for millennia. So, what is the solution?

Well, I'll leave it up to you to decide if I've come up with a solution or not. I only decided to cover the topic of social justice and place it in Volume 1 due to the ever-increasing events surrounding these subjects. So keep in mind that I will only touch on this topic matter in this sub chapter, but I assure you that I am going to address the problem and offer the solution with resolute and profound revelation. You although will need to bear with me because you have not yet read the full two volumes therefore you do not have the broad understanding of what I am about to relay. Hopefully, you will be patient with this explanation and continue to read and understand the two volumes and not jump to a conclusion, one of which is that this is just too radical a thought or belief. I also think that I should mention that Volume III involves the advanced spiritual wisdom for a mature Believer and the proceeding presentation follows suit to that.

If you had at least already read Volumes I & II, I would ask you to take a comprehensive 10,000ft. view of what you have learned, to ponder it, meditate and pray on it. This not only would summarize in part the foundation of our spiritual journey, it would also in part reveal God's predestined purpose for mankind. With having said that, it is about the "**choices**" we make with regards to loving our neighbor, as thyself. Jesus only gave a couple of handfuls of commandments and it is imperative that you realize the utter importance of them and the impact they have on our journey if we abide by them. The one commandment which is in context with my explanation is stated in:

> **(Matt. 22: 34-40)**KJV "But when the Pharisees had heard that Jesus had put the Sadducees to silence, they were gathered together. Then one of them, which was a lawyer, asked Him a question, tempting Him, and saying, Master, **which is the greatest commandment** in the law? Jesus said unto him, Thou shalt love the Lord thy God with all thy heart, and with all thy soul, and with all thy mind. This is the first and great commandment. And the second is like unto it, **Thou shalt love thy neighbor as thyself.** <u>On these two commandments hang **all** the law and the prophets.</u>"

Take a moment and meditate on this scripture and how it relates to social justice. Well, you can see how it relates, that is if we were <u>all</u> able to achieve this that it would solve the problem of social injustice. Although speaking in absolutes as it pertains to man is not realistic because it is impossible for all of mankind to accomplish the one same objective. And if you take this one line of scripture, even if it is the second greatest commandment, that it will not accomplish anything, in and of itself and with people only familiar with it and not practicing it. But if you take the comprehensive teachings as I suggested, and you along with a significant portion of the collective church body were to work at fulfilling this commandment, it would undoubtably make a difference.

What specific comprehensive teachings am I referring to? I'll get to that but let's first assess the problem. Ponder and consider the thousands of years of social injustice, racism, and related conflict throughout the world. It is mind boggling, but one thing is for certain and that is from as far back as Cain and Abel moving forward to the present, mankind has fallen way short of the second greatest commandment. Thus we live in a fallen world and with that there will always be strife, conflict, prejudice, racism, social injustice, and on and on. But that does not mean that all of those negatives have to be the dominant culture of our times and that there are solutions that can minimize it and allow for us to live abundantly while on this journey.

Okay, if I'm going to keep this brief then I'm going to have to take what will seem to you as a quantum leap with this explanation, in covering a bit of summarization of what you'll read in Volume II. Also, you will need to read Vol. I and especially Vol. II to understand and comprehend what I am about to relay. We are spiritual beings with an earthly body; we are comprised of a spirit, soul and earthly body; the body is natural, whereas the spirit and soul are supernatural; the body will someday die, but the spirit and soul will never die, rather will live for an eternity whether in heaven or hell; our spirit and soul are so intwined and inter-connected that they may seem as one and often misinterpreted and falsely taught that they are one in the same, but the Word of God can divide the two; this is important because of the following: due to mankind's fallen (Adam & Eve's) nature, we are soul dominant (our emotions, personality, will, etc.), but God meant for us to be spirit dominant (of His Spirit; supernatural realm – not natural; utilizing all His attributes: mercy, grace, forgiving, giving, loving, compassionate, tolerant, peaceful, etc...); you've already read that sanctification is an ongoing process in this life and into eternity (the process of becoming Holy, becoming like Jesus, etc.); this can only truly be achieved when we humble our "self's" (soul), have self-control (soul), focus on Jesus and living a righteous life (spirit) for God (for one: loving one another as thyself), which ultimately means that "all that we think, say, and do, glorifies God," which must come from a place within us of spirit dominance which now has put the soul into a place of subordinance (although still very important for it is the "who" that we are); see Vol. II for these and more details.

But that is not all, now hold onto your hat for the quantum leap into Vol. III advanced spirituality, for us Believers who have been saved and will go to heaven for an eternity (absent from the body, present with the Lord), where at a blink of an eye, we are transformed to spirit dominance (that we cannot fathom right now in the natural on earth), and the other good news is that we retain our soul (the "who" that we are) although in the proper measure and proportion that God originally planned from before the beginning of time!!! As mentioned, the sanctification process continues although now from an entirely different perspective and even with all that God has to teach us, it will be one that will quickly be achieved. Can you now understand and see that this experiential spiritual life journey on earth is in preparation for eternity, and that if we as a collective are able to become somewhat close to being spirit dominant, that our lives WILL BE ABUNDANT during this journey.

Whew! Now that I've blown your mind and hopefully you all stick with me through this, social injustice will only improve by the same measure (extent) that we "human beings" and children of God, are able to live abundant lives by renewing our minds daily with the Holy Spirit via the Word of God (Bible)...in a spirit dominant, soul subordinate, and love your neighbor as yourself, while in this **experiential spiritual life journey on earth!** That is referencing an individual standpoint first, but let me make it clear that in order for it to positively impact our culture and daily life, this must be taken to the next levels and occur within a major population of the collective church body. BTW, you can take the above sentence in which I have social injustice underlined and replace it with practically any social ill and it too will apply! i.e. racism, poverty, homelessness, drug abuse, etc.

Where does that leave us? Well for one, *** Identify the root problem (racism); then determine how to fix it with a root fix (Jesus). As mentioned, we have thousands of years of experience for reference, the root problem defined, and we have the root fix. So we can reverse engineer to come up with solutions. In the beginning of this book, I think that I made my point clear that we need a spiritual reformation (not revival, not a violent revolution) but rather a reformation in which we change ourselves from within and we change the system and processes that are corrupt in our society. Easier said than done? Well it has cycled back and forth throughout the millennia and the majority of the time, social injustice (primarily due to racism) was dominant, but I truly believe that if it can happen anywhere and anytime that in America now is as good a time as any to put this into motion. Remember, a journey begins with a first step...and if it is to be, it is up to me. And this reformation begins with you and me.

Side note: there are a multitude of opinions for solutions on social injustice, with many well intentioned, although far off base. Point is, the solution that I've lined out is the only one that may have positive, overarching and lasting results if we can pull it off. All the others I've encountered are a lot of talk and at most only possibly a band-aid.

I'll begin with a pastor being interviewed on a prominent Christian television network at the onset of protests and rioting. He exhibited that he was uncomfortable at first with the topic matter and the impromptu questioning, although you would have thought he'd have prepared somewhat to speak on these topics. He began with what it is like to be black and grow up in this society and gave a number of examples. Then he shifted to communicating the oppression of over 400 years, then he got into the topic of slavery, and it was obvious that he went way outside his wheelhouse and knowledge base, although spoke it as though it was accurate. He appeared that he was attempting to say the right things and remain somewhat politically correct, although he fell way short. Meaning, that which was coming out of his mouth was from his biased heart (not his spirit, but his dominant soul instead) and so he was saying what was on his mind (soul) to draw an abysmal picture. I wanted to illustrate that context of the interview and his communication, in order to put the main point into perspective. He then stated that the only way this can get fixed is "IN the church." To my point, not the collective church body, but IN the church. He knows what the difference is, yet he was saying what was on his mind, which in a way is good so that we at least know where he stands on this topic. Maybe his candid narrative was due to the impromptu situation or for some other reason I can only speculate, nonetheless I do believe that this was coming directly from top of mind. In the past he has bragged about his Rolex watch and the vehicles he owns, so it is clear that he believes that internally "IN" his church, he can deal with the matter of social injustice. Again, I can only speculate but my explanation and my historical observations of him may tend to give a first impression that he is using his platform for other blacks who aren't so fortunate and do not have a voice, when in actuality he spoke in first person, in a wronged and victimized stance, playing up to the overwhelming media hype and drama (I'm not downplaying the importance of this topic matter, only relaying what took place in his interview). Another thing to take note of is that it was his congregation (flock) that paid for the watch, vehicles and other conspicuous luxuries, and it is his congregation that apparently agree with his beliefs and support him and his approaches and in this case as it pertains to social injustice.

Thing is, what will be the result of it? Little to nothing, or on the contrary, probably a fueling of the fire.

In hindsight, it was obvious that his message was not for the masses, but rather for his congregation who was watching (it is not a megachurch although has approximately 9K in its congregation), and I would also assume that he believes little to nothing will be accomplished in our society regarding this topic, as has been the case. I do not give him credit that he was even close to being correct especially in regard to the context in which he was stating it, but what he unknowingly had correct is that it must begin IN the church. And that is where I pick it up and expound on it, in that it must begin in the church with the collective church body (whether in the U.S. or worldwide, involving all or most denominations) coming together and working through Jesus as spirit dominant Believers, or working on becoming so, as stated prior. Thing is, to live spirit dominant is how God wants us to live, yet so few in the church even recognize it and fewer teach it, maybe because they would rather dilute their messages and avoid anything that poses difficulty. Additionally, when you are Spirit filled and walking in the Spirit and with Grace consciousness, at that point it is really not that difficult to achieve spirit dominance. Imagine the quality of life in the U.S. in which a large population of Believers through Jesus and via the Holy Spirit were led to be spirit dominant and treated their neighbor as themselves, and the spirit dominated words from the heart that come out of their mouth were: just, kind, loving, considerate, tolerant, compassionate, and on and on.

The next example could easily be an illustration of tens of thousands of virtual discussions or blogs with similar content. Somehow this particular virtual meeting must have gone viral and ended up in mainstream media online and I happened to stumble across and out of curiosity watch a portion of it. A young 25-30 something attractive black female host (who seemed more concerned about her appearance and her bubbly personality, more so than the topic being discussed), had invited a 50 something white female secular psychologist to give her viewpoints, and had a number of participants of all millennial black females. One had a not so notable comment, although does has its place within the context of this subchapter. She first gave an example that had taken place that morning, another the day before and another the day before that and in frustration concluded by saying, "It is not my job to "teach" white people how to treat or how not to treat me, or how they are to act." I think it speaks for itself and I will not comment regarding it, you draw the conclusion on how it relates to speaking one's mind, from an emotional viewpoint, from the soul and not the spirit, as well as how you think this would contribute to positively impacting the topic of social injustice or racism for that matter. Regarding the secular psychologist, nothing she had to say was productive, rather she was preaching to the choir and fueling the fire of the participants with what came across as her opinions and not a professional viewpoint (having been secular she probably believes that it was professional); in addition she was pushing to the participants the ever increasing and ever popular (and extremely destructive "I feel, therefore I am" philosophy) "this is the way I feel, therefore I am right and justified in believing it as the truth." Problem is, when you are soul dominant, your emotions are your moral compass and general guide regarding your choices in life...enough said.

I'll still applaud the efforts behind this and as mentioned tens of thousands similar discussions, but that's just it, they're all talk and no substance, whatsoever. No redeeming quality, no matter how hard you try evaluating it. Unfortunately, the majority actually does more harm by fueling the fire from another perspective, therefore perpetuating a vicious circle of racism that continues to reach all-time lows.

People can always criticize and find fault in things, so what's important is being a part of the solution and not adding to the problem. Fortunately, the Holy Spirit has given me this revelation and is not only a viable approach to finally correcting the vicious circle that is spinning out of control, but it is "THE" approach that our Lord wants us to take. Not only was it THE plan before the beginning of time for us to be spirit dominant while on our experiential spiritual life journey on earth and to have an abundant life, but for those Believers who do not mature to that point in their walk, they WILL in a blink of an eye be spirit dominant in heaven and love every minute of it.

A couple of miscellaneous points to ponder:
- A solution is not to defund the police.
    - If our society continues to remove God, remove Jesus, remove religion, etc. from our lives, you won't be able to hire enough police officers or military personnel to handle the ensuing unrest and violence.
- Many of the riots were due to factions of terrorists' cells embedded among the sincere peaceful demonstrators, provoking the police to violence against all of the participants.

- o As stated previously a number of times in this subchapter, change needs to happen, but it must be non-violent and begins within each and every one of us.
- o Those who want change and protest with signs and marches are sincere, but they are also a part of the lost generation, because they know they want change to happen but have no idea what to do to achieve it successfully.
  - ▪ Change is what they want. My point is that change is what is needed and that the change must come from each of those individuals, Note: the word "repent" simply means to change your ways, although it is far from simple for most to consider change, let alone actually change.
- o Those in the minority who were throwing rocks and rioting, everyone else who were trying to comprehend and understand what was taking place needs to understand three things: a) as mentioned, they were either terrorist cells doing their best to create chaos and instability or they were far left radicals doing the same thing. b) And probably a significant amount were just plain thugs and losers. C) Ponder this, if Jesus were present for the protesters and rock throwers, He very likely would have challenged them with, "Those who are without sin, bias and prejudice, let him/her cast the first stone."
- See, it is social ills as these that involves every individual in one way, or in many ways.
  - o *We need to take a long hard look in the mirror, and then remove the plank out of our own eye, before we complain and attempt to remove the speck out of our brothers' eye!
  - o (Matt. 7:1-5)BSB "Do not judge, or you will be judged. For with the same judgment you pronounce, you will be judged; and with the measure you use, it will be measured to you. Why do you look at the speck in your brother's eye, but fail to notice the beam in your own eye? How can you say to your brother, 'Let me take the speck out of your eye,' while there is still a beam in your own eye? You hypocrite! First take the beam out of your own eye, and then you will see clearly to remove the speck from your brother's eye."
- ***Consider doing this, when you speak to others, consciously speak from your spirit with the intent of speaking to their spirit.
  - o First, you have to identify how to speak from your spirit and not from your soul (that you have probably spoken from for your lifetime). Volume II and III will assist you in understanding it,

but the process itself involves the Holy Spirit as your active personal coach.

- o I personally do not go around consciously attempting to do this day in and day out, rather I do so as a specific intention for when I am giving Godly advice, praying with others, etc. For me it is a work in progress that I have actually accomplished in the past, but at times get off track, fall into old habits due to my circumstances, but the Holy Spirit will get my attention and get me back on the correct path. Thing is, it should be at all times if we truly live in a dominant spirit. This is very similar to what I covered in a previous chapter, glorify God in all that you think, say and do. When you make a conscious effort to do that each and every minute of each and every day, and you accomplish it the majority of the time, then you must be in a spirit dominant mode.

- o Let me also briefly touch on a couple of characteristics as to the "how" that's involved in being spirit dominant. First, recall the concept of glorifying God by the things we think, say and do. Therefore think and do things "in the right" spirit; and speak words of the Spirit that bless others and not curse. There are numerous lines of scriptures that point out specific words from the Spirit, as well as what the proper mindset is of one who is in the Spirit and of the right spirit.

Contemplate and meditate on what you have just read. Also seek the Holy Spirit to validate all that I have relayed by taking you through numerous scriptures in the Bible. Keep in mind that I threw a considerable amount of God's principles and predestined purposes in very short and concise couple of paragraphs and I do not expect you to fully comprehend it, nor fully understand it. As mentioned, I spent hundreds of pages in Volumes I & II to lay the foundation to help you in understanding those principles, so be sure to continue reading to gain a greater understanding. Additionally, meditate on what you believe you should do as a Believer and as an individual to move forward regarding this topic and/or any other social ills. Finally, determine what you can do to contribute to a positive change in our society and then act on it.

Well, I thought I was going to end the topic, but the Holy Spirit nudged me to continue with some deeper explanations that are very important, related to this topic and need to get communicated. Even though I have covered this social ill and others quite extensively in Volume III, I cannot move on from this topic without expounding on it. So here I go again pulling **insight and advanced**

263

teachings from Volume III but I think that this is one of those occasions that it may help you to get exposed to it and there is no harm done if you do not fully comprehend the information. You can circle back around to it once you've had a chance to read Vol. I & II in their entirety. Just a couple of pages prior, I suggested that you take a comprehensive look at the BIG picture after having read Volumes I & II. Here I'm relaying that it is imperative that all Believers take a BIG picture 10,000ft view <u>of the Bible (the Word of God)</u> and to do so **in context** from cover to cover. This way you are able to see topics that get illuminated by the Holy Spirit and are interlinked one to another, then you can see comprehensively how it applies to our lives both individually and to the collective church body (and hopefully a reflection on society). Be careful in doing this, because without guidance you can combine things that should not be combined or vice versa. Whether you utilize "A Father's Wisdom" as your guide or you use your church home and pastor, that is up to you.

Let me give you a brief example of what I am referring to, although off topic, and keep in mind this is a brief explanation and to fully expound on it would take many pages or even a few chapters. Mentioned elsewhere in Vol. I is the Age of Grace that we are in due to the finished works by Jesus on the cross. God's grace has erased our sins and by faith through Jesus we are allowed a relationship with the Heavenly Father. In the Old Testament, the only way to have a relationship with Him was by divine appointment or by fulfilling the Ten Commandments which were laws set forth by God, that no man could fulfill. Many Christians mistakenly believe that even today we must "work" at fulfilling those laws. Jesus communicated specifically in **(Matt 5:17-18)**BSB "<u>Do not think that I have come to abolish the Law</u> or the Prophets; I have not come to abolish them, but to fulfill them. For I tell you truly, until heaven and earth pass away, not a single jot, not a stroke of a pen, will disappear from the Law until everything is accomplished." He came to fulfill the Law, so in other words, the Law is not nullified rather we uphold the Law and we should use it daily as our moral compass. Now to the main point, we are no longer in bondage to the Law and facing death for not fulfilling it, (remember death in this context is being separate and without God). So, to wrap this example up, there are some teachings and precepts from the OT that apply in the NT (as I am going to point out in the upcoming paragraphs); there are teachings and precepts from the OT that still apply but have changed somewhat from the original application (as seen in this example); and there are definitely teachings and precepts from the OT that do not at all apply in the NT, nor do they apply to us now. Again, it takes wisdom, knowledge and understanding of the Word via the Holy Spirit;

or from a source like "A Father's Wisdom"; or from a source like your pastor to guide you in understanding.

As just mentioned, the following are relevant teachings from the NT and one extremely important teaching from the OT that is still applicable today. Review the following scriptures to give you an idea of what I am referring to "in context" as a whole and from cover to cover (OT and NT), with regards to this topic of racism and loving your neighbor:

(Matt 22:36-40)BSB "Teacher, which commandment is the greatest in the Law?" Jesus declared, "'Love the Lord your God with all your heart and with all your soul and with all your mind.' This is the first and greatest commandment; And the second is like it: **'Love your neighbor as yourself.'** All the Law and the Prophets hang on these two commandments."

(Mark 12:30-31)BSB "Love the Lord your God with all your heart and with all your soul and with all your mind and with all your strength.' The second is this: **'Love your neighbor as yourself.'** No other commandment is greater than these."

Our Lord here teaches us that we should have these two precepts in our minds continuously and before our eyes, and direct all our thoughts and words and actions by them, and regulate our whole life according to them! Mentioned just prior in this subchapter and in various parts of this book, is my take on how we glorify God daily, in the things that we think, say and do, and do so every minute of every day. As I had mentioned, this alone transformed my life significantly for the better, and it surprised me that it really did not impinge on my daily life, nor would require a major change in what I did in my day or night. This is just one scripture that conveys that we can glorify God, **(Matt 5:16)NKJV "and **glorify your Father in heaven." Just imagine what would happen if a major portion of the collective body focused on glorifying Him with all that they think, say and do, not to mention what it would do for them individually, but the mighty impact it would make on so many other people in this world!

The following is one aspects of the BIG picture view that I wanted to emphasize, meaning that although Jesus declared a pivotal commandment in Matthew and Mark, ****a very important point that often gets overlooked or simply ignored is,

(Levit. 19:16-18)BSB "You must not go about spreading slanderous rumors among your people. You must not endanger the life of your neighbor. I am the LORD. You must not harbor hatred against your brother in your heart. **Directly rebuke your neighbor**, so that you will not incur guilt on account of him. Do not seek revenge or bear a grudge against any of your people, **but love your neighbor as yourself.** I am the LORD."

- Rebuke in this context means to correct or convict your neighbor for his or her sin/wrongdoing against God and the collective body of Christ.
  - o **Many have this very wrong, and this confusion has led our society down a treacherous path of destruction. It does **NOT** mean to turn your cheek and/or be tolerant and allow them to "do as they please." Boy, I could go down a deep rabbit hole on this topic but have saved it for Volume III, in order to keep us on topic here.
  - o Please take note of correction and conviction (which you have learned about in a previous chapter on the Holy Spirit) that it is not referring to condemnation of your neighbor. Here I am referring to the degree of conviction, where if you overstep those bounds falls into the category of condemnation and it is not up to you to pass judgement (only One passes judgement).
- To paraphrase Dietrich Bonhoeffer: Not to speak is to speak, which in turn corrupts the collective body of Christ and you can incur guilt by that account.
  - o **(Ezek. 33:7-9)** KJV God said to Ezekiel, "As for you, O <u>son of man</u>, I have made you a **watchman** for the house of Israel; so hear the word from My mouth and give them warning from Me. If I say to the wicked, 'O wicked man, you will surely die,' but you do not speak out to dissuade him from his way, then that wicked man will die in his iniquity, yet <u>I will hold you accountable</u> for his blood. But if you warn the wicked man to turn from his way, and he does not turn from it, he will die in his iniquity, but you will have saved your life."
  - o Note, this is another OT scripture that very much applies today and is in direct context with the topics we are covering.
  - o Just an FYI, you've heard me mention that I was <u>called</u> as a carpenter with a purpose of helping to build up others, and <u>sent</u> as a messenger, with a twist during its evolution to now also a watchman.

We are expected to "Love thy neighbor as thyself," and we are equally expected to have an understanding of the wisdom of God (Jesus / Bible), or have the Holy Spirit give us discernment at any moment, so that we can rebuke our neighbor with "Truth in love," as illustrated in the following scripture.

(Eph 4:15)NIV "Then we will no longer be immature like children. We won't be tossed and blown about by every wind of new teaching. We will not be influenced when people try to trick us with lies so clever they sound like the truth. Instead, we will **speak the truth in love**, <u>growing in every way more and more like Christ</u>, who is the head of his body, **the church**. <u>He makes the whole body fit</u>

together perfectly. As each part does its own special work, it helps the other parts grow, so that the whole body is healthy and growing and full of love."

- Can you recall Jesus' travels and how outspoken he was? He spoke the truth in love, time and time again. Aren't we supposed to grow in every way more and more like Jesus in our daily walk and our sanctification process on earth and into eternity?

- The contemporary understanding/translation of "Speaking the Truth in Love" is: telling someone (whether correcting or convicting) of their wrongdoings, from a Godly perspective and position, without emotion and bias, but instead from being led by the Holy Spirit in your spirit (as stated and in context with Leviticus 19 above). In the same right yet on the other side of the spectrum, it also applies to us speaking the truth to our neighbor, which means giving Godly advice when asked, the fullness of wisdom that we as Believers believe in and makes up our beings…to speak the truth in love to everyone we come in contact with (this applies to one of the many meanings when Jesus said, "You must take up your cross daily").

- When doing this be careful not to pass judgment, rather only "rebuke" their sinful actions. **(Matt. 7:1-2)**BSB "Do not judge, or you will be judged. For with the same judgment you pronounce, you will be judged; and with the measure you use, it will be measured to you." It may seem like a fine line between correcting or convicting someone of their sinning, versus passing judgement, but if you are led by the Holy Spirit, He will keep it from becoming judgmental as long as that is your true intention and you are making a conscious effort not to pass judgement.

- In addition, take heed to this passage **(Matt 18:15)**NIV "If your brother or sister sins, go and point out their fault, just between the two of you. If they listen to you and repent, you have won them back. But if they will not listen, take one or two others along, so that 'every matter may be established by the testimony of two or three witnesses.' This is a lesson for today's society, to keep things private and not to air dirty laundry, but to do it "speaking the truth in love."

Continue reading the following scriptures to finalize this exercise in applying a BIG picture view of the Bible with regards to the topic of racism. Additionally, this is a huge paradigm shift for most (see paradigm defined in the Introduction in Vol. I). After an entire life of conditioning, you view life through your lens (paradigm) and therefore very difficult to adjust, not to mention change, but change is what all Believer's have in common and are familiar with doing. This topic of racism and social injustice will require us to change first before the balance of society might understand, thus opening up opportunities for change throughout the corrupt system. The next scripture covers multiple topics related to the subjects being covered here. As mentioned, continue reading with the previously stated objectives in mind.

(**Eph. 4:21-26**)BSB "Surely you heard of Him and were taught in Him, in keeping with **the truth that is in Jesus**. So put off your former way of life, your old self, which is being corrupted by its deceitful desires; to **be renewed in the spirit of your minds**; and to put on the new self, created to be like God in true righteousness and holiness. Therefore each of you must put off falsehoods (telling lies) and **speak truthfully to his neighbor, for we are all members of one another**. 'Do not sin by letting anger control you.' Do not let the sun set upon your anger, thus giving the devil a foothold." (foothold is equivalent to a portal and discussed extensively in Ch 9 & 10)

Here Paul is expressing an example of truth in love by telling the Ephesians to put away lying, because as a church body those sins misaligns it and he points out that we are all members, one of another. The following scripture points out how a church body is fitly framed together, and when that is so, the collective can move mountains.

(**Eph. 2:19-22**)BSB "Therefore you are no longer strangers and foreigners, but fellow citizens of the saints and **members of God's household**, built on the foundation of the apostles and prophets, with Christ Jesus Himself as the cornerstone. In Him **the whole building is fitted together and grows into a holy temple in the Lord**. **And** in Him **you too** are being built together into a dwelling place for God in His Spirit."

The "whole building" is referring to the body of Christ, growing into a temple "in" the Lord. And be sure to understand the "And" connection, that we too (in Him) are being built together into a dwelling place for God's Holy Spirit (1Cor. 6:19 "Do you not know that your body is the temple of the Holy Spirit, given to you as a gift of God?") We are to be striving to become a building that is fitly framed together and growing unto a Holy Temple "IN" the Lord. Keep that thought for my connecting of the dots summation.

(**John 15:4-6**)BSB "Remain in Me, and I will remain in you. Just as no branch can bear fruit by itself unless it remains in the vine, neither can you bear fruit unless you remain in Me. I am the vine and you are the branches. The one who remains in Me, and I in him, will bear much fruit. **For apart from Me you can do nothing**. If anyone does not remain in Me, he is like a branch that is thrown away and withers. Such branches are gathered up, thrown into the fire, and burned."

Your efforts without Jesus are a waste of time, from apart from Him you can do nothing.

(Eph. 3:16-19)BSB "I ask that out of the riches of His glory He may strengthen you with **power** through His Spirit in your inner being, so that <u>Christ may dwell in your hearts through faith</u>. And I pray that you, being rooted and grounded in love, will have power, together with all the saints, to <u>comprehend the length and width and height and depth of His love</u>, and to know the love of Christ that surpasses knowledge, that you may be filled with all the fullness of God."

(Eph. 3:20-21)NKJV "Now to Him who is able to do exceedingly abundantly above all that we ask or think, <u>according to the power that works in us</u>, to Him be glory in the church by Christ Jesus **to all generations**, forever and ever. Amen."

This is a connecting of the dots, from loving thy neighbor as thyself; to rebuking your neighbor when it is appropriate and needed; to doing so by communicating truth in love; to advancing the kingdom by renewing our minds daily via the Holy Spirit, who dwells in us and is building us up, along with building up our fellow Believers who are striving to accomplish these like-minded processes, which results in us all being members of God's household and thus the collective body of Christ is being fitted together as one holy temple, who must include Jesus as the integral center of this process, for with Him we can do all things, great and small, moving mountains and changing social ills; who gives us supernatural power via our faith in Him dwelling in our hearts (dominant spirit), with a foundation of being rooted and grounded in the fullness of His love that surpasses all knowledge and understanding, is able to do exceedingly abundantly above all that we ask or think, and with that comprehensive understanding to accomplish those things that we have never as a church body has ever been able to do before, according to the power that works in us and through us...this is applicable and achievable for all living generations that hope, trust, have faith and Believe in the Lord!

- A note of warning: as just mentioned, Jesus must be the integral center of these processes, but I haven't heard much by anyone discussing the topic of racism and social injustice, pastor or otherwise, mention Jesus or mention anything like what I am proposing. They focus on changing laws, rights and privileges, how to elect officials, cultural influence and change to the society, etc. and their centric emphasis is on themselves, or their plight, or the injustice they've endured, or the inequalities faced, or their anger, or their resentment, and on and on, but they do not have their first focus on Jesus. I'll make this point brief, if you exclude Jesus from the processes mentioned above that needs to be changed, you might get some favorable laws changed, but that will be all you accomplish. Subsequently, the injustice will increase and so will the racism from each race and ethnicity of peoples! This will continue to perpetuate until you change yourself by the renewing of your mind and always first focus on Jesus as you fight your battles! It is fair to say, "Jesus is the answer!"

- **A Jesus centric life** is key to us having an abundant life in this experiential spiritual life journey on earth, and it is key for mankind to get his (or her) act together. As pointed out, He is a key component in positive change in this world. The following is a huge paradigm shift (as defined in the Introduction of this book) which is a problem with the lens that people view their life through and a problem with not being able to change and overcome it (victoriously; as in Jesus overcame the world; meaning He was victorious over the world; So do you approach the world from your own victimized viewpoint or from the stance of a victor, as Jesus did). Having said that, a related problem is with those who feel victimized, or cheated out of life, or taken advantage of, etc. with regard to social injustice, is that they or someone they know may have been going to church for years or even decades and have prayed on the topic relentlessly and to their dismay their list of wants did not get answered and they do not believe their prayers will ever be answered (to their liking; and often without any <u>action</u> taken by them that is in relation with the prayer). So now they exclude Jesus from the process and have taken matters into their own hands. Whether you analyze this from an individual standpoint or from a collective church body, it is the same thing. We all know that when you take things into your own hands, to do your "self," He will rest as you work and He will even bless you to an extent, but you are no longer under the fullness of His grace or blessings. The only way to truly change things is to rest in Him and get guidance from Him in what to do and how to do, along with benefiting from His full grace and blessing continuously throughout the process. And consider this, if we do not start working on changing to our spirit dominance now, then just as with past generations, we will probably never be able to change the future for those upcoming generations that we should be so concerned about.

Hopefully, you were able to grasp a few or all of the meanings I just conveyed. Just keep in mind that with me compiling this into one lump of teaching (albeit advanced), the information can be confusing for some of you, so as mentioned be patient and finish reading Vol. I & II then return to this subchapter and you should by then have a greater understanding with regards to this range of topics. This exercise we just went through in this subchapter will also give you an idea of the wisdom and advanced teachings that constitutes Volume III.

COVID-19

The world has been through pandemics before and ultimately survived and overcame them. COVID-19 was no different. It was amazing though that the world was NOT better prepared to deal with and lessen its impact. But mankind let its guard down and got comfortable and complacent with the status quo and believing they had gotten to the point of either being invincible or godlike in terms of "I am the captain of my world, I've built the career, the wealth and the lifestyle and I can withstand any storms that comes my way, etc." Everyone knew that at its peak and its duration, it would take many, many lives, which would be painful for most, depressing and then devastating for some. What they had no idea was that it would transform life as they knew it, or at least alter the norm to a "new normal" and significantly inconvenience their precious bubble of a life they have been living in. A plethora of articles, medical journals, government policies, books, etc. have been written on this topic, so no need to elaborate other than a few points that directly relate to the context of this book.

I've previously discussed elsewhere in this book, that mankind was created to be social beings. To be in a relationship with God (as a spiritual being) and to be in positive and mutually productive relationships with others (as a social being). That is how life is supposed to work, that is if we do not turn our backs on God and on others, whether out of selfishness, laziness, greed, hatred, and the list goes on and on. So the result of COVID-19 was that some people learned some very hard and extremely difficult lessons, while others are destined to continue to repeat things via their fleshly and selfish ways. Most that learned the lessons are Believers, or people that are in the process of becoming born again Believers. Having said that leads into what I have to say next, which I want to make perfectly clear that COVID-19 was not from God, but rather from mankind (just as all previous pandemics, diseases, etc.), therefore of fleshly origin, thus opening up a portal for demonic activity. In this case, incredible amounts of demonic activities due to our society being primed for satan/devil to further divide people from God and from each other!

"Social Distancing" was a term coined for the times. Where in actuality the better explanation would have been "physical distancing," which communicates for people to keep a physical distance between themselves and others to keep from transmitting the virus; and in reality would have relayed the appropriate message more effectively to the masses who may have responded better, as well as heeded and adhered to the warnings. *Is it just coincidence the term "Social Distancing" received the green light, when satan works so diligently on creating social divide for a people who were created by God to be in a righteous relationship with each other??? *It is against our nature to distance ourselves and especially to isolate

271

ourselves from others. So having to comply with that directive further breaks down the individual's spirit while opening additional portals of doubt, fear, etc. for satan/devil to capitalize on and further negatively impact those people's (unbelievers) lives that allow this to occur, not to mention making strides with those Believers that allow it to occur and thus moving them away from the Lord! *A word of warning, do not allow society or satan to distance us from each other! It's understandable that during a pandemic to stay safe and distance until a cure is found, but the government, the media and society as a whole overreacted especially after the worst of it had passed. Remember that we were created to be social beings and do not allow that to be taken from you.

Didn't I say, "Incredible amounts of demonic activities?" (see also Ch9, Ch10) Another very impactful demonic tactic was to ruin people's livelihood, losing their jobs, losing their businesses, losing their savings, losing their houses, losing their investments, losing, losing, losing! All the while causing much pain and sorrow for nonbelievers and Believers alike.

> **(Duet 31:6)**BSB "Be strong and courageous, do not be afraid, for it is the LORD your God who is with you; He will never leave you nor forsake you." (also Heb. 13:5)
> **(2 Cor 2:3-4)**NKJV "Blessed be the God and Father of our Lord Jesus Christ, the Father of compassion and the God of all comfort, who comforts us in all our troubles so that we can comfort those in any trouble with the comfort we ourselves have received from God."
> **(Rom 15:13)**BSB "Now may the God of hope fill you with all joy and peace as you believe in Him, so that you may overflow with hope by the power of the Holy Spirit."

Regarding those losses previously mentioned, please understand that it was because of God and through God that you acquired those things and it will be because of God and through God that you regain those things. What satan has stolen from the Believer, God according to His purpose for you, will make things right (e.g. the Book of Job). I can attest to this from my own personal experiences (as noted in Ch1, Ch2, Ch9, Ch10), my accumulated wealth was lost and then returned to me as I matured as a Believer (persevere and believe)! God's Word (The Bible) has scripture upon scripture regarding God providing us with all things, He is the God of Providence (Jehovah Jireh), God providing us with hope, and Jesus instructing us not to be fearful or sorrowful but to rest (trust) in Him, and on and on. You either Believe (trust in faith) or NOT.

> **(Mat 6:31 paraphrase -33)** "Therefore do not worry, saying, 'What shall we do now that we lost these things?' For the pagans strive after all these things, and your Heavenly Father knows that you need them. But seek

first the kingdom of God and His righteousness, and all these things will be added unto you."

(Mat 6:19)BSB "Do not store up for yourselves treasures on earth, where moth and rust destroy, and where thieves break in and steal. [20]But store up for yourselves treasures in heaven." (The thief, satan/devil will steal what you believe you have made on your own; and those things prove to be only temporal. But rather invest first in the Lord and all these things according to His will, will be given unto you; and your investment and commitment to the Lord will pay off for you for an eternity).

(Prov 19:20-21)BSB "Listen to counsel and accept discipline, that you may be wise the rest of your days. Many plans are in a man's heart, but the purpose of the LORD will prevail."

Mentioned just a few topics prior, **Jesus is the foundation of our medicine, our remedy and our cure**, so how does that work when it comes to our healing? As mentioned, you must be a Believer who is walking in the Spirit daily and renewing your mind. Jesus plays an integral role in your healing. Before I continue, let me relay some additional background information that should assist you in processing this topic.

I had Covid19 right at the peak of the hysteria and I must say that with all the media hype along with the mounting death tolls, that it was scary (stressful with much anxiety, even as a strong Believer). I had recently moved in order to take care of my 95yr old aunt and therefore was living alone with no friends or family within hundreds of miles, so being alone and battling the virus at the same time was difficult to bear. The prospect of getting sick and dying in just a matter of days, weeks or months was an eye opening, unnerving, unsettling, humbling and revealing experience (I never anticipated ever having to experientially live out something like this, and the prevailing questioned loomed: **am I prepared to die today?**). By the way, thankfully a Christian broadcasting station interviewed two popular pastors who contracted Covid19 in the N.Y. area during the peak of the hysteria and you could tell that the interview was not scripted or attempting to project an agenda. I say that because the interview was so explicit and revealing in terms of how these to Godly men feared for their lives. Both pastors were extremely scared and spoke of the dark times they experienced (including dreams, nightmares and hallucinations), that was a contributor to them not wanting to go to sleep and in addition to that they had this strange sense that when they would go to bed that they didn't know whether they would wake up; the death that surrounded them in the hospital; one who was high risk at 60yrs old and lifetime of asthma had to be on a ventilator just to be able to breathe, he relayed some grave aspects of his bout and grave aspects of other people that were in ICU with him and those that died; the other 40yrs old with a young family and fortunately not as serious a situation as the other, but enough to check into the hospital along with an assistant pastor, he too expressed the darkness of the events and said that it was difficult to stay positive and maintain his faith in trusting in the Lord, which he commented that he is not built that way his entire life and to experience the thought of potential death was an experience he found difficult to put into words. Obviously, both had good endings in which both of them overcame the virus, checked out of the hospital and participated in the interview via video conferencing. I just mentioned a few of the takeaways and although there were quite a few, the standouts had to be: pastors who feared for their life and experienced a dark journey with the disease; they expressed their concerns of the "darkness" which involved a number of scenarios from death, to uncertainty, to the insidious nature of the disease, nightmares, helplessness, weakness, paralyzing the body and also much to the extent the mind, etc.; they were "distracted" (devil) with the events unfolding around them; even though they both had a collective of Believing prayer warriors praying for them, yet they still questioned why (whether why me or why now, etc.) and they prayed fervently to be healed; they praised the health care workers and they praised the Lord!

Additionally, they mentioned the stigma attached to Covid and how people are dying at home because they did not want anyone to know they contracted it, and therefore did not seek medical attention, etc. I can relate to this myself and want to take this opportunity to relay that whether Covid or any other illness, disease or infirmity, do not worry what others may think, but rather seek help both professional and spiritual. I know, easier said than done…I did not seek help and did not tell a single person and suffered the consequences of the isolation and paranoia.

As just mentioned, I was ill during this time and was wondering if I should be watching this interview, but at the same time thinking that I need to watch it in order to gain as much insight as possible. During this time period I was careful not to get an overload of information, and especially fake news and misinformation which was and always remains rampant on just about every major topic. One of the biggest stressors for me was how the Covid attacks crucial organs and specifically the lungs. My symptoms began like most have experienced, similar to a cold but quickly went into my lungs. You can cope with cold like symptoms, but it is the things you do not have control over that puts the fear into you. I was experiencing both shallow breathing and shortness of breath and especially at night I would wake up gasping for breath and would be up for a couple of hours (or the rest of that night) in calming myself down and focusing on taking deep breaths and praying that it did not get any worse. One morning the Holy Spirit brought to my attention that a couple of months prior in my move across the country, I did not throw out a lung exercise tool that I received at the hospital after having major surgery 15yrs ago. Yes, I held onto it for that long and it was in an unopened sealed bag. You inhale through it for 6 reps at 3 sets each and the meter reads whether you are hitting the "normal" lung capacity goal, or you push yourself to get there. I unpacked it and exercised my lungs every three hours of every day. Eventually it did the trick as well as helping to reduce my anxiety and allowed me to look forward to going to sleep and getting the rest needed to get better. This is another of the thousands of examples in which the Holy Spirit gave me the discernment to do something that would help my situation.

One of the biggest ploys of the devil is to get us distracted from God and our relationship with Him. As I pointed out with my example of the two pastors in the hospital, they were distracted to the point of losing sight of how to battle the darkness, but fortunately their years of commitment, habit and knowledge along with the extended helping hand of Jesus to pull them out of that pit, allowed them to focus on what is the most urgent and important things to do under these extreme circumstances: pray, declare your "rights" in Jesus's name, walk with the Holy Spirit and renew the mind (spiritual mind, soul and body) in the Word. Believe me, this is what I did and I wanted to share another what I think is an extremely important point: I was in the process of editing the final copy of this book, therefore I was listening to it (all 550+ pages) first at regular narrator speed and then a couple of times at 1.25 speed; I could say that this kept me from being idle and freaking out about Covid and my illness, and especially from allowing the devil to distract me, which both were the case and are relevant, but I experienced my greatest healing when I listened to the narration of this book for hours on end and in addition to it I had fasted the weekend before and I was taking the Last Supper (Holy Communion) every night after shutting off the narrator and computer. Note for weeks prior to that, I was praying and reading and quoting scripture and declaring healing in the name of Jesus and quite frankly was anxiously thinking which scriptures I should focus on that will "make a difference." I'm not attempting to "pitch" this book for healing, the point is that there are so many scriptures and subsequent true to life explanations along with my intense listening (for editing purposes) that my mind was racing and taking it all in; note, this would apply to any similar book or especially the Bible audiobook. Bottomline, in only a couple of days I noticed the difference and the Holy Spirit helped me in connecting the dots and I then experienced dramatic improvement and healing! Glory be to God! Honestly, at one point I didn't know whether I should go to the hospital or not, and quite frankly did not know what to think or do. I did although rely on the Holy Spirit to guide and direct my path, and He did!

I also wanted to add another observation that I had but am not suggesting it applies to anyone else, so do not utilize this as advice for you or anyone you know, to execute it. If you've ever experienced a bad case of the flu, you typically go to bed and get under the covers and sleep as much as you can to get over it. I think that Covid is just the opposite and it was for me, I never "gave into it" so to speak and never relaxed or rested, but rather I exercised as normal every single morning and evening whether I felt like it or not; at one point I lost my appetite, so from then on it was bone broth and steamed vegetables only, to reduce the stress on my digestive system, but I ate four times a day to keep my energy up; I focused on past, present and future positive thoughts and especially positive future faith; I prayed more often than normal with prayers primarily of praise with very few petition requests; as mentioned, I listened to this book and I took Holy Communion in which the triune are present and I ask to enter their presence (explained elsewhere in this chapter and others); and I walked in the Spirit 24/7 as I always do and rested in the assurance that Jesus would guide the Holy Spirit to guide me into recovery and wellness; as He did! As previously mentioned, this worked for me but do not attempt it for your self-remedy, I just felt it was important to relay to never give in to the Covid19 or ever let your guard down.

(FYI, 1.25 speed will cover both volumes of the book in approx. 50hrs although difficult to absorb key points; also I do not recommend at all listening at 1.5 speed I could not edit the grammar, but my point is you would not be able to comprehend anything let alone even the most crucial points)

I hope that this was some good background information for you on the topic of "Jesus as the medicine, the remedy and the cure." That was a pretty comprehensive story for you to extrapolate the information you need out of it, leaving the question, what is there left to say about this topic. Well, another book could be written on it. (see subchapter the medicine, the remedy and the cure; also Ch4 on prayer; but in reality, it is this book from cover to cover and the Bible!)

The Lord is here for us and He will never leave us nor forsake us. Honor Him, trust in Him, and Believe in Him! Receive His blessings, His grace, and His love! **Pray in victory!** Have **Positive Future Faith** always and He will close doors and open new ones, and He will provide exceedingly abundantly above all that you can ever utilize, need, desire or dream of!!!

Victory

I stand in a place of victory and **I pray** from a place of victory!

- All that is behind me, is the past (whether bad times or good times).
  - o The "old" man I was, without Christ, is behind me (and I keep him there).
  - o The past troubles and challenges are behind me.
  - o I do not dwell in the past (nor do I "dwell" on even past successes).
  - o I do not strive for victory in my daily life, because of what Jesus did for me on the cross, He made it so that I am already victorious and it took me almost a lifetime to understand that and embrace it.
- So, I stand in victory with my thoughts and prayers of positive future faith...and it is all the while fueling my present!
  - o "To have life and have it abundantly!" Today, in the present!
- Praying from a place of victory with God confidence and always moving forward.

Positive Future Faith – Fuels our Present***

The concept of Faith is one of the most misunderstood and confusing topics a Believer has been given to utilize in their daily repertoire. See the lengthy discussions on Faith in Chapters 2 & 7 for detailed elaboration of this topic. Both chapters deal with separate contexts, so it was important to maintain them, therefore I've written this subchapter separately so that the others would not to be too wordy, or changing context, thus adding to any current frustrations, or adding to any confusion. I have to admit that I myself has struggled with understanding a couple of the many aspects of Faith. Now, thanks to the Holy Spirit having given me this revelation about positive future faith, I've passed that threshold of uncertainty and can hopefully assist you in doing so as well.

Jesus said **(John 10:10)**KJV, "I have come that you may have life, and may have it more abundantly."

He delivered a very important message, "I <u>have come</u> so that…" therefore we are meant to live life abundantly in the present (not some date sometime whenever it might happen, or after they do this good or that good, as some people mistakenly think). Another takeaway for you is that you should always be "Moving Forward" in life! We are to mirror Jesus, and the Lord is always moving forward. Take the Bible from a 30,000ft view and the 4000+ years that it encompasses, and yes even the Lord had setbacks but He's always in motion and He's always moving forward. Just as you should always be doing, even with setbacks, you have to keep your eyes on Jesus through it all and continue to move forward while walking in the Word and in the Spirit.

We are all going to experience setbacks in our lives, but as a Believer you are in God's favor and in looking at your life in retrospect the positive times far outweigh the bad times, and as you mature as a Believer you will have the outlook and understanding of what tomorrow will bring and the next and the next, based on your relationship with Jesus and the experiences you've encountered. As mentioned, even with a setback or two thrown into the mix, you are able to get back on track and on the right path to abundant living. Note, this is NOT living it up for today only (i.e. carpe diem or otherwise), also if this was your approach, you would definitely not know what tomorrow brings and your days would resemble a roller coaster ride.

To continue, we see our lives bettering and moving forward which is the evidence of things experienced and seen and/or the substance of things hoped for. This gives us confidence in God, which in turn builds up within ourselves "God Confidence." Personally, my life transformed when I approached positive and negative situations with "God Confidence." We <u>believe</u> that God is <u>providing</u> and bettering our lives and moving it forward, all supernaturally (unseen; and the evidence of things not seen) that do indeed move our lives forward for the better (both positive and negative situations; God has storms of correction and storms of perfection that are designed to teach us lessons to better us). Now without God Confidence, the Believer is not living in the light but rather somewhat in the dark (in other words a bad place to be). With no real potential for growth, and not using the gift of hope that he has given us, limits drastically the potential for "positive future faith."

> **(Heb 11:1)**BSB "Now **faith** is the <u>assurance</u> of what we <u>hope</u> for and the <u>certainty</u> of <u>what we do not see</u>."

This is not only the most accurate definition of faith, but it is part of the process we must go through to gain our God Confidence, as described previously.

So what is Positive Future Faith? For one thing it is the culmination of many of Jesus's teachings relayed throughout this book, as in: executing the Hope and Faith gifts from God that you are given; executing what is your responsibility in Trusting and Believing in the Lord; not dwelling in the past, leaving the past in the past by standing in the place of victory and always moving forward; not being fearful or anxious of the future, nor being fearful or anxious in the present; but to have life and have it abundantly in the present; and the only way you can truly accomplish this is by having God Confidence in your present and future, and this is accomplished via your relationship with the Holy Spirit, Jesus and the Heavenly Father!

- **Our faith is "SEED"** for our positive future, and that future faith in turn takes care of our positive present (when everything mentioned above is interacting and at play in our daily lives).
  - This is a **supernatural principal** (unseen) that involve the mysteries of God and eternal actions, i.e. your positive future faith is continuously fueling your present (from day, to day, to day…). Worded another way, a faith filled future fuels our present (it's perpetual as long as you keep your foot on the gas and you have all of Jesus's principles toggled on and working in unison).
  - So, if you were to toggle off your positive (attitude), or toggle off your faith (trust), or toggle off your God Confidence, etc. then your present is left up to your own devices (and this is the sad truth), from this day forward until hopefully you are guided onto this right path to abundant living, by toggling them all on.
  - This is KEY to having a truly abundant life; although confessedly difficult to attain at first and can be a struggle at times, but as you mature as a Believer and follow the steps outlined above it is not only attainable but achievable as well as sustainable.
  - Ask yourself, "What do you need to toggle 'on' in your daily walk with the Lord?" Or, "What did you toggle 'off' that has put you in the rut you are currently in?"

***What's so special about our Heavenly Father is that He has provided the majority of the mechanisms for the process of achieving abundant life and these are conveyed through His Word, his son Jesus Christ. Our faith (His gift) is fueled with our hope (His gift) and when we exhibit our trust and believing with God Confidence our positive future faith, He sees to it that it fuels our present abundant life! Hallelujah and amen.

The Medicine, The Remedy and The Cure (Your path to Healing)

The path of least resistance "is human nature," the easiest way, or the fastest way, are all examples of how today's society approaches daily life. So a corresponding statement would be that it is easier for us to ask Jesus for healing versus having to act on and execute a number of variables such as reading the Word, walking in the Spirit, maintaining a relationship with Jesus and the Heavenly Father, receiving all the Father has already provided for us, and focusing on our believing, faith, trust and hope for a healing. Another factor that's playing a role in the confusion of healings and how we access healing power, is the improper translation and teaching of the Word. All too often people are told that they lack faith, while not being told and taught how to not lack in faith. And again, all too often people are taught to pray to Jesus (the Healer) for their healing and that is where it is left. Probably because there is example after example of Jesus's healing of others in the Bible, even to the extent that He rose people from the dead, as well as all the various miracles He performed. But the problem is, asking Jesus for healing alone with no action tied to it the outcome 98% of the time will have little to no results. What about the remaining 2% of the time? Jesus does work miracles!

Do not get me wrong or misunderstand, and please be patient and continue to read through this explanation. The teaching that "Jesus is the Healer" is accurate, and the proof is revealed regarding His healings throughout the New Testament, but now Jesus is the healer in conjunction with reading the Word, walking in the Spirit, maintaining a relationship with Jesus and the Heavenly Father, receiving all the Father has already provided for us, and focusing on our believing, faith, trust and hope for the healing. One thing that is confusing about this Godcept is that it is paradoxical, just as many of the mysteries of God that are revealed in the Bible. It's paradoxical in that Jesus is the Healer, but that now He only plays a significant and dominant role and is not the sole reason for healings.

When Jesus died on the cross for you and all mankind, He said, "It is finished." What that meant was that He did everything and achieved everything for us while on the cross. That in turn put God's "new" plan for mankind into motion and while that plan involves every individual's plan, it also relies on a number of variables one of which is us being obedient and in relationship with God as outlined primarily in the New Testament. For example, your faith is a gift from God through Jesus via God's Grace. And let me tell you that your faith does NOT move God to action, because His plan for you is already in place. Therefore His Grace upon you and your subsequent action of positive future faith, activates and puts God's plan for you into motion! And as mentioned, it is a combination of variables along with your faith that activates your healing. The culmination of this puts some or all aspects of God's plan into motion, based on His predestined purpose He has for you. In other words, we have to "receive" what He has already given us. So when you relay a prayer of petition with regards to a healing, all these things are factored into whether that healing takes place or not.

The succinct statement, "Your faith in Jesus, is what heals you," is accurate but in and of itself would be misleading. This is a principle that many are guilty of, and that is to take one statement or Godcept out of the Bible and its full context and "believing" it to be a blanket truth.

> Jesus said **(Mat 17:20)**NKJV, "Ye of so little faith, for truly I tell you, if you have faith the size of a mustard seed, you can say to this mountain, 'Move from here to there,' and it will move. <u>Nothing will be impossible for you.</u>"

**<u>It is not Jesus that heals you, however it is your faith in Jesus that heals you</u>! (along with the other previously mentioned variables involved). Yes, it may be paradoxical and at first difficult to comprehend but continue to work through this by utilizing the Holy Spirit to give you guidance and instruction in the Word. Your faith does not move God or Jesus to act without the responsibility of your actions, and also it was revealed that, your faith does move mountains! That is, your mountains. Mountains are a metaphor for your problems. And in Jesus's realm a problem is no different than an illness, disease, infirmity, etc. So a problem can be corrected, and a health problem can be healed, and <u>both are done by you and through Jesus</u>. It was also revealed by Him in that scripture that, "Nothing will be impossible for you!"

Let's shift gears for a moment and refer to when you take The Last Supper / Holy Communion. This act is so special on so many levels (see also Taking Holy Communion for additional information on this topic), because it has to do with you focusing on stepping into Jesus's, the Father's and the Holy Spirit's presence and sharing an intimate dialogue with them, and on occasion asking for healing or other needs.

> Jesus said, **(John 6:53-54)**BSB "Truly, truly, I tell you, unless you eat the flesh and drink the blood of the Son of Man, <u>you have no life in you</u>. Whoever eats My flesh and drinks My blood has eternal life, and I will raise him up at the last day."

The flesh and the blood is again another metaphor, as for eating of My flesh represents us "Hungering daily for His wisdom (via the Word and in relationship)," and as for drinking of My blood, represents "Thirsting daily for the Abundant Life He offers." **This Godcept is a microcosm of what I'm conveying in this subchapter as well as throughout the book. If you focus on Jesus by walking in the Word with the Holy Spirit to gain wisdom as a maturing Believer and in obedience with God (adhering to the many variables of the plan), you will experience Abundant Life on this journey as well as being raised up for Eternal Life! That abundant life consists of an even keel journey (rather than a roller coaster one), which means that you are taking control of your life the way God meant for it to be. So when it comes to correcting problems or needs fulfilment such as healings, the aggregate of what you Believe along with your actions are the factors that cause these things to occur. There are three primary pieces of this puzzle: **The Holy Spirit in (scripture) the Word is your medicine**! And the aggregate that makes up **You as a Believer is the remedy**! And **Jesus is the cure**! It requires all three working in unison for your healing!

So let's pull this together into a few succinct statements: remember first things first, Jesus is the foundation of our medicine, our remedy and our cure. I've conveyed throughout this book the importance of walking in the Spirit. In doing so, you are renewing your mind (spiritual mind, soul and body) daily. In turn, you are also renewing your body. Remember that we are comprised of a spirit, a soul and a body and all three are renewed when you are in the Word daily while walking with the Holy Spirit of God. In discussing this topic with others, I have found that there is some confusion that primarily stems from the following mindset and question: "So, am I supposed to 'think' myself well?" Well no, not exactly. The following short and concise reply to that question will although give you the basis for researching this topic more in depth: "You do not 'think' yourself well, in and by itself; rather you are to renew your mind (spiritual mind, soul and body) daily via the Bible, the Holy Spirit and Jesus." See the subchapter on Covid19 for additional information to use as a guide on this topic; also Ch4 and but in reality, it is this book from cover to cover and the Bible to answer all questions concerning this topic.

As mentioned previously when Jesus said, "It is finished," in reality His work had only just begun. Now, is that contradictory to what I relayed prior? No I communicated, God's new plan was put into motion, also that Jesus had accomplished everything as it pertains to God's new plan. What I am referring to now is that Jesus is presently in relationship with all of us and isn't it His responsibility to assist the Holy Spirit in guiding us and directing us through the Word and onto the right path? And didn't I mention that He performs miracles that include miraculous healings? Therefore His work has only just begun. An analogy of this is when I complete writing this book and get it published in order to be available worldwide that I am finished, but in reality, my work has only just begun. Regarding miraculous healings, people who are at the end of their rope should not hesitate to go to Jesus in prayer for a healing, because it just may happen. Just don't confuse this with the pastors that claim that they perform healings. To begin, it is Jesus that actually does the healing miraculously, and often times it is the individual using their positive future faith without being conscious of it because they have not been taught or instructed on it (the "healing pastors" are too busy wowing their congregation than giving proper instruction). With that being said, many of those "healing pastors" might admit the truth if confronted, that most of those healings are temporary and it is due to the individual continuing down the same path and inviting the same illness/disease/infirmity back into their being. They do not understand what took place, they do not renew their minds daily in the Word, they do not die of the "old person" and their old ways; they do not become an altogether "new person in Christ" day in and day out; etc.; so without the new outlook and the tools to achieve it, they fall into the same rut that they were in before. Those so-called healing pastors should spend more time on teaching than on promoting their self-proclaimed gift of healing.

Please note, that I've referred to "faith, plus all the other variables involved" a number of times in this subchapter, and although it is a profound topic matter, it is only a couple of pages of teachings. You should keep in mind that I teach about faith and all the other principles throughout this book, therefore you must read the entire book in order to glean all the intricate details to understand, practice and execute God's plan for you successfully.

Step into God's Presence
Another factor that hampers or hinders a Believers growth, maturity and prosperity is when they pray, they do not envision talking with God, or they mistakenly believe that they "invite" God supernaturally into their presence. But the Father, Jesus and the Holy Spirit is always and forever here and now (omnipresence). Therefore, it is up to us to "step into His presence" when we pray, or worship, or are at church, etc. It is making the conscious effort to connect, that improves your spiritual walk and relationship tremendously. This can be done when you are reading scripture, quoting scripture out loud, speaking in tongues, prayer, worship and I strongly suggest stepping into Their presence during Holy Communion, because scripture reveals that all three of them are present while doing this (see Ch7 subchapter on the Last Supper /Holy Communion).

It is commonly stated that people love going to church to be in God's presence which is an overwhelmingly great feeling, refreshing, stimulating, motivating, etc. and then on Monday its back to the reality of the hard knocks of life. To the extent that they cannot wait for Wednesday service to come, or others who have to wait for the following Sunday service, or for those who attend sporadically they have to do without. But doing without does not have to be the case, you can experience the same uplifting benefits anywhere you are by stepping into Their presence.

Thing is, this is initially another dichotomy: you do need to go to church to be in His presence and you do not need to go to church to be in His presence.

- You do have to go to church to learn what it means and feels like to be in His presence.
- It is also important to understand and experience the collective power of 30, 300, 3000 people who are focused on being in His presence (and hopefully are intentionally stepping into His presence)
- But you don't have to go to church to step into God's presence. As mentioned, church provides the understanding of the experience, but having now known what that is gives you the experience to practice in your quiet place in meditation, prayer or worship (and especially in Holy Communion).

Stepping into God's presence and bridging the natural with the supernatural takes you up another notch in your growth and maturity as a Believer. It also assists you in your relationship and in turn assists you in communicating with God, which then assists you in knowing what He has done for you and what blessings to receive and what you need to do to act on those blessings.

> **(Mat 28:20)**NKJV Jesus said, "And <u>surely I am with you always</u>, to the very end of the age."

So always and forever, show your love and devotion by stepping into Their presence, especially when you are speaking directly to the Father, Jesus or the Holy Spirit.

Sometimes the most profound messages come from Jesus in the simplest of ways.

By His Stripes You are Healed

In **Ch7** (Ch4 is the prayer only), I was thorough in covering the many processes involved in praying the Last Supper / Holy Communion. For example, one KEY group of related *** components: a) "You must eat of my flesh," b) "As often as you do this, do it in remembrance of me," c) Meaning that we must hunger for His wisdom daily, d) To break bread represents His broken flesh and broken body, e) That as often as we break bread it should be representative of the "breaking" of His body (note: to be more exacting His body was beaten/whipped, not broken; also note: this fulfilled the prophecy that no bones would be broken **[Psalm 34:19-20 and confirmed by John 19:31-36]**; the "stripes" (translated from Hebrew meaning blows) were the punches, kicking and whipping that He endured (again to be more exacting, the scourge/whipping with the cat of nine tails is designed to "break" the flesh and often with it removing skin and muscle, thus representing the "stripes" that it would leave on His back and arms), f) "And by His stripes we are healed" (to cure, to mend, as in made whole and no longer broken), g) With us now being made "whole," we <u>might</u> no longer be held in bondage to satan/devil, for Jesus began to <u>disarm</u> their powers over us during <u>this process</u> and successfully completed the disarmament **(Col. 2:15)** when the Father raised Him from the dead.

> **(Isaiah 53:4-6)**BSB "Surely <u>He took on our</u> infirmities and carried our sorrows; yet we considered Him <u>stricken by God</u>, struck down and afflicted. <u>But</u> He was **pierced** for our **transgressions**, He was <u>crushed for our iniquities</u>; the punishment that brought us peace was upon Him, and <u>**by His stripes we are healed**</u>. We all like sheep have gone astray, each one has turned to his own way; and the LORD has laid on Him the iniquity of us all."

He was pierced (thorns, nails, spear) for our transgressions (sins, offenses), He was crushed (bruised) for our iniquities (our guilt and due punishment).

This is exactly an area not to take legalistically, in that believing that passage verbatim in terms of the piercing as only being how He took on our sins and subsequently us being forgiven when He was on the cross. To clarify, it is the culmination of the beatings, whippings and piercings that transferred our sins onto Him, and it was His death that ultimately led to God forgiving us. Put another way, * the piercing, the bruising, the beating and the whipping are all the ways in which He took on all of our past, present and future sins, and He having done so, we are healed (and supernaturally made whole).

That was very similar to the explanation I gave in Ch7 although with some additional elaboration. **BUT there is much more.** In Ch7 I attempted to keep topics on track without adding too many other topics on top of them and possibly diluting the primary points or causing confusion, I chose not to expound on this until now. For most, the following is very important and significant because it was never included as part of most Believers past teachings nor expounded upon, as I am about to do. It is a game changer so to speak in ** understanding the relationship and changes that take place between our soul, our spirit and our fleshly nature as it relates to this topic and our transformational rebirth and potential for an abundant life.

Since we are visual in nature, it is no surprise that we are subject to thinking and visualizing in the natural realm and not the supernatural ("things not seen," see below **Heb. 11:1**); therefore concerning the passion of Christ, we envision the beating and whipping. I've been in a number of church services in which the pastor graphically described the violent nature of it and/or showed an animation video of it, and Hollywood has depicted it as well in the most graphic detail. I think that what most of us correlate here is what we envision (the violent nature of the beatings) along with what we are told (that He took on our punishment as well as taking on the sins of the world), and we therefore are seen as holy and blameless in the eyes of God **(Col. 1:22)**. This is accurate and a correct perception of the events at play, but as mentioned there is much more to it.

The Holy Spirit gave me this revelation when I was drawing the illustrations for this topic, regarding our soul, spirit and fleshly nature. For some time I had been praying the Last Supper in Holy Communion and when I would say that "You chose to have your body broken because You knew that as it was occurring, instantaneously I would be made whole (and all others who Believe)." Just as with what was previously mentioned this too is accurate, but I failed to realize was that concurrently another supernatural event was taking place. Every one of my sins were being erased by Jesus, with every one of the stripes He was enduring. And while that was occurring, this is what I was missing, ***that as every sin was erased the outer "fleshly nature shell" of my soul was being chiseled away/minimized and thus allowing my true spirit and soul to emerge. And would remain that way as long as I did my part in accepting Jesus as the Lord of my life and walking in the Spirit to get my guidance and instruction (renewing of the mind) and to have a relationship with Jesus and the Heavenly Father. So to reiterate, I understood that by His stripes we are healed, but what I did not comprehend was the additional supernatural component of freeing my spirit and soul from its fleshly nature bondage. Also, it's important for you to remember that there is a requirement (which holds true for the majority of God's processes) and that is in order to perpetuate that freeing up component: that we must "**Believe**" and "**act**" in order for the things of God to get implemented and come to fruition. In this case in point, we must "act" by walking in the Spirit (renewing our mind) and be in an obedient and intimate relationship with the Lord.

After I had received this revelation, the following passage jumped off the page at me!

(1Peter 2:24-25)BSB "He Himself bore our sins in His body on the tree, so that we might die to sin and live to righteousness. 'By His **stripes** you are healed.' For you were like sheep going astray, but now you have returned to the Shepherd and ***Overseer of your SOUL."(That is the profound statement that jumped off the page at me)

Hopefully this explanation helps you in better understanding the illustrations on the previous page and connecting the dots on how this process of God works (see below **Col. 1:25**) "by the dispensation of God," which means the systems and processes of God.

Please note that the opposite of what was just relayed can occur instead and it too being another process of God's system which is important for you to understand. That is, **the "fleshly nature outer shell" will re-form and become dominant if you revert back to thinking, talking and acting on things as per your fleshly nature. Next, you need to accept that this is a consequence of your choices, therefore the re-enabling of the corruption is entirely on you. Meaning it's a matter of choice, of you allowing your fleshly nature to play a dominant role, rather than allowing Jesus to be the Lord of your life and allowing the Holy Spirit to lead, guide and direct your thoughts, words and actions. Jesus's works on the cross disarmed the evil part of you (see below Matt 7:11), but it is entirely up to you after your "conversion" to choose to be dedicated and committed in your relationship with God and with His processes **(Col. 1:25)**, in that, you leave the old man/woman a thing of the past and the reborn man/woman as your new abundant life in Christ.

> **(Matt 7:11)**KJV "If you then, being **evil**, know how to give…"
>
> **(Col. 1:25)**KJV "Whereof I am made a minister, according to the dispensation of God, which is given to me for you, to fulfil the word of God;" (Dispensation means to administrate **the systems and processes** [in this case: **of God**])

Additional passages of importance and relevance to this topic:

> **(Luke 13:31-32)**BSB "At that very hour, some Pharisees came to Jesus and told Him, "Leave this place and get away, because Herod wants to kill You." But Jesus replied, "Go tell that **fox**, 'Look, I will keep driving out demons and healing people today and tomorrow, and on the third day I will reach My goal.' (Note the Passion "third day" parallels: sufferings are demons/infirmities = healing at the cross; goal is the resurrection); ****Look to Jesus's works on the cross for restoring your health and healing your infirmities, then also the resolving of your problems which are sufferings due to the devil/demons in your soul.**
>
> **(1John 3:8)**BSB "The one who practices sin is of the devil, because the devil has been sinning from the very start. This is why the Son of God was revealed, **to destroy the works of the devil.**"
>
> **(1Cor. 15:3)**BSB "For what I received I passed on to you as of **first importance**: that Christ died for our sins…"
>
> **(Heb. 4:12-13/16)**BSB "For the word of God is **living and active**. Sharper than any double-edged sword, **it pierces even to dividing soul and spirit**, joints and marrow. **It judges the thoughts and intentions of the heart.** Nothing in all creation is hidden from God's sight; everything is uncovered and exposed before the eyes of Him to whom we must give

account." "Let us then approach the throne of grace **with confidence**, so that we may receive mercy and find grace **to help us in our time of need.**"
(Col. 1:21-22)NKJV "And you, who once were alienated (by God) and (having) **enemies in your mind** by **wicked works (evil)**, yet now He has reconciled in the body of His flesh through death, to present you holy, and blameless, and above reproach in His sight."
(Col. 2:15)NKJV "Having **disarmed** principalities and powers, He made a public spectacle of them, triumphing over them in it." (Note, he was not defeated in a battle)
(Heb. 2:13-15)KJV "And again: "I will put My trust in Him." And once again: "Here am I, and the children God has given Me." Therefore, since the children have flesh and blood, He too shared in their humanity, so that **by His death He might destroy him** who holds the power of death, that is, **the devil**, and **free** those who all their lives were held in **bondage** by their fear of death."
(Rom. 8:3)BSB "For what the Law was powerless to do in that it was weakened by the flesh, God did by sending His own Son in the likeness of sinful man, as an offering for sin. He thus condemned sin in the flesh." (Not condemning us but sin in the flesh)
(1Cor. 15:54)KJV "When the perishable has been clothed with the imperishable and the mortal with immortality, then the saying that is written will come to pass: "Death has been swallowed up in victory."
(2Tim 1:10)BSB "And now He has revealed this grace through the appearing of our Savior, **Christ Jesus, who has abolished death and illuminated the way to life and immortality through the gospel.**"
(Heb. 11:1)KJV "Now **faith** is the substance of things hoped for, the evidence of **things not seen.**"

How many times have I relayed that we serve an awesome God! Regarding this matter, we never lose what Jesus did for us. The example of reverting back and allowing the "fleshly nature outer shell" to become dominant can and will occur if we so choose to, then if and when we come back to our senses in obedience to Christ, it will **minimize that fleshly nature and allow our spirit and soul to be dominant once again**. In other words, we can backslide multiple times and His works over 2000 years ago continue to perpetuate. Thing is for most true Believers, it only takes one or two occurrences such as this to happen and they figure out that an abundant life in fellowship and obedience to God is the only way to go and end up never returning to that past lifestyle!
   *(Rom. 13:14)BSB "Instead, **clothe yourselves with the Lord Jesus Christ**, and make no provision for the desires of the flesh."
   (Eph. 5:2)KJV "And walk in love, as Christ also hath loved us,"

We are to clothe ourselves everyday <u>with</u> Jesus Christ and walk in **love, in His image and His attributes which the Holy Spirit indwelling us will guide us initially in how to do this and subsequently will lead, guide and direct us daily in our walk in the Word and with the Lord.

The following applies directly to this topic: ***<u>Repentance</u>, <u>Humility</u> and <u>Meekness</u> are antiquated words that no one uses or necessarily understands in this day and age. Repentance means a true commitment to change, of their actions, thoughts and words; and may mean having and exhibiting true remorse; so rather than using this word I've simply relayed the importance of changing the way we think, say and do when it comes to sinning (doing things contrary to God). Humility means to humble yourself which in turn means: no ego is involved. **(Matt 5:5)**KJV "The meek shall inherit the earth," meekness has numerous meanings, but Jesus was referring to meek as in obedient; the obedient to God shall inherit the earth. So with regards to this book, for those who are obedient to God while on their experiential spiritual life journey on earth, they will inherit the earth and the goodness thereof in living an abundant life during their journey.

Jesus "Full Circle" in His Ministry

Jesus began his ministry on the shore of Galilee, and on the shore of Galilee (full circle) is where He chose to transfer his ministry torch to his disciples to carry the ministry forward. What is also interesting was that His disciples were told by Jesus twice and his Angels once at the tomb that Jesus would meet up with them later in Galilee, yet the disciples were in such grief that they didn't pick up on it and they went back to the house instead of going to Galilee in anticipation of meeting up with Jesus. Also, when the disciples did go up to Galilee and they went out to catch fish, they did not recognize Jesus standing on the shore. It was not until Jesus called out to them to ask if they had caught any fish, is when a couple of them realized it was Jesus. One point here is that it is so very important to <u>listen to others with the intent to hear and understand</u>, and especially in this case it is doubly important to <u>listen to Jesus when he says something to you and especially when He tells you to do something!</u>

(Matt 4:18-19)BSB at beginning of the ministry; As <u>Jesus was walking beside the Sea of Galilee</u>, he saw two brothers, Simon called Peter and his brother Andrew. They were casting a net into the lake, for they were fishermen. "Come, follow me," Jesus said, "and I will send you out to fish for people."

(Matt 28:7)NKJV at Jesus's tomb; The Angel of the Lord said to Mary, "Then go quickly and tell his disciples: 'He has risen from the dead and is going ahead of you <u>into Galilee</u>. <u>There you will see him</u>.' Now I have told you."

289

(Mark 16:7)NKJV The Angel of the Lord said to Mary, "But go, tell his disciples and Peter, 'He is going ahead of you into Galilee. There you will see him, just as he told you.'"

(Matt 28:10)BSB Then Jesus said to the disciples, "Do not be afraid. Go and tell my brothers to go to Galilee; there they will see me."

(John 21:4-5)NKJV Jesus stood on the shore; yet the disciples did not know that it was Jesus. Then Jesus said to them, "Children, have you any food?"

(John 21: 12-14)NKJV Jesus said to them, "Come and eat breakfast." Yet none of the disciples dared ask Him, "Who are You?"—knowing that it was the Lord. Jesus then came and took the bread and gave it to them, and likewise the fish. This is now the third time Jesus showed Himself to His disciples after He was raised from the dead.

Jesus Supplies Redemptive Opportunities for All

John was the first to recognize that it was Jesus standing on the shore, so when he told Peter who it was, Peter wrapped his garment around himself, jumped into the water and speedily swam to shore.

(John 21:15-19)BSB When they had finished eating, Jesus said to Simon Peter, "Simon son of John, do you love me more than these?" "Yes, Lord," he said, "you know that I love you." Jesus said, "Feed my lambs." Again Jesus said, "Simon son of John, do you love me?" He answered, "Yes, Lord, you know that I love you." Jesus said, "Take care of my sheep."
The third time he said to him, "Simon son of John, do you love me?" Peter was hurt because Jesus asked him the third time, "Do you love me?" He said, "Lord, you know all things; you know that I love you." Jesus said, "Feed my sheep. Very truly I tell you, when you were younger you dressed yourself and went where you wanted; but when you are old you will stretch out your hands, and someone else will dress you and lead you where you do not want to go." Jesus said this to indicate the kind of death by which Peter would **glorify God**. Then he said to him, **"Follow me!"**

Peter was hurt because at the time he did not realize what Jesus was doing. If you recall, Jesus told Peter **(Matt 26:34)**KJV "Truly I say to you that this very night, before a cock crows, you shall deny Me three times." Peter after having done so could not forgive himself and was distraught over it to the point it was dominating his mind in an extremely negative manner. By Jesus asking him three times if he loved Him, it was Jesus going out of his way in giving Peter a redemptive opportunity not just once, but He matched the three times. Jesus truly wants the best for each of us and He will go out of His way for you, in providing you a redemptive opportunity time and time again so that your journey may flourish, be prosperous, have life and have it abundantly. He loves you that much!!! Our obligation is to be obedient to Him, one of which is to "feed His sheep" with the Gospel (the Good News) to all the nations.

Just as Jesus conveyed to Peter, I was a perfect picture of doing whatever I chose and whenever I chose to do it back when I was young and not saved. Then at mid-life I chose to stretch out my hands to Jesus to have him lead me on a path that I had previously been unfamiliar with and would not have chosen to take, but I followed Him nonetheless and glorified God in doing so! Good thing I did, because my life now is so very blessed and abundant beyond my wildest dreams! Just as He promises.

A Father's Wisdom for a Lost Generation does not stop here, refer to the table of contents to view chapters and topics for Volume II. The WISDOM continues there...

Diagrams

(GPS) God's Positioning System
Choose Your Path "Wisely"

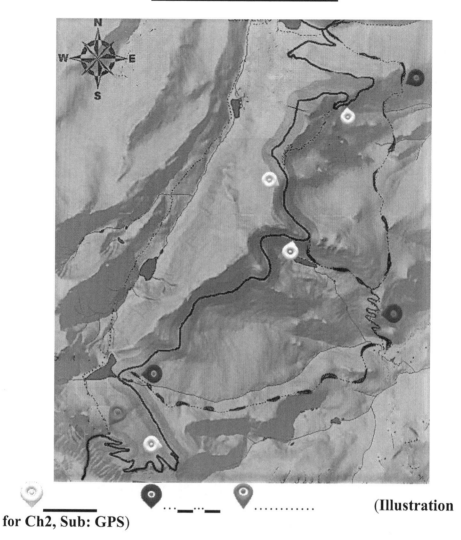

(Illustration for Ch2, Sub: GPS)

This is a topographic map that highlights a mountain with valleys on both sides. The journey begins at the bottom of the map and as illustrated by the <u>solid line</u> that heads north as an early point in life but due to poor choices, lack of guidance, a life without God, etc. goes backwards, sideways, takes wrong turns, etc. until arriving at the first white pointer (born again; accepting Jesus as the Lord of their life). Note that the <u>dotted lines</u> and gray pointer illustrates a point of also being born again and path often taken by Believers who choose a "safe" and convenient route. It is one in which they probably don't pursue their dreams or purpose, or they don't understand the power and blessings available from God so they hover just above the valley (lows) and are so close to the valley low that when they encounter trials and tribulations it doesn't vary much from what they are used to and do not benefit from the lessons they provide. Also, they miss out on experiencing the mountain highs that the other two paths do. Next, the <u>dash and dots</u> of the black pointer is an alternate route that a Believer might choose and this often occurs when they do not walk in the Spirit and renew their mind daily, in other words a babe in Christ whose either ignorant and not pursuing learning, or not changing their lifestyle and sporadically or continuously sinning. You can see that the path leads down hovering close to the valley and straddling the side of a mountain and the second black pointer is showing a wilderness experience in which upon exiting there are two path options, one staying on the same course, or the other one that climbs the side of the mountain (methodically with the guidance of the Holy Spirit/Guidebook/Bible) to reach near the top intersecting with the solid line that is itself coming out of getting off track and in the wilderness by now is on the way to the mountain top, which includes experiencing the abundant life along with living a purposeful life that God had predestined and purposed. If on the other hand the black pointer remains on its original (pseudo-Christian) path, as you can see it is pretty rough terrain with many smaller mountains and hills heading up to the third black pointer that is a sheer cliff and requires scratching, clawing and climbing the steep mountainside to finally get out of the hectic erratic lifestyle while nearing the end of their journey. With respect to the white pointer and solid line path, they experience an initial progressive ascent to get near the top of the mountain and as mentioned in the chapter, a Believer's life still has its ups and downs and occasional wrong turns and wilderness experiences (see 2nd white pointer; Wilderness = getting off God's right path) but thankfully due to the Holy Spirit the trials, tribulations and wilderness experiences are short lived and not occurring very often, which affords them a more joyful and abundant living while on their sojourn with God and quest to "have life and have it more abundantly, that is exceedingly abundantly." The 3rd white pointer illustrates a joyful, contented, purposeful, exceedingly abundant life, mountain top high, that is Jesus in all His fullness and glory. And yes, you too can live this kind of life and God desires it for all His children. Note, **this solid line path is God's "RIGHT" path designation**. As mentioned, anyone can get off course if something (health, work, sin, etc.), or someone close to you, impacts your journey and sends you into retrograde as illustrated by the 4th white pointer, requiring the Holy Spirit to relay to you "<u>repositioning or recalculating your direction</u>" and change the way you think, say and act, while changing your current path. Note, all paths lead to God (for those who are obedient, committed and believe). Since all paths lead to an eternal life with God for the Believer, then the difference is how and what you want to get out of this experiential spiritual life journey on earth. It's your choice, choose it "wisely" in utilizing the wisdom of God (Jesus) via the Guidebook/Bible with the Holy Spirit as your personal guide.

FYI: The black marker is the route I chose to take after having been saved (no one coerced me to take it, although the evil worldly influences from others are always present and I allowed that to influence me). I thank God that Jesus and the Holy Spirit helped me to claw my way up the side of the mountain to reach His desired and "right" path for me.

Take note of the difference in perspectives:

- A desolate valley: whether desert, or dirt, or rock, desolate doesn't require elaboration; you get the picture and what it would mean to you.
- A valley made up of a dense forest; can't even see the side of the mountain, or judge where you are at (stagnation; state of confusion; stress, anxiety); and you can't see or tell the size of the forest for the trees that are surrounding you and blocking your sight.
- Side of the mountain (higher elevation); not only can you not see clearly above and below you (only horizontally), but that physically your footing and body is forced to lean to the angle of the mountain (in other words, you are off kilter [unbalanced; possibly confused or disoriented] and maybe not prominently but still off kilter nonetheless). Therefore you may not have a clear perspective of where you are presently, nor where you are headed in the future. Although mentally (spiritually) you know you must continue to persist towards reaching the top of the mountain with the help, direction and guidance of the Holy Spirit and the word of God.
- Mountain top: is when everything becomes clearer in perspective and allows for the opportunity to live abundantly.

Other topics from Ch2, sub: GPS that pertain to this illustration, a) the Lord is always moving forward, b) and requires you to have your "faith in motion;" c) in the natural realm, the shortest distance between two points is a straight line, but in the supernatural realm the shortest distance between two points is up to God, d) there are paths for Believers that lead to abundant living and then eternal life; and there are paths for Believers that can be chaotic, dysfunctional and challenging; and there are paths that lead to destruction (not illustrated; the path that non-believers have chosen), e) Yes, God is in control but not of your choices; your choices all have consequences (positive, neutral and negative), f) GPS (God's Positioning System) allows for all Believers to walk together with the Holy Spirit (GPS) and be positioned for success, g) the Holy Spirit (GPS) is our primary tool along with the Guidebook/Bible that will guide us onto the solid line path (God's

"RIGHT" path on the illustration) to abundant living, God's predestined purposes for you, and a fulfilling life while on this experiential spiritual life journey on earth.

> **(Prov. 3:5-6)**BSB "**<u>Trust</u>** in the LORD with **all your heart** and lean not on your own understanding; in all your ways acknowledge Him, and **He will make your paths straight.**"

Refer back to Ch2, subchapter "GPS," for additional information on this topic matter.

Illustration for Ch2, sub "A discourse on our soul and spirit"

I've previously established that **we are comprised of spirit, soul and body**. Our body is visible, so obviously doesn't require clarification, but what about our spirit and our soul and does either even require elaboration? Throughout the book I've outlined a detailed explanation of our spirit and soul, and having done so believe that an illustration is needed, but only for those who will benefit by it and it assisting them in understanding what I am relaying, regarding the systems and processes of God, as it relates to this topic matter. Our body is of the natural realm and therefore visible, but our soul and spirit are of the supernatural realm and therefore not visible to us.

For those who are wondering the direction I'm taking with this explanation and the following illustrations, first, ponder the following: "Could our spirit and soul be linked to our individually unique DNA; or might it be that our spirit and soul is an invisible "object" either located in our chest ("heart"/spirit), or head ("mind"/soul), or both; or it is not only invisible, its shape fits and encompasses our entire body although confined within? Note that I did not ask for you to pray on this, meditate on it, or research it, because to try to come up with a solution to these or any similar type questions is moot (too uncertain to come to a conclusion and there is no relevance accomplished in deriving a conclusion). Point is, it cannot be answered and there is no relevance to do so, but it is ***extremely important** for you to understand the processes that are taking place within your spirit and within your fleshly nature self and the true you that is contained within your spirit and soul.

Please understand that the following is for **ILLUSTRATION PURPOSES ONLY**.

As relayed, our soul and spirit are intertwined to the point that only the Sword of the Spirit (Word of God) can slice between and divide the two (Heb. 4:12 & Eph. 6:11) and that prior to being born again and during times of transgressions afterward, our soul and spirit has a rough (evil) outer shell that dominates us in everything we think, say and do, and is referred to as our fleshly nature.

Briefly, Jesus's works on the cross chisels away that rough (evil/fleshly nature) outer shell when we are born again, then the Holy Spirit leads, guides and directs our path so that we ourselves continue the chiseling away process as we walk in the Spirit and renew the mind (soul), thus exposing the real you who God meant for you to be!

296

This 3rd illustration reveals YOU, when you are **spirit dominant**: in the center is your spirit intertwined with the Holy Spirit of **God** ("I am in you and you are in me"); surrounded in blue representing your soul (your true you; now exposed by God, who designed and created YOU); and the fleshly nature (evil self) is minimized (although always present) in the upper left corner and as specks (either hiding out in specific areas of your mind or entering through portals created by sin; i.e. the devil, **see Ch9 & Ch10**).

Note: all illustrations can be seen in color at **www.afatherswisdom.org** or eBook reader.

God-Centric Goal / Wheel of Life (Ch7) (WWJD vs. WWYD)

JESUS

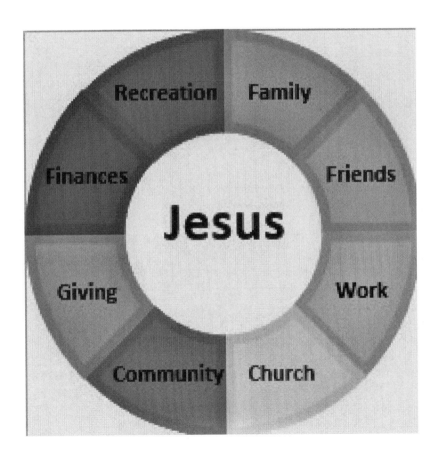

Glimpse of Volume II Table of Contents

CONTENTS

About the author:

Know that God is ever-present (unfortunately DW didn't know this), from his teens (20+yrs before being saved) he knew that his purpose in life was to help others but as this world would have it, he was instead a perfect fit in this lost generation and unknowingly lost focus of his purpose (referred in the Bible as drifting). In his mid-forties (5yrs after being saved), he had a miraculous talk with God, in which he received directives along with an impassioned drive like he's never experienced before in writing a journal based on revelations from the Holy Spirit during their walk in God's Word, the Bible. Commissioned as a messenger to compile 15yrs of impassioned Bible research, walking in the Spirit and relay his findings to you in an easy to relate and understandable way, while filtering through doctrines of men and traditions of men (false teachings) so that you have a clear understanding of your Lord and the opportunity to have an exceedingly abundant "experiential spiritual life journey on earth." Although committed to the goal to convert the journal into the book God told him to write, life happened whether family, a successful and time-consuming business, friends, etc. and the journey took 15yrs till now to produce (and an incredibly abundant journey along the way). Now, it's perfect timing for you to harvest and reap the benefits of it but do so in a fraction of the time! BTW who DW is, is not important... a few of his messages, "All honor, glory and any legacy go to Jesus and the Kingdom of God;" "To know God and make Him known;" and DW truly wants "To tell everyone of the treasure he has found," and he sincerely hopes that you will benefit from his books and find similar peace, joy, contentment and abundant living that the Lord has blessed him with. Written and brought to you by the most unlikely uncommon "DW" Carpenter (with many similarities you yourself possess).

www.afatherswisdom.org

Made in the USA
Columbia, SC
23 October 2020